BRITAIN'S BEST WALKS

BRITAIN'S BEST WALKS

Twenty long-distance walks through Britain's spectacular countryside

TOM QUINN

Photography by
PAUL FELIX

TED SMART

This edition produced for
The Book People Ltd
Hall Wood Avenue
Haydock
St Helens WA11 9UL

First published in 2003 by New Holland Publishers (UK) Ltd
London • Cape Town • Sydney • Auckland

www.newhollandpublishers.com

Garfield House, 86–88 Edgware Road, London W2 2EA, UK
80 Mckenzie Street, Cape Town 8001, South Africa
14 Aquatic Drive, Frenchs Forest NSW 2086, Australia
218 Lake Road, Northcote, Auckland, New Zealand

10 9 8 7 6 5 4 3 2 1

ISBN 1 84330 639 5

Publishing Manager: Jo Hemmings
Senior Editor: Kate Michell
Assistant Editor: Rose Hudson
Copy Editor: Sue Viccars
Design: Alan Marshall
Cartography: William Smuts
Production: Joan Woodroffe

Reproduction by Pica Digital Pte Ltd, Singapore
Printed and bound in Singapore by Kyodo Printing Co (Singapore) Pte Ltd

Publishers' Note
The maps contained in the book are intended as 'locators' only; detailed, large-scale maps should be consulted when planning a trip. It is important to note that access details vary as new transport methods and facilities develop. Although the publishers and author made every effort to ensure that the information in this book was correct at the time of going to press, they accept no responsibility for any loss, injury or inconvenience sustained by any person using the book.

Illustrations appearing in the preliminary pages are as follows: half title: Weather Vane in Thixendale village (Wolds Way); title page 2: This green and pleasant land: a Cotswold valley (Cotswold Way); page 3: Ladram Bay (Jurassic Way); page 5: Withiel village (Saints' Way); page 6: (top) Stackpole Head (Pembrokeshire Coast Path), (bottom) Derwent Water, as seen from Ashness Bridge (Cumbria Way); page 7: (top) A Cornish Wall near Fowey (Saints' Way), (bottom) Broadway Tower in winter (Cotswold Way).

Contents

INTRODUCTION

Above all else do not lose your desire to walk.
KIERKEGAARD

Below: *Sheep-farming earns many people a livelihood in the Lake District (Cumbria Way).*

Bottom: *Pretty cottages in Broadway (Cotswold Way).*

Scientists now believe that the earliest humans who left the forest to live on the African plains several million years ago were nomadic. In other words they walked. But they didn't walk just to fetch water or to find food; their walking was a perpetual migration as they followed the movements of the animals they hunted or as they moved with the seasons. The evidence of our ancient walking ancestry is built into the very design of our bodies: apes' feet are flat, ours have sprung arches, confirming us as creatures made to walk. It is said that babies left to lie still will often cry and scream because instinct tells them that if they have been still for more than a few minutes and cannot sense movement their mothers must have continued on their long walk without them.

In many cultures walking has a religious importance – the idea of a journey into the wilderness alone and on foot has a profound resonance for Christians and Jews. Muslims should make the pilgrimage to Mecca on foot at least once in their lifetimes. Aborigines may walk from one side of their enormous continent to the other. When a Hindu's family duties have ended, his children grown up and left home, he is supposed to go on a long walk without money or possessions, relying only on the charity of those he meets for survival. The journey gives him time to assess his life and prepare for the next. A Buddhist in China was once asked what he had done during the long years of persecution during the Cultural Revolution – he replied that he had gone for a walk in the mountains.

The history of rambling

Closer to home, some of our greatest writers and poets – Charles Dickens, Thomas Hardy and, most especially, the Romantic poets – were enthusiastic walkers. Clearly, walking and creativity are closely allied. Two of the greatest Romantic poets, William Wordsworth and Samuel Taylor Coleridge, were also largely responsible for creating the modern enthusiasm for the Lake District and other 'wild areas'. Until the late 18th century, the Lake District had been seen as an untamed place, barbarous and uncivilized;

Below: *The rolling green hills of the South Downs attract not only walkers, but mountain-bike enthusiasts and horse riders (South Downs Way).*

Above: *Half-timbered cottages in the quaint English village of Henley-in-Arden take walkers back in time (Heart of England Way).*

walking through such a region for pleasure would have seemed utterly incomprehensible. For Wordsworth and Coleridge, however, walking through the Lake District became a route to poetry and inner meaning.

Of course, changes in our perception of the countryside and our desire to gain access to it have a lot to do with the fact that modern man – at least in the developed world – has plenty of leisure time. In times past in Britain, the Industrial Revolution and the long hours of drudgery it imposed on millions of poor people left no time for anything other than the daily struggle to stay alive. The same was true for those who lived in the countryside. A ploughman who walked perhaps a dozen miles a day behind his team of horses was not likely to set off on a leisurely walk across the fields during what little free time he might have.

Gradually, however, as living conditions improved and the economic surpluses of the post-industrial age enabled us to enjoy our free time, walking became something of enormous importance. The vast network of footpaths across Britain came back to life. For centuries they had only been used by country people simply to get from one place to another; now they became important for their own sake. Many began to realize that when it came to walking it was the journey that was more important than the destination. Footpaths gave people freedom: freedom from the dictates of the machine age, from the speed and stress of cars and aeroplanes, from stressful working lives and from busy, noisy, dirty roads.

The famous trespass on Kinder Scout in the Peak District in April 1932 began a movement that has protected and extended our network of footpaths so that now, in addition to thousands of miles of ancient footpath and bridleway, we have dozens of long walks, hundreds of short trails, woodland walks and nature trails. Walking, in short, is hugely popular. And for the real enthusiast there is nothing quite like our National Trails. These official long walks – many of which are included in this book – are generally very well waymarked and they cross some of our most historic and beautiful landscapes.

Walking the walks

Thanks to the excellent waymarking of these long walks this book did not need to be a step-by-step account of the 20 routes it covers, and is instead a general guide highlighting the varied attractions of each one. A detailed description for each route would fill a book the length of this one, and besides, such books already exist in large numbers.

Although I hope that this book will be welcomed by the serious dedicated walker, it is really aimed at anyone and everyone who enjoys walking, whether they prefer an afternoon's stroll along a quiet river or a more arduous 10-mile (16-km) trek into the hills. I hope it works as an introduction – the first of its kind – to the whole idea of long walks and to the extraordinary range and variety available. For the truth is, it really doesn't matter whether you tackle these long walks a bit at a time on odd weekends, or if you decide to do one complete walk each summer. Just being on part of a walk that, perhaps, crosses from one side of the country to the other or retraces an ancient trade route is magical, even if you have no plans to cover the whole of it.

Above: *All the trails are well signposted; this marker guides walkers over the green, green grass of Wales and up to Hay Bluff (Offa's Dyke Path).*

Most of the long walks included are very easy, one or two are a little more demanding, but none is beyond the abilities of anyone of average fitness. They vary in length from about 30 miles (48km) to more than 200 miles (322km), covering everything from Scotland's newest long-distance trail to quiet inland routes in the Midlands and South-East, spectacular coastal paths and historic ways that retrace ancient pilgrim routes. As the book is aimed at those who want to enjoy the journey rather than race to get to the final destination, I've also tried to add as much information as possible about landscapes and buildings of interest along the way – these may be a mile or more from the walk proper, but are included if I thought the detour was worth it.

I have made no great efforts to be entirely consistent about the way the walks are treated. Shorter walks tend to be more detailed, longer walks less so, particularly where there is a great deal to see en route. But finding your way will rarely be a problem on any of the walks.

Mostly this is a book for those who enjoy walking for its own sake and in as wide a variety of landscapes as possible. It is for those who understand that walking is not a competition, and that it can and should be enjoyed by anyone whether they are aged 9 or 90. The first time I walked The Ridgeway I walked it as fast as I could; I'd set myself a deadline and was determined to get to my destination on schedule. Sadly, when I got to the end I realized that I'd seen very little along the way. I have never made the same mistake again.

This guide is primarily for those who like to walk at a pace that allows them to absorb the history, archaeology, wildlife and geology of the landscape through which they are travelling. It is also concerned with the built environment, the towns and villages, even, in the case of the Thames Path, the city. On some walks – most notably the Greensand Way – the villages are so close together that as you walk they seem at times to crowd one upon the other, but no matter. If this walk is not for you, try one through remote Northumberland, Wales or Scotland – for there is, I hope, something here for everyone.

CAUSEWAY COAST WAY

The coastline of Northern Ireland has a rugged beauty, and the Causeway Coast Way through County Antrim is designed to take full advantage of the best of the windswept cliffs and bays. The route runs from Portstewart to Ballycastle and includes one of Europe's most spectacular landscapes: the Giant's Causeway, an extraordinary natural formation of polygonal pillars of basalt that has all the appearance of being man-made.

The way – which is well marked throughout – begins at Tubber Patrick (St Patrick's Well) on Portstewart Strand. Sites dedicated to St Patrick, Ireland's patron saint, are common right across the island, but St Patrick (who died in AD 461) was almost certainly Welsh by birth. He is best known for converting the Irish to Christianity and – legend has it – banishing snakes from Ireland.

The walking is easy along this first stretch of sand and rough tussocky grass. Throughout the walk you should keep an eye out for the wide range of fascinating, sometimes rare plants and animals that live in or around the coast. These include pink campion, ragged robin, bird's-foot trefoil and several species of orchid. Grey seals are fairly common off the coast, too, along with an occasional dolphin and porpoises at Barmouth. On the path itself you may see rabbits and hares, foxes and stoats. Badgers are common, too, but rarely seen during the day.

Castles and clans

Once you leave the beach at Portstewart the path climbs the cliffs and passes Portnacapple ('the landing place of the horses') and the extraordinary early 19th-century O'Hara's Castle. Horses have always been a passion among the Irish, and until well into the 1950s there were regular horse fairs all along this coast; horse dealers from Gaelic-speaking Inishowen in Donegal once landed at Portnacapple to sell their foals. That may sound romantic, but there is nothing romantic about O'Hara's Castle. Grim, almost fortress-like, it was built in 1834, becoming a convent school in 1917 and today it is a grammar school.

GETTING AROUND THE CAUSEWAY COAST WAY

Start: Tubber Patrick, Portstewart Strand, County Antrim.

Finish: Ballycastle, County Antrim.

Length: 33 miles (53km).

Transport Links: *Portstewart*: By car: Take the A26/A37 to Coleraine, then turn off onto the A29; by bus: regular Translink services operate from Coleraine to Portstewart and Portrush; by train: Portrush, 2–3 miles (3–5km) up the coast, and Coleraine, 5 miles (8km) south. *Ballycastle*: By car: the A2 and B15 run through the town; by bus: regular buses operate from principal towns; by train: Ballymoney, 16 miles (26km) away.

Ordnance Survey Maps: Discoverers 4 and 5 Northern Ireland (1:50,000).

Guidebooks: *The Complete Ulster Way*, Paddy Dillon (The O'Brien Press, 1999); *An Illustrated Guide to Walking the Causeway Coast Way* (Countryside Access and Activities Network for Northern Ireland).

Website: www.countrysiderecreation.com.

Further notes: The Causeway Coast Way is part of a much longer walk, The Ulster Way. At the time of writing not all of the Ulster Way was accessible.

The way soon reaches Portstewart Harbour and its blow-hole in Gun Rock. During storms, great spouts of water shoot up through a natural hole. From Portstewart continue along the cliffs past Ringaree Point (Ringaree means 'green') and Harbour Mill Strand to Portrush.

Shortly after passing Portrush the way reaches Ramore Head and then continues along a clear path to Portandubh Harbour and Portrush Nature Reserve, which has an interesting display of fossils outside the visitor centre. Soon you will be on sand again at Curran Strand. The path makes its way along the beach to the white rock, an isolated chunk of limestone with an arch through it, before going uphill and along a small road to hit the main A2 road. Continue along the road to Dunluce Castle, passing en route the wonderful viewing point at Magheracross.

Dunluce Castle is a glorious ruin. Once home to the chiefs of the MacDonnell clan, the castle was built in the 17th century but had been abandoned by the mid-18th century. From the castle continue along the A2 to Portballintrae. Soon after reaching the junction with the B145 the path crosses fields to Portballintrae village and then continues past the harbour to the beach.

From the beach car-park you head into the most spectacular section of the walk, for just beyond Portballintrae lies the amazing geolgical feature that is the Giant's Causeway. You can get to the Causeway Visitor Centre by either walking along the river and alongside the tram track or you can follow the beach.

Above: *Dunluce Castle was built in the 17th century as a home for the MacDonnell clan. However, by the mid-18th century it was already a ruin collapsing into the sea.*

Opposite: *There has been a rope bridge at Carrick-a-Rede for over three centuries. Originally used by salmon fishermen, it is now the domain of tourists.*

A unique landscape

From Portnaboe ('the port of the cow') to Benbane Head is a UNESCO-designated World Heritage Site. Within the site, the Giant's Causeway itself and a total of 6 miles (10km) of clifftop as far as Benbane Head is looked after by the National Trust.

The stacks of basalt rock that make up the Giant's Causeway were formed during volcanic eruptions more than 60 million years ago. Molten rock was forced up through fissures in the chalk bed and then cooled – variations in the cooling rate produced the columnar structure we see today. By any standards the stacks are extraordinary, resembling pillars packed side by side. As well as being geologically fascinating, the Causeway is important for wildlife: the north-facing cliffs are home to fulmar, peregrine falcon and chough, all nationally rare species.

From the visitor centre continue along the cliff path or take the shepherd's steps from the Causeway itself and rejoin the path a little further along. An easy grass path follows the bays and headlands of one of Europe's most beautiful coastlines to reach Benbane Head and Bengore Head with its 330-foot (100-m) high viewing point at Hamilton's Seat. All along here the wind that gusts in off the Atlantic can be ferocious, and the local council closes the cliff path when the weather is particularly bad. Even on days of moderate wind it's easy to imagine being whirled out to sea in an instant!

Head on to Portmoon and the ruins of Dunseverick Castle, built by the MacDonnells in the mid-1500s and destroyed by the English in 1641. From the castle the way takes a clearly defined grass track round the clifftops to Dunseverick Harbour and on past rocky bays to Portbradden and the broad sweep of Whitepark Bay. There is an alternative route to Whitepark Bay via an inland road, useful when the tides are high. The bay is a haven for a number of rare plants including black bog rush and bog asphodel. From Whitepark Bay it's an easy walk via a grassy track and sand dunes to Ballintoy Harbour.

A dare-devil crossing

From the harbour the way winds uphill to a church before crossing fields to Larrybane and a splendid view out across the sea to Sheep Island and Rathlin Island, where a distinct version of Irish Gaelic, now long gone, was once spoken. Rathlin was home to more than a thousand people before the Great Potato Famine of the 1840s; now about a hundred people live there. If you have time, take the ferry over for a day of exploring.

A short way east of Ballintoy is Carrick-a-Rede (meaning 'rock in the road' – the road referring to the route the salmon take along the coast here), where a rope bridge connects the tiny rocky island to the mainland over a 79-foot (24-m) drop. Visitors are allowed across the spectacular rope bridge to the National Trust-run island in summer. Razorbill, twite and kittiwake are among the birds that nest here. The bridge – used originally by local salmon fishermen – has been here, constantly renewed, for more than three centuries.

The section of the Causeway Coast Way from Carrick-a-Rede to the end of the walk at Ballycastle is slightly disappointing as it forces walkers onto the road – the B15; but given that

Below: *Before the advent of tourism, sea-edge communities such as Portbradden relied entirely on agriculture and fishing.*

Northern Ireland's roads are generally not that busy, and that the views from the road are pretty good, this is not a complete disaster.

From the car-park at Larrybane the B15 goes over Knocksoghey Hill to reach Portanveevey, from where there are wonderful views out to Rathlin Island. When you reach Cregaboy you can take a left to return to the cliff edge and the ruined castle of Kinbane.

Back on the road it's now just a few miles to Ballycastle from where there is a ferry out to Rathlin. When you reach the sea-front in the town you can continue to the Diamond – an open space in the town centre – and from there (if your legs are up to it) start another long walk: the Moyle Way, which takes you inland and through the beautiful glens of County Antrim for a little over 20 miles (32km).

Above: *The rock stacks that make up the magnicent landscape of the Giant's Causeway were formed during volcanic eruptions more than 60 million years ago.*

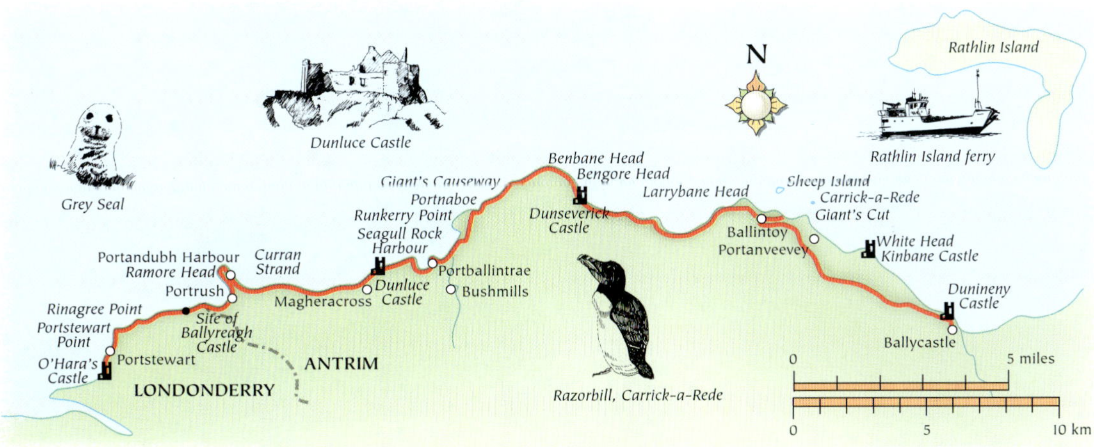

COTSWOLD WAY

The Cotswold Way runs north-eastwards through quintessentially English countryside from just outside the Cotswolds at Bath to Chipping Campden. The route probably takes in more consistently pretty towns and villages than any other long walk in Britain; even the village names – Wotton-under-Edge, Old Sodbury and Winchcombe, for example – seem to epitomize our concept of English village life.

Much of the beauty in this region is attributable to the remarkable creamy-yellow-coloured Cotswold stone from which almost everything – from great churches and manor houses to tiny cottages – is built. In fact, Cotswold stone is not confined to this area at all; it actually comes from a broad underlying swathe of oolitic limestone that runs from the Dorset coast as far as Stamford in Lincolnshire and beyond, to re-emerge on the North York Moors.

Away from the villages, a large section of the walk takes you through the uniquely beautiful Cotswolds Area of Outstanding Natural Beauty and there are numerous National Trust-owned houses and areas of open countryside along the way.

The Cotswold Way took an extraordinarily long time to be given official National Trail status – the idea for a long-distance Cotswold path was suggested as long ago as 1950, but official recognition was finally granted in 1998. Most of the walking is easy, although there are a few steep climbs – most notably to the top of Cleeve Cloud ('cloud' meaning 'hill'), which at 1,083 feet (330m) above sea level is the highest point on the walk. But this walk, like all the others in this book, is meant to be fun – if you don't want to climb Cleeve Cloud, you don't have to!

Bath – a Georgian spa town

The walk starts at Bath in Avon. What can be said of Bath that has not been said a thousand times before? It is justly one of the world's most-loved cities,

GETTING AROUND THE COTSWOLD WAY

Start: Bath, Avon – beside the cathedral.

Finish: Chipping Campden, Gloucestershire.

Length: 101 miles (163km).

Transport Links: *Bath*: By car: accessible from the A4, A36 and A46; by bus: local buses run six days a week from Moreton-in-Marsh, Chipping Campden and Stratford-upon-Avon with links via Bath, Tetbury and Stroud; by train: Bath. *Chipping Campden*: By car: located on the B4035; by bus: local bus links from Bath, Moreton-in-Marsh and Stratford-upon-Avon and Cirencester; by train: Moreton-in-Marsh, 7 miles (11km) away.

Ordnance Survey Maps: Explorer 155 Bristol & Bath, 167 Thornbury, Dursley & Yate, 179 Gloucester, Cheltenham & Stroud (1:25,000); Outdoor Leisure 45 (1:25,000) .

Guidebooks: *The Cotswold Way*, Kev Reynolds (Cicerone Press, 1994); *The Costwold Way*, Mark Richards (Constable, 1999); *A Guide to The Cotswold Way*, Richard Sale (Crowood Press, 1999); *The Cotswold Way*, Anthony Burton (Aurum Press, 1995.).

Website: www.cotswold-way.co.uk

and completely deserving of its recent elevation to UNESCO World Heritage Site status. The National Trust looks after the Assembly Rooms in Bennett Street, which were built in the 1760s to designs by John Wood the Younger, and it is easy to imagine Jane Austen – who visited the town on several occasions and used it in a number of her novels – here among the local gentry on the hunt for suitable partners.

Though its heyday as a 'must-see' spa resort of the rich and fashionable came to an end as long ago as the late 18th century, and despite its decline as a place of importance since then, Bath survived the follies of town planners and modernizers in the 1960s and '70s to emerge once again as a town that no visitor should miss. The Royal Crescent – that great sweep of grand 18th-century houses – Pulteney Bridge, still with its tiny Georgian shops, the astonishing Roman baths, all make Bath a place of wonder and delight.

The presence of hot-water springs gave the site enormous ritual importance in Celtic and earlier times, long before the Romans arrived. No doubt even prehistoric man found something of extraordinary significance in a place where hot water poured continually from the earth. For the Romans, with their love of bathing, Aquae Sulis (as Bath was then known) was ideal, and the Roman baths should not be missed on any visit to the city.

In the 18th century, 'taking the waters' was seen as a cure-all, and for particular ailments enormous quantities were prescribed (18 pints a day was recommended for gout!). Taking the waters stopped briefly towards the end of the 20th century after potentially harmful bacteria were found in the hot waters causing major panic. This led to the installation of a special filter, and Bath water is now back on tap and being drunk again.

The Cotswold Way starts by Bath's 15th-century vaulted cathedral, Bath Abbey. From here you need only wander vaguely north-east, taking in those parts of the town (or all of it) that please you. For some sustenance you could do worse than try a Sally Lunn bun – invented 300 years ago in the little shop (reputedly the oldest building in Bath) at 4 North Parade Passage where it is still sold today.

Above: *Even in pre-Roman times the presence of hot water springs gave enormous ritual importance to Bath.*

Opposite: *Cistercian monks founded Hailes Abbey in 1249, but it was largely destroyed during the Dissolution of the Monasteries (1536–40).*

Soon you will pass the Royal Crescent – which looks down and across a wide swathe of parkland – and then almost before you know it Bath is left behind and open country beckons. Along this first section there are views across the valley of the River Avon and towards the distant Mendip Hills. The path soon reaches Hanging Hill before setting off across a string of little valleys, dotted with farms and houses built from the characteristic local stone. From Cold Ashton, where there is a delightful, if largely hidden, 17th-century manor house, the path continues to that most wonderful early 18th-century house Dyrham Park.

Cooper's Hill Cheese Rolling

Broadway Tower

Sudeley Castle

Dursley Market House

'Wool' Church, Wotton-under-Edge

Royal Crescent, Bath

Grand houses and fine gardens

Dyrham, which is owned by the National Trust, took over 10 years to complete. It was built between 1691 and 1702 for William III's Secretary of State William Blathwayt – none of that sounds particularly special, until you realize that the interiors and contents of the house are almost exactly as they were when Blathwayt was alive. Each item of furniture is recorded in household records compiled in the 18th century.

From Dyrham the path crosses farmland, reaches the M4 and then dips to Dodington Park, a heavy, brooding house built in 1795 and with gardens designed by the prolific Lancelot Capability Brown (1716–83). The beauty of Dodington's surrounding parkland reminds us that many of our oldest oak trees exist only because they were enclosed – and therefore protected – within the walls of the grounds of these old houses.

Above: *Although just off the walk, Coaley Peak near Stroud is worth the detour since it offers some of the best views of the Severn Valley.*

A little beyond Dodington is the curiously named village of Old Sodbury, which itself lies just 3 miles (5km) from the Duke of Beaufort's grand estate at Badminton, famed for its annual international horse trials. From Old Sodbury the way passes the Iron Age hillfort of Horton Camp and a Tudor battlefield before reaching National Trust-owned Horton Court. This lovely house, part Norman and part Tudor, has been described as the oldest rectory in England. Continue on over country that rises and falls and soon you leave the modern county of Avon and enter the ancient county of Gloucestershire.

The path reaches the tiny village of Alderley and skirts Newton Park (also with grounds by Capability Brown, and now home to Bath Spa University College) before reaching Wotton-under-Edge where the houses are curiously mixed: some in typical Cotswold stone, others timber-framed and more reminiscent of Herefordshire or Suffolk. This architectural mélange is a reminder that in medieval times timber was still the preferred building material in this area, and that many Cotswold stone houses conceal behind their golden façades far older houses constructed of oak. From Wotton – taking care first not to miss its splendid 'wool' church – climb up to the wooded ridge, the 'Edge' from which the village gets its name. Walk on to Nibley Knoll where there are wide views of the distant River Severn to the west. On a good day you should also be able to see the Black Mountains of Wales beyond the Severn. William Tyndale (*c.* 1494–1536), one of the earliest translators of the Bible into English, has a 100-foot (30-m) high commemorative tower here.

The path continues down a steep hill into North Nibley and then on to Stancombe Park, where there are landscaped gardens and a Victorian 'secret garden'. The house is not open to the public. Soon you will reach Stinchcombe Hill before descending to Dursley, once famous for its great butter market, and now worth stopping in to admire the numerous fine early houses and the splendid early 18th-century market hall.

Above: *The Devil's Chimney – a stone pillar created by centuries of erosion – stands on Leckhampton Hill. From this wonderful viewpoint the whole of Cheltenham can be seen.*

The wealth of wool

Now we are in the heart of Cotswold country. The great manor houses and splendid churches that remain throughout this region are testimony to the enormous wealth generated by the medieval wool trade. Even the name of the region – the word 'Cotswold' – derives from 'sheep cote'. It is said that in medieval times more than 70 per cent of taxes received by the Crown came from wool, and that the best wool came from the Cotswolds. Eventually, exports of raw wool gave way to finished products, but of the 150 woollen mills that once dotted this part of the world not one working mill remains.

From Dursley it's a short but steep walk to Uleybury and its Iron Age hillfort. A little further on can be found another ancient monument, the wonderfully named Hetty Pegler's Tump – a 3,000-year-old Neolithic long barrow. The burial mound is named after a widow who owned the land in the 17th century.

From here the path heads through easy, partly wooded country towards another long barrow near Nympsfield and then on, still sticking to the ridge, towards Middleyard. When the path reaches the River Frome there is a splendid cloth mill, closed as recently as 1954. In its heyday it was one of the biggest and most important mills in the Cotswolds. Soon after this the path crosses the Stroudwater Canal, a road and a railway before heading for the high ground again and the National Trust's Standish Wood. Beyond Standish the National Trust also owns Haresfield Beacon, from where it's just a

few miles to the village of Painswick, one of the highlights of the Cotswold Way

Painswick is filled with beautiful ancient houses all built with money earned from wool exports in medieval times, but now mostly inhabited by antique dealers. In Painswick churchyard don't miss the wonderful yew trees and the distinctively local table tombs where so many wealthy wool merchants found their final resting place. From Painswick the path soon reaches Painswick Hill Iron Age hillfort. From here you can see the town of Gloucester. Stop and admire the view and then head on towards Birdlip through woods and across soil that sticks to your boots in wet weather. The path skirts Prinknash Abbey; although the name sounds old, the building is a recent and unpleasant example of the worst kind of 20th-century architecture. The path continues through occasional woodland to Cooper's Hill where a traditional cheese-rolling race is held each year. There has been talk of banning the race on the grounds that it is dangerous – the hill is so steep that it's simply a question of throwing a cheese over the edge and then chasing it downhill!

Ancient routes and monuments

Just before the village of Birdlip the way goes round the head of Witcombe Valley where the remains of a Roman villa can be seen. Birdlip sits high up on these hills and lies on the route of the old Roman road from Cirencester to Gloucester, otherwise known as the Ermine Way.

Above: *The village of Stanton is golden – thanks to the prolific use of Cotswold stone – and unspoiled.*

From Birdlip head up to Barrow Wake with views across Gloucester. Cross a road and begin the climb to Crickley Hill, again looked after by the National Trust, then on to the curious rocky outcrop known as the Devil's Chimney on Leckhampton Hill south of Cheltenham. From here the way crosses a common to the settlement at Severn Springs.

From Severn Springs the path heads for the Chelt Valley before climbing up to Cleeve Cloud (the highest point on the walk), and then heads back south-east towards Wontley. From the top of Cleeve Cloud all England seems spread out before you.

March on to Belas Knap with its impressive restored Neolithic long barrow and then descend through a wood to Winchcombe, where the church has more medieval stone gargoyles than any other in Britain. A gentle downhill stretch brings you to Sudeley Castle, once the home of Henry VIII's widow Katherine Parr, but apparently popular with most of Henry VIII's wives. The castle dates back a thousand years but was largely destroyed during the English Civil War (1642–49) and then restored during the 19th century by Worcestershire glovemakers John and William Dent.

Beyond Sudeley the way crosses the little River Isbourne and continues over fields to Hailes Abbey, a Cistercian foundation of 1246. Like so many monastic foundations, Hailes Abbey was largely destroyed during the Dissolution of the Monasteries (1536–40) following the Pope's refusal to let Henry VIII get divorced. The site, owned by the National Trust, has a museum and the remains of the cloisters.

Right: *St Peter's Church, Winchcombe holds the unusual record for the greatest number of gargoyles found on any church in England.*

Cotswold eccentricities

The path continues through Stanway with its unmissable 14th-century abbey barn and beautifully preserved Jacobean house. Stanway House has been home to the Earls of Wemyss (pronounced 'weems') for more than 700 years. Though open to the public, the house is still owned and lived in today by the same family. Tours are conducted by the present Lord of the Manor and the house contains some fascinating furniture, including a sprung chair designed to give the sitter the kind of exercise he or she would normally get on a horse! Tenants of Lord Wemyss still pay their rents using a round table built specially for the purpose 200 years ago.

Beyond Stanway a lovely stretch of the way leads to Stanton, justly famed for its 'timeless perfection'. From Stanway the path climbs steadily via Shenbarrow Hill where a little detour will take you to the National Trust's Snowshill Manor, an extraordinary 16th-century house filled with items collected by Charles Paget Wade, who owned the house in Victorian times. Here you will find countless bicycles, prams, carts, tricycles, clocks, toys, musical instruments, bits of linen and pretty much anything else man-made that you can think of.

After Snowshill the walk passes through the village of Broadway to the tower high on Broadway Hill. This splendid sandstone Gothic tower was built by the 18th-century Earl of Coventry so he could eat breakfast while keeping an eye on his estate!

After Broadway Tower the path crosses field and woods to reach Dover's Hill, where English sports and games like skittles and wrestling were held annually for 250 years until 1853. They were known as the 'English Olympicks', and were revived in 1963. This area of what was once commonland commands a wide view over the surrounding fields and farms and, like so much on this walk, is owned and managed by the National Trust.

Chipping Campden is just a short walk from Dover's Hill. It is a town that manages to combine beauty with utility to the detriment of neither, as it has managed to save itself from the worst of the efforts of the modernizers; a fitting end to the Cotswold Way. The wool hall – built in the 14th century – is a gem. The town also has a row of wonderful early 17th-century almshouses, and the house where England's richest medieval wool merchant – William Grevil – once lived still stands.

Above: *The gardens of Snowshill Manor are just as enticing as the manor house itself, which is crammed full of bizarre artefacts collected by Charles Paget Wade who lived here at the end of the 19th century.*

CUMBRIA WAY

Running for a little under 73 miles (117km) through some of the most spectacular and popular landscapes in Britain, the Cumbria Way is a walk through the Lake District, but one with a difference. After leaving the archetypal Lakeland village of Ulverston the way threads through rich farmland to the coast north of Morecambe Bay. It then climbs into the wild heights of the Lakes before descending once again to farmland and the city of Carlisle.

Opposite: *The view from Ashness Bridge to Derwent Water and the peaks of Skiddaw beyond is just a sample of the much-loved rugged landscape that the Cumbria Way passes through.*

Like most Cumbrian towns, Ulverston, where the way begins, is relatively unspoiled – it still has many cobbled streets and numerous interesting and historic buildings. It has a fascinating glass-blowing museum and Laurel & Hardy museum too: comedian Stan Laurel, the town's most famous son, was born here in 1890.

The Cumbria Way starts, rather unromantically, at a car-park by the glass-blowing museum and heads up a path by the side of a stream. After a while it climbs steeply past a wood and then heads for Old Hall Farm. Once through the farmyard the way reaches a wood and climbs until the first view of the hills and fells of the Lakes spreads out ahead. The path continues along a stream, crosses fields and stiles and then reaches Higher Lath Farm. From here a road descends until a left turn takes the path along a wall, past farms and a stream. Soon you reach a lane from which high moorland and farmland lower down can be seen. A footpath then continues up to the slate-built church of St John where the path follows signs for Broughton and then Broughton Beck. At the stream the route heads towards a wind farm, eventually crossing the stream and going steeply downhill to a road. Follow the road to find another track, then pass through more fields and past another farm to a road that leads to Gawthwaite village.

A Viking past

Villages and other place names ending in 'thwaite' (a clearing) or 'thorpe' (an outlying farmstead) are common in the Lake District. They reveal the Viking origin of many settlements, and the local word for a stream – 'beck' – is also Norse. For many years it

GETTING AROUND THE CUMBRIA WAY

Start: Ulverston, Cumbria – next to the glassblowing museum.

Finish: Carlisle, Cumbria.

Length: 72½ miles (117km).

Transport Links: *Ulverston*: By car: located on the A590; by bus: Stagecoach services between Ulverston and Barrow, Coniston and Kendal, National Express services run to Ulverston; by train: Ulverston, servced by Arriva North West; *Carlisle*: By car: the A7, A69 and A595 all run into the town, take Junctions 42–4 of the M6; by bus: National Express services from key towns and exhaustive local services; by train: Carlisle, on the West Coast mainline.

Ordnance Survey Maps: Outdoor Leisure 7 The English Lakes – South Eastern Area, 4 The English Lakes – North Western Area, 5 The English Lakes – North Eastern Area (1:25,000); Explorer 315 Carlisle, Bramptom, Longtown & Gretna Green (1:25,000) .

Guidebooks: *The Cumbria Way*, Anthony Burton (Aurum Press, 1999); *The Cumbria Way and Allerdale Ramble*, Jim Watson (Cicerone Press, 1997); *Cumbria Way*, John Trevelyan (Dalesman Publishing Co., 2002).

was believed that the Viking raiders of the Dark Ages attacked English settlements, took what they wanted and set off home, but more recent research suggests that this is only part of the story. Like the Roman invaders before them, the Vikings (or at least some of them) married local women and settled here for good.

The way goes straight through Gawthwaite and uphill by road until the Old Man of Coniston – one of Lakeland's finest summits – comes into view. We are now within the Lake District National Park, established in 1951 and the largest national park in England and Wales. Soon a rough farm track followed by a footpath takes you to High Stennerley. A tiny road comes next and then the route passes through a farmyard on a trackway before heading uphill to a grass path which leads above the Crake Valley. This is a beautiful stretch of the way but with little of the drama to come.

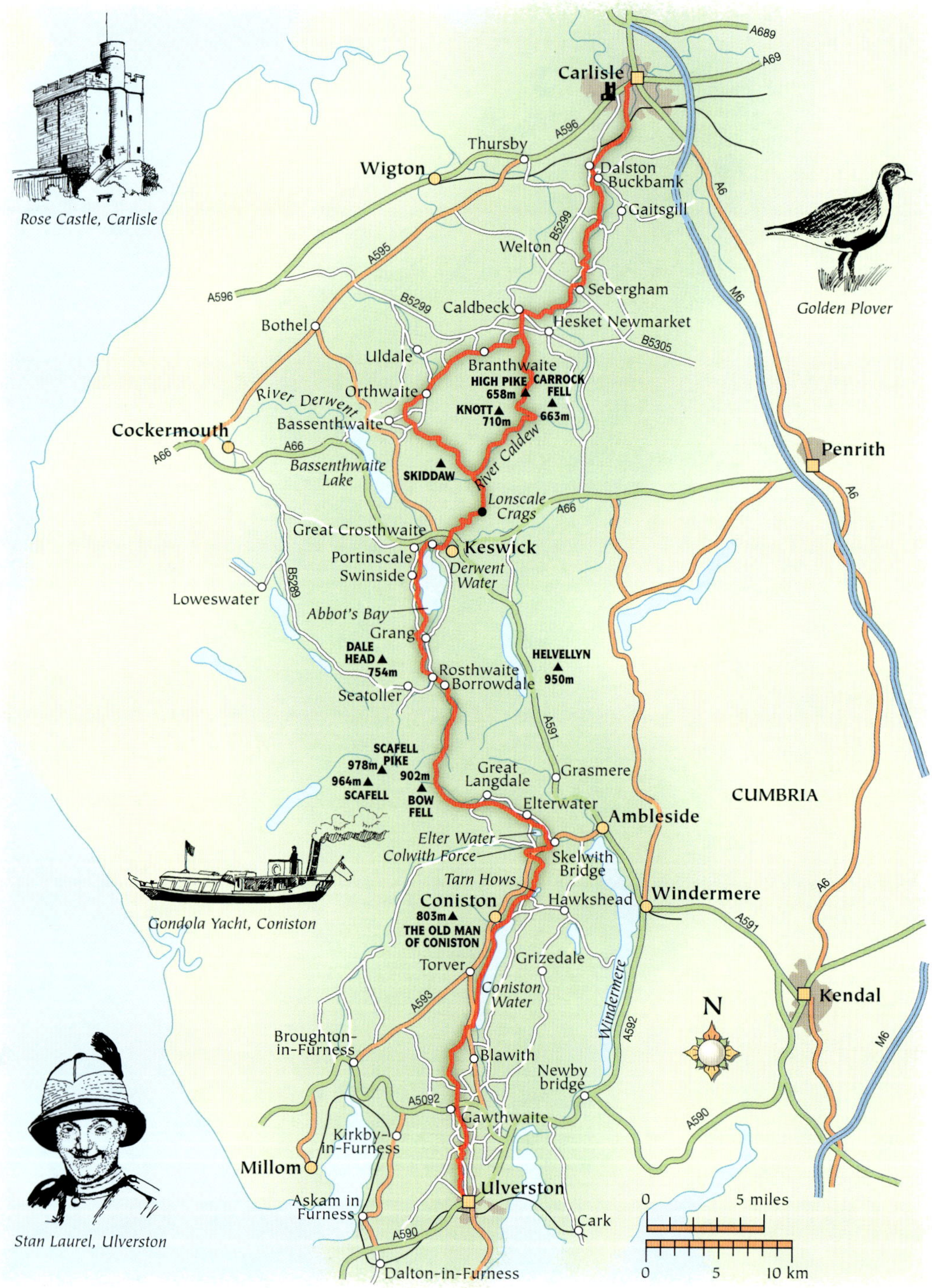

Rose Castle, Carlisle

Golden Plover

Gondola Yacht, Coniston

Stan Laurel, Ulverston

The results of the Ice Age

Until the Romantic era of the late 18th century, when the great literary figures of William Wordsworth, Samuel Taylor Coleridge and the like began to favour the region, the Lake District was invariably seen as barren, inhuman and threatening; and of course it was, and still can be, dangerous. When the mists come down and the high tops are covered the danger of accidents is ever present and lives are lost each year.

Nevertheless, the high tops are also unquestionably beautiful. The three rock types in the area – the volcanic rocks of the Borrowdale series, the sedimentary Skiddaw slates and Silurian rocks – were moulded and gouged by the glaciers of the Ice Age to produce the superb landscapes associated with the Lake District today: high, craggy tops and weathered peaks, tranquil corrie lakes high above deeply incised glaciated

Above: *The National Trust-owned* Gondola *was launched in 1859 and has been fully restored to sail Coniston Water.*

valleys and, of course, 16 lakes. And what would the Lake District be without water? Wherever you look becks, streams, bogs, marshes and rivers attest to high levels of rainfall.

Back on the way, continue along tracks and field paths up hill and down dale, but still this is relatively easy walking; little so far could be described as particularly arduous though you will have climbed considerably since the start of the walk. Then, at last, a steep climb brings us to Beacon Tarn, seemingly isolated and untouched by man. Yet this landscape has long been home to man despite its wild, untamed appearance. Sheep have roamed the hills for more than a thousand years and, in addition to agriculture, parts of the Lake District have long been mined for graphite and copper and quarried for slate. During the Neolithic period, stone axes – made from the hardest volcanic rocks – were produced at sites such as that in Great Langdale, and exported elsewhere.

The way on from the tarn is easy to spot: take the path through a gap in the hills and then follow the valley to the boggy ground of Stable Harvey Moss. Much of the route is marshy here, but the sense of space is intoxicating. Soon a road is reached, then a track, which leads past an old reservoir and down to a footbridge over Torver Beck. The wide waters of Coniston Water should now be visible up ahead.

Speed junkies

It was on Coniston Water in 1967 that Donald Campbell died while trying to break the world water speed record. The lake is still popular, but for slower vessels now, including the spectacular National Trust-owned steam yacht *Gondola*, which was launched in 1859 and still sails from Consiston Pier daily throughout the summer. The yacht's interiors (though heavily restored) are a wonderful example of Victorian opulence.

Below: *The memorial to speed king Donald Campbell, who died on Coniston Water in 1967.*

Despite the size of Coniston and the other lakes there is surprisingly little in the way of wildlife beneath the surface of the water. These lakes are just too cold and too poor in nutrients to sustain much. Occasional cannibal trout are reputed to grow to titanic proportions, but they are rarely caught. Smaller trout are common as well as char, relics of the Ice Age. Although locally common, char are rare this far south of the Arctic Circle and can only be found in Britain in the Lake District, Scotland and Wales.

Literary Lakeland

Coniston Water is surrounded by trees, but the path down to the lakeside is clear. The way clings to the water's edge until it reaches Torver Jetty from which ferries cross to the other side of the lake. It's worth taking the ferry to visit Brantwood, John Ruskin's home from 1872 until his death in 1900. Ruskin, who was perhaps the greatest art critic of the 19th century, as well as a social reformer and poet, was also a bit of a prude: infamously, he destroyed hundreds of erotic drawings by J.M.W. Turner in a bizarre attempt to create a 'whiter-than-white picture' of the great artist. Ruskin lost his wife to the pre-Raphaelite painter John Everett Millais and finally became insane.

The best-known Lakeland writer was the great Romantic poet William Wordsworth who, through his books, helped popularize the Lake District as a place of beautiful landscapes, poetic drama and inspiration. Another famous local author was the children's writer Beatrix Potter, who lived at Hill Top, Near Sawrey, a 17th-century farm. Her home is now in the hands of the National Trust and is exactly as she left it. In the late 19th century, Arthur Ransome spent childhood holidays near Coniston Water, later the setting for his famous *Swallows and Amazons* stories.

Below: *Remote uplands, such as these below Langdale Fell, may be beautiful but they are hard to tame and farming here has always been a struggle against the landscape and the elements.*

Soon after the path swings away from the lake it reaches a road that leads into the town of Coniston. If you are feeling energetic, you can climb from here to the top of the Old Man of Coniston from where there are the most breathtaking views – the summit is more than 2,460 feet (750m) above sea level. Be careful, however, because the weather can change suddenly at that height and when the mist comes down it may be difficult to find your way.

Back in Coniston the way continues past the church and

along the Ambleside road for a short distance before cutting into a field and then along a stream. Much of this ancient meadowland is owned by the National Trust. The way then heads uphill through gorse, then conifers and then beautiful broadleaved woodland. Where the woods end the distant fells open up ahead. The route is clear from here to Tarn Hows. A path by a stream leads to an uphill trail through woodland and on to Tarn Hows Cottage, which must have one of the best views of any house in England. A road and then a path lead down to the tarn itself, which was created from several smaller tarns.

Above: *Honister Pass near Keswick is, like any mountainous area, subject to dramatic and sudden changes of weather. Care must always be taken when walking in such remote areas.*

Waterworld: lakes, tarns, rivers and falls

The Cumbria Way skirts the tarn on a clearly discernible path and continues on past another tarn and along a meandering path until at last it reaches a road and then woodland. The road passes High Park Farm and then a footpath leads through more woodland to a sign for Skelwith Bridge. A short detour here will take you to the spectacular waterfall, Colwith Force (signs will direct you to it). A long clear path heads down to Skelwith Bridge, crosses the bridge and then turns sharp left towards Elter Water. You pass Skelwith Falls (a 20-foot/6-m drop over sheer rock) then field paths lead to Elter Water. Follow the lakeside for a while before turning off to the very pretty village of Elterwater. The way then passes old slate quarries on a road before turning onto a footpath past a chapel and farm across a river and then on to Great Langdale.

All along this steep-sided, craggy valley rivulets tumble down the hillsides. The path follows the main stream for a while then turns away and continues along the foot of the hills. Fields and farm roads follow; signs lead right to Stickle Tarn and New Dungeon Ghyll Hotel, but you must keep straight ahead. The path is quite clear along the sides of this beautiful, lonely valley, at the head of which you must bear right towards Stake

Right: *The red squirrel was once widespread throughout the United Kingdom, but under pressure from its more aggressive grey cousin it can now be found only in a few isolated areas, one of which is the Lake District.*

Pass. As the path climbs steadily steeper the landscape becomes tougher and more unforgiving, particularly at the top of the pass where the ground is boggy and hummocky, but the views are spectacular. A steep descent to the Langstrath Valley follows, and the path runs beside the stream along the near-level valley to reach farmland and a gentler landscape once again.

Follow the stream into Borrowdale and then head on to Rosthwaite. Pass through the village to reach Yew Tree Farm before joining the River Derwent, which is crossed at New Bridge. The way follows the river then branches off to woodland past a long-disused slate quarry, then downhill to the River Derwent and finally onto a track that leads through Hollows Farm and along the valley slopes past the village of Grange.

Woodland and moorland

Many Lakeland woods still provide a home to the much-threatened red squirrel, whose range has declined so dramatically over the past 50 years. Its last refuges – outside Scotland – are here in the Lakes, a small area of Norfolk, woodlands near Formby in Lancashire, and the Isle of Wight. Deer, particularly roe, are also common in Lakeland woods, and on the high moors you might see red grouse – that favourite target of the well-to-do – as well as golden plover and curlew. Along the streams and rivers wagtails and dippers are common.

Below: *Sheep and the effects of their grazing have shaped the appearance of much of the countryside along the Cumbria Way.*

Back on the path and with Grange behind you comes your first glimpse of Derwent Water. A good stretch of field walking is followed by a short distance on a road and then a footpath which brings you to the edge of Derwent Water. As the way follows the lake edge towards Keswick it becomes more crowded, particularly in summer. Woodland paths lead past Abbot's Bay and along the lakeside until at last you swing away and join a road that leads into the village of Portinscale. The route follows the road for a short while, then branches off on a footpath through woodland, across fields and along smaller roads to reach Keswick itself by a more scenic route.

Keswick is well worth a visit; it has many Victorian and earlier buildings, a weekly market and a good museum of Victorian curios. When you leave to continue the walk go along the Cockermouth road, then take the Carlisle turn and finally the signs to Skiddaw. Soon a bridleway takes you off into woodland and then along an open stretch overlooking Derwent Water before reaching a car-park at a magnificent viewpoint. From here the way heads into a wide moorland landscape. The path passes Lonscale Crags and heads up the long valley of the Glenderaterra Beck. Having passed Skiddaw House Youth Hostel the path takes you past grouse butts, old mineworkings and over streams to the highest point on the walk at High Pike, 2,159 feet (658m) above sea level – it is an arduous climb, but not to be missed if the weather is good. When you've reached the peak and enjoyed the view back over the Lake District, descend gradually to Caldbeck village.

If the weather is bad the alternative route also takes you across lonely moorland with only sheep and the occasional grouse for company. Fells and boggy ground follow, cut across here and there by streams, and the way climbs steadily before descending again. The valley is beautiful but tamer than the high tops and the way continues towards Bassenthwaite before bearing right via Orthwaite. Little Tarn and then fields and stiles lead to a road that climbs past a reservoir and across more moorland with views of the Solway Firth to the north. A farm track leads down to a road, on to Burblethwaite and then on past Branthwaite, Fell Side and, at last, Nether Row where the low- and high-level alternatives join up again.

Above: *Streams and becks, such as Grainsgill Beck below Coombe Hight, are a dominant feature of these high-rainfall uplands, and they continually cut through the higher parts of the Cumbria Way.*

Towards a Roman city

From Nether Row the way steals across fields and streams, through farms and along roads to Caldbeck with its church – a mix of Norman and 18th-century craftsmanship – and early 18th-century mill still pretty much intact. From Caldbeck you are on the last leg of your journey to Carlisle. Take the road past the church and onto a path that follows the river before climbing through trees and fields to reach a forest road, then descend once more to the river. A good stretch of riverside walking leads to a climb to Sebergham Church with its outside staircase to the tower. Beyond the church the way reaches the River Caldew which it then follows almost all the way to Carlisle. This last stretch is a wonderful end to the walk. The river is always interesting and you will pass several old houses, such as Rose Castle, with its 15th-century pele tower, and Georgian Hawkdale Hall. The Cumbria Way ends where the river reaches the outskirts of Carlisle, but the city centre, with its castle and cathedral, should be visited.

Situated at the end of Hadrian's Wall (see pages 62–69), Carlisle was a Roman fortress and then a key target for Viking invaders. William the Conqueror saw it as vital to his control of the north, but so wild was this area that until well into the 18th century the border reivers (raiders) crossed back and forth from Scotland stealing cattle with impunity. Most of what we see of the castle today dates from the end of the 13th century.

DALES WAY

The Dales Way links two of Britain's loveliest national parks – the Yorkshire Dales and the Lake District – and crosses some of the most remote and picturesque parts of England on the way. It combines riverside walking with rough upland and passes numerous historic villages and hamlets.

Above: *One of the great pleasures of the Dales Way is the many different stiles, gates and stone wall steps encountered along the route, such as this stile and dog gate near Barden Tower.*

Fairly early on, the route passes through the Yorkshire Dales National Park, famed for its spectacular scenery, resulting from the underlying belt of Carboniferous limestone. The area is characterized by large areas of upland limestone pavement, crags and gullys, caves and potholes, rolling heather moorland and deep, narrow, fertile river valleys – the dales. Names such as Wharfedale, Deepdale and Nidderdale conjure up images of sparkling rivers and solid farmsteads in the sheltered valleys surrounded by neat drystone walls, small fields and stone barns. The local agriculture is largely based on sheep-farming, particularly on the higher ground, and cattle. Much of the moorland is managed for grouse shooting, and the heather moorland we see today is as much a product of modern farming management as of the ancient pattern of fields and drystone walls. This has always been a difficult landscape in which to make a living, and those who work on the land will often have two or even three jobs in order to make ends meet.

As the way goes west towards the Lake District a hard sandstone – millstone grit – predominates as the underlying rock. Thus, the eastern section of the walk – with its highly permeable underlying limestone – drains well, while in the west the gritstone prevents the water soaking away and as a result the ground can be boggy and marshy. Along much of the route abandoned or converted woollen mills are testament to a vanished age of industrial prosperity.

Start with a cup of tea

Although you can start walking the Dales Way in Leeds – it was extended in the mid 1990s – the walk officially starts in Ilkley, a solid, attractive town that flourished in the 19th century as a holiday destination where people came to take the waters, and is today famed for Betty's wonderful tea-rooms in The Grove. The way goes through the town and then along the bank of the River Wharfe to the beautiful stone bridge that was built in the late

GETTING AROUND THE DALES WAY

Start: Ilkley, Yorkshire.
Finish: Bowness-on-Windermere, Cumbria.
Length: 81 miles (130km).
Transport Links: *Ilkley*: By car: Ilkley is on the A65; by bus: Local services operate from Ilkley to local villages and towns; by train: Ilkley. *Bowness-on-Windermere*: By car: Bowness is on the A592 and A5074; by bus: Daily buses to Windermere from local villages and towns; by train: the First North Western line runs to Windermere.
Ordnance Survey Maps: Explorer 297 Lower Wharfedale & Washburn Valley (1:25,000); Outdoor Leisure 2 Yorkshire Dales – Southern & Western Areas, 30 Yorkshire Dales – Northern & Central Areas, 7 The English Lakes – South Eastern Area (1:25,000).
Guidebooks: *Dales Way Route Guide*, Arthur Gemmell and Colin Speakman (Stile Publications, 1996); *The Dales Way*, A. Burton (Aurum Press, 2001); *Dales Way*, Paul Hannon (Hillside Publications, 2000); *The Dales Way*, Terry Marsh (Cicerone Press, 1992).

1700s. From here the path follows the river except in one or two places where it avoids the wide bends.

All along here the Wharfe tumbles over rocks, and the surrounding broad-leaved woodlands are a haven for birds and other wildlife. Among the birds, dippers and wagtails predominate. Along the river you may – if you are lucky – see an occasional otter. The way passes several disused mills, continues along the riverbank through meadows and then follows a small road away from the river for a short distance to a wood at which point it turns back to the river. Soon you reach the ruins of the 12th-century Augustinian Bolton Priory, one of the highlights of the whole walk. Much of the priory is now a ruin, but at the time of the Dissolution in the mid-16th century the locals managed to save part of the building which was turned into the parish church.

Above: *Bolton Priory near Skipton was founded in 1154 and grew in magnificence over the next four centuries until 1539 when, during the Dissolution, it was ransacked and partly demolished.*

The church and abbey ruins are by the river, a little to the north of Bolton Abbey village. Just as you reach the ruins, the way crosses the river via a footbridge and then continues along the bank heading steadily upstream. Grass and meadow walking follows and then oak woodlands, which are beautiful in autumn. Soon the path reaches a road, crosses a stream and then the river itself to reach Strid Wood. Still the path clings to the river, but here the river is very different – when you first met the Wharfe it was almost placid compared to this turbulent, noisy stream. The way climbs steadily now as the river valley narrows through a region of exceptionally hard rocks. At one point it looks almost jumpable – don't try it!

Soon the route leaves the woodland and returns to the higher ground well above the river. Cross a footbridge and return to the river's edge before reaching the extensive ruins of Barden Tower. This mainly 17th-century house wasn't demolished, rather its remoteness made it unpopular with the descendants of the family who built it and it was subsequently abandoned and left to simply fall apart.

Idyllic villages

The path continues along the river bank with minor diversions here and there, passing woods and farms until it comes parallel with Appletreewick, an attractive little village worth detouring to and long famous for its annual onion fair, an event that began in the early 14th century. Beyond Appletreewick continue along the river with occasional forays across fields. The path crosses Burnsall Bridge, where it is pleasant to spend an afternoon in the

Above: *The village of Burnsall, comfortably nestled in a dale, has several pretty 17th-century houses and a church that has been left untouched since the 16th century.*

village. There are 17th-century houses here and a church unrestored since the 16th century.

Soon the way passes Grassington parish church (visible on the opposite bank) and two tumbling weirs that were once involved in providing power for a thriving woollen mill. Built in the mid-18th century, the mill only closed in the 1980s. Grassington is a perfect Dales village with a small main square of ancient cobbles surrounded by early stone houses. Take a moment to visit the interesting Wharfedale Museum. The route cuts right through Grassington, past the old theatre where the great 19th-century tragedian Edmund Kean once played, and out through a farm onto the hillside.

A forgotten industry

Now the route really climbs and some of the best views on the walk are spread out before you. Ancient field patterns can be seen in the valley and the way crosses areas of limestone pavement that typify this area. Field paths and stile crossings lead on past the remnants of limekilns that once dotted the landscape. They were built to burn limestone which, when heated with coal, broke down into a crumbly powder that was a useful fertilizer used to improve these thin upland soils.

Higher still the path takes us to the most spectacular spot of all, Conistone Pie, a rocky peak surmounted by a cairn. From here look out across one of the best-loved landscapes in England – a classic Dales scene of small stone-walled fields. Across the river from here are Kilnsey – the village – and Kilnsey Crags, overhanging limestone rockfaces that are popular with seasoned rock-climbers.

From this high point the way begins to descend, crossing stiles and cutting through woods and past a very ugly building (Scargill House) to a lane that leads through small fields to the outskirts of Kettlewell, another delightful village. Here the village church has Arts and Crafts stained glass. There are several pubs, for Kettlewell was an important stopping place in the days of coach and horses.

Opposite: *The Dales Way is a wonderful mix of meadow – such as that in Wharfedale seen here – field, upland and marsh walking.*

Leave the village and return to the riverside, crossing countless stiles and gates, continuing along farm tracks and field paths through boggy ground past Starbotton village (also worth a detour) and on through meadowland to enter a wood. Pass Buckden – a short hop across the river – and then continue along the riverside edge to Hubberholme.

From dale to dale

Hubberholme marks the end of Wharfedale and the beginning of Langstrothdale. The

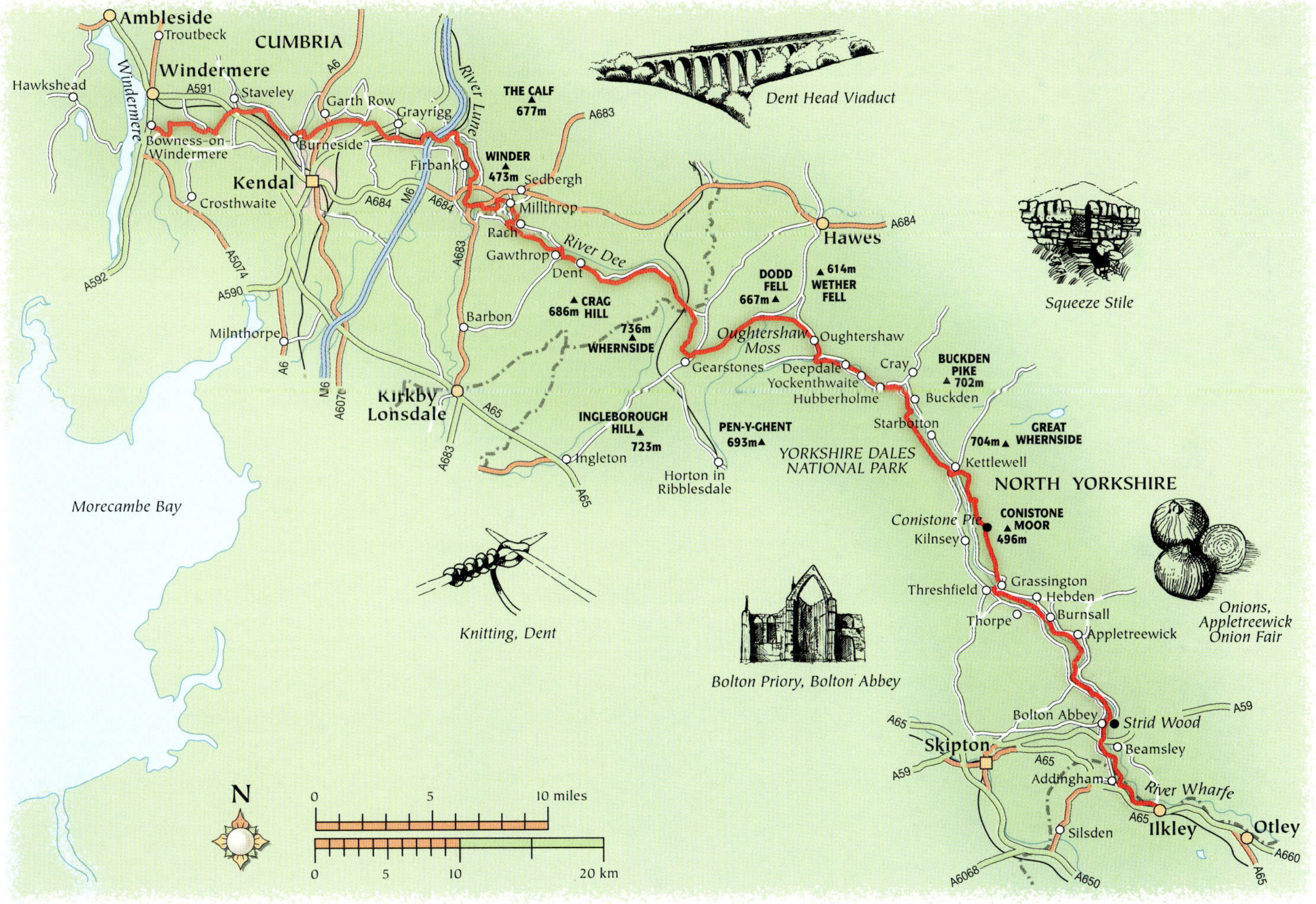
Ambleside
Troutbeck
CUMBRIA
Windermere
Hawkshead
Windermere
A591
Staveley
A6
Garth Row
Grayrigg
River Lune
THE CALF
677m
A683
Dent Head Viaduct
Bowness-on-Windermere
Burneside
Kendal
Crosthwaite
A684
M6
A684
Firbank
WINDER
473m
Sedbergh
Millthrop
Rash
River Dee
Gawthrop
Dent
Hawes
A684
A5074
A592
A590
A683
Barbon
CRAG HILL
686m
736m
WHERNSIDE
DODD FELL
667m
614m
WETHER FELL
Squeeze Stile
Milnthorpe
A6
M6
A6070
Kirkby Lonsdale
A65
Oughtershaw Moss
Gearstones
Oughtershaw
Deepdale
Yockenthwaite
Hubberholme
Cray
BUCKDEN PIKE
702m
Buckden
Starbotton
GREAT WHERNSIDE
704m
Kettlewell
INGLEBOROUGH HILL
723m
Ingleton
A683
A65
PEN-Y-GHENT
693m
Horton in Ribblesdale
YORKSHIRE DALES NATIONAL PARK
NORTH YORKSHIRE
Morecambe Bay
Conistone Pie
CONISTONE MOOR
496m
Kilnsey
Knitting, Dent
Threshfield
Grassington
Hebden
Burnsall
Thorpe
Appletreewick
Onions, Appletreewick Onion Fair
Bolton Priory, Bolton Abbey
Bolton Abbey
Strid Wood
A59
A65
Skipton
Beamsley
A59
A65
Addingham
River Wharfe
A65
Ilkley
Otley
Silsden
A6068
A650
A660
A65
N
0
5
10 miles
0
5
10
20 km

Above: *The Ribbledale Viaduct on the Settle to Carlisle line is a spectacular sight on the Dales Way, along with the Dent Head and Lune viaducts.*

Below: *The Dales is a popular venue for grouse-shooting; the red grouse relies for its survival on carefully managed heather uplands.*

route skirts the church and follows the sparkling waters of the Wharfe along the dale. A succession of stiles and gateways leads to the tiny hamlet of Yockenthwaite, passing through and round farms until once again you refind the trackway above, but still alongside, the river.

After passing a small ancient stone circle the way leaves the river, crosses a stream and reaches the village of Deepdale. From here the path goes steadily higher, crossing a rocky landscape cut through by numerous streams and rills. After a footbridge and some road walking you will be in the high moorland country of Oughtershaw Moss.

Continue over high ground close to the infant Wharfe, passing lonely farms, to reach the watershed, the point at which rainwater filtering down through the rock ceases to head back towards the North Sea, but instead goes west.

The way reaches a large wood and then skirts it, heading uphill to meet the Pennine Way (Britain's first national trail, running for 268 miles/431km from Edale in the Peak District to Kirk Yetholm on the Scottish borders) and a trackway known as Cam High Road. Cam High Road was the route of a Roman road and has breathtaking views. On leaving the track you enter grouse country; there are shooting butts all around and you may disturb the birds, which whirr like clockwork up from the heather at a terrific pace before skimming and banking over the contours of the land till they are out of sight. Despite high concentrations of birds on moors such as this, grouse are not nationally a common species. They rely on the fragile ecosystem of these heather uplands, which have to be managed carefully to ensure the birds' long-term survival.

Victorian engineering

Soon the route descends to a track and the road into Gearstones. From Gearstones a trackway leads onto more heather moorland. Grass paths and farm tracks lead across streams to a road, and on to the Victorian Dent Head railway viaduct on the Settle–Carlisle line. The viaduct is a superb ten-arch stone structure that replaced the tiny but still perfectly serviceable packhorse bridge over Fell End gill beneath it.

The way continues along a road into Dentdale and then on to the stream at the bottom of the valley. Like the Wharfe earlier (and all these limestone watercourses)

the stream has little in the way of fish life other than diminutive trout: there are plenty of them, but they rarely grow to weigh more than a few ounces.

Along the stream you reach Scow Force, a splendid waterfall, before crossing a footbridge, passing a riverside pub – the Sportsman's Arms – and then passing near to England's highest railway station (about 1,150 feet/350m above sea level), which is well worth a detour, at Dent. The route follows the stream, wider now, and then leads over fields and stiles, trackways and narrow roads before crossing the stream and entering a dark conifer plantation. Soon you are below the peak of Whernside, which rises to over 2,400 feet (732m). More farm tracks and field crossings follow, together with numerous narrow squeeze stiles which have been a feature of the walk throughout. It is said squeeze stiles would let a man but not a sheep through – but that was on the assumption the man had not had a good lunch!

The way meanders round several farms and over rough, hillocky fields before hitting a road and then heading back down to the river. Soon the path crosses Tommy footbridge, continues along the bank and then re-crosses the river by another bridge. This is delightful riverside walking (with a few diversions) until we reach the lovely village of Dent, about 4 miles (6km) from its fell-top station!

Above: *The village of Dent dates back to Norman times and has numerous claims to fame, from pioneering geologist Adam Sedgwick (1785–1873), knitting in the 18th century, cobbled streets and historic cottages to its more recent meditation centre.*

The 'terrible' knitters of Dent

Dent is almost too pretty to be true – cobbled streets, old whitewashed cottages and hardly a structure out of place. It's the sort of village that brings out all the clichés – timeless, quaint and unspoiled – but in this case all the clichés are justified, which is why so many tourists come here each year. It's an excellent place for a walker to stop for a drink and something to eat. But Dent's greatest claim to fame is – or was – the speed at which the locals were able to knit! They were known as the 'terrible knitters of Dent', almost as if there was something slightly demonic about their haste!

Back at the bridge the walk continues along the river, which is considerably wider here than when you first met it. Soon you are on a road through a wooded valley, until

Opposite: *The River Wharfe is a magnificent waterway that changes character from gentle stream to roaring rapids as it progresses through the heart of the Yorkshire Dales.*

reaching Rash where river and way part company. Follow the contour of the hills until the path descends into Milthrop, a very attractive village with small slate-hung houses and an ancient, comfortable air. You could take a short detour here to the much bigger town of Sedbergh where Bonnie Prince Charlie is said to have hidden in a chimney (the house – in Weaver's Yard – can still be seen) after the failed Jacobite Rebellion of 1745–6. The Jacobites, mostly Highlanders, had risen against the English Hanoverian King George, and Bonnie Prince Charlie, Catholic grandson of James II, had returned from exile in France to lead them.

From Milthrop the way runs across fields and up hill and down dale for many miles. The well-worn path through the grass, running from stile to stile, is obvious. Leaving Milthrop the route passes several disused mills, and follows a millstream to the River Dee. It crosses a disused railway embankment and passes close to Brigflatts, made famous by Basil Bunting in his poem of the same name and by the wonderful Quaker meeting house established by George Fox in the middle decades of the 17th century and still in use today. Brigflatts, like so many of the settlements along the Dales Way, is idyllic if rather isolated. After Brigflatts there is a short section of road walking before the way heads across fields again. Lanes and field paths then lead on to the River Lune and the spectacular Lune Viaduct, built in the 1840s. Once through the eight-arched viaduct the path climbs the hill diagonally. From the hilltop the Howgill Fells appear ahead like a great upturned bowl.

After a good stretch of field and meadow walking, the way returns to the side of the River Lune, which has declined dramatically as a salmon river over the past few decades. Much of the path by the riverside is marshy and uncomfortable but it soon joins a track and then crosses the M6. The West Coast main railway line runs here too, along with older drovers' and packhorse routes. For the last mile or so before the bridge over the M6 try not to let the continual roar of traffic spoil an otherwise pleasant walk.

After the motorway the path is clear across fields past a farm to a wood. Beyond the wood the village of Grayrigg comes into view before you reach and cross the railway line. Farmland and field walking follows, leading to the little River Mint. Trackways and more field walking gradually head uphill with views across the fells until Kendal comes into view.

Border raids

The route crosses the A6, runs by hedges and past a farm until a wide and glorious vista confirms that at last you have reached the Lakeland fells. The way passes Sprint Mill,

dating back to the 18th century, and then passes close to medieval Burneside Hall, a fortified house built during the days when raids across the border from Scotland were still commonplace. The route passes close to Burneside, a village that has little of the charm of other settlements passed on the walk, before continuing across fields to the River Kent. The river here is delightful and the way follows it, through grassland and along rough tracks and then road, to Staveley, where the path goes under the Lakes railway line. Continue along narrow lanes and trackways before reaching a road that climbs steadily. At the brow of the hill there is another stunning view over the Lake District. The narrow road descends to a farm and then follows a bridleway across a rocky landscape to hill pasture, and then on to reach another road.

Trackways continue, and then fields and more tracks lead to a roadway that takes us to the edge of Windermere. Pass through seemingly endless kissing gates and fields until at last the waters of the lake come into view. A stone seat by woodland on the very edge of the built-up area of Bowness-on-Windermere marks the end of the walk. And after such an achievement what better way to spend the rest of the day than to wander around this attractive (albeit touristy) town before taking a trip on the lake.

GLYNDŴR'S WAY

Walking Glyndŵr's Way is a wonderful voyage of discovery through a relatively neglected but very beautiful and historic part of mid-Wales. It runs through north Powys taking in ancient sites, lonely farms and spectacular hilltop views over countryside unspoiled by modern development.

Above: *The clock tower at Knighton where the way begins. At various times in history Knighton has been officially in both England and Wales.*

Opposite: *Glyndŵr's Way starts as it means to go on and almost immediately enters the green and rolling countryside for which Wales is famous.*

The idea for the walk was first mooted in the early 1970s, but it wasn't until 2002 that the way received full national trail status. Much of the walk runs across high country where low cloud can make navigation difficult – take warm clothes and a compass with you.

Owain Glyndŵr, Prince of Wales

It's worth looking at the life and times of the man after whom the route is named. Owain Glyndŵr (*c.* 1354–*c.* 1417) was a Welsh warrior who almost defeated the English in the early 15th century in his attempt to set up an independent, united Wales. The walk named after him crosses much of the wild country he knew and includes many sites made famous by his great rebellion. Halfway along the walk is Machynlleth where Glyndŵr held his great Parliament of Wales.

Little is known of Glyndŵr's early life, but he was certainly an educated man who is said to have studied law in London. His father was descended from the Princes of Powys and his mother from the rulers of that other great medieval Welsh kingdom Deheubarth. Glyndŵr is thought to have served in Richard II's army before returning to his homeland. His rise to fame began in 1399 when a local dispute over land with his neighbour Lord Grey of Ruthin got out of hand and exploded into a widespread and bloody campaign for Welsh independence. Just a year later, Glyndŵr declared himself Prince of Wales.

His first great battle against the English occurred at Hyddgen in the remote hills just south of Machynlleth. Vastly superior English forces ambushed Glyndŵr's small band of armed men, but against all the odds Glyndŵr won the day. This victory elevated him to the almost godlike status as legendary hero that he has enjoyed ever since. He then won

GETTING AROUND GLYNDŴR'S WAY

Start: Knighton, Hereford & Worcestershire – by the clock tower.
Finish: Welshpool, Powys.
Length: 132 miles (220km).
Transport Links: *Knighton*: By car: located on the A488; by bus: local services run to and from Newtown, Hereford and Ludlow; by train: Knighton station, on the Heart of Wales line from Shrewsbury to Swansea. *Welshpool*: By car: located on the A483 and A458; by bus: a National Express service runs to and from London, local Contact Arriva Cymru services run to and from Oswestry, Shrewsbury and Newtown; by train: Welshpool station, on the main Birmingham–Aberystwyth line.
Ordnance Survey Maps: Explorers 201 Knighton & Presteigne, 214 Llanidloes & Newtown, 215 Newtown & Machynlleth, 216 Welshpool & Montgomery & 239 Lake Vyrnwy (1:25,000).
Guidebooks: *Owain Glyndŵr's Way*, Richard Sale (Gwasg Carreg Gwalch, 2001); *Owain Glyndŵr's Way*, Chris Catling & Ronnie Catling (Cicerone Press, 2000); *Owain Glyndŵr's Way*, Gillian Walker (MU Publishers, 1990).

a famous victory in 1402 just south of Knighton at a place called Pilleth. Such was his reputation by this time that it was even said that Glyndŵr could control the weather.

The English army was defeated, and by 1404 Glyndŵr had captured a number of the greatest English strongholds in Wales, including Harlech and Aberystwyth castles. The first Welsh Parliament under Glyndŵr was held in Machynlleth in a building that stood on the site of the present Parliament House building, which now houses a permanent exhibition to the hero. But the glory days were not to last; by 1406 support for the rebel leader was fading. He lost Aberystwyth and Harlech to the English, and retreated to the hills where, using guerrilla tactics, he continued to harry the English occupiers. He was never captured or killed so far as we know – he simply vanished.

Rolling hills and valleys

Glyndŵr's Way starts at the clock tower in the market town of Knighton, where a section of the Offa's Dyke National Trail also starts (see pages 96–103). Knighton is on the Welsh side of the England–Wales border, but at various times through history has moved between the two countries. The town still has a few historic areas and a weekly market.

Wind through narrow streets to a steeply descending path that crosses a road and then follows the Wylcwm Brook upstream. The path goes through the suburbs of Knighton, past bungalows and then out towards the northern slopes of Garth Hill, which it crosses. From Garth Hill there are wonderful views across the Teme Valley and Knighton itself.

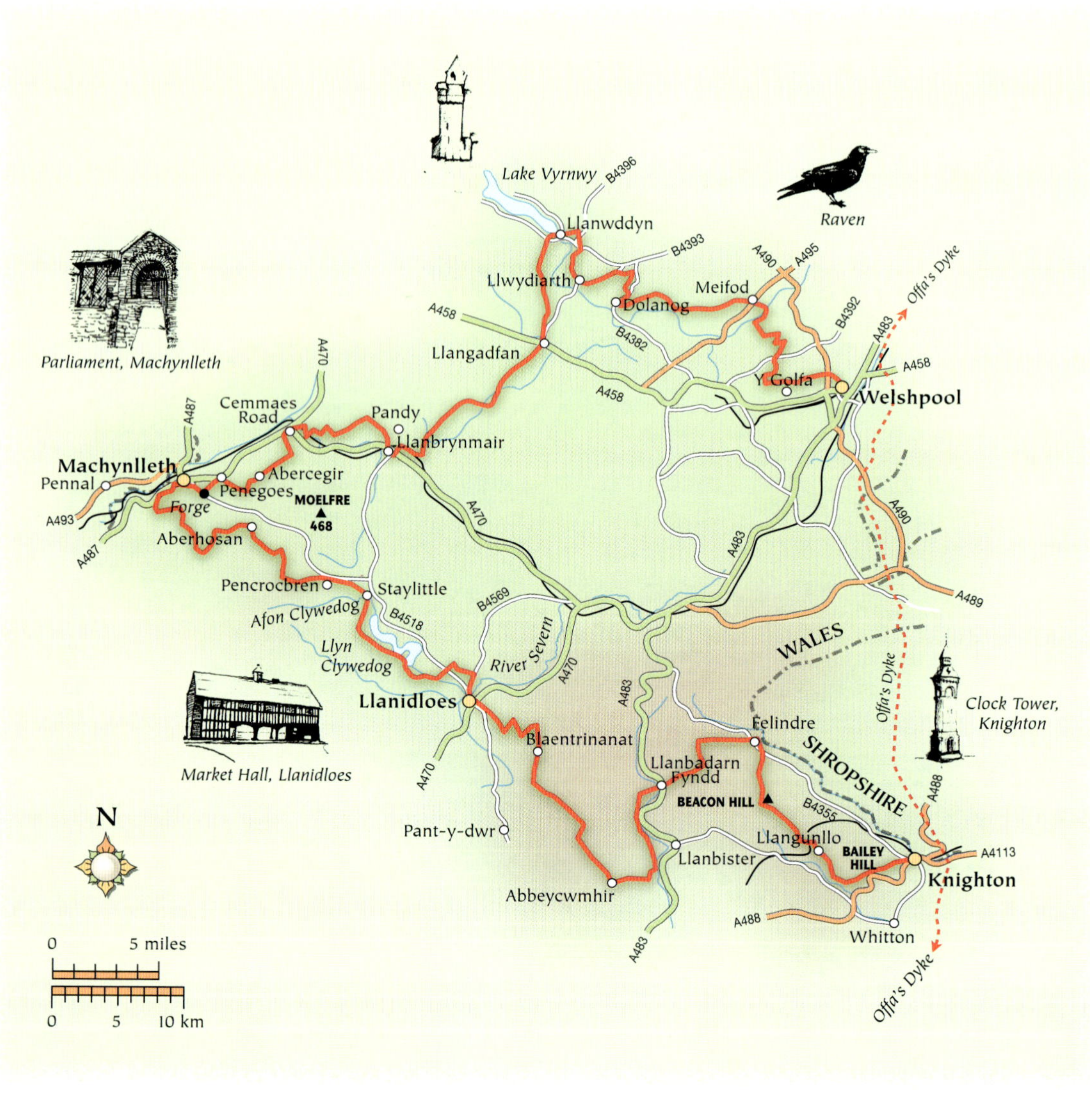

Beyond Garth Hill the path quickly enters woodland, then a narrow lane before reaching a small, unmarked road. Follow the waymarks along the road through a series of rights and lefts until taking a final left turn into Ebrandy Lane. The path continues uphill past a farm until it reaches Bailey Hill. It then descends to the valley bottom and crosses the little Dingle Brook. From here the path crosses fields and sunken trackways until it reaches another

stream, then on through quiet tracks and lanes, past lonely farms until it reaches the village of Llangunllo.

Above: *Glyndŵr's Way takes you through remote country that is a mix of wild, heather-covered upland, farmland and pasture.*

Cross-country through the heart of Wales

From Llangunllo you must head north along a road before crossing fields and going through an underpass beneath the Heart of Wales railway line, which runs from Swansea to Shrewsbury. A trackway takes you up past a belt of conifers, then across fields and pasture to the head of the Ferley Valley. Here you meet a crossroads, but the route continues up the narrow lane onto Beacon Hill Common before crossing a short ditch, an earthwork dating from pre-Roman times when tribes in the area – the Deceangli, Ordovices and Silures – were continually at war with each other.

The path now crosses through heather over Pool Hill to Cwm Pennant. The path here – basically a green lane – is clear until it crosses a stream and then climbs to Stanky Hill. From the hilltop the way takes you round the eastern side of Black Mountain before descending and then crossing Warren Bank. The way climbs again, and soon reaches a road. The path clings to the ridge here before joining a trackway and descending through bracken to Felindre.

From Felindre the way rises steadily through tracks and lanes to high pasture before dropping to Gwernlas Brook and then crossing wide fields of pasture until it reaches the medieval Wolf Castle earthwork (Castell-y-blaidd). Descend towards the Ithon Valley and the village of Llanbadarn. From the New Inn the footpath runs parallel with the A483 before passing the church and setting off down a minor road. At the top of the hill cross several fields and then continue onto a bracken-covered common. The path is clear here, but boggy in places.

More heather and gorse follow until you reach a green lane on the slopes of Moel Dod (1,532 feet/467m). The path descends past conifer plantations and areas of gorse before passing the high outline of Castelltinboeth, a medieval earthwork (1,320

Above: *Near the village of Llanbadarn the walk follows country roads. The surrounding area would have been well known to the great 14th-century Welsh hero, Owain Glyndŵr.*

feet/400m), which sits on top of the wooded hill in the distance. Next, a narrow metalled road leads to a bridleway, then more conifer belts, then an area of gorse, until you reach Ysgwdfford (1,444 feet/440m). At the peak is a triangulation point and magnificent views.

Back on the bridlepath the way descends into the valley and reaches Neuaddfach Wood. Continue heading down, cross a brook and you will reach a minor road. Turn left and follow the road for a little over a mile (1.6km). Cross fields and stiles and then more woodland before reaching Abbeycwmhir village. At Abbeycwmhir the scant remains of a medieval monastery that once had the third largest nave in Britain, measuring over 230 feet (70m) long, can be seen. March on through woods, and then across the Clywedog Brook, before continuing over more fields and another brook to Upper Esgair Hill. The path then goes round Lanfraith Hill and joins a track before reaching the hamlet of Bwlch-y-sarnau. When you leave the village the way descends via a deeply cut path into another area of woodland before crossing the Afon Marteg Bridge, after which there's more than a mile (1.6km) of forest walking. You then pass from Radnorshire into Montgomeryshire and enter the village of Blaenrinant.

From Blaenrinant the path cuts through a farmyard, crosses a ford and passes by an old quarry before reaching wide pastures. Tracks and cattle paths lead on to the Nant Feionion Valley. At the bottom of the valley the way leads upstream before rising quickly through fields across a hillside above a lonely cottage and across another stream. At the head of the valley (after crossing another stream) the path goes uphill, on across fields and past another old quarry. Soon you will reach pasture before gradually descending and crossing a footbridge. A narrow road now leads past Newchapel Baptist church and into a little valley where you cross the Nant y Bradnant footbridge. From here climb above an ancient oak wood and then down into Llanidloes.

Above: *The ornate Gothic dam wall at Lake Vyrnwy is part of the man-made reservoir built by the Corporation of Liverpool between 1881 and 1888 to supply the city with water. This extensive project involved submerging the village of Llanwddyn, and in dry summers, if the water level drops far enough, the ruins of the old village reappear.*

Past inhabitants

Tumuli (burial mounds) on the hilltops around Llanidloes reveal that this area has been inhabited since at least the Bronze Age, which began about 2000 BC. The Romans built roads here and mined for lead. The Celtic saint Idloes is said to have laid the foundations of the earliest church overlooking the Severn, but the town only really began to expand after the Norman Conquest. A castle was built (of which nothing remains), and in 1280 Llanidloes obtained its first Charter, granted by Edward I. The Old Market Hall, the only half-timbered hall of its kind in Wales still in its original position, was completed *c.* 1610.

From Llanidloes the way crosses the River Severn, which is full of barbel, and goes up into Allt Goch Wood through a golf course and then across fields, past farms and onto the B4518 at Bidffald. The path then cuts through a farmyard before continuing on past an abandoned lead mine to a footbridge beneath the Clywedog Dam. After the dam the path climbs to a specially built viewpoint, and then descends slowly to the edge of the reservoir before diverting along a small stream as far as the road. From here a bridleway crosses several fields and enters a forest. Beyond the forest the way reaches pasture again before descending into the valley of the Afon Biga and continuing through woods and fields and across marshy ground.

At this point of the way you simply need to keep the hedge on your left before descending to cross the Afon Clywedog. The route then ascends tracks and lanes till it crosses Llechwedd Du (2,014 feet/614m). Soon you are on the windswept top of Pencroebren. Bridleways lead you to the edge of the upper Clywedog Gorge, where a good footpath descends to a bridge. The path passes old mineworkings before rising and crossing moorland overlooking Glaslyn. The distant landmark of Foel Fadian (1,850 feet/564m) should now be visible. At the head of Nant Fadian the path becomes rocky before leading down across fields to a road that leads towards Aberhosan.

Above: *The tower at Lake Vyrnwy strongly resembles a fairy-tale castle – which is precisely what the 19th-century builders intended. On first appearances, Lake Vyrnwy has all the characteristics of a natural lake. In 1889 it was stocked with 400,000 Loch Leven trout, and people have been fishing for them ever since.*

Modern technology and an ancient parliament

The path descends to a road and crosses the Dulas Valley before climbing again to Cleiriau-Isaf. Follow a green lane down across pasture, and continue along trackways and woodland paths to Bwlch y Groesen before climbing again to skirt Cwmcemrhiw. A lane then takes you down onto a rocky, bracken-covered ridge. Climb through steep pasture to a forest and then cross Parc Common. Soon Machynlleth, where Glyndŵr held his great Parliament of Wales, comes into view. Here you can visit the Owain Glyndŵr Centre and the fascinating Centre for Alternative Technology.

The Machynlleth area has been inhabited for at least 3,000 years; recent research suggests that copper was being mined here during the Bronze Age. The Romans came too, building roads and a fort at Cefn Caer 4 miles (6km) west of the town. Edward I granted Machynlleth its Charter in 1291, which included the right to hold a market every Wednesday, a tradition that continues to this day. Visit the medieval Royal House, which gets its name from the legend (and it is no more than that) that Charles I stayed here, near the centre of the town. Another legend has it that David Gam was imprisoned in Machynlleth in 1404 for attempting to assassinate Owain Glyndŵr.

From Machynlleth turn east along Heol Maengwyn and through the village of Forge before setting off across fields to Penegoes and then, via a lane, making your way to the head of the valley. Cross the edge of Bryn Wg Common to reach a stream at Bryn Wg Isaf, go over it and then head downhill to the village of Abercegir. From here you must cross fields, climb a track to pastures and a stream to finally reach the A470. Follow the road towards Dolgellau, but quickly turn right into a track that continues beneath bracken-covered slopes before climbing to pasture again. Having crossed the next valley, the way continues along a track that climbs until a group of space-age wind turbines can be seen in the distance. Soon you reach another road, then a trackway that leads up through more pasture with the high top of Moel Eiddew on the left. The path continues across fields and by woods and fields until the wide Afon Rhiwsaeson Valley comes into view on your left. The way descends to the A470 and the village of Llanbrynmair.

Head north towards Pandy, crossing a long series of fields and stiles before rising towards the ridge of Cerrig y Tan. More forest walking follows, and then a green lane that leads down into the valley. The way now wanders past farms and along lanes to cross Pen Coed Common before descending through conifer plantations to Llagadfan.

Lake Vyrnwy

A narrow road takes you north-east before the way turns left to a farm and crosses fields and pasture to reach a road at Penyffordd. On a forestry track make a long descent to a footbridge and then take another road, which leads – after a mile (1.6km) or so – to Ddol Cownwy. A series of green lanes and gravelled tracks, plantations and fields lead to the spectacular dam at Lake Vyrnwy and the relocated village of Llanwddyn. Lake Vyrnwy may look natural, but it is actually a giant Victorian reservoir, completed in 1888.

A minor road and a green lane take you from Llanwddyn on to Abertridwr. Then a narrow road and forestry track lead uphill past plantations and pasture until you hit another road and the village of Llwydiarth. The way follows the Vyrnwy stream, then goes uphill to a road, before continuing along bridleways and little roads and on through fields to Allt Dolanog Common. Cross the common and descend to Dolanog.

Left: *A male common crossbill is one of the species that makes its home in the RSPB reserve at Lake Vyrnwy.*

Founding fathers

From Dolanog the path follows the river downstream and crosses fields before climbing through gorse and woodland towards Pont Robert. It then crosses the River Vyrnwy, which has excellent trout fishing, and climbs to the Zion chapel before crossing a series of fields towards Dolobran Hall and the restored Dolobran Quaker meeting house. Seventeenth-century Dolobran Hall was built by Charles Lloyd (of Lloyds Bank fame), whose brother Tom sailed to America with William Penn, the founder of Pennsylvannia.

Cross farmland on tracks past woodland to reach Meifod, and then head south-east to cross the River Vyrnwy again. Once over the river turn right to head through a field until you can see the remote lake of Llyn Du. The way then hits a road before turning left into a green lane and continuing through fields and a farmyard to another road. Pasture leads to Craig Wood, and then you head south, skirting fields until reaching Golfa Hill and climb to the peak of Y Golfa (1,119 feet/341m). From this spectacular viewpoint you can see far away to Cadair Idris, the Arans and the Berwyns. Finally, make the long descent to the A490 and into Welshpool, a busy market town surrounded by the Montgomeryshire hills with a number of historic houses and home to Europe's largest sheep market.

Below: *The once-threatened polecat, which was hunted for its fur in the 19th century, has made a comeback in Wales, and may be found in the pine forests around Lake Vyrnwy.*

GREAT GLEN WAY

This long-distance route runs the length of the Great Glen, known in Gaelic as Glen Mor. The Glen, and the walk, effectively joins the Atlantic to the North Sea, marking the line of a 400-million-year-old geological fault and crossing some of the wildest, most beautiful landscapes in Britain.

The Great Glen Way – which was opened in 1992 – starts at Fort William at the head of lochs Eil and Linnhe in west Scotland and ends at Clachnaharry near Inverness, 73 miles (117km) away on the east coast. For a third of its length the Great Glen is filled by one of Europe's biggest areas of freshwater – Loch Ness. Apart from being home to the most famous monster in the world, Loch Ness is an extraordinary body of water by any standards: it is 23 miles (37km) long, has an average depth of more than 400 feet (122m) and at its deepest – more than 750 feet (229m) – is deeper than anywhere in the North Sea. It is so deep that however cold the weather it never freezes.

Monsters of the deep

Loch Ness is also home to an extraordinary creature, a relic of the last Ice Age 20,000 years ago – and by this I don't mean the fabled monster, but Arctic char. Deep in the waters of the loch there are still healthy populations of this little-known fish. The Arctic char looks vaguely like a trout, but with an extraordinary crimson-coloured belly. Until the mid-1980s even the Natural History Museum did not have a specimen. Like many cold northern waters, Loch Ness is not particularly rich in life forms. Apart from the char

GETTING AROUND THE GREAT GLEN WAY

Start: Fort William, Highland – by the railway station.
Finish: Clachnaharry, near Inverness, Highland.
Length: 73 miles (117km).
Transport Links: *Fort William*: By car: located on the A82; by bus: Buses run to and from all major towns, and there are also local services; by train: Fort William, served by Scotrail. *Clachnaharry*: By car: take the A82 or A9; by bus: the principal service provider is Scottish Citylink, with routes stopping at larger towns; by train: Inverness, served by ScotRail.
Ordnance Survey Maps: Explorer 392 Ben Nevis & Fort William, 400 Loch Lochy & Glen Roy, 416 Glen Affric & Glen Moriston (1:25,000); Landranger 26 Inverness & Loch Ness, 34 Fort Augustuts, 41 Ben Nevis (1:50,000).
Guidebooks: *The Great Glen Way*, Jacquetta Megarry (Rucksack Readers, 2002); *The Great Glen Way: A Low-level Walking Route from Fort William to Inverness*, Heather Connon and Paul Roper (Mainstream Publishing, 1997); *The Great Glen Way*, Brian Smailes (Challenge Publications, 2002); *The Great Glen Way Accommodation and Services Guide* (Highland Council).
Website: www.greatglenway.com.

Above: *Almost all of the Great Glen Way is easy walking through glens such as Nevis, and there are wonderful views throughout. The more energetic can always opt for a detour to the high peaks, however.*

Opposite: *Inverlochy Castle, built in 1260, is one of the oldest castles in Scotland. It is now a ruin, having been made redundant as the military focus of the area by the building of a more modern citadel – Fort William – at the head of Loch Linnhe by Oliver Cromwell in 1654.*

there are numerous small trout and the occasional gigantic (up to 20lb/9kg) – but rarely seen – ferox or cannibal trout. And, of course, there is the Loch Ness monster...

Over the thousands of years that this part of Scotland has been inhabited there was no recorded mention of a monster – apart from a creature banished from the area by St Columba in the 6th century – until the 1860s, when a local newspaper mentioned a 'huge fish' that had been spotted in the loch. Similar rumours persisted until 1934, when a Dr Wilson published what is still the most famous image of 'Nessie' – a grainy black-and-white photograph of a long, serpent-like creature with its head raised above the water and its body undulating behind. The photograph was later denounced as a hoax, but sightings of Nessie have continued on and off ever since. Despite numerous searches in the 1980s using highly sophisticated submarines and radar, nothing has been found to substantiate the various sightings. On the balance of probability Nessie couldn't actually exist – the amount of food in the loch simply wouldn't sustain a big, dinosaur-like creature – but it's a delightful story and has done wonders for local tourism.

The Caledonian Canal

Much of the way is relatively easy walking, particularly along the towpath of the Caledonian Canal – but there are also moorland and forest paths, and some steep climbs. The walk starts at Fort William. Originally known as Inverlochy, and based around a fort built by General George Monck in 1654, the town of Fort William (named after William of Orange) grew up around the replacement stone fort built in 1690 by General Hugh Mackay. Hardly a scrap of the fort survives – it was largely destroyed by the arrival of the railway in the 1890s – but the town has an interesting visitor centre and a spectacular setting beneath the slopes of Britain's highest mountain, Ben Nevis (4,410 feet/1,344m).

From the station head north-west and across the River Lochy, passing close to Inverlochy Castle. Built in 1260, the ruin is one of the oldest castles in Scotland.

The walk begins at the towpath section of the Caledonian Canal in Fort William. The canal, built by William Jessop and Thomas Telford, cuts through 22 miles (35km) of the Great Glen. Completed in 1822, after nearly 20 years of work, it links lochs Oich, Lochy and Ness to create a navigable waterway between the North Sea and the Atlantic, saving ships the long, dangerous journey round the Pentland Firth. However, it was never a great commercial success and is now used largely by leisure craft. The canal has 29 locks, including Neptune's Staircase, a spectacular flight of eight locks rising 65 feet (20m).

This early part of the towpath walk continues as far as the village of Gairlochy, crossing en route four aqueducts that pass *under* the towpath. Just before Gairlochy you cross the swing-bridge at Moy, but the best feature of this first part of the walk is the glorious view of the mountains rising on either side of the Great Glen.

The Jacobite rebellions

Beyond Gairlochy you are in true Jacobite country: the ancestral lands of the Camerons of Lochiel whose ancestral home, Achnacarry House, was destroyed after the Jacobite rebellion of 1745. There is a Cameron Museum a little off the route beyond Gairlochy.

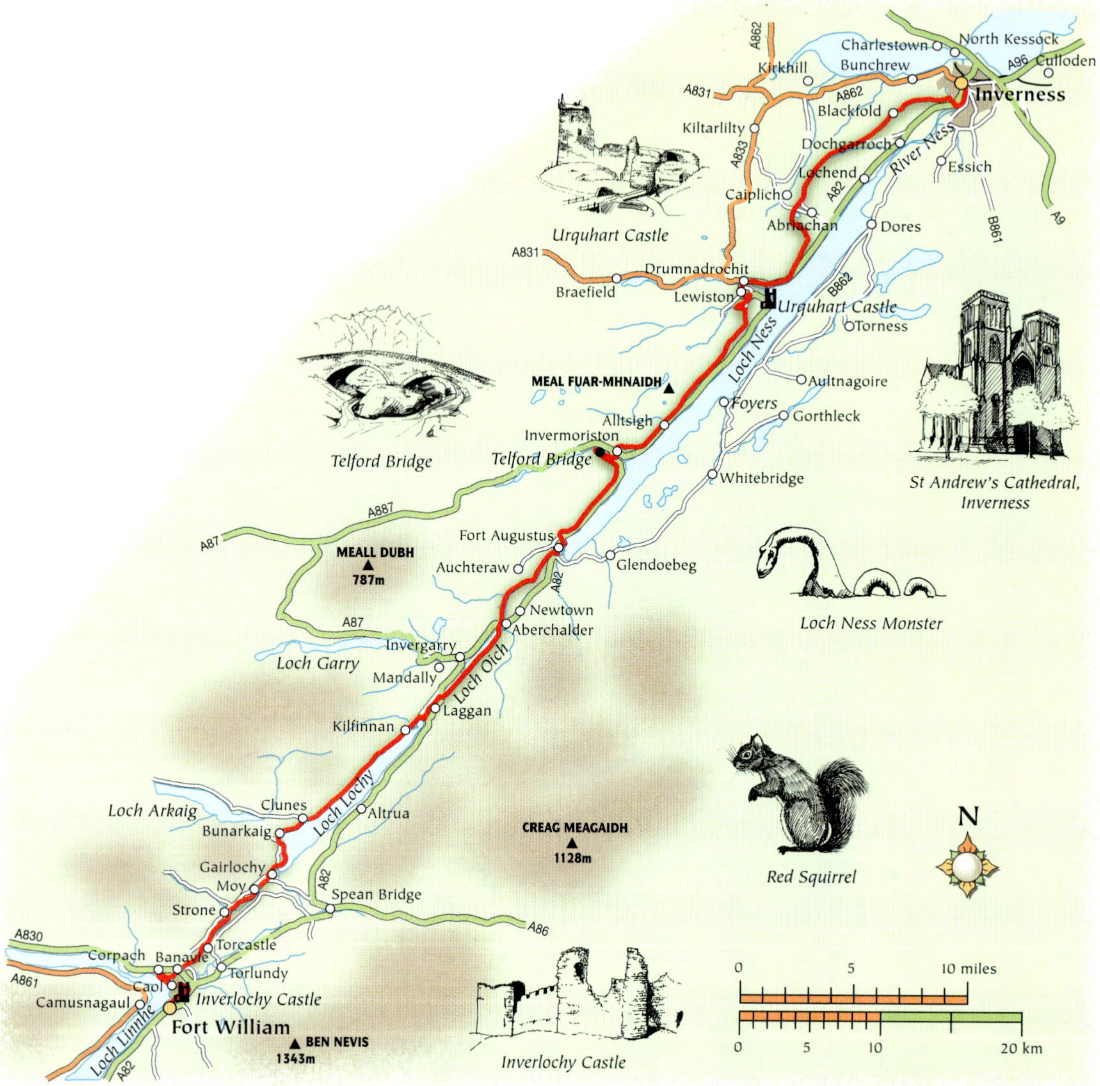

The Jacobite rebellions of 1715 and 1745, and the savage suppression of the Scots by the English that followed, changed the face of Scotland forever. Hundreds of miles of road were built – largely by the English General Wade – in an attempt to control the Highlands; landowners like the Camerons lost their local power base, their houses and even their lives.

The rebellions stemmed from the deposition of Catholic James II (also James VII of Scotland) in 1688 in favour of his Protestant daughter Mary, wife of the Dutch Protestant William. Despite the fact that William was heartily disliked by the British public there was little sympathy for

those (particularly in Scotland) who wanted to put James's son – also James, but known as the Old Pretender – on the throne. The 1715 rebellion failed and then, more famously, the Old Pretender's son Charles Edward Stuart – Bonnie Prince Charlie – failed in his attempt to regain the throne in 1745–6. This final rebellion ended in the bloody slaughter at Culloden on 16 April 1746.

From Gairlochy the way takes you to Clunes and then hugs the edge of Loch Lochy along forest paths until it reaches Kilfinnan. Here and there you glimpse the mountains rising above the loch. From Kilfinnan there is a short stretch of road walking until you reach Laggan Locks. Continue along the canal until you reach Laggan swing-bridge, then Great Glen Water and on into an area of mixed woodland, the Leiterfearn Nature Reserve, where you may see a red squirrel – Scotland is one of this species' last strongholds. The way now follows the line of the tracks of the long-vanished Spean-to-Fort Augustus railway, which closed just after World War II, for a short distance. The route then quickly reaches a stretch of Colonel Wade's Military Road, and before you lies Loch Oich with the ruins of Invergarry Castle in the distance. The castle, ancestral home of the MacDonnells, was destroyed during punitive raids after the 1745 rebellion.

The way leads on to Fort Augustus via Aberchalder and the Bridge of Oich. The latter – a wonderful design based on cantilevered chains supported between stone arches – was built in 1850 and carried motor traffic until just before World War II. For much of this stretch the route runs through attractive mixed woodland with the River Oich close on the left and the canal on the right. A short distance before you reach Kytra Lock the canal almost imperceptibly widens to form a small loch, above which, to the left, can be found one of Scotland's most ancient settlements. Torr Dhuin is one of a string of 10 hillforts along the Great Glen that date back to the Iron Age. Head up the slopes to the right towards the communications mast on the peak of Meall a Cholumain (3,389 feet/ 1,033m) if you want to enjoy spectacular panoramic views across lochs and mountains.

Above: *Neptune's Staircase on the Caledonian Canal consists of eight locks rising over 65 feet (20m). The locks were originally operated by lock keepers but have now been adapted to work via hydraulics. Built by William Jessop and Thomas Telford between 1803 and 1822, the canal cuts through 22 miles (35km) of the Great Glen.*

'Butcher Cumberland' alias 'Stinking Billy'

Back on the way you quickly reach Kilcumein, or Fort Augustus as it has been known since 1730 when General Wade – not the most popular man in Scotland – renamed it after

William Augustus, Duke of Cumberland, known in Scotland as 'Butcher Cumberland' or 'Stinking Billy'. Fort Augustus marks the beginning of the route along Loch Ness. The fort, where Wade's men were based during the Jacobite rebellion, was – ironically – eventually bought by Lord Lovat, a descendant of an executed Jacobite. Lovat gave the fort to a group of Benedictine monks. There is the interesting Caledonian Canal Heritage Centre here, and the Clansman Centre gives a good insight into Highland history.

Leave Fort Augustus and climb steeply through woodland with occasional views down to the huge expanse of Loch Ness. Look out for one of Britain's rarest birds above the loch – the osprey – which lives by fishing. More commonly you'll see herons, kestrels and some sea-birds that have wandered inland, such as kittiwake and fulmar. In the woods you may see crossbills and siskins, buzzards, owls, deer and red squirrels. Best of all, these woods still offer a home to the very rare pine marten as well as the ubiquitous rabbit and fox.

A few miles from Fort Augustus you will reach Invermoriston with its beautiful old stone bridge, built by Thomas Telford in 1814. When the stone bridge was no longer considered sturdy enough to carry modern traffic the Scots had the sense to build a new bridge to carry the cars, leaving the old bridge for pedestrians to enjoy.

Beyond Invermoriston the way takes the high slopes above Loch Ness for much of the route, avoiding the main A82 road. Cross the stream known as Allt Saigh just above a fine old packhorse bridge before reaching Grotaig. From here the brave and energetic may like to climb Meall Fuar-mhonaidh, which at 2,296 feet (700m) above sea level gives glorious views ahead to Inverness and back towards Fort William.

Urquhart Castle – a fine detour

Most of the path is now forest track until just before Drumnadrochit, where the way joins the A82 for the last half-mile (0.8km) or so. If you want to know anything and everything about the Loch Ness monster, Drumnadrochit is for you. There are two visitor centres and you can take a loch cruise. This is also the point at which you should take a detour to Urquhart Castle, which encompasses everything that typifies a Scottish castle. Perched high on a rocky outcrop on the edge of a natural bay of the same name, the castle – built in the mid-13th century – commands a view over the full length of the loch. Its five-storey tower house, built in the 1500s, has survived the ravages of time remarkably well, but much of the rest of the castle has been badly damaged by countless wars and sieges over the centuries. It has an excellent visitor centre.

From Drumnadrochit follow the A82 for a couple of miles (3km) before climbing through conifer plantations and woodland, much of which is preserved for its wildlife and amenity value by a local trust. Pass Loch Laide and then head towards Blackfold. Only a few hundred yards away is the prehistoric village of Caiplich,

Below: *Loch Lochy was linked to lochs Oich and Ness by the Caledonian Canal in the early 19th century to create a navigable waterway between the North Sea and the Atlantic. Some believe that Loch Lochy is home to Lizzie, the little sister of the Loch Ness monster, so walkers beware.*

where traces of the 2,500-year-old field system and hut circles can still be seen. Beyond Blackfold, woodland paths lead down towards the valley bottom. Loch Ness is now behind you, and the way follows the River Ness through the Great Glen towards the North Sea.

Above: *Castle Urquhart is the epitome of the Scottish castle: perched high on its rocky outcrop above Loch Ness, the 16th-century tower and 13th-century walls are now partly ruined, yet the castle still manages to house an excellent visitor centre.*

A cathedral city

Continuing downhill the way meets a road, houses and then an underpass. It skirts a golf course and then the river enters the Caledonian Canal again. The route crosses the canal and heads for Whin Park before crossing the river, and soon Inverness is reached. The Great Glen Way actually continues beyond the city to the point where the Caledonian Canal reaches the North Sea at Clachnaharry. There are monuments to the great engineer Telford here, as well as a splendid little lighthouse and, for railway buffs, an old signal box.

Archaeology tells us that there has been a settlement on the site of Inverness for at least 7,000 years. The twin-towered cathedral of St Andrew's was completed in 1870 at a time when much of the city was being developed as a result of new prosperity stemming from the railway and the Caledonian Canal. The city has an excellent museum and art gallery, and a delightfully open feel – most of the buildings are still on a human scale and the broad waters of the Ness, which still has a good run of salmon, sweep through the city.

Two excursions from the town are an absolute must: first to mid-18th-century Fort George, a little over 10 miles (16km) to the north-east. Much of the fort appears now as it did when it was first built. Those who take the journey 5 miles (8km) east of Inverness will reach Culloden, site of the final battle between supporters of the British Crown and the Jacobites in 1746. The story of Culloden seems to be the epitome of all battles fought for a lost cause. Although there is little to see beyond the visitor centre and a wide empty landscape, this is one of the most evocative places in the British Isles.

GREENSAND WAY

The Greensand Way runs along a narrow horseshoe-shaped ridge below the chalky North Downs of south-east England, from Haslemere in Surrey to Hamstreet in Kent, taking in old villages, hilltops and sites of industrial and much earlier archaeology. In many places it runs through National Trust land and officially designated Areas of Outstanding Natural Beauty.

The greensand ridge is composed of layers of sandstone filled with varying amounts of the green mineral glauconite. The greensand was laid down more than 100 million years ago; over succeeding millennia it was overlaid with sandstone and then chalk, before massive earth movements pushed the whole area up. Over time it has weathered and worn to leave a softer central belt – the Weald – with harder, more resistant chalk downs to the north and south. The narrow greensand ridge runs between the Weald and the downs, and is more prominent just inside the North Downs. The Greensand Way leads through other areas of great geological interest: in the Reigate area of Surrey there is firestone, and in Kent there is blue-grey ragstone.

Back to the Bronze Age

Four thousand years ago prehistoric people began to clear the dense woodland of the ridge and downs. Bronze Age people continued the process, leaving behind burial mounds as evidence of their occupation. Then came Celts, Saxons and Romans, all of whom left their mark on the landscape in the form of farming patterns, churches, ruined villas and so on.

The Romans called this area 'Andredsweal', meaning the great wood lying behind Anderida, now Pevensey. In medieval times the people of the ridge and downs relied on

GETTING AROUND THE GREENSAND WAY

Start: Haslemere, Surrey – by the Town Hall.

Finish: Hamstreet, Kent.

Length: (105 miles) 169km.

Transport Links: *Haslemere*: By car: located on the A286; by bus: Stagecoach links Haslemere with Guildford, Chichester and Bognor Regis, Midhurst, Godalming, Aldershot and Farnham; by train: Haslemere, on the London Waterloo to Portsmouth South West Trains line. *Hamstreet*: By car: take the A2070 or B2067; by bus: a Kent Coaches service runs hourly from Ashford; by train: Hamstreet, on the Ashford to Hastings line.

Ordnance Survey Maps: Explorer 133 Haslemere & Petersfield, 137 Ashford, Headcorn, Chilham & Wye, 145 Guildford & Farnham, 146 Dorking, Box Hill & Reigate, 147 Sevenoaks & Tonbridge, 148 Maidstone & the Medway Towns (1:25,000).

Guidebooks: *Along and Around the Greensand Way* by Bea Cowan (Kent County Council).

Website: www.kent.gov.uk/countrysideaccess.

sheep and – before the north of England became industrially predominant in the late 18th and 19th centuries – small-scale iron production was a staple in many communities along the ridge. As late as the 18th century, this region was so remote that London, just 35 miles (56km) away, might as well have been on another planet.

By the 17th century, most of the ancient woodland had gone, although tiny pockets perhaps 300–400 years old remain even today. The National Trust has done much to preserve particular landscapes along the ridge, and this helps to protect the wildlife of the area. At the Surrey end of the walk, agriculture is based on pasture for sheep and cattle and on arable crops. In Kent, the rich loamy soils have enabled extensive fruit growing and the cultivation of hops, for centuries. The distinctive Kentish oast house was developed several centuries after the introduction of hops. Hops transformed a nation of ale drinkers into a nation of beer enthusiasts; they were an import from Holland, and oast houses, which began to be built in the 17th century, were designed to improve the drying process. Many oast houses remain today and hops are still grown, though on a lesser scale than in years past.

Above: *This stained-glass window in St Bartholomew's Church, Haslemere was made to designs by the pre-Raphaelite painter Sir Edward Coley Burne-Jones (1833–98) and commemorates the Victorian poet laureate Alfred Lord Tennyson (1809–92).*

The first commuter towns

Both Kent and Surrey developed rapidly as dormitories for London commuters in the 19th century, and many houses from this period – including splendid examples, such as Munstead Wood near Godalming in Surrey by the great architect Sir Edwin Lutyens – remain. The Victorians also tore through many ancient medieval churches and then restored or rebuilt them.

The Greensand Way begins in Haslemere. This still pretty town was once a centre of the glass-making industry. It has an excellent local history museum and retains a number of beautiful 16th- and 17th-century buildings. St Bartholemew's Church has a stained-glass window to the memory of the poet Alfred Lord Tennyson, who spent his summers from 1868 until his death in 1892 at nearby Aldworth on the edge of Blackdown; the window was designed by the great pre-Raphaelite artist Burne Jones.

From the town hall the way takes you along the High Street to the Georgian Hotel where you turn left. Continue along Church Lane, over the railway and across two roads before taking a field path. The route goes through woodland and round gardens into a valley and then on towards the A3 before doubling back to Hindhead Common and Gibbet Hill. A cross here commemorates a sailor murdered by three men who were hanged on the hill in 1776. Cattle and horses have been reintroduced to try to restore Hindhead Common to its medieval appearance, at which time it would have been heavily grazed by commoners' animals.

Opposite: *The quaint post office at Hambledon Common sits in an area that was famous for glass-making in medieval times.*

The Devil's Punch Bowl

From Gibbet Hill the way leads across the A3 and along the side of the Devil's Punch Bowl. Legend has it that this splendid natural amphitheatre was created by the devil throwing a clod of earth at the god Thor; he missed, and the clod made a big hole in the ground. In fact, natural erosion caused by underground springs over countless

Above: *The Devil's Punch Bowl near Hindhead is a large tract of lowland heath containing a rich variety of flora and fauna. One of the best times to visit is on a sunny afternoon when it has been warmed by the sun.*

Opposite: *The church of St Michael and All Angels, Thursley, has Saxon windows on the north wall – the only ones in England with their original timber frames. The churchyard also has a number of interesting table tombs.*

millennia created the bowl. Charcoal-burners and broom-makers lived in hovels here until at least the early 20th century, and traces of these primitive shelters can still be seen.

A sunken path leads through woodland along a road and then across fields to Thursley with its Saxon church and 18th-century chest tombs. The main street in Thursley is also worth a look as it includes many 17th- and 18th-century houses. The route continues on past 16th-century Cosford Mill and then runs on across fields to Heath Hall, built in the 1800s. Parkland and woodland walking then bring you to the A286 and the little village of Brook, where the Dog and Pheasant pub gives the walker a rare chance to have a drink inside what was originally a medieval hall house.

From Brook we soon pass Witley with its 16th-century houses and Saxon church complete with 12th-century wall paintings. A path opposite the village pub, The Woodpigeon, takes you to a road and then a sandy track leads to Hambledon Common. Hambledon, a centre of glass-making in medieval times, is now home to garden designer Gertrude Jekyll's (1843–1932) collection of Surrey bygones – humble artefacts once used by ordinary people and never destined to become antiques; these are housed in the National Trust's 17th-century timber-framed Oakhurst Cottage.

Hambledon Church

Ewhurst Windmill

New church, old pond

The way goes past Hambledon Church and through woodland. March on below the wonderful line of beech trees that is Burgate Hangar and you will eventually reach Hascombe. Here, as in so many greensand villages, the medieval church was demolished and rebuilt in the 19th century. This is good Victorian work, however, and the roof is especially fine: it is designed to look just like an upturned fishing boat. Hascombe's pond once provided the village with an excellent supply of fish.

From Hascombe head uphill into woodland until you reach a road. Soon after this you reach 17th-century Scotsland Farm before more field walking and woodland bring you to Gatestreet Farm. A path then takes you – mostly on a track – to the A281 where you cross a railway and the line of the long-vanished Wey & Arun Canal. This canal was an extraordinary feat of engineering, rising 48 feet (14.5m) in just 6 miles (10km) through seven locks. It cost the Earl of Egremont a fortune to build but was a failure from the start; it closed in 1870.

Bilberries and juneberries

Soon you reach Long Common and then cut across fields to Shamley Green where ironworking was once the dominant industry. From here you pass ancient farms before climbing to Winterfold Heath and Winterfold Hill. All around was once common land, taken without compensation from the commoners during the major period of enclosure at the end of the 18th century. Much of the land

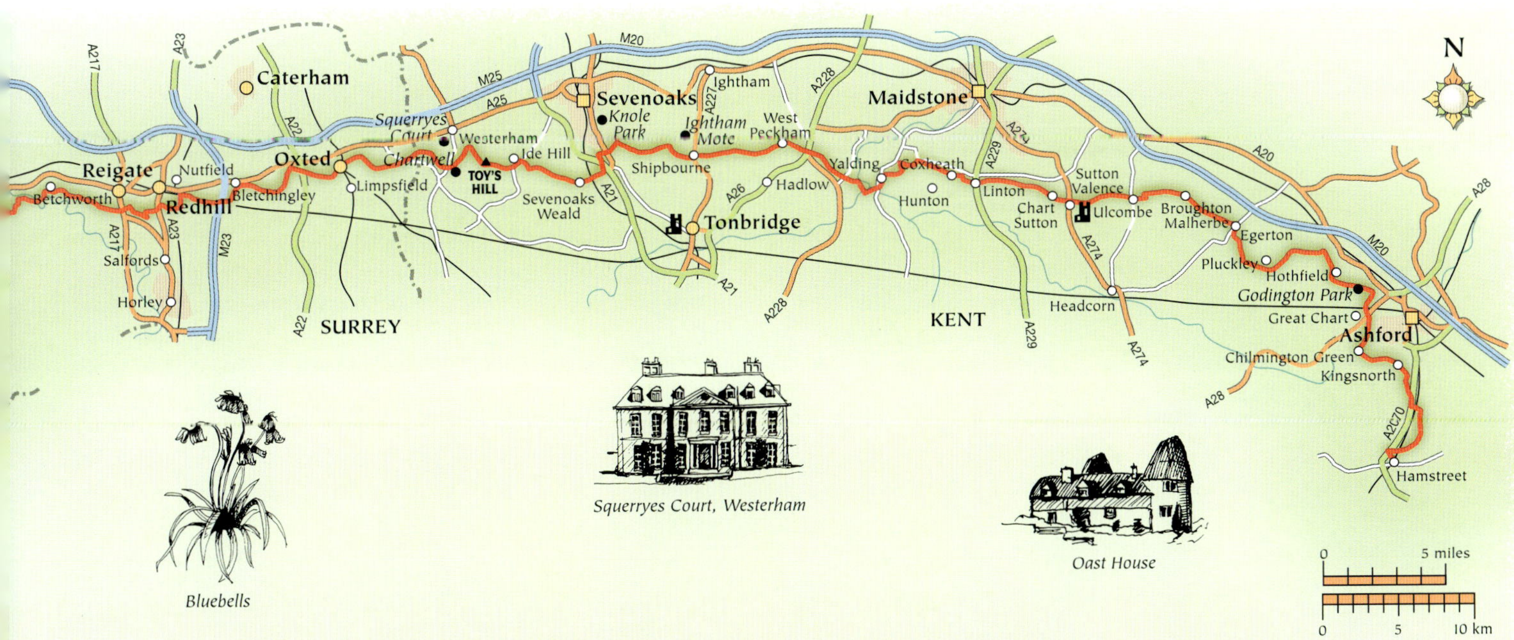

Above: *Leith Hill Tower on Leith Hill is the highest point on the Greensand Way. On a clear day London and 12 other counties can be seen from the summit. It was built by Richard Hull, who provided visitors to the tower with prospect glasses, a type of miniature telescope, through which they could view the sea some 30 miles (48km) distant.*

was given back to the people by local landowner Sir Reginald Bray in the 1920s. The area is now part of Hurtwood, named after the hurts, a kind of bilberry that grows on the sandy soils.

The way continues through woodland and along tracks to reach Ewhurst windmill. Built in 1840, the windmill closed just 40 years later. From here you descend, only to climb again to Pitch Hill where attractive American juneberries grow over much of the slopes. Descend Pitch Hill, almost going back on yourself, and continue along paths and trackways, cross a road and head into woodland before reaching Hurtwood car-park and heading uphill. Pass Holmbury Iron Age hillfort and then descend to the Abinger Hammer road. Turn right and then left, before taking a track uphill towards Leith Hill Tower. In 1766, a wealthy local man named Richard Hull, disappointed that his beloved Leith Hill (967 feet/295m) failed to be a mountain by just 35 feet (12m), obtained permission from the Lord of the Manor, a descendant of the great 17th-century diarist John Evelyn, to build a tower that would take the hill over the 1,000-foot (305-m) mark (1,029 feet/341m to be precise). It is the highest point on the walk and the highest hill in the south-east. The tower was enlarged in the 19th century, and is surrounded by hazel and oak woods. The area is famous for its colourful display of rhododendrons in May and June.

Wildlife watching

From Leith Hill the route descends to Broadmoor before crossing the River Tillbourne. Woodland walks and trackways follow before you reach Westcott and the Nower, a wide area of heath and woodland. Westcott still has a few pretty 17th-century houses and a church – Holy Trinity – designed by Sir George Gilbert Scott (1811–78), one of the more sympathetic Victorian church improvers. The Nower, also once commonland, is now an important area for wildlife: kestrels and other raptors, owls, woodpeckers and many rare insects thrive here, and the bluebells are splendid in spring.

The Nower is on the edge of Dorking – about which the less said the better – through which the path makes its way. Just beyond Dorking, however, Glory Wood is a gem. Given to the local people by the Duke of Newcastle in 1928, it is rich in wildlife and offers wonderful views of the North Downs.

From Dorking the way leads across fields and over the River Mole into Betchworth. Here Deepdene House once stood. This property had three incarnations: as a wonderful 17th-century house much admired by the diarist John Evelyn, as a Palladian house and, finally, as a Gothic house of 1805; this last was demolished in 1969. The local church of St Michael's contains an interesting monument to Thomas Morsted, surgeon to kings Henry IV, V and VI, who left an annuity to the church of 16 pennies to help with repairs. William Benjamin, surgeon to Queen Victoria, is also buried here.

From Betchworth cross fields and tracks to Reigate golf course before climbing to a

windmill. Descend to a road before climbing again to woodland and along a road to Reigate Park. Reigate still has the remains of its castle, while its priory – which was founded in the 13th century and converted into a mansion in the 16th century – is now a school.

Above: *Oast houses were introduced from Holland several centuries after the arrival of the hop itself, and were designed to speed up the hop-drying process; they can now be found all over Kent.*

Firestone

Reigate gives its name to Reigate stone, or firestone as it is sometimes known. Fullers earth, a silicate of ammonia whose absorbent properties were needed in the cloth making industry until relatively recently, was also extracted from a seam in the greensand hereabouts, but particularly at Nutfield and Bletchingley. Much of the way through Reigate and the surrounding area is along roads, small commons and a golf course. After crossing the main railway line the trail follows Redhill Brook and crosses fields before returning to the road. Having crossed the M23, the way skirts Bletchingley and continues across fields to Tandridge, where St Peter's Church has a bell-tower that was built in 1300 and a yew tree that is said to be the oldest in Britain. Walk from Tandridge to Oxted (about 1 mile/1.6km), where you will find splendid 15th- and 16th-century houses and the Old Bell inn, whose overhanging timber-framed first floor should not be missed.

The route now crosses Limpsfield Common to the village of the same name. Limpsfield Chart comes next – members of the Fabian Society, including dramatist and writer George Bernard Shaw, met here in the late 19th and early 20th centuries – and then Mariner's Hill, which was given to the National Trust by Ocatavia Hill, one of the trust's founders.

As the way passes to the south of Westerham it skirts Squerryes Court, a superb example of a gorgeous red-brick William and Mary house.

Churchill at Chartwell

From Mariner's Hill the way leads to Chartwell, Winston Churchill's home from 1924 until his death in 1965, and now owned by the National Trust. A trackway leads to a bridleway and then on to Toy's Hill which, at just over 800 feet (244m), is the highest point in Kent. Formerly tree-covered, the hill was badly hit by the storms of 1987.

Continue downhill across fields and tracks to Ide Hill – where much of the surrounding land is designated a Site of Special Scientific Interest because of its improved pastures – and then head for Goathurst Common. Pleasant field and woodland walking eventually leads to Sevenoaks Weald, a village that developed as a result of London commuters discovering Kent early in the 20th century.

Below: *Chartwell was Sir Winston Churchill's home from 1924 until his death. Now owned by the National Trust, the rooms and gardens remain much as they were in Churchill's day, making this house a veritable museum of the great statesman.*

After crossing the A21 the path cuts across the estate of Knole Park, one of the greatest houses in England. The house was built in 1456 and was given to the Sackville family, who still live there, by Elizabeth I. The house has a unique collection of 17th-century textiles and furniture. The 1,000-acre (405-ha.) estate is unique in that it has never been ploughed or sprayed with chemicals.

Once out of the park the way continues past Carter's Hill, Rooks Hill, Shingle Hill and Wilmot Hill to arrive at Ightham Mote (also National Trust), surely the most romantic moated house in England. Tucked away in its own little valley, it dates from 1330 and was never a particularly grand house, which makes its survival all the more extraordinary.

Shipbourne comes next, and then Roughway and the River Bourne, a tributary of the Medway that once powered numerous paper mills. Roughway must also have been an important Roman settlement as two Roman villas have been excavated nearby.

Field and farm tracks bring you to the Peckhams, West and East. West Peckham's St Dunstan's Church has many memorials to the local grand families, the Colepepers and the Gearys. West Peckham also has the splendid 15th-century Duke's Palace which, despite the name, was associated with the Knights of St John, an order of chivalry dissolved by Henry VIII. At Moat Wood begin the descent to the Medway Valley, which takes its name from the Celtic word 'medu' meaning sweet water. The River Medway was once one of the most important trade routes in Europe, particularly for iron, timber, corn and lime. Yalding, the next village along our route, has retained its medieval bridges.

The garden of England

As we reach Hunton and Linton we enter the rich fruit-growing lands of Kent. From the high point occupied by the splendidly named Boughton Monchelsea Place – built in 1567 – there are wonderful views across to the South Downs. At the end of the garden is the church of St Peter with its 16th-century lych-gate. The church itself was rebuilt in the 19th century.

Kent has long been one of the most heavily settled parts of England, as evidenced by the fact that, from here to the end of the walk at Hamstreet,

Above: *Fifteenth-century Knole House is set in a magnificent deer park. In 1603, the original house was enlarged and embellished by the 1st Earl of Dorset, one of Queen Elizabeth's 'favourites', and has remained unaltered ever since.*

villages come thick and fast. Chart Sutton and Sutton Valence are next. This is hop-growing country where, until World War II, generations of Londoners came annually to pick a crop once derided by the English as the spoiler of ale. At Sutton Valence the way passes one of our oldest schools, founded by William Lambe, a clothmaker, in the 1560s. Lambe's almhouses, built at about the same time, are worth visiting, as is the tomb of John Wells (1760–1835) in St Mary's churchyard. Wells, to the outrage of his diehard colleagues on Surrey County cricket team, first permitted overarm bowling in cricket.

East Sutton comes next, then Ulcombe whose church has some excellent medieval wall-paintings. Pluckley, a village reached across fields and orchards, is said to be the most haunted village in Britain; look out for the red lady and phantom coachman! The village church of St Nicholas has an extremely rare pre-Reformation screen. From Pluckley cross gently undulating countryside through farm and woodland to Little Chart (where paper has been made since 1770) and Hothfield Common, home to such plants as bog asphodel and St John's wort and an important wildlife site for insects, amphibians and birds.

After Little Chart you quickly reach Godington with its 17th-century manor house, and then Great Chart, a one-street village with a church built partly with stone plundered from a nearby Roman road. Beyond the village the way rises to a point at which the River Great Stour can be seen in the distance with the North Downs beyond. Kingsnorth village more or less dates from the 19th century, although the church is 14th-century. The trail is now mostly level, and at Ham Street Woods enters an area of international importance for wildlife; this is the last remnant of an ancient forest and dates back to the last Ice Age.

At last we reach Hamstreet and the end of the Greensand Way. Before the arrival of the railway, Hamstreet was an isolated spot, deeply mired in winter and inaccessible to all but the most determined traveller – which may explain why the notorious Ransley gang of poachers hid their booty here in the 18th century.

HADRIAN'S WALL PATH

Given the beauty of the remote landscape that Hadrian's Wall crosses between the Tyne and the Solway in the north of England and the historic siginificance of the Wall as a northern outpost of the Roman Empire, it is astonishing that the Hadrian's Wall coast-to-coast walk did not become an official National Trail until May 2003, although it did become a World Heritage Site in 1987. This has always been a difficult area to govern, however; as late as the 18th century it was still considered completely lawless, subject to cattle-raiding and bloody feuds between the borderland families.

Opposite: *The Roman turret at Walltown Crags along the central section of Hadrian's Wall is a significant ruin, as much of the rest of the wall has been plundered over the centuries for building materials used in roads and houses.*

The wall itself has only been protected in relatively recent times. For centuries its stone was plundered by local farmers and road-builders. An eye-witness account from 1801 backs this up: having made a month-long tour of the wall the Reverend John Skinner wrote, 'The mutilated figure of a woman standing at the back of an animal has lately been put in a wall enclosing a plantation … [and] … some masons who were making a new wall near a turn-pike confessed to me they had broken up many big stones covered with inscriptions.'

From Wallsend to Bowness-on-Solway, the wall was built deliberately to take advantage of any high ground. After the Jacobite rising of 1745 massive sections were plundered by King George's soldiers to build an east–west road by which they hoped to control the turbulent north. The line of this Military Road – under modern tarmac – remains to this day. Today the wall still exists for much of its length, but rarely stands higher than about three feet (1m). When first built it would have been over 20 feet (6m) high with milecastles, turrets and forts dotted along its 80 Roman (73 modern) miles (117km). The wall can be seen stretching away over the hills into the distance in one or two areas. Traces are visible here and there even in the now heavily urbanized areas of Newcastle, Wallsend and Byker.

GETTING AROUND HADRIAN'S WALL PATH

Start: Wallsend, Newcastle upon Tyne – by Segedunum fort.

Finish: Bowness-on-Solway, Cumbria.

Length: 81 miles (130km).

Transport Links: *Wallsend*: Segedunum Fort is located on the A186/7; by bus: principal operators are Go Ahead, Arriva and Stagecoach. Hadrian's Wall Bus Service is a special service operating daily throughout summer along most of the length of the wall, stopping at key locations; by train: Newcastle station, on the major West Coast and East Coast lines between London and Scotland. From Newcastle, take the Tyne and Wear Metro to Wallsend. A branch line running parallel to Hadrian's Wall connects Carlisle and Newcastle via Haltwhistle and Hexham. *Bowness on Solway*: By car: take the B5307 to Kirkbride, from which the remote Bowness is a 12-minute drive; by bus: The Stagecoach Cumberland/Arriva 685 bus service follows the A69 between Newcastle and Carlisle; No. 93 runs between Bowness and Carlisle railway station; by train: Carlisle Station, a 25-minute bus journey away.

Ordnance Survey Maps: Explorer OL43 Hadrian's Wall, 314 Solway Firth, 315 Carlisle, 316 Newcastle upon Tyne (1:25,000).

Guidebooks: *Hadrian's Wall Path National Trail Guide*, Anthony Burton (Aurum Press, 2003).

When Hadrian's Wall and its great ditch, the Vallum, were built all the land north of the wall was inhabited by the Picts, a tribe about whom little is known. The Scotti, an Irish tribe from the area around modern Dublin, arrived in AD 454, after the Romans had departed, and gave modern Scotland its name. The Roman Emperor Hadrian came to Britain in AD 122 and ordered the wall to be built – probably by legionnaires rather than slaves – to mark the northernmost boundary of the Roman Empire and to keep out raiding parties of what they called barbarians.

We know that the eastern end of the wall was built first. A deep ditch was dug to the north, and 17 large forts, some of which still have substantial remains, were built at intervals. The forts would have been part military camp and part civilian settlement, with houses, grain stores, baths and so on. The milecastles (as the name suggests, built at mile-long intervals) would each have had a garrison of eight soldiers. Between each milecastle were two watchtowers, each manned by two soldiers.

A suburban start

The path starts in the post-industrial heartland of Wallsend. Here, where shipbuilding was a large part of the 19th- and 20th-century industrial base, are the remains of Segedunum Fort. A good, if short, stretch of Hadrian's Wall leads away from what would have been the west gate of the fort. Little remains here other than the lowest courses of the walls, but they give a clear indication of the general layout, which is best seen from the observation tower; there is also an excellent museum here. After this short section the wall disappears and you pass through Walker along a disused railway before reaching Walker Riverside Park and then the recently developed Quayside that leads into the heart of Newcastle. Before leaving Newcastle visit Bessie Surtees's late medieval house on the newly restored quayside. The 'new' castle, though badly damaged by the coming of the railway, retains its Norman keep (*c.* 1160) and is also well worth visiting. It stands on the site of the Pons Aelius Fort (*pons* meaning bridge).

The official path takes a route through the post-industrial landscape of Scotswood and Denton, but you can deviate from this and leave Newcastle by Westgate Hill, beyond which intermittent traces of the wall are visible alongside the suburban road. Then, in the middle of a great swathe of 1930s housing, you can take a short detour to a miraculous survival: the Roman Temple of Antenociticus, which sits neatly between two houses. Turn off Westgate Hill into Broomridge Avenue where the first few stone courses can still be seen. When the temple was discovered its apse and a few pillars also remained. The pillars are now in Newcastle Museum and have been replaced on the site by replicas.

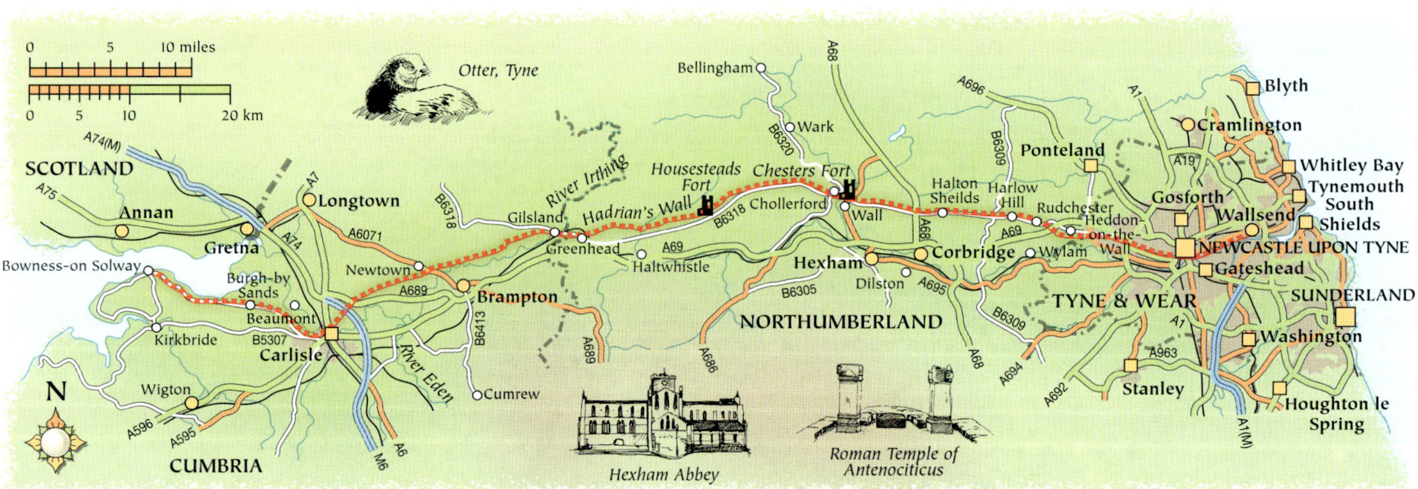

Above: *The Roman fort at Housesteads covers five acres and much of the layout of the granary, stores, and latrines can still be seen. In the latrines even the loo seats are still in position!*

From here the path continues towards Wylam where the great engineer George Stephenson was born in 1781. There is also the splendid 18th-century Close House, now owned by Newcastle University. For more than a century, until the 1990s, the lower reaches of the Tyne were some of the dirtiest waters in Europe. Now the salmon have returned, and otters are seen occasionally within 10 miles (16km) of the centre of Newcastle. The official route reaches Wylam via Newburn and the Tyne Riverside Country Park

Ancient placenames

At Bulcher parts of the wall are again visible, as is the Vallum (ditch). The path then reaches Walbottle (whose name means 'the farmstead on the wall'). All along the route many place names derive from the presence of settlement along the wall; Benwell, for example, means 'within the wall'.

The path continues to Throckley ('the burial mound of Throcca'). A little beyond the village the broad open valley of the Tyne appears. Continue past Heddon Hall to Great Hall village and the first really impressive stretch of wall; here well over 300 yards (100m) can be seen, all of it standing more than 3 feet (1m) tall. But it's not just the wall that is so impressive – it's the setting in this still wild, relatively uninhabited countryside. Although it has been heavily restored, the wall does appear now much as it would have looked when the Romans patrolled it, as they did for around 300 years.

From Heddon to Rudchester the path follows the wall high up and parallel to the Tyne. At Rudchester there are the remains of a temple dedicated to Mithras, a Roman god associated with bull sacrifice. Many of the farms nearby were almost certainly built from stone taken from the temple. The path continues on to Horsley and Nafferton Castle via Whittle Dene, a wooded valley seemingly undisturbed by the modern world.

A short detour south from the wall brings us to Corbridge with its ancient river crossing and medieval pele tower, the stone of which may well have come from the wall. Corbridge was for many years best known for its splendid Unwearoutable Sock shop. The shop is gone now, but the town has many lovely old houses. Nearby was the Roman fort of Corstopitum, which sat on the north–south crossing of Roman Dere Street (part of Watling Street), which ran from York to the Firth of Forth, and the east–west-running Stanegate, which ran from Carlisle to Corbridge. Several stone courses remain and the drainage systems can still be seen. The names Corbridge and Corstopitum may both derive from a Celtic tribe, the Corio, that once inhabited this region.

Beyond Corbridge the path passes close to Dilston Castle, a 15th-century house once owned by the Jacobite Duke of Derwentwater, who was executed after the 1715 uprising.

Hexham Abbey

Our next detour is a little to the south to Hexham with its great abbey, market and pretty streets. The Saxon crypt in the abbey, dating from the middle years of the 7th century, is well preserved. The rest of the church is late 12th- and early 13th-century, and contains a number of Roman carvings and inscribed stones. Don't miss the 14th-century moot hall and its Border Library Trust, which has a unique collection of Northumberland pipe music. Leave Hexham by the bridge north over the Tyne and head for Acombe village.

The Military Road now underlies the B6318. Near Planetrees Farm there is another fine stretch of wall, and it was here that it reduced in width from 10 feet (3m) to 8 feet (2.5m). No one knows the reasons behind this, but the point at which the change occurs is still clearly visible. Here, too, the Military Road diverges from the route of the wall and we reach some of the very best-preserved sections.

Below: *The wall at Cawfield is one of the best preserved sections. These sections are to be found, generally, in the wildest and most remote countryside, which looks today much as it would have looked 1,800 years ago when the wall was first built.*

A little further ahead survives the remains of Brunton Turret, still 8 feet (2.5m) high, and then you reach Chollerford with its delightful 18th-century bridge. The remains of a Roman bridge can be seen over the Tyne at Chesters, and Chesters House holds large numbers of Roman artefacts, collected by the Victorian antiquary John Clayton. Without Clayton's intervention far less of Hadrian's Wall – and more particularly the monuments and inscribed stones found along it – would have survived.

Above: *A superb stretch of wall near Housesteads leads the walker on towards Carlisle. Here it is possible to see how the Roman engineers took advantage of the high, easily defended ground.*

The path runs close to Cilurnum Fort, almost certainly a cavalry garrison, where the lavatory system is still clearly visible. The bath house here even has traces of its internal plaster, as well as niches in the walls that may have held the statues of Roman deities. The fort is situated close to the North Tyne, a tributary of the Tyne proper and the haunt of good populations of otters, salmon and trout. The salmon benefited enormously from the decline of traditional Tyneside industries, the pollution from which had made it impossible for them to get upriver to their breeding grounds.

A wild, remote landscape

Along this stretch there are wide views across the North Tyne Valley, with Redesdale and the Cheviot Hills beyond. It is spectacular countryside, and one can see why Northumberland was one of just three or four places in England recently defined by the Campaign for the Protection of Rural England as genuinely wild. This part of the route runs along the edge of the Northumberland National Park, through country that was once the land of the Border reivers or raiders. Families like the Charltons and the Robsons had feuded with each other for centuries, ignoring the laws by which most of Britain was governed, until punitive raids by 18th-century militia put a stop to their activities.

The next substantial remains are those of the temple of Mithras, just below the ruins of Brocolitia Fort. Nearby, too, is a well where offerings were thought to have

Above: *Walkers must expect sheep to be regular companions along Hadrian's Wall.*

Opposite, top: *The Roman quarry at Walltown is just one part of the impressive structure that is Hadrian's Wall. Unlike many other massive early defence works, such as Offa's Dyke, Hadrian's Wall is not thought to have been built by slaves.*

Opposite, bottom: *Carlisle Castle was built by William Rufus in 1092. The oldest and most impressive surviving part of the castle is the large 12th-century stone keep.*

been made to the goddess Coventin. When it was excavated, the well was found to be full of small inscribed pieces of lead – mostly inscribed with curses – as well as numerous bits of pottery and thousands of coins.

A little further on you reach Sewingshields Farm and the best and most famous stretch of Hadrian's Wall, where it runs for hundreds of yards along the black dolomite ridge of Whin Sill. At Beaumont the wall lies about a quarter of a mile from the ditch; the ground was simply too hard immediately below the wall. At Winshield Crag, a little further on, the situation is similar; the wall perches on an 800-foot (244-m) high rock outcrop that the ditch has to skirt round.

At Sewingshields Milecastle there is an extraordinary feature: a Saxon grave has been dug right up against the wall for reasons that we are never likely to discover. Nothing else like it exists.

Across this bleak, open landscape – too remote for stone robbers – the main line of the wall is clear. At Knag Burn you can see not only the wall stretching away, but also a Roman gateway, still with its two guardrooms. Then we reach Housesteads, an extraordinarily well-preserved fort, known to the Romans as Vercovicium. It covers 5 acres (2 ha.) and originally included a granary, hospital, latrines – still with their multiple seats in position and a stone basin for washing – and barracks. Glass bottles, used for keeping oil for cleaning purposes, have been found. It is thought that the Romans poured the oil over their bodies and then used a strigil to scrape off oil and dirt.

From Housesteads follow the wall to Cuddy's Crags, then on over the still remote country to Rapishaw Gap, Hotbank Crags, Milking Gap and Crag Lough. At Sycamore Gap the National Trust has rebuilt, using original stones, a stretch of the wall. At Mons Fabricus the foundations are broader than the wall itself, suggesting that the plan for Hadrian's Wall was in place before it was actually built. Near Peel Crags a swastika can be seen carved into a stone in one of the lower courses, a symbol of good luck in Roman times. Look back from Steel Rigg towards Peel Crags – a wilder, more impressive view would be hard to find.

Cawfields Crags is a popular place for day-trippers out to see one of the best parts of the wall. From here the path crosses the north–south Pennine Way, then crosses Haltwhistle Burn and on to Great Chesters. At Cockmount Hill traces of cultivation terraces, believed to be of Roman or earlier origin, can still be seen. The path continues to Mucklebank Crag and Walltown Crags where the 7th-century Northumbrian King Edwin is said to have been baptized. Irthing Gorge comes next and the gaunt ruins of Thirlwall Castle. The castle was built in the 13th century using stones from the wall. From this point rivers and streams begin to flow westwards instead of east.

Towards the Lakes

At Gilsland, an old spa town, we leave Northumberland and enter Cumbria. From here the path heads towards Birdoswald Fort, overlooking the River Irthing. A bridleway that heads for Bewcastle from here follows the route of the old Roman road. From Birdoswald the views towards the Lakeland Fells are spectacular.

The path passes Comboglanna Fort, which was plundered in 1779 when nearby Castlesteads House was built. At Newtown detour to the delightful red sandstone town of Brampton, with its Georgian moot hall and a centre miraculously ignored by 1960s planners and architects. Back on the path we reach Bleatarn before crossing the M6. The path passes Drawdykes Castle – an 18th-century house – and leads on to Carlisle. This lovely red sandstone city has a romantic castle and the splendid Tullie House Museum of Roman artefacts. The path leaves Carlisle and follows the River Eden, still a good salmon-fishing river, before continuing on along the river to Grinsdale, Beaumont and Burgh-by-Sands, then on past Drumbergh Castle.

The way ends at Bowness-on-Solway, an ancient settlement on the edge of the Solway Coast Area of Outstanding Natural Beauty. The Solway Estuary is an internationally important wintering ground for ducks, geese and wading birds, including plover and oyster-catchers. Seals and dolphins are common offshore and the coastal sands are one of the last strongholds of the natterjack toad. Bowness once had a Roman fort, but little remains of it today, instead its stone is visible in the walls of the church and the oldest village houses.

HEART OF ENGLAND WAY

The Heart of England Way gives the lie to the idea that central England is almost entirely industrial and urban. The way runs through the charming Cotswolds, the magical Forest of Arden and on to Cannock Chase. It is particularly rich in historical and literary associations – largely thanks to William Shakespeare. First suggested in the 1970s, the Heart of England Way finally received official recognition in 1990.

Above: *The Grand Union Canal, which is crossed during the walk, was completed in 1806 and links the Thames to Birmingham.*

From the Cotswolds, the Heart of England way moves north to the Vale of Evesham's orchards and arable fields before reaching the River Avon at Bidford. Flatter country gradually gives way to more hilly landscapes around Arden, the suburbs of Berkswell and the glorious open country around Meriden, the geographical centre of England. Then comes the industrial Tame valley, the wooded hills around Weeford, the cathedral city of Lichfield and, finally, the woods and heaths of Cannock Chase.

The walk starts at Bourton-on-the-Water, an attractive but touristy town in the heart of the Cotswolds. The village's oldest houses are early 17th century, built from the lovely creamy-yellow Cotswold stone – oolitic limestone – that characterizes all the local settlements. Bourton, however, can trace its story back more than 2,000 years, when a number of ancient trackways converged on the settlement. The most important of these was the Roman Fosse Way, which ran from Lincoln to Bath. Iron Age finds, such as grave pottery, suggest even greater antiquity.

A 'sheela na gig' in Lower Swell

From Bourton-on-the-Water the path crosses the A429 and makes its way along the River Eye until it reaches the village of Lower Slaughter, with a fascinating restored mill

GETTING AROUND THE HEART OF ENGLAND WAY

Start: Bourton-on-the-Water, Gloucestershire.
Finish: Milford, Staffordshire.
Length: 100 miles (167km).
Transport Links: *Bourton-on-the-Water*: By car: take the A429/A436; by bus: local bus services connect with most train stations. Pulham's (from Cheltenham) and Beaumont 55 operate services to the village. National Express coaches run between London and Cirencester or Cheltenham; by train: Moreton-in-Marsh is the nearest station, from here you can take a bus to Bourton-on-the-Water. *Milford*: By car: located on the A513; by bus: The No. 825 runs hourly from Stafford; by train: Stafford is the nearest station.
Ordnance Survey Maps: Explorers OL45 the Cotswolds, 205 Stratford-upon-Avon & Evesham, 220 Birmingham, 221 Coventry & Warwick, 232 Nuneaton & Tamworth, 244 Cannock Chase & Chasewater (1:25,000).
Guidebooks: *The Heart of England Way*, John Roberts (Walkways, 2000); *Heart of England Way*, Richard Sale (Aurum Press, 1998); *The Heart of England Way from the Cotswolds to Cannock Chase*, Roger Noyce (Sigma Leisure, 1999).
Website: http://hoe-way.port5.com/

Above: *The River Windrush flows gently through pretty Bourton-on-the-Water. The town's, numerous low bridges spanning the river have caused it to be often captioned 'the Venice of the Cotswolds'.*

and several pretty bridges across the river. The word 'slaughter' comes from Old English 'slough', meaning a marshy area. Continue across fields until you cross the little River Dikler. It's easy to follow the way along this stretch as it continues over two bridges and passes Slaughter Woods to Hyde Mill. From the mill take a wide green lane, pass Nether Swell manor house (built in 1900, but in a vaguely 17th-century style) and head on into the village of Lower Swell, which has a partly Norman church, a small triangular green with a memorial and a decent pub. The church has a 'sheela na gig', a bizarre, vaguely pornographic carving of a woman on its Norman arch.

Lower Swell is just a short distance from Stow-on-the-Wold, which lies a little off the route. Stow, perched on a hill rising to 800 feet (244m), is the highest settlement in the Cotswolds; and the couplet 'Stow-on-the-Wold, where the wind blows cold' is certainly true during the winter months. Stow has a splendid ancient market square where regular farmers' markets are now held. The cross in the square was to remind the sheep traders who once gathered here that God was watching to see if they cheated each other! Each May and October Stow horse fair, which began as a hiring fair in the Middle Ages is held just outside the town.

Like most Cotswold towns and villages, Stow has an abundance of antique shops, but it also has lots of interesting pubs, including the Royalist Inn, said to be one of the oldest in Britain. Some of the structure certainly dates back to the middle of the 10th century. The Royalist started life as a monastic foundation dedicated to the support of travellers, becoming an inn after the Dissolution in 1545.

Betjeman country

Back on the path at Lower Swell continue across fields, passing over several stiles until you reach the pretty hamlet of Upper Swell. From here the walk follows the road for half a mile or so to once again cross the River Dikler. Continue until you cross the A424 onto a trackway through fields and past woods and stiles to the delightfully named Love Walk Lane. This takes you into the village of Longborough with its 12th-century church and two pubs. The nearby long barrow (ancient burial site), from which the village takes its name, is 5,000 years old. Go past the church, whose bells inspired the late poet laureate John Betjeman (1906–84) to write:

At six o'clock from Bourton-on-the-Hill
The bells rang out above the clumps of oak
A lighter peal from Longborough lingered on
Moreton-in-Marsh came echoing from the vale.

Continue on through fields with lovely views of rolling countryside. You will pass Sezincote House – a remarkable early 18th-century house built in an Indian style, where Betjeman stayed in the 1920s – and soon that most lovely Cotswold town Moreton-in-Marsh comes into view. The way bypasses Moreton, but you should make a detour to have a look at the town. There are lots of good pubs and an interesting old curfew tower. The way continues on into Bourton-on-the-Hill, which has a pub, several attractive houses and a very pretty church. All these Cotswold villages are so picturesque that it's almost impossible to resist the temptation to explore each one, including those off the way. This is a route best not attempted in a hurry!

From Bourton head off over small hedged fields that appear little changed since the 18th century. The way passes the Batsford Estate, with its arboretum and 19th-century mansion (open to the public), and goes on to Blockley. From Blockley you must set off across rolling countryside to Broad Campden and then Chipping Campden with its wonderful old market hall, almshouses and church. Like so many of the settlements in the Cotswolds, Chipping Campden's past wealth was based on the medieval wool industry; today tourists have replaced sheep as the major source of income.

After leaving Chipping Campden the way crosses school playing fields before heading out over farmland to Blake's Hill. As you descend Blake's Hill there are splendid views across the valley, and then the trail reaches the village of Mickleton, the most northerly Cotswold village. Head north-east across fields and stiles and round Meon Hill to Upper Quinton with its thatched cottages and medieval church. More field walking leads to Long Marston and Dorsington.

Below: *The historic Butter Market at Chipping Campden shows how beautifully Cotswold stone weathers. The town is also famous for its beautiful early almshouses and its medieval church.*

The Throckmortons

From Dorsington the way soon crosses the River Avon and then follows its course to Bidford-on-Avon, which has an excellent 15th-century bridge and a 13th-century church, much restored by the Victorians. Descend into the town and then follow the Bidford–Broom road until you reach the village of Broom, famous until well into the 20th century for basket-making and knife-grinding. The way then takes you through fields that pass Moor Hall, touch the River Arrow, and pass Wixford, which was until recently still occasionally called 'Papist Wixford' because of the strong influence of local Catholic landowners, the Throckmortons.

The path wanders past the village church and climbs towards 19th-century Oversley Castle; there was a building here in the 12th century too. A trackway takes you round the castle and over the A46 into Oversley Green. From here it's just a short distance into the Roman town of Alcester with its splendidly preserved almshouses, Tudor cottages round the church and 17th century town hall. Nearby are Ragley Hall and Coughton Court. Ragley Hall sits on the brow of the hill overlooking the Warwickshire countryside; designed in 1680, it was not completed until the end of the 17th century. It is now the home of Lord and Lady Hertford. Coughton Court, on the other hand, is an early and spectacular Tudor house owned by the National Trust and lived in by the Throckmorton family since the early 15th century. It has a superb collections of furniture and pictures, as well as gardens and two churches.

Lichfield Cathedral

William Shakespeare

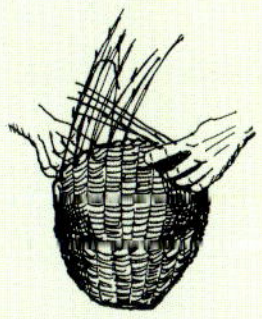
Basket weaving, Broom

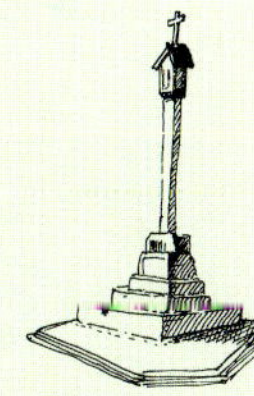
Cross at Stow-on-the-Wold

England's favourite bard

From Alcester cross the river and then climb to the triangulation point, which is 215 feet (66m) above sea level, and look back over the rooftops of Alcester and beyond. Warwickshire is most associated with William Shakespeare (1564–1616), whose birth-place, Stratford-upon-Avon, is 7 miles (11km) from Alcester. The house where he was

born was built from timber from the nearby Forest of Arden, made famous in *As You Like It*. New Place, Shakespeare's retirement house in Stratford, can also be seen, along with one of the most visited houses in the world: Anne Hathaway's cottage at Shottery, a mile (1.6km) to the west of Stratford. Anne was the wife to whom Shakespeare bequeathed his 'second best bed'.

The trail continues over an old railway bridge onto a trackway and then a lane. This takes you past Alne Wood and Newlands Wood – both famous for their glorious display of bluebells in spring – and on through picturebook countryside until you hit the A4189. Here the way takes a footbridge over the railway line and becomes a hedged path before reaching Henley-in-Arden, a small market town with houses dating back to the mid 1300s and two ancient churches. The town's 15th-century guildhall is open to the public.

Now the way climbs steeply to the Mount, a hill outside the town where long-vanished Beaudesert Castle once stood. Although the Mount isn't particularly high, it does offer wonderful views across the surrounding countryside. After descending the Mount, the trail crosses miles of undulating countryside to reach Lowsonford and the Stratford-upon-Avon Canal, begun in 1802. The path then crosses the M40 and the Grand Union Canal – completed in 1806, and linking the Thames to Birmingham – and reaches Rowington.

Leave Rowington via the churchyard – the church is Norman – and go north-east over fields past an old windmill, now converted to a house, and pass by 15th-century Baddesley Clinton manor house (National Trust). If you visit just one house along the Heart of England Way, Baddesley Clinton must be it. With its moat and three priest's holes – it was a Catholic stronghold – the house is extraordinarily romantic and hardly changed since Shakespeare's day.

Continue through woods that are azure with bluebells in May, across fields, over a footbridge and down a lane to Chadwick End. The way then climbs to Priest's Park wood over fields and trackways, past a glorious black-and-white timber-framed farmhouse; the landscape is no longer dominated by distinctive yellow Cotswold stone, for the dominant building material of Warwickshire was timber in earlier times. Cross more fields until you hit the A452 where the path goes left and then heads north-east to Berkswell, named after the spring owned by Bercus, a Saxon chieftain. Berkswell's 12th-century church – one of the best in the Midlands – has a crypt with some Saxon stonework. Fields and lanes then take you past Meriden, then Eaves Green, and over the M6. From here cross the B4114 before following the way along a railway past Shustoke Reservoirs (popular with

fly-fishermen, sailing enthusiasts and cormorants) and across more fields to Foul End, then Hurley and Kingsbury.

Lichfield – a medieval city

From Kingsbury's church the way crosses the River Thames, goes under the M42 and continues along the Birmingham & Fazeley Canal (completed in 1830) to Drayton Basset. A lane then leads to the A453 before crossing farmland and rising to Gorsey Hill. Farther on, the path crosses a brook and reaches the A5, from where a farm track leads to Weeford, a small village in the picturesque vale of the Black Brook. The path then takes a north-westerly course crossing the A51, A38 and A5127 to the cathedral city of Lichfield.

Lichfield was the birthplace of the lexicographer Dr Johnson (1709–84) and his great friend David Garrick (1717–79), the actor. Johnson's house and Garrick's birthplace both still stand. Dr Johnson's house in the main square was owned by his father who was a bookseller in the town; it is now open to the public. With its three spires – known as 'the Ladies of the Vale' – Lichfield is unique among medieval cathedrals. It was restored during the 17th century and then again by the Victorian architect George Gilbert Scott.

From the cathedral the path is waymarked through a car-park, across a golf course, back over the A51 and across fields to Bilson Brook. From here go on to Gentleshaw Common and the village of the same name. It is now just a short distance to the Iron Age hillfort at Castle Ring, from which you head north-west to Cannock Chase on a trackway through Beaudesert Old Park. After crossing several roads you reach a little valley with a stream and then hit the A460, which the way crosses. Go up a track through trees to Brindley Heath and the Cannock Chase visitor centre. Keep on the same track, which eventually goes through woodland up to the Katyn Memorial to the Polish dead of World War II.

From here the path descends to Anson's Bank from which there are splendid views. The way continues before descending to Milford (where the walk ends) and Shugborough Hall. Shugborough is a wonderful place, having been restored by the National Trust as an example of a working Victorian estate.

Above: *The wild, unmanaged appearance of Cannock Chase reminds us of how much of the Midlands must have looked before urbanization and modern farming methods.*

Opposite, top: *The moated manor house of Baddesley Clinton was built in the 15th century. It was a haven for persecuted Catholics and still has three priest's holes.*

Opposite, bottom: *The three spires that make medieval Lichfield Cathedral unique are known as the Ladies of the Vale. The central spire rises to 258 feet (79m).*

ISLE OF WIGHT COASTAL PATH

The Isle of Wight Coastal Path gives you that wonderful feeling of having completed a circumnavigation of a mini-country. It doesn't stick exclusively to the coast – there are one or two little detours inland and sections through woodland and across farms – but for most of the route there are wonderful views across the Solent to the mainland or out across the English Channel.

Despite occasional forays inland, this is mostly cliff walking with all the sense of space cliff-tops invariably induce – the Isle of Wight is, in short, a great chunk of white cliff adrift in the English Channel. A chalk ridge runs east–west from Culver Cliff to the Needles, and a second mass of chalk lies behind Ventnor: the Southern Downs. The highest point on the Isle of Wight is St Boniface Down, at Ventnor at 787 feet (240m). The north, south-east and south-west coasts of the island consist of soft sandstone and clay cliffs.

As this is a circular walk you can obviously start anywhere, but the official start point is at Cowes. Cowes is one of the world's great yachting centres, playing host to huge numbers of international boats during Cowes Week (usually held during the first week of August) and the massive annual Round the Island Race, held in June.

Set off from the floating bridge on the West Cowes side of the River Medina. Head west through the High Street past the sailing club, making your way gradually to the promenade. Go along the sea wall past beach huts and then on up to Gurnard Cliff. Follow the signs through houses till you reach a clear path through the gorse. The path runs across the chalk cliff-top for several miles from here, but as this area is subject to serious erosion the exact route changes constantly – whatever you do, don't go too near the edge.

All roads lead to Yarmouth

Continue to Thorness Bay before continuing along the beach, through a holiday village, farmland and woodland until emerging on a road at Porchfield village. Follow the road

GETTING AROUND THE ISLE OF WIGHT COASTAL PATH

Start & Finish: Cowes, Isle of Wight.

Length: 65 miles (105km).

Transport Links: *Cowes*: By car: Several car-ferry services operate to the island, but only Red Funnel Hi-Speed Ferries run to Cowes (from Southampton); by bus: a regular Southern Vectis bus service from Newport connects with Red Funnel Hi-Speed ferries at Cowes. Southern Vectis also operates a good bus network around the island, with most services centred on Ryde and Newport; by train: the Stagecoach Island Line provides regular services between key towns including Shanklin and Ryde, connecting with walking routes. There are train links at Yarmouth pier head with Wightlink catamarans to Portsmouth Harbour for onward rail connections.

Ordnance Survey Map: OL29 Isle of Wight (1:25,000).

Guidebooks: *A Walker's Guide to the Isle of Wight*, Martin Collins and Norman Birch (Cicerone Press, 1995); *The Coastal Path and Inland Trails on the Isle of Wight* (Isle of Wight Tourism); *The Complete Isle of Wight Coastal Footpath*, Brian Smailes (Challenge Publications, 2000); *The Isle of Wight Coast Path*, John Merrill (Walk & Write, 1997).

Website: www.islandbreaks.co.uk/walking.

Above: *Godshill village, about 4 miles (6km) inland from Shanklin, is the prettiest village on the Isle of Wight, so well worth a detour. With no industry to speak of, almost everywhere on the Isle of Wight has a peaceful, almost forgotten air.*

signs for Shalfleet and Yarmouth, then take the road for Newtown. Cross several fields and roads until you reach Newtown Bridge. From here the path leads to Shalfleet Mill, and then leaves the village by the Yarmouth Road. A footpath takes you off the road to the right and down through fields and across stiles to the seashore again, before diverting inland past Bouldnor Cliff.

Field and trackways lead back to the cliff edge, and continue for about a mile (1.6km) before going down to a shingle beach. The path quickly turns inland again and runs parallel to the cliff edge, but still through woodland. It reaches a gravel road, then makes its way down to the main road and Yarmouth itself. Relatively unspoiled, Yarmouth is a fishing, ferry and yachting port with a deep-water harbour and several lovely old pubs and 18th-century houses.

Go west from Yarmouth past the ferry terminal and along the sea wall before going up through woodland to a lane. Continue along the route of an old military road through woodland to Cliff End Battery. The path goes along a farm track before reaching a road and then the sea wall to Totland Pier. Go past the pier, up a steep flight of steps and follow the footpath signs to Alum Bay. Much of the woodland cliff-top path here is overgrown, but is always passable.

From the early 16th century until recently, alum – a mix of potash and aluminium – was mined in the bay, hence its name. It was used in the paper-making and leather-tanning industries. The cliffs where it was mined are famous for their extraordinary stripey, multi-coloured appearance, caused by bands of chalk and dark or black clays which smell of sulphur and produce a yellow efflorescence.

Tributes to Tennyson

From the pleasure park go south towards Tennyson Down. The path will take you up the white chalk cliffs towards The Needles, famous striking offshore stacks of chalk. West of Freshwater is Tennyson Down, named after Alfred Lord Tennyson (1809–92), the Victorian poet who lived at nearby Farringford House. The Tennyson Cross, a monument to his memory, stands on the top of the downs, on the spot formerly occupied by the Nodes Beacon. Made of Cornish granite, it stands nearly 38 feet (11.6m) high, and was unveiled on 8 July, 1897. The inscription on the east face reads, 'In Memory of

Alfred Lord Tennyson this cross is raised, a Beacon to Sailors, by the People of Freshwater and other Friends in England and America'. Tennyson made a daily pilgrimage to this spot, whatever the weather, and told a friend that 'the air on the Downs is worth sixpence a pint'. Few modern visitors would disagree, for this is truly one of the loveliest spots anywhere in the south of England. A visitor remembered seeing Tennyson sitting for hours gazing out to sea, 'his big, black, broad-rimmed hat and his military cloak wrapped around the tall, bent form, making him a picturesque figure familiar to everyone'. On a clear day there are breathtaking views from the downs across the island and over to the mainland. Cormorant, razorbill, shag and fulmar nest on the cliffs here.

At the coastguard cottages take the route along West High Down, past the Tennyson monument and on past the Iron Age earthworks to Freshwater Bay. Having walked round the bay, climb the cliff steps to follow the old military road to Compton Chine. The local word 'chine' means a steep narrow ravine (caused by thousands of years of rainwater erosion) that leads to the sea. Cross the chine and notice that chalk gives way to sandstone. Next comes Shippard Chine, and then Brook Chine. Pass the lifeboat house and you are back on the clifftop. At Chilton turn inland along the chine before returning to the clifftop, from where a track leads to Grange Chine, the military road and then Grange Road, which leads to Brighstone village at the foot of the high chalk downs.

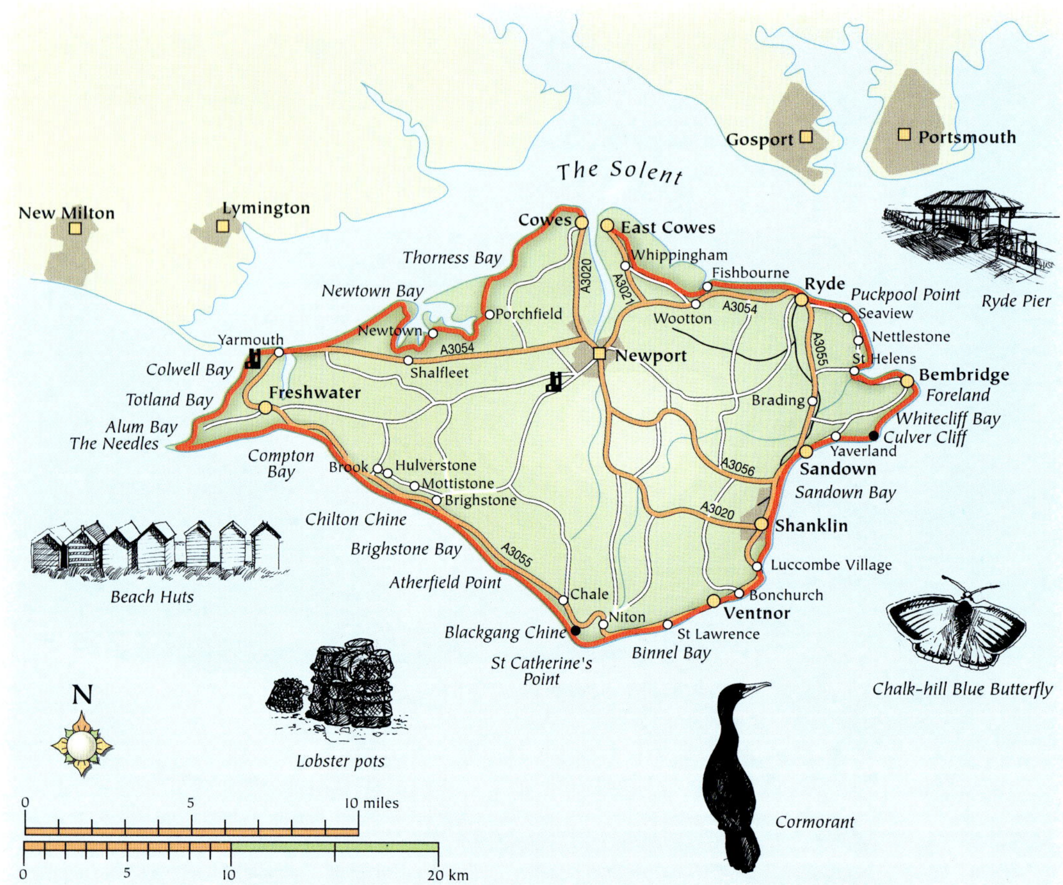

Above: *These three chalk stacks are known as the Needles; they are the eroded remnants of chalk cliffs and are the Isle of Wight's most famous landmark.*

A local micro-climate

From the sea, the walk continues along the cliff overlooking Brighstone Bay and then on to Cowleaze Chine before diverting inland to go round the chine. Back on the clifftop the path soon reaches Shepherd's Chine and then Atherfield Point. When you reach Whale Chine the path runs parallel with the military road to Ladder Chine, Walpen Chine and the village of Chale. Chale was once a great centre of smuggling. You can take a little detour here to Blackgang Chine, an example of the extraordinary, almost tropical micro-climate that exists in these narrow rocky valleys. Blackgang Chine is also said to be the oldest theme park in the world. It's been run by the same family since the late 19th century but, unusually, has always been passed to the youngest rather than the eldest son.

The cliffs at Blackgang and many other places on the island sit on a layer of gault (known locally as blue slipper), which makes the upper layers of rock extremely unstable. Water percolates down through the chalk, hits the impermeable gault and builds up, thereby undermining the cliffs above. Massive falls are inevitable from time to time, and at Blackgang the cliff is disappearing at a rate of over 11 feet (3.5m) a year. Three huge cliff falls occurred in 1928, 1961 and 1994.

Opposite: *The old town hall at Newtown is one of the few remnants of this near-deserted medieval town, which was one of three deliberately planned medieval communities on the island. Newtown began to decline as its harbour silted up.*

Pepper Pot and Salt Cellar

From Chale the trail crosses the main road and heads up to the cliffs again. The path is clear along the clifftop and runs above what is called the undercliff (where a large section of cliff has slipped seawards to form a sort of secondary cliff), past St Catherine's Point and Rocken End – an isolated rocky outcrop offshore – to Barrack Chute and the village of Niton. St Catherine's Point is home to many rare plants, including milk vetch. Insects found here include the rare glanville fritillary.

Serious erosion of the cliff base has led recently to a number of undercliff houses having to be abandoned, and in 1928 the whole undercliff road collapsed into the sea. High up above Niton are two buildings known as Pepper Pot and Salt Cellar. The former is the remnant of a late medieval lighthouse; the latter the remains of a never-completed Georgian lighthouse.

From Niton the path sticks to the cliffs past Binnel Bay and Puckaster Cove before heading for the village of St Lawrence where it follows the main road through the village and then heads for Woody Bay, Woody Point and Orchard Bay. After reaching Ventnor Botanic Garden – the displays of temperate and tropical plants are well worth seeing – the way descends to Steephill Cove and round the huge concrete sea defences of Castle Cove. The cliff path then descends to Ventnor, which 70 years ago was just a farm and a few cottages. When a well-known doctor recommended Ventnor for the benefits of its sea air, something of a mad rush from London developed – it is now a classic, but not overly attractive, seaside resort.

From Ventnor the path continues along the top of the concrete sea wall to Bonchurch and past the 13th-century Bonchurch old church, one of the smallest and most beautiful little churches in the country.

Beyond Bonchurch the path reaches an area accurately known as the landslip, and then Luccombe Chine. Luccombe Cliffs are looked after by the National Trust. The path continues through Luccombe village and then along the beach before heading back up to the cliffs, continuing along the path signposted to Sandown.

Below: *Bembridge Harbour is now home to more leisurecraft than fishing boats, since, like most places on the island, Bembridge relies on tourism for its income.*

A rare butterfly and a classic seaside pier

Walk along Sandown esplanade and head towards Culver Down. From Bembridge Down head for the monument to the Earl of Yarborough, a local benefactor, on Culver Cliff. Culver Downs are looked after by the National Trust and support a wide variety of wildlife species, including the chalk-hill blue butterfly.

The path then descends through woodland towards Whitecliff Bay, passing what used to be Bembridge boys' school through playing fields and woods and on towards Bembridge Point. The path follows the road round Bembridge Harbour, crosses the River Yar, and then continues along the old mill dam wall. After negotiating a few roads, then crossing fields and lanes, the way eventually reaches the sea again before finding its way to the village of Seaview (a multitude of 1950s and '60s bungalows!). Here the High Street leads to the sea wall, which the path follows past the sailing club and coastguard cottages and then on through Appley Park Woodlands into Ryde.

At nearly half a mile long Ryde Pier is the second longest in the UK, after Southend Pier in Essex. From the pier head west along the esplanade, through several streets to Spencer Road which, after a few hundred yards, becomes a gravel

road. A public footpath then takes you past Ryde House and on to Binstead church. This Victorian building replaced a Norman church, but retains an interesting medieval carving of a man sitting on a ram's head!

From Binstead church the path goes through woodland, reaches a road and then passes both the ruins and new buildings of Binstead Abbey before hitting another road. Turn left here and follow the path to Kite Hill. More woodland follows before the path reaches a stream and then the main road. A downhill stretch brings you to Wootton Bridge where you cross the main road to pass the Sloop Inn, and then go along an unmade road past houses and garages to Church Road. After working its way through more streets the path reaches a bridge over Palmers Brook, and then climbs into woodland before reaching the main road into Cowes, passing Osborne House on the way.

Above: *Spring flowers on the cliffs above Freshwater Bay may well have once inspired the Victorian poet laureate Alfred Lord Tennyson. Tennyson is known to have made a daily pilgrimage to the nearby Downs where, he told a friend, 'the air is worth sixpence a pint'.*

Victoria's retreat

Osborne House, built for Queen Victoria from 1845–51, is the one really grand house on the island. It was a country retreat where the Royal family could be free from state ceremonial. Today, the drawing, dining and billiard rooms and the private apartments are laid out almost exactly as they were in Victoria's day. Queen Victoria's passion for the island helped make it one of Britain's most sought-after destinations before package holidays became popular.

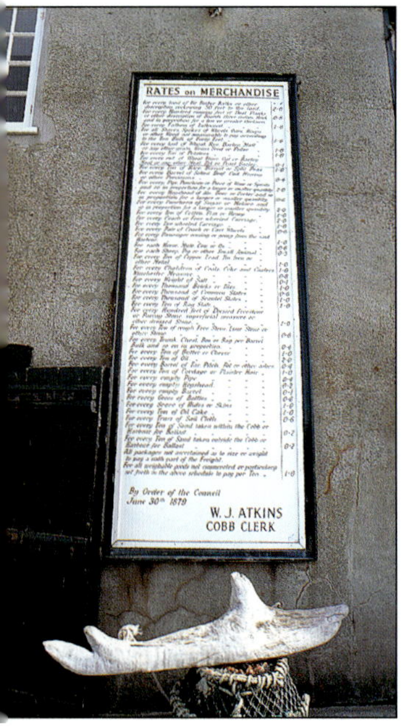

Above: *An old plaque on the Cobb at Lyme Regis shows the harbour's rates of merchandise in shillings and pence, and is a remnant of the town's days as an important port.*

JURASSIC WAY

Following the decision by UNESCO to designate the East Devon and Dorset coast stretch of the UK's longest national trail, the South-West Coast Path, as a World Heritage Site – largely because the chalk cliffs here are both very beautiful and incredibly rich in fossils – it was decided that the Exmouth–Poole section should be renamed the Jurassic Way. The route includes cliff, beach and woodland walking, taking in the main fossil-rich section of cliffs centred on Lulworth and Lyme Regis, as well as a number of ancient sites and historic towns and villages.

Purists and fans of the 630-mile (1014-km) South-West Coast Path may balk at the creation of the Jurassic Way, particularly considering there is another long-distance route of this name that runs from Stamford to Banbury, but no one can deny that this 95-mile (153-km) stretch of coast is unique. If you start at Exmouth you will probably get there via Exeter with its wonderful 12th-century cathedral and – slightly less well known – its unusually early lock canal. Those who think canals are entirely a product of the 18th and 19th centuries will be astonished! It was built after a dispute between the citizens of Exeter and the Countess of Devonshire. Some time in the 1280s the countess asked the city for tithes, the city refused, so she built a weir on the Exe that put paid to wool exports from Exeter. The city retaliated by digging a canal to get the boats round the weir.

As you head from Exeter to Exmouth you pass through Topsham, with its pretty Dutch-style gabled houses and Georgian lympstone. A footpath here runs alongside the Exe all the way to Exmouth where the walk proper begins. You need to get to the eastern end of Exmouth esplanade and then simply follow the path onto the cliffs. After only a short distance the town will already seem far away and there are wonderful views back across the Exe Estuary and the sea.

GETTING AROUND THE JURASSIC WAY

Start: Exmouth, Devon – the eastern end of the esplanade.
Finish: Poole, Dorset.
Length: 95 miles (153km).
Transport Links: *Exmouth*: By car: Turn off at Jct. 30 of the M5 and take the A376 down to Exmouth – or take the B3178 if you are coming from the east; by bus: National Express runs to Exmouth, and there are frequent local services from Exeter, with bus links to other towns in East Devon; by train: Exmouth. *Poole*: By car: the A350 runs directly into Poole; the B3068 runs through the town; by bus: Wilts & Dorset Bus Company is the principal service provider; Yellow Buses also run from local towns; by train: Poole.
Ordnance Survey Maps: Explorers OL15 Purbeck & South Dorset, 115 Exmouth & Sidmouth, 116 Lyme Regis & Bridport (1:25,000).
Guidebooks: *South West Coast Path: Exmouth to Poole*, Roland Tarr (Aurum Press, 1989).
Further notes: There is another Jurassic Way running from Banbury to Stamford. The Dorset Jurassic Way is part of the South-West Coastal Path.
Website: www.swcp.org.uk

Above: *The beach at Budleigh Salterton still has something of the air of an unspoiled Georgian seaside resort, with its lobster pots and beach huts. The layers of pebbles found in the cliffs nearby are some 400 million years old.*

Protected beaches and seaside resorts

The way quickly reaches beautiful Orcombe Rocks, looked after by the National Trust. Although most of this part of the south coast is protected from development under its UNESCO World Heritage site status, on a day-to-day basis much of it is under the care of the National Trust or various national or local conservation organizations, including the RSPB and local wildlife trusts. You can get down to the sandy beach here below Orcombe Rocks before continuing to Orcombe Point. From here the path cuts across the neck of Straight Point to avoid a firing range, and then descends to a little valley. No sooner are you down than it's time to climb again – to a high point known as The Floors. From here the path soon reaches West Down Beacon where you can admire the view from the triangulation point before descending past a golf club and into Budleigh Salterton, a seaside town that still has the air of a relatively unspoiled, late Georgian resort. The layers of pebbles found in the cliffs here date back more than 400 million years to the Triassic period.

Beyond Budleigh Salterton the path detours a short distance to cross the River Otter at South Farm and then returns to the coast via a Devon Wildlife Trust nature reserve. Back on the coast you pass Danger Point, Black Head and Brandy Head before reaching shingly Ladram Bay. From here the path heads back up onto the cliffs to High Peak with its Iron Age hillfort – at 564 feet/157m one of the high points on the south Devon coast – then through woods to Peak Hill with its lovely views over Sidmouth and Lyme Bay ahead. Descend through woods to a road that continues into the classic Regency seaside town of Sidmouth, which developed from a fishing settlement into a fashionable holiday resort in the late 18th century.

At the far end of the town the path crosses the River Sid and then climbs steeply to beautiful Salcombe Hill, a little way inland, before returning to the coast and Higher Dunscombe Cliff. The way meanders down to Lincombe Valley, climbs again and then reaches Weston Mouth, an area particularly rich in wild flowers.

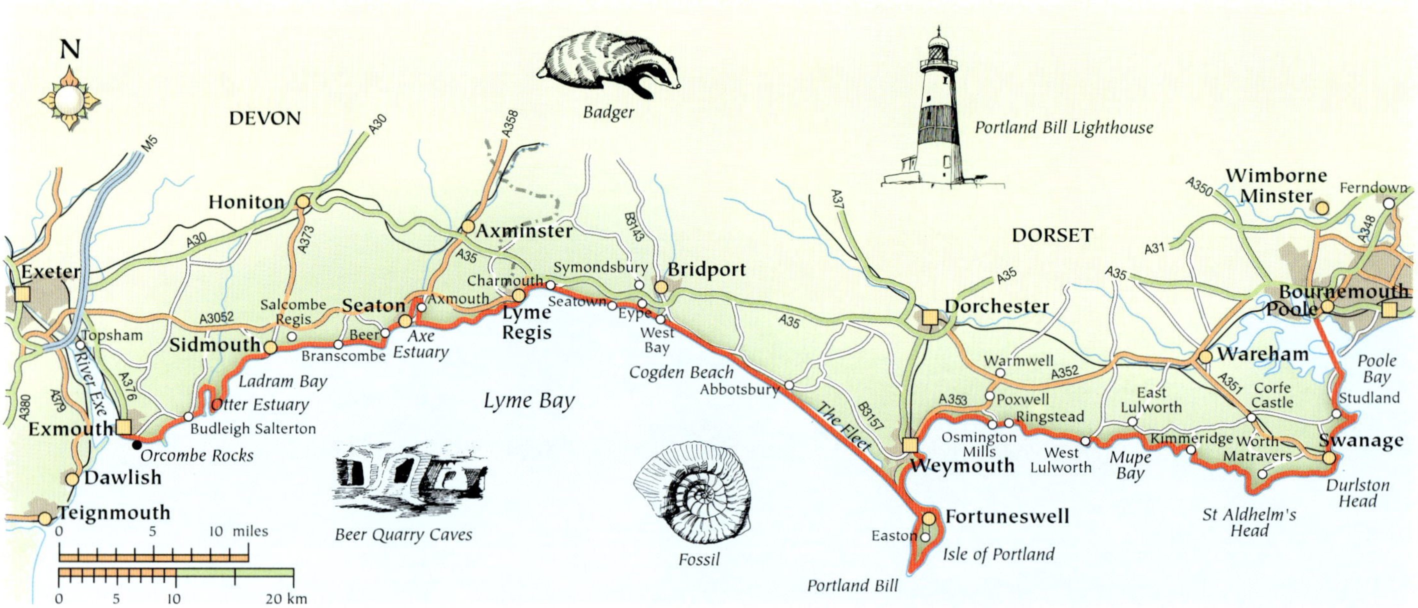

Below: *The rock masses of Ladram Bay date back to the Triassic period when the area was a desert; the red colour is due to the presence of iron in the rock.*

Pubs, Beer and beer stone

Back on the cliff path you cross fields to Littlecombe Hollow and then more easy field walking brings you to woodland and then Branscombe Mouth. You can take a detour here to two good pubs in Branscombe village, and to have a look at the wonderful 11th-century church with its squat Norman tower. The path continues along the coast to Beer, with fine views all the way. Beer Quarry Caves can be visited – beer stone has been used over the centuries for many great English buildings, including Exeter and Winchester cathedrals – and flint has been mined on the cliffs here since Neolithic times.

The path is easy to follow through Beer, where little fishing boats lie pulled up on the beach. Beyond Beer the path goes down through Seaton – a rather unprepossessing town – to cross Axmouth Bridge across the mouth of the River Axe. The village of Axmouth is actually a little to the north of the way, but with its ancient pretty church and good pub it's worth the detour.

Once over the bridge the path crosses a golf course a little way inland and then returns to the cliffs and the Axmouth–Lyme Regis Undercliff National Nature Reserve. The exact boundaries of the reserve, and the edges of the cliffs themselves, are constantly changing as a result of erosion. But for the next 6 miles (10km) you'll find yourself walking through dense, wildlife-rich woodland. Deer, nationally rare plants and flowers, birds of prey, badgers and foxes are all common here, and though the sea views we have come to expect are now only spasmodic through the almost jungle-like vegetation, this part of the walk is a delight and has the feel of real primeval forest.

Lyme Regis's famous Cobb

You will pass Humble Point, Pinhay Cliffs and Ware Cliffs before crossing at last from Devon into Dorset just before Lyme Regis. Like so many of these Dorset and Devon coastal communities, Lyme Regis developed as a fishing community and a port for the medieval wool trade and, later on, smuggling. The town's ancient cobb – or harbour wall – was made famous through several books and films, including Jane Austen's *Persuasion* and John Fowles's *The French Leiutentant's Woman*. St Michael's Church, which dates from 1100 and is largely unmodernized, should also not be missed.

Above: *The Cobb at Lyme Regis has been mentioned in many books, but Jane Austen's* Persuasion *and John Fowles'* The French Lieutenant's Woman *made it world famous.*

The limestone cliffs from here to Charmouth are rich in fossils – the commonest are ammonites, but complete fossils of marine and other creatures have also been found. Digging for them is strictly forbidden, but bits and pieces can often be found simply lying on the beach, especially after stormy weather. In the early 19th century a local boy, Joseph Anning, found the skull of a fossil 'seadragon', and his sister Mary found the rest of the skeleton a year later. Mary became hugely famous for her collection (and extensive knowledge) of fossils gleaned from the cliffs around Lyme; interest in fossils was extremely fashionable at the time, and many of Mary's discoveries were sold to collectors from London.

From Lyme Regis the way continues to Charmouth, although frequent landslips can alter the exact route dramatically. In Charmouth follow the path to the seafront and the Heritage Coast Centre, then continue along the road eastwards and over a footbridge back to the cliff path. The landscape and sea views are unsurpassed through this National Trust-owned stretch and the route is clear over Golden Cap; at 627 feet (191m) above sea level, this spot is the highest point on the whole south coast. Descend then to Seatown where the River Winniford can be crossed by a bridge.

Back on the cliffs, Ridge Cliff and Doghouse Hill offer fabulous views before the way descends to Eype Mouth where a short detour inland brings you to the village of Lower

Opposite: *The beach near Seatown is just one spot on the island that was once famous for smuggling; particularly popular contraband was French brandy.*

Eype, where there is a pub. Staying on the path, however, will lead to a climb to West Cliff from where you can leave the coast path and find a way inland to Bridport, still relatively unscarred by modern developments. From medieval times until the end of the 19th century Bridport was an important centre of rope-, net- and sail-making; there's a pretty medieval church, early almshouses and a good little museum. The town was also once important for fishing (from its port at West Bay), but most of the town's income now comes from tourism. It has over a thousand listed buildings.

Chesil Beach

Back on the way, drop down into West Bay and then follow the path from the eastern end of the beach to climb onto East Cliff, go past a golf course and a caravan site, across the River Brid and past picturesque Burton Bradstock, just inland and worth a visit.

The path passes Burton Beach before climbing down to Cogden Beach, part of that extraordinary length of pebbles and shingle – created by storm waves driven by the prevailing south-westerly winds – known as Chesil Beach. This huge ridge, 18 miles (29km) long and running almost from West Bay to Portland, is one of the world's great barrier beaches. The pebbles here are mostly quartz and chalcedony – a crystal that is harder than steel – and the coarsest pebbles occur at Chesil, diminishing in size towards Bridport. Fishermen landing at night are said to judge their position on the ridge by the size of the pebbles! The surface is difficult to walk on – trying to cover any distance along the ridge is exhausting!

The way continues behind the beach to West Bexington and Cloud's Hill, home of T.E. Lawrence (1888–1935) of Lawrence of Arabia fame, who bought the cottage in 1925. The trail passes (a little way inland) Chapel Hill with its 15th-century chapel, before turning inland for a while and then returning to the coast. However, you can take a detour to historic Abbotsbury with its ruined abbey, extraordinary medieval tithe barn and Swannery. The many pretty early cottages in the village are almost certainly built from stone taken from the abbey after its demolition was ordered by Henry VIII.

Back on the way you reach the Swannery car park and head east, climbing and descending until Hodder's Coppice is reached, passing through a small wood before heading seawards again. The way reaches the River Fleet and then returns to the sea's edge. All the river estuaries and beaches along this Jurassic coast are home to huge numbers of bird species including tern, redshank and oystercatcher.

Below: *Weymouth still has one of Britain's busiest harbours. The town developed rapidly as a tourist centre after George III began to make regular visits at the end of the 18th century, and it has retained its largely Victorian esplanade.*

Portland Bill

Continue on the coast past the Moonfleet Hotel and on to Weymouth. Take a detour around the Isle of Portland and Portland Bill where there is a visitor centre. Most people know the word 'Portland' from the magnificent high-quality pale stone quarried here; St Paul's Cathedral and the buildings of Regent Street in London are of Portland stone. Tout Quarry, now a Site of Scientific Interest, was one of the main quarries

Above: *The arch, known as Durdle Door, through this isolated chunk of limestone just off the coast at Lulworth has been created by centuries of wave erosion.*

and now houses a fascinating sculpture park.

A road walk around Portland Harbour, hand-built by Victorian convicts, leads into Weymouth. Though modernized in part, Weymouth – at least along the magnificent esplanade – is still an attractive place. Like Brighton, Weymouth developed rapidly after it found favour with George III in the late 18th century. The way follows the coast road (past the remains of 16th-century Sandsfoot Castle) leading eventually to the ferry. Take the ferry across the harbour (or go inland a short way to the bridge) before continuing along the sea front and out of the town past Lodmoor (an RSPB reserve) and Bowleaze Cove to Osmington Mills. Near here you can see fossilized ripple marks from ancient beaches, said to date from a time tens of millions of years ago, when this area was tropical. There is a pub at Osmington Mills but little else of interest. From the pub car-park take the coast path to the clifftop, past the deserted medieval village of West Ringstead – the layout of houses and lanes can be seen in aerial photographs – to Burning Cliff and its nearby nature reserve.

Follow the path along the clifftop, with spectacular views across Weymouth Bay, to Durdle Door. This, an impressive arch through a massive isolated block of limestone a few hundred yards offshore, was produced by centuries of wave action ('durdle' is derived from the Saxon for 'through'). Lulworth Cove, a little further on, is usually awash with tourists and is spoiled by having a car-park bigger than the village itself!

Climbing the steep cliffs out of Lulworth in summer you'll pass through an area alive with butterflies and insects. Soon you will find yourself on the edge of the massive army ranges that take up much of the coastline here. The route along the edge of the ranges is usually open as firing seems a rare event these days, but you must stick to the designated paths through the ranges because of the danger of unexploded shells. Wildlife in this area has benefited enormously from the army's 'protection', free from disturbance from building development, agro-chemicals and people. Just beyond Little Bindon is the remarkable Fossil Forest, an area of ancient fossilized tree stumps more than 100 million years old, visible at low tide.

An abandoned village

The path sticks close to the cliff edge from here, past Mupe Rocks with glorious views out across the sea. Beyond the beach at Arish Mell, the path climbs to Rings Hill and Flower's Barrow (an Iron Age hillfort) before going down to Worbarrow Bay, where the village of Tyneham, which was evacuated by the Army in 1943, lies. At certain times of the year you can visit the village; most of the buildings still stand, though they are badly damaged, and the place has a forlorn air. It is a sad reflection on the military authorities that local residents who were told that they would be able to return to the village when the war ended were eventually forbidden to do so.

Above: *When you reach the chalky island known as Old Harry, just beyond Swanage Bay, you know you are just a short walk and a ferry ride from the end of the walk.*

The way continues along the cliff path to Gold Down and Gad Cliff and then descends to Kimmeridge Bay. Halfway round the bay the path reaches one of Britain's only oil wells – it's been producing steadily (if in small amounts) since the 1950s. From the well continue along the clifftop to Clavel Tower, a 19th-century coastguard lookout, and on to Rope Lake Head and Freshwater Steps before reaching a high point at Hounstout Cliff. Precise waymarking may change here as a result of landslips.

After Hounstout the path turns inland for a short distance to the tiny village of Hill Bottom before returning to the coast, running across West Hill and Emmetts Hill to ancient St Aldhelm's Chapel on St Aldhelm's Head. The chapel, which is largely 12th-century work, is dedicated to a 7th-century Celtic Bishop of Sherbourne.

Beyond St Aldhelm's Head the Isle of Wight can be seen far ahead. Pass the Windspit Valley (where the way makes another short detour inland), disused quarries at Seacombe, then Dancing Ledge before reaching National Trust-owned land that takes us to Durlston Country Park and on to the Victorian Anvil Point lighthouse.

The path skirts Durlston Bay and passes through woods to Peveril Point and then Swanage. Swanage is not the prettiest town in England, but it has an interesting museum and nearby Studland Bay was the English Riviera for the well-to-do in Edwardian days. Continue along the Swanage seafront and then out of the town round Swanage Bay to the spectacular rocks known as Old Harry and Old Harry's Wife. From here it is easy to continue the last few miles to South Haven Point, from which you can catch the ferry into Poole where the walk ends.

NORTH DOWNS WAY

The North Downs Way is generally an easy walk over chalk downland, with some heavily wooded sections and farmland and pasture, too. It takes you through areas that have been inhabited for thousands of years, but also includes places that feel remarkably remote yet are astonishingly close to the sprawl of London.

As with the South Downs, these northern chalk hills are made up of the compacted remains of countless billions of tiny sea creatures. Millions of years ago they settled at the bottom of shallow seas, building up over the millennia into massively thick layers, with earth movements creating the ridges of the Downs we know today.

The Pilgrims' Route

As with the Ridgeway (see pages 120–127), the North Downs Way follows the high tops of the Downs along a route that dates from prehistoric times, avoiding the then dangerous and sometimes marshy wooded valleys below. The route has been used ever since: in medieval times the great shrine of St Thomas Becket at Canterbury was accessible from London and the coast via the North Downs. Becket, who publicly and repeatedly voiced his criticisms of Henry II, was murdered in the north transept of Canterbury Cathedral on 29 December, 1170. Immediately he became a martyr and the cathedral a centre of pilgrimage. The way also incorporates much of the route taken by Geoffrey Chaucer's pilgrims in the *Canterbury Tales*. Pilgrims also followed the route west from Canterbury – to Winchester – to attend the great pre-Reformation festivals of the Catholic Church associated with the 10th-century saint St Swithin. The pilgrimage tradition pretty much died after the Reformation since the whole idea was tied up with holy relics and the holiness of the physical place –it was believed that just being at the place where St Thomas Becket died could cure sickness or cleanse a sense of sin – ideas that were rejected by the Reformation.

GETTING AROUND THE NORTH DOWNS WAY

Start: Farnham, Surrey.

Finish: Dover, Kent.

Length: 155 miles (249km).

Transport Links: *Farnham*: By car: located on the A31 (Farnham Bypass), which can also be accessed by taking Junction 4 or 5 from the M3; by bus: there is a daily National Express coach service between Farnham and London, and local services connect Farnham with local towns; by train: The start of the North Downs Way is a 5-minute walk from Farnham Station, serviced by South West Trains. *Dover*: By car: the A2 and A20 are the two principal roads running into Dover; by bus: National Express services regularly run to and from London and Stagecoach is the main local operator, with frequent buses to local towns; by train: Dover.

Ordnance Survey Maps: Explorers 137 Ashford, 138 Dover, Folkestone & Hythe, 145 Guildford & Farnham, 146 Dorking, Box Hill & Reigate, 147 Sevenoaks & Tonbridge, 148 Maidstone & the Medway Towns, 150 Canterbury & the Isle of Thanet, 149 Sittingbourne & Faversham (1:25,000).

Guidebooks: *North Downs Way*, Neil Curtis and Jim Walker (Aurum Press, 2002); *North Downs Way*, Kev Reynolds (Cicerone, 2001).

Website: www.nationaltrails.gov.uk/northdownsframeset.htm

The North Downs Way incorporates two Areas of Outstanding Natural Beauty, the Surrey Hills and the Kentish Downs. The route also enjoys numerous literary and musical associations: it was loved by Charles Dickens, Lewis Carroll and the composer Vaughan Williams, among others.

Above: *The route along the North Downs follows the River Wey along heathland at the foot of the hill known as the Hog's Back; it is only a quarter-mile (0.4-km) detour north of the walk to visit the beautiful church at Seale, seated below the Hog's Back.*

A gentle and genteel start

The walk starts at Farnham, a town whose lovely Georgian and earlier buildings were largely spared the dreadful efforts of town planners and architects in the 1960s and '70s. Farnham's most famous son is William Cobbett, the radical writer and pamphleteer, born here in 1763. Nearby on the River Wey are the beautiful ruins of Waverley Abbey, the first Cistercian abbey in England. It was founded in 1128 by William Gifford, the Bishop of Winchester and is now looked after by English Heritage. The path follows the River Wey – once noted for its giant chub – along heathland at the foot of the Hog's Back (which rises to 500 feet/168m above sea level), skirting that symbol of stock-broker-belt Surrey: a series of golf courses. The path reaches the village of Puttenham, a quiet backwater with numerous pretty houses, before continuing to Guildford and the

Above: *St Martha's Hill near Guildford rises to 574 feet (175m). At the top, isolated and alone but with a fantastic view, stands the mid-Victorian church from which the hill takes its name.*

Opposite: *The outline of oast houses typifies the Kentish countryside; built to dry hops, most have now been converted into houses.*

River Wey again. Like the curate's egg, Guildford is good in parts – many decent buildings remain, but the cathedral – completed in 1961 – is rather grim. Guildford has a ruined Norman castle and retains much of its original medieval street plan, together with one or two delightful early 17th-century houses.

A Royal honeymoon

From Guildford the path climbs St Martha's Hill (573 feet/175m) to where St Martha's Church – built in 1850 – stands among the conifers isolated and alone. On then to Newlands Corner; stop for a while here and enjoy the distant views that were greatly loved by writers Robert Louis Stevenson and Lewis Carroll, among others. The path continues to Hackhurst and then Ranmore Common where the North Downs church of St Barnabas can be found. National Trust-owned Polesden Lacey is nearby in a spectacular setting. This Regency villa was remodelled in Edwardian times and it is virtually unchanged since society hostess Mrs Ronald Greville held parties here for the rich and famous before the Great War. King George VI and Queen Elizabeth, the Queen Mother, stayed here during their honeymoon in 1923.

The trail passes just to the north of Abinger Hammer, a village at the heart of an area famous

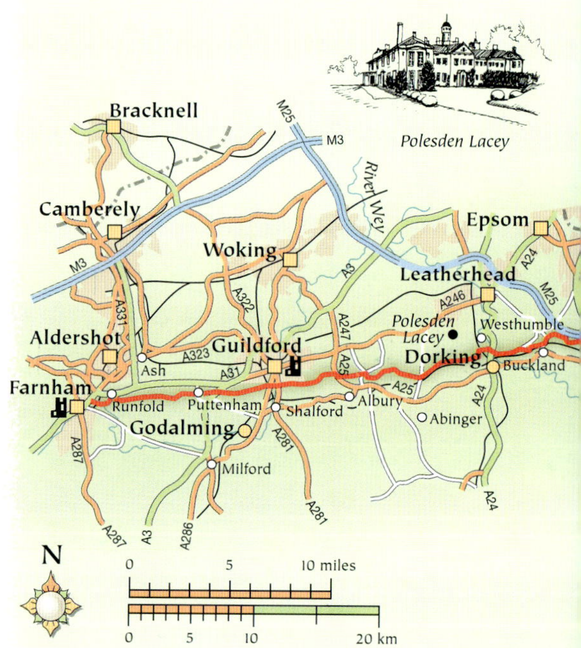

from medieval times until the 18th century for iron-smelting. Abinger Hammer – a hamlet with a pleasant green – takes its name from the old hammerponds or dam heads on the Tillingbourne, which are all that survive of the medieval iron industry. These ponds were subsequently used for watercress growing. The Victorian Abinger Hammer clock is a superb piece of work; it includes, appropriately enough, the figure of a smith who strikes the bell every hour with his sledgehammer.

Next the path reaches Dorking, a busy, noisy town with little to recommend it. Just north of Dorking you reach the Mole Gap and the even noisier A24. The River Mole is crossed by a famous series of stepping stones. You could take a break at the nearby Burford House Hotel where the poet John Keats (1795–1821) wrote *Endymion.*

Country retreats of the good and the great

On to Box Hill, a favourite place for Sunday picnics for more than a century and offering the most wonderful views. From here the path makes its way to Juniper Hill, Colley Hill and then Reigate Hill with its Georgian temple. Now the roar of the M25, which you will cross by a footbridge, can be heard. The village of Merstham comes next, with its pretty, tile-hung houses, many dating from about 1700. The path climbs Oakley Hill (on the other side of the motorway) before continuing parallel to the M25 but high up on the ridge of the hills until Botley Hill, just north of Titsey, where the downs reach their highest point at 882 feet (269m). The way goes through Titsey Park (its early 19th-century house is open to the public) before crossing into Kent at Oxted. Next comes Chevening, the Foreign Secretary's country seat, the equivalent to Chequers for the Prime Minister

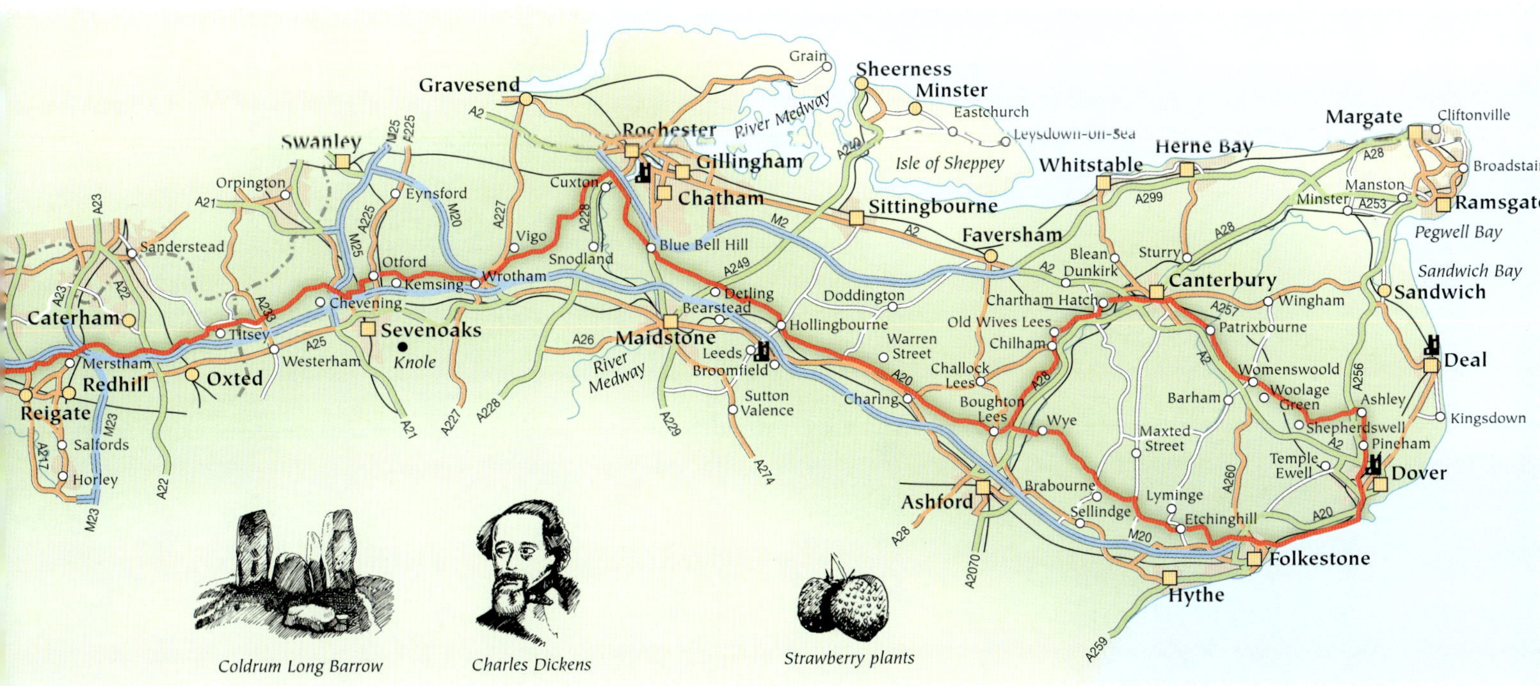

Coldrum Long Barrow

Charles Dickens

Strawberry plants

Above: *Sitting on the River Stour, the former Holy Cross church at Canterbury's West Gate is now the city's Guildhall. Ever since the brutal murder of Thomas Becket in 1170 in Canterbury Cathedral, the town has played host to an endless stream of pilgrims.*

The nearby village of Westerham is worth a visit, particularly to see Chartwell, the home of former statesman Winston Churchill and now owned by the National Trust. The 15th-century house, home of the Sackville family for more than four centuries, remained unmodernized throughout the 17th, 18th and 19th centuries, and now remains pretty much as Churchill, who lived here from 1924 until his death in 1965, left it.

Nearby is Knole, perhaps the greatest medieval house to survive in England. It has all the appearance of a walled medieval village and its interiors are as unspoiled as its exterior. It also has nearly 1,000 acres of parkland. It was the childhood home of the writer Vita Sackville-West (1892–1962), whose life was blighted by the fact that, as a woman, she could not inherit the house and title.

Back on the path we have reached the Darent Valley and the way descends to cross the River Darent and reach Otford, where Thomas Becket once lived. There is a steep climb out of Otford before you reach Kemsing and then Wrotham where you cross the M20. The path follows the top of the downs to Coldrum long barrow, a Neolithic burial mound now cared for by the National Trust.

Soon the broad expanse of the River Medway comes into view. Here the Downs were much frequented by novelist Charles Dickens who lived at nearby Gad's Hill from 1856 until his death in 1870. Today a road bridge takes you quickly over the Medway. In medieval times such a crossing would probably have involved a guide to lead you across the marshes and then a ferry ride.

After crossing the river, a long climb takes you away from the noisy valley bottom to where you can enjoy windswept hills and distant views. Pass along Blue Bell Hill and then by Kit's Coty, another ancient burial site. The path takes you to Detling and then across farmland before climbing again to the high ridge and Hollingbourne. You are now on, or at least near, the route Chaucer's pilgrims would have taken. The path crosses Charing Hill and goes round Eastwell Lake to Boughton Lees and Wye.

Above: *The skyline of Dover Castle remains pretty much today as it was in medieval times, and continues to dominate the surrounding landscape. In its shadow, however, stands a more remarkable survival – a Roman lighthouse.*

Endless orchards

At Boughton Lees you have a choice. If you want to visit Canterbury, take a loop towards the wonderful village of Chilham before going on to the cathedral city. Chilham is a compact unmodernized village still with its ancient manor house, leaning timber-framed houses and quiet square. From Chilham the route leads through orchards and farms to the edge of Canterbury, from where a 20-minute walk will bring you to the gates of the great cathedral.

From Canterbury to Dover the walk – roughly 18 miles (29km) – is easy and well marked. Leaving the city to the south the route crosses strawberry fields and seemingly endless orchards before reaching the Kent coalfields, the last of which – Betteshanger – closed in 1985. Just south of Canterbury, the way passes through the village of Patrixbourne with its flint medieval church, and then runs parallel and next to the A2 for a short distance. A clearly defined track continues via woodland, fields and orchards, skirting Woolage village and then rising onto Three Barrow Down. The trail then descends, crossing more fields, to 18th-century Waldershave House and the A256 which it crosses via a bridge. Soon you will reach the village of Ashley before continuing on a narrow bridleway to the village of Pineham. The path soon reaches the A2 again, crosses it and then descends into Dover.

The Devil's Kneading Trough

The alternative route from Boughton Lees continues towards the coast. Take the path uphill to Wye Down and the Devil's Kneading Trough, an unspoiled valley nearly 2 miles (3km) long. From here the path heads towards Etchinghill and Stowting before it reaches and combines with another long-distance path, the Saxon Shore Way, which runs for 163 miles (262km) from Gravesend to Hastings. The two paths run together to Folkestone and then along the famous white cliffs to Dover and journey's end. Dover Castle is a must, but even more evocative of the past is the still intact Roman lighthouse.

OFFA'S DYKE PATH

The Offa's Dyke Path, which has been an official long-distance path since 1971, leads from the Bristol Channel to the Irish Sea along one of the most remarkable man-made landscape features in the world. The modern path – just under 180 miles (290km) in total – follows a little over 60 miles (97km) of the original 80-mile (129-km) dyke. But who was Offa, and why did he build this huge earthwork?

We know that the dyke was built between AD 757 and AD 796 because Offa was king of the Mercians between those dates. The dyke is thought to have been constructed as a defensive barrier against the Welsh and it was, in fact, the original boundary between Wales and England.

Like the Romans before him, Offa found that he could not subdue the Welsh, who were seen as wild men occupying an inaccessible landscape. The Romans hoped to keep the 'barbarians' in the north at bay by building Hadrian's Wall; Offa appears to have had a similar motive. Certainly the dyke was carefully planned: it follows the natural contours, hugs the easily defended heights and uses rivers and natural barriers where possible. However, where the natural features disagreed with Offa's route he ignored them and simply routed his dyke over difficult terrain. Almost certainly dug by thousands of slaves, the dyke is constructed with its bank to the east and its ditch to the west. The distance from the bottom of the ditch to the top of the dyke can be as much as 30 feet (9.2m) in places, and before erosion and infilling reduced its bulk the earthwork must have been an extraordinary sight. We know very little about Offa other than that he traded with Emperor Charlemagne (742–814) and tried – unsuccessfully – to marry his son to Charlemagne's daughter. He also introduced a new currency and a new code of laws; but his one lasting monument is the great earthwork that bears his name.

GETTING AROUND THE OFFA'S DYKE PATH

Start: Sedbury, Monmouthshire

Finish: Prestatyn, Denbighshire

Distance: 180 miles (290km)

Transport Links: *Chepstow*: By car: located on the A48; by bus: local buses run from Gloucester, Newport, Monmouth and Bristol; National Express coaches also run from London; by train: Chepstow. *Prestatyn*: By car: located on the A548, also accessible by the A547; by bus: local bus service from Rhyl, Chester, Holywell, Mold and Dyserth; by train: Prestatyn.

Ordnance Survey Maps: Explorers OL14 Wye Valley & Forest of Dean, OL13 Brecon Beacons National Park, 201 Knighton & Presteigne, 216 Welshpool & Montgomery, 240 Oswestry, 256 Wrexham, 265 Clwydian Range (1:25 000).

Guidebooks: *Offa's Dyke Circular Walks: Southern Section*, Ian Coulthard (Sigma, 2000); *Offa's Dyke Circular Walks: Northern Section*, Ian Coulthard (Sigma, 2001); *Walking Offa's Dyke Path*, David Hunter (Cicerone, 1994); *Offa's Dyke Path South (National Trail Guides)*, Ernie & Kathy Kay and Mark Richards (Aurum, 2000).

Website: www.offas-dyke.co.uk

Historic Chepstow to Monmouth

The path begins on the cliffs at Sedbury, near the Wye Estuary. From the cliffs you can see far out across the Severn Estuary, but turn inland and make an immediate detour – it's only a couple of miles (3km) – to Chepstow. Chepstow's Norman castle is surprisingly largely intact; despite many facelifts, it is basically 11th-century. Chepstow – the name means 'market place' – also has a splendid and very early iron bridge, built by the engineer John Rennie in 1816. The town has a group of very attractive 17th-century almshouses, as well as Brunel's spectacular early 19th-century railway bridge. The metal tubes (now removed) in which the trains originally ran were positioned in the most remarkable way: Brunel waited for a suitable high tide and then simply floated them up into place.

Back at Sedbury look for the stone that marks the beginning of the walk and then head for Buttington Tump. The early part of the walk leads through suburbia, but you soon reach a good stretch where the dyke is clearly visible. Impressive views of the dyke continue at Buttington Tump itself, though sadly here it is cut through by a road. The way continues to Tallard's Marsh via Pensylvannia village and a sewage works.

From Tallard's Marsh the path follows the River Wye before crossing a railway and heading on to Tutshill. There is a steep lane opposite Chepstow bridge; go up this and cross the A48. When you get to St Briavel's road you will see the 16th-century Tutshill Tower, now a ruin.

Continue via Chapelhouse Wood to Broadrock and Wintour's Leap, named after the Royalist Sir John Wintour who, during the English Civil War (1642–49), is supposed to have leaped from the edge of this 200-foot (60-m) cliff on his horse to escape the pursuing Parliamentarians – and survived. Anyone who has seen the cliff will be sceptical to

Above: *Although Chepstow Castle has been restored and refurbished many times over the years, the castle is still basically an 11th-century structure.*

Opposite: *The leaning medieval church at Cwmyoy near Abergavenny is worth detouring to. The remoteness of ancient monuments like this on and near the path is one of the reasons that most have remained unspoiled by modernization.*

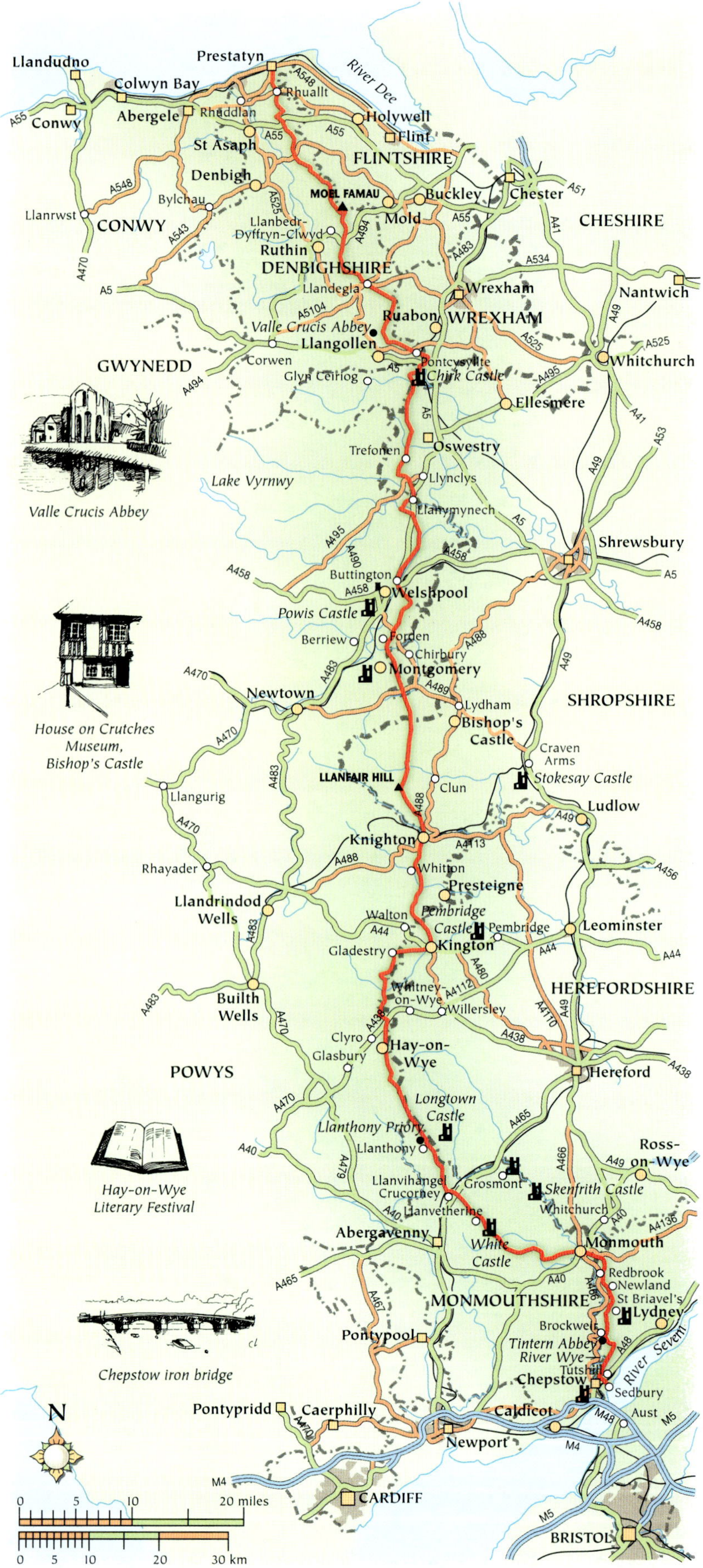

say the least, but it is a nice story. Soon after passing the leap the path reaches Spital Meend Iron Age hillfort, then passes the Twelve Apostles (giant outcrops of rock). Wyndcliffe, just across the river, soars to 800 feet (245m) and offers wonderful views of the winding River Wye below.

Five miles (8km) north of Chepstow is the romantic ruin of Tintern Abbey – the subject of one of Wordsworth's greatest poems. Founded in 1131 by the Marcher Lord of Chepstow, Walter de Clare, Tintern was a Cistercian foundation suppressed by Henry VIII in 1536. The abbey, or what was left of it, was sold to the

Crown in 1902 by the Duke of Beaufort whose family had owned it since Henry VIII's time. Like so many great monastic foundations, it is situated well away from the noise and bustle of the world.

From Tintern – which was beautifully painted by J.M.W. Turner (1775–1851) on one of his tours of Britain – the path follows the Wye via Brockweir to Bigsweir, or you can take a slight detour and climb to Caswell Wood where a splendid section of the dyke can be seen. On the alternative route there are the ruins of a great medieval castle at St Briavel's – traces of prisoners' carvings and graffiti can still be seen on its walls.

Anyone born within the hundred (an ancient division of a county) of St Briavel's may become a freeminer – a coalminer in the Forest of Dean. This right was first granted after one of a series of 14th-century sieges of Berwick by Edward II was successful due to miners from the Forest of Dean digging under the walls of Berwick Castle. Their reward was to be given the right to mine the forest in perpetuity. The partly Norman church at St Briavel's is also worth a visit – especially if you are what the late poet laureate John Betjeman would have called an inveterate 'church crawler'.

Above: *After a steep climb up to Hay Bluff, a promontory with fantastic views on the edge of the Black Mountains, you will descend into the town of Hay-on-Wye, where the castle which dates from 1200 has an attached 17th-century house.*

Continue to Redbrook where the Wye Valley railway once terminated. It was axed – unusually – in the Great War, long before Baron Beeching decimated the rest of the network in the 1960s. You then reach the pretty village of Newland with its monument-filled church, including one to a medieval freeminer, his thick leather breeches and jacket beautifully delineated.

The path rises 800 feet (244m) to the Kymin, a beautiful hill now looked after by the National Trust. From here you can see the Black Mountains, the Brecon Beacons and the distant town of Monmouth. There are two buildings at the top of the Kymin: the Round House, built in 1794 as a dining club for 'the gentlemen of Monmouth', and the Naval Temple, erected in 1800 to commemorate the Battle of the Nile in 1798. Lord Nelson, with Lord and Lady Hamilton, apparently had breakfast here in 1802.

Above: *Selling books in Hay-on-Wye: the town's reputation as a centre for the second-hand book trade and for its annual literature festival held in May is now worldwide.*

The path drops down to Monmouth, where you could be forgiven for not knowing whether you were in England or Wales. For centuries the town has been dealt with in Parliamentary matters as if it were English, but so far as the army is concerned recruits from here join the Welsh Guards. Monmouth has a wonderful Nelson Museum – Nelson visited Monmouth twice, both times receiving a rapturous reception – where the great man's sword can be seen, along with other fascinating memorabilia. Parts of Monmouth's castle remain, but the real attraction of the town is its many surviving 16th- and 17th-century buildings. Monmouth also has the distinction of being the only town in Britain with a medieval fortified gateway (13th-century) on Monnow Bridge.

Over the Black Mountains and beyond

Just a few miles from Monmouth is the well-preserved 13th-century Pembridge Castle. From there you must follow the path to eventually reach the beautiful Vale of Ewyas and the atmospheric ruins of Llanthony Abbey (Priory), founded in 1103. Most of the surviving structure dates from 1115. The Llanthony Estate nearly bankrupted the writer and poet Walter Savage Landor (1775–1864), who owned it between 1807 and 1814 and spent a fortune on planting and landscaping work. The path leads along the ridge to pass near Hay Bluff (2,219 feet/677m), with glorious views, then drops to Hay-on-Wye, an attractive town tucked below the scarp of the Black Mountains and best known for its huge number of second-hand bookshops. Its castle, built around 1200, was added to later; the house adjoining it dates from the 17th century.

From Hay, the path heads towards Kington through countryside made famous by the Reverend Francis Kilvert, curate of the parish of Clyro, near Hay, from 1865 to 1872. Kilvert began to keep a diary in 1870, extracts from which were published in the 1930s, giving readers a rare picture of country life in the late Victorian years.

Presteigne (or, if you prefer, in Welsh Llanandras) comes next, although the path passes to the west of the town. This beautiful Georgian town has a 15th-century curfew bell, which is still rung each night in an unbroken tradition dating back at least two centuries. Next the path reaches Knighton, the halfway point on the walk. A town of steep narrow streets, it has a slightly forgotten air.

After 5 miles (8km) of open country you can detour to Clun, which takes its name from the river of the same name. Clun will forever be associated with the poet A.E. Housman (1859–1936) and his long poem, *A Shropshire Lad*, in many ways a celebration of the Shropshire countryside and a lament for the innocence of childhood days:

Into my heart an air that kills
From yon far country blows
What are those blue remembered hills
What fields what farms are those?

This is the land of lost content
I see it shining plain
The happy meadows where I went
And cannot come again.

Above: *Lord Hereford's Knob above Hay-on-Wye, is just part of the area described so well in Kilvert's Diary. Francis Kilvert was curate of the parish of Clyro in the 19th century, and his diary, first published in the 1930s, has long been a bestseller.*

Opposite, below: *Llanthony Priory dates from the early 12th century. Although now ruined, it is still a popular draw for tourists, who can stay at the attached hotel.*

Above: *Not far from Knighton the path reaches its highest point – Llanfair Hill, which rises to 1280 feet (420m). This area of the walk has many well preserved stretches of the dyke and affords spectacular views of the earthwork.*

On one of his rare happy days Housman also wrote: 'Clunton, Clunbury, Clungerford and Clun, Are the quietest places under the sun'.

Beyond Knighton is the highest point of the walk – Llanfair Hill, 1,280 feet (420m) above sea level. Nine miles (14km) east is Stokesay Castle, a unique survival of a fortified unmodernized medieval manor house.

The next town to detour to is Bishop's Castle, 3 miles (5km) east of the path. It has many early black-and-white timbered buildings and a wonderful Georgian town hall, the smallest in England. All around Bishop's Castle traces of the medieval strip-field system are still visible. The path makes its way to Montgomery. The town still has the remains of its medieval castle, and is the smallest county town in Britain. The church of St Nicholas still has a rood screen, a very rare pre-Reformation survival, although brought here from another church. The church also contains the family tombs of the great 17th-century metaphysical poet George Herbert, famous for his rather sturdy attitude to God, expressed typically in lines such as: 'Batter my heart three person'd God'.

The path goes on to Welshpool, known as the Gateway to Wales. Welshpool is worth visiting for Powis Castle (National Trust), one of the many castles built along the border between England and Wales in an attempt to control the unruly, frequently rebellious Celts who could not easily be pursued into the mountainous terrain. Built around 1200, only the shell is medieval; like so many other castles, Powis survived by being turned into a fashionable house, home to generations of the Herbert and the Clive families.

From Welshpool the trail follows the Severn for nearly 10 miles (16km) until you reach the town of Llanymynech, famous for having the Welsh–English border running

Above: *Powis Castle near Welshpool is an impressive stone keep-and-bailey fortress. Originally built in the 13th century by Welsh princes, it was heavily restored in the early 1900s.*

down the middle of the main street!

Relatively easy walking follows, up hill and down dale, to reach the Ceriog Valley. More undulating, unspoiled countryside leads to 14th-century Chirk Castle, a medieval fortress with a largely 18th-century interior and beautiful parkland, now owned by the National Trust.

After Chirk a good stretch of the dyke in all its glory lies ahead. On your way to Llangollen visit Pontcysyllte where, in 1795, the engineer Thomas Telford built a canal viaduct that soars nearly 130 feet (40m) above the valley.

Llangollen and its twin town Llandegla are separated by a moor near the site of Valle Crucis Abbey, founded in 1201. Though ruined, the abbey still has its fishpond and it is not difficult to imagine the monks netting their carp here every Friday – fast-growing and delicious, carp were part of the staple diet at most monastic houses.

Beyond Llandegla the path is easy to follow. For the final few miles before we reach Moel the land – wild, high and open – is owned and protected by the National Trust. From Moel the path makes its way to St Beuno's, where the 19th-century poet Gerard Manley Hopkins studied at the Jesuit College.

Beyond St Beuno's you pass through wild border country and a line of six Iron Age hillforts, each with impressive and elaborate earthworks. This is tough walking. The long Vale of Clwyd provides glorious views deep into Wales as far as Snowdonia. The path passes close to Rhuddlan – where Offa died in battle in 796 – and then descends into Prestatyn. Like so many seaside towns that have declined as tourists head for holidays in Spain and elsewhere, Prestatyn has a slightly down-at-heel air. The path brings you down into the High Street and the end of the walk.

PEDDARS WAY

& NORFOLK COAST PATH

Above: *Blakeney's sign hints at the village's history – in times past it was famous for its harbour, international trading and piracy.*

Opposite: *The estuary at Thornham: as with most of North Norfolk, it is one of Britain's top birdwatching spots.*

Peddars Way is the best preserved Roman road in Norfolk. It defines parish boundaries and was probably built over an existing route that had already been in use for thousands of years. The path is a mix of wooded country, heathland, marsh and – given that the route crosses East Anglia – hardly any hills at all.

The path starts right on the Suffolk–Norfolk border at Knettishall. Here, at the first of many wildlife-rich sites along this walk, is the Knettishall Site of Special Scientific Interest. The sandy soil supports large numbers of lizards, snakes and traditional heathland plants such as harebell and tormentil. Here, too, are traditional English partridges, redleg or French partridges, kestrels and owls. The path leaves Knettishall and crosses the River Little Ouse, which marks the county boundary. Sadly, this once sparkling little stream has been spoiled and straightened by water authority works, and damaged by the leaching of agricultural chemicals from the surrounding farmland.

A wealth of wildlife

We are now in Breckland, also known as The Brecks, an area described by 18th- and 19th-century travellers as bleak, derelict and inhospitable. It is a land characterized by light, sandy soils, 19th-century conifer plantations and a high rabbit population. It's hard to say which of the latter two is less popular. The path goes through Forestry Commission plantations at Thorpe Woodlands and then reaches the little River Thet, from which Thetford takes it name. From the Thet you soon reach the busy A11 and a railway line, which is crossed using an underpass. Next the path reaches the ancient route known as Harting Drove, once a well-trodden way through the low-lying fenland when it still consisted of thousands of square miles of reed bed and dangerous swamp. The whole of this area – being well below sea level – was once sodden marsh, until Dutch engineers, brought over in the 17th century, began to drain the thousands of square miles to

GETTING AROUND THE PEDDARS WAY

Start: Knettishall, Suffolk.
Finish: Cromer, Norfolk.
Distance: 93 miles (149km).
Transport Links: *Knettishall:* By car: just off the A1066 east of Thetford; by bus: local buses run from Norwich, King's Lynn and Cambridge; by train: Thetford, on the Cambridge–Norwich line. *Cromer:* By car: take the A148/A149; by bus: local buses run to and from local towns and villages, plus National Express services from London; by train: Cromer.
Ordnance Survey Maps: Explorers 229 Thetford Forest in The Brecks, Thetford, 236 King's Lynn, Downham Market & Swaffham, 250 Norfolk Coast West, 252 Norfolk Coast East (1:25,000).
Guidebooks: *National Trail Guide No. 15: Peddars Way and Norfolk Coast Path*, Bruce Robinson (Aurum, 2002); *Peddars Way and Norfolk Coast Path: A Guide and Accommodation List – Walking the Peddars Way and Norfolk Coast Path with Weavers Way* (Ramblers' Association, 2001); *Norfolk Songline: Walking the Peddars Way*, Hugh Lupton (Hickathrift, 2000).

produce some of the best agricultural land in Britain. Remnants of true fenland may still be found in a few places, such as at the National Trust's Wicken Fen in Cambridgeshire.

The walking here is pleasant and open, but very flat until you reach East Wretham and then Thompson Water. The latter is a wonderful place for many species of wildfowl – ducks, geese and waders – as well as reed warbler and reed bunting. Mammals are represented by the secretive, but distinctive, muntjac as well as roe deer. Thompson Water, now a nature reserve, was created by damming the River Wissey more than 150 years ago to provide water for the herds of animals being driven to London and other towns along the Harting Drove; this area has the lowest rainfall level in Britain. The annual rainfall here is 24 inches (623mm) compared to, say, 41 inches (1,047mm) in south-west Cornwall.

The path crosses Sparrow Hill and heads over land owned by Lord Walsingham. Soon we reach the Brandon road and then Little Cressingham. From here the path continues mostly over farmland – too intensively farmed to be attractive. The occasional ancient hedge – lucky survivors of the 1970s destruction of hedges to accommodate bigger and more advanced farm machinery – reveals the ancient line of the Peddars Way.

Below: *In 1090, the Norman William de Warenne, inspired by the abbey at Cluny in France, founded the priory at Castle Acre. The priory was surrendered to Henry VIII during the Dissolution of the Monasteries and is now a cluster of ruins, which include this 15th-century gatehouse.*

Grimes Grave

At Grimes Graves, just north of Brandon, we reach one of the most fascinating and important places on the walk. Grimes Graves is a Neolithic site where more than 1,700 circular pits, dug originally 4,500 years ago by flint-miners, have been found. Another sort of mining in this area was carried out in medieval times when warrens were dug because rabbits were a delicacy. The rabbits' descendants now live wild and thrive on the light, dry soils, despite occasional bouts of myxomatosis. This is a land of army bases, airfields and conifer plantations, but it still has in parts the wasteland feel: lonely and bleak. Thetford Forest nearby has one great wildlife claim to fame: it is one of the last places in England where the red squirrel may still be seen.

From Little Cressingham the path leads to Pickenham Hall, an undistinguished Edwardian house that replaced a beautiful 18th-century mansion. South Pickenham's medieval church has a lovely round flint tower. From here the trail quickly reaches the valley of the River Wissey, well known among anglers for its splendid roach, dace and chub fishing.

At North Pickenham the path crosses the road that leads to Swaffham. You are now on what is known as Procession Lane, a green lane that was once walked by pilgrims on their way to the great Catholic shrine at Walsingham. The shrine was established by Richeldis de Faverches in 1061 after he dreamed that the Virgin Mary asked him to build a replica of the House of the Annunciation in Nazareth.

Walking through an historic landscape

All along the Peddars Way you will find evidence of Dr Beeching's 1963 axing of the branch-line railways. East Anglia suffered more than most areas; overgrown embankments and renovated stationmaster's houses

can still be seen right across Norfolk and Suffolk.

The path reaches the A47 and then the villages of Great Palgrave and Cotes, but these are 'DMVs' – deserted medieval villages. Norfolk has many of these. Most were abandoned after outbreaks of the Black Death, but the 18th-century agricultural depression – documented at length by the countryside writer and radical William Cobbett (1763–1835) – also took its toll on Norfolk's villages and hamlets. Having passed these long-vanished villages the path winds on, across the pretty little River Nar, to the lovely and historic village of Castle Acre.

Above: *Legend has it that lavender was first brought to Britain by the Romans, who were aware of the plant's healing, soothing and insect repellent properties. Lavender has been grown in Norfolk for centuries, and the lavender fields on the royal estate at Sandringham are a sight to behold in the summer months.*

Castle Acre has pretty brick-and-flint cottages, old pubs and the beautiful and substantial ruins of its medieval priory. Take a look at the remains of the Norman castle, where the gatehouse and earthworks can be seen. This area is rich in remarkable survivals: just 5 miles (8km) to the east in the village of Great Dunham is a church with its original Saxon tower. Close to Castle Acre and worth a detour is the town of Swaffham, where the sport of greyhound racing is said to have originated. It's now a busy market town, with many old pubs and houses; sadly most of the pubs, though attractive from the outside, have been modernized within and are filled with fruit machines and piped music. Swaffham church has a magnificent hammerbeam roof.

Towards the coast

From Castle Acre it is an easy, level walk to the coast, through an area that man has cultivated, shaped and managed for at least 10,000 years. It was one of the richest and most densely populated areas in the country in the days when agriculture was enormously labour intensive, though agricultural depression and modern farming practices have largely emptied it. The sites of abandoned villages dot the route all the way, and here and there bumpy ground reveals the site of long-vanished cottages.

The path passes Great Massingham, with its pretty red tiled houses and church overlooking the pond. As you make your way towards the coast, the trackway winds over gently undulating ground – a relief after the flatness of earlier sections. Only a few areas of commonland remain here, as the Enclosure Acts in the late 18th and early 19th centuries reduced the extent of commons and took commoners' rights with little or no compensation. The need for maximum food production in World War II put paid to the few remaining commons in the country, which were ploughed up as part of the 'Dig for Victory' campaign.

Above: *At Hunstanton the Peddars Way meets the North Norfolk Coastal Path. Fossil-hunters should head down to the beach as the cliffs, which have a white chalk upper, a band of limestone known as Red Chalk in the middle and a lower band of red-brown carstone, have been known to throw up some wonderful specimens. Beware rock falls from the cliff, however.*

Soon you cross the A148 and pass a group of old marl pits. Marl was dug in the 18th century and spread on the land to improve its fertility. This part of the walk also passes numerous Bronze Age burial mounds. You can detour to Sir Robert Walpole's beautiful early 18th-century house, Houghton Hall. Sir Robert decided he wanted to landscape his grounds, but there was a problem – there was a village in the way. The solution in those far-off undemocratic days was simple: he demolished the village and had it rebuilt farther away! It's also worth visiting nearby Sandringham, which is open to the public if the Royal family is not in residence. The house, built in the 1870s to replace a far more attractive earlier building, is no architectural masterpiece but has long been the most favoured royal residence. The gardens are the real appeal. At nearby Great Bircham, one of Norfolk's last working corn windmills is open to the public.

Before you reach Fring Cross the landscape will have become slightly hillier, more overgrown and definitely more attractive. The Norfolk lavender industry was once centred on Fring, and there are still fields of lavender to be found, particularly near Heacham.

From Fring Cross the path climbs a slight hill, passes Dovehill Wood and then crosses the B1454. Here you can take a little detour to see the splendid Sedgefield Magazine, a 17th-century armoury. Soon you reach Ringstead, where flint as the dominant building material gives way to browny-red carstone. It's now just a few miles to the sea and in the far distance on a clear day you can see The Wash, home to tens of thousands of migratory birds of all species. Nearby Snettisham was put on the map in 1948 when a huge hoard of Iron Age gold was found. This unique collection of large, beautifully made torcs (which are to be worn around the neck) is now in the British Museum. The word 'torc' means 'twisted'. However Snettisham, and nearby Titchwell, a little farther east along the coast, are both famed for their RSPB reserves. This part of the north Norfolk coast is one of the most internationally important for wintering wildfowl.

Opposite: *Cley windmill dominates the surrounding marshland. Built in the early 1800s, the mill stands on what was once a quayside. The mill was still in use until just after World War I, and it is now a guesthouse.*

Below: *Blakeney has an excellent sailing school, should you choose to swap your landlegs for sealegs.*

Along the coast of north Norfolk

The path takes you to Holme-next-the-Sea. At the point where the path crosses the River Hun it ceases officially to be the Peddars Way and becomes the Norfolk Coast Path. At Holme Dunes a little under 300 bird species have been recorded over the years; the whole of the north Norfolk coast is a birdwatcher's paradise. The Holme Dunes – a fragile and vitally important habitat – cover just over 220 acres (89 ha.).

Much of the way from here to Yarmouth is sand dune and coastal path – described by Charles Dickens as 'the strangest place in the wide world' – but rich in numerous species of wildfowl and waders. From Holme the path heads for Gore Point past the dunes and on to Thornham village. Here the path is forced away from the coast for a short while, to skirt Titchwell before returning to the coast at Brancaster. At Brancaster are the remains – and there really is little to see – of the Roman fort of Branodunum, one of several defensive forts in the area.

Burnham Thorpe is the next village reached by the path, and Lord Nelson was born here in 1758. From Burnham Overy Staithe ('overy' meaning 'over the water') the path heads for the high dunes of Gun Hill and then Scolt Head. The dunes along this coast are preserved either by the National Trust or by the North Norfolk Naturalists' Trust, and it is vitally important that visitors and walkers do not damage them – they may look solid, but this is a fragile ecosystem. From here the path hugs the coast for many miles and there are breathtaking views out to sea across the wide creeks, dunes, marshes and sandbanks.

Holkham Bay comes next. At 10,127 acres (4,100 ha.), this is the site of the biggest coastal nature reserve in Britain and home to countless thousands of wildfowl and waders as well as natterjack toads. The nearby Holkham Estate has been in the Coke (pronounced 'cook') family for centuries. An 18th-century Lord Coke introduced crop rotation and dramatically improved agricultural practice throughout the world. Holkham Hall is also the original home of the bowler hat. Though later the chosen wear of the city gent, the bowler was originally designed for Lord Coke's game-keepers, at which time – the mid-1800s – it was known as the billycock.

Next, the path reaches Wells-next-the-Sea where it follows the beach road round the harbour. From Wells you pass Warham Saltmarshes to reach Stiffkey. Above the River Stiffkey is the impressive earthwork of an Iron Age fort, enclosing more than 3.7 acres (1½ ha.). From Wells you can take a delightful light railway ride inland to Walsingham, for centuries a place of Catholic pilgrimage.

From Stiffkey the path heads along the edge of the sands to Morston and then Blakeney, a pretty village of narrow lanes and tiny cottages. In medieval times Blakeney was an important wool-exporting point, but the harbour has long ago silted up and the village relies now entirely on visitors. Blakeney's 14th-century guildhall should not be missed. The long sand-and-shingle spit of Blakeney Point, managed by the National Trust, is a

National Nature Reserve, home to terns, geese of several species, ducks, waders, seals and rare plants.

Bird-rich creeks and inlets continue right along the coast. Cley-next-the-Sea is soon reached, and for the birdwatcher the Cley Marshes Nature Reserve will be tempting with its permanent hides and large population of wildfowl and waders. From Cley continue straight along a shingle bank to Salthouse Marshes, Gramborough Hill and then Weybourne. The path reaches Weybourne Hope and then continues to Sheringham, where a splendid preserved steam railway runs to Holt. All along this part of the walk the views are wonderful as the path hugs the coast. The trail reaches Beeston Hill and goes on to the Runtons – East and West – and then Cromer. Just before Cromer don't miss one of the best early houses in Norfolk, 17th-century Felbrigg Hall. The Hall, owned by the National Trust, still contains its original furniture and paintings.

Below: *The north Norfolk coast is world-famous for its birdlife. Here, a huge flock of knot pack tightly together as they gather at their roost.*

Between Beeston and Cromer the path is pushed inland and it ends in Cromer at the seafront. Norfolk still has more surviving medieval churches than any other English county, and the tallest of them is Cromer's, at just under 165 feet (50m). More than a thousand churches are recorded and at least 600 are still in use. The explanation for these numbers is simple: in medieval times Norfolk was hugely wealthy as its income, as in so many parts of Britain, was largely based on wool.

PEMBROKESHIRE COAST PATH

Inland from the wild, windswept coast, the countryside of Pembrokeshire has been settled for at least 5,000 years. There are many stone tombs dating from this time all along the Path, as well as the remains of Iron Age hillforts and evidence of the earliest Celtic Christians who came to this wild landscape to spread the Word and, later, to escape the temptations of the world.

Right: *The tiny chapel of St Govan's literally clings to the cliff edge. It was built in the 13th century well away from civilization – indeed it is difficult to imagine a more austere, unworldly place! Intrepid visitors can take a path down to the chapel which is usually open. However, the path can be very slippery when wet.*

GETTING AROUND THE PEMBROKESHIRE COAST PATH

Start: St Dogmaels, Pembrokeshire
Finish: Amroth, Pembrokeshire
Distance: 186 miles (299km)
Transport Links: *St Dogmaels*: By car: turn off the A487 to the B4546 at Cardigan; by bus: the Poppit Shuttle links St Dogmaels with local towns; by train: no railway line nearby, take a bus from Carmarthen. *Amroth*: By car: located on the A487; by bus: a regular local bus service, roughly hourly, to and from many local towns; by train: Saundersfoot, 3 miles (5km) away.
Ordnance Survey Maps: Explorer OL35 North Pembrokeshire, OL36 South Pembrokeshire (1:25,000).
Guidebooks: *Pembrokeshire Coast Path*, Brian John (Aurum, 2001); *Pembrokeshire Coast Path*, Jim Manthorpe (Trailblazer, 2003).
Website: www.pembrokeshirecoast.org.uk

Monks would have landed from Ireland, Cornwall and Spain, and pilgrims would have left these shores by boat for the great European shrines at Santiago de Compostela in Spain and elsewhere. The Vikings left their mark in place names such as Milford Haven and Skomer Island. By the late Middle Ages, castles had been built in several places along the coast – including 13th-century Pembroke Castle – symbols of a foreign dominion that still stand today.

The dominant feature of the Pembrokeshire Coast Path is rock – red sandstone, limestone and millstone grit – and sea. Some of the oldest rocks in Britain are here, dating back 700 million years. Around 300 million years ago the forests died, and it is their buried remains that form the basis of the coal deposits that are now a feature along the southern part of the Pembrokeshire coast.

Above: *From the path near St David's, the route ahead of you is clearly visible, as it hugs this wonderful coastline almost the whole 186 miles (299km).*

Into the National Park

The walk starts at St Dogmaels on the River Teifi near Cardigan. The Teifi was once a great salmon river, but high-seas netting (taking the fish on their feeding grounds) and

Right: *St David's Cathedral was built in the 12th century from red sandstone on the site of a monastic centre founded by St David, the patron saint of Wales.*

Below: *Newgale Sands is just one of several remote, windswept beaches all along the Pembrokeshire Coast. For walkers, as for the early monks, it is truly a place to escape from busy, noisy lives.*

pollution have damaged it, perhaps beyond repair. Visit the ruins of the 12th-century abbey – the monks must have had a ready supply of fish from the river.

The path follows the river and reaches the estuary. Half an hour's walking will bring you to the edge of the Pembrokeshire Coast National Park. The path then leads on to Cemaes Head, and on through fields and rocky cliffs and a series of climbs and descents through seemingly endless stream-cut valleys. All along here the rock forms, twisted and moulded by ancient tectonic plate movements, are fascinating. Look out to sea and you may be lucky enough to spot that most rare bird, the chough, a large member of the crow family.

A prehistoric past

When you reach Newport Bay – the village of Newport is on the far side – you are close to the Preseli Hills. Around 4,000 years ago Neolithic peoples are thought to have transported huge blocks of bluestone all the way from here to Salisbury Plain, to be used in the construction of Stonehenge. From Newport the path follows the Nevern Estuary bank

through pretty Parrog village, past Cat Rock and on to a succession of small bays.

Fish as bright and colourful as any tropical species can be found in the waters here. Wrasse – whose colour varies from bright red with blue spots to bright yellow with red spots – hug the rocks all along this coast.

Just over an hour's walking from Newport is the abandoned church of St Brynach at Cwm-yr-eglwys. The church was severely damaged in a storm in the 1850s and never rebuilt. From here the trail takes you round Dinas Head, a spectacular promontory with views across to Needle Rock with its colonies of gulls and guillemots. Look south-west from the top of Dinas Head and you are likely to see ferries destined for Ireland waiting in Fishguard Harbour.

Beyond Dinas the route is across very rough, tiring country around Castle Point and on into Fishguard. Here the path follows the beach before climbing once again to the clifftops. The path leads on to Strumble Head with its lighthouse and coastguard station and then reaches Pwllderi Bay, Aberbach and Abermawr before continuing to Abercastle village where a rocky island, known as the Grave of Sampson's Finger, sits massive and brooding. Inland is Carreg Sampson, a Neolithic cromlech (burial chamber) dating back at least 3,000 years.

Next comes the village of Trevine, then a series of little bays, past slate quarries and long-abandoned quarry tramways to St David's Head where the remains of prehistoric fields and an Iron Age hillfort can still be seen. From here the path quickly descends to the broad sweep of Whitesand Bay.

Remote religion

A few miles further on we reach the smallest cathedral city in Britain – St David's. Named after a 6th-century Welsh monk, St David's replaced an earlier monastic foundation, also named after the saint, that was deliberately built in a remote place. The idea was that the monks would be free to contemplate God and the hereafter in peace. The monastery also had the great advantage of looking out towards that most holy place – Ireland. The 12th-century red sandstone

Above: *The pretty little fishing village of Solva has been a port since the 1300s, and was once home to wreckers who used lights to lure passing ships onto the rocks from which their cargoes could then be spirited away.*

Opposite: *Porth Clais near Tenby attracts rock-climbers to its rugged cliffs. Walkers and climbers alike are well aware that the this coastline can be bathed in sunshine and gentle breezes one day only to be battered by gales and storms the next.*

building has one particularly striking feature: its floor slopes upwards towards the altar. The ruins of the bishop's palace can also be seen.

Back at Whitesands Bay the path continues to St Bride's Bay, named after St Brigid of Kildare. From the bay you can see the island of Ramsey, across a turbulent stretch of water known as The Bitches. All along here the windswept, dramatic coast is looked after by the National Trust.

Deliberate wreckers

The fishing village of Solva, a port since the 1300s, sits in a narrow valley with a sheltered harbour and an ancient reputation for villagers using lights to lure passing ships onto the rocks. Under the old law of the sea any wreck could be plundered with impunity if there were no survivors – an open invitation to the unscrupulous to ensure that there *were* no survivors!

Beyond Solva the path takes you past long disused limekilns – limestone was burnt and used as fertilizer – and across the clifftops until a few miles farther on it reaches the long sandy beach at Newgale. After about a mile (1.6km) the route takes you onto a road and past St Caradoc's Chapel. Six miles (10km) farther on you reach Musselwick, having passed the tiny villages of Nolton Haven, Broad Haven and Little Haven along the way.

The village of St Bride's comes next, with a little chapel dedicated to the Irish saint. From here the path continues along the storm-battered clifftops to the beach at Martin's Haven, then past ancient volcanic rocks to the southern tip of St Bride's Bay with views out to the island of Skomer, famed for its colonies of Manx shearwaters and grey seals.

Then comes Gateholm and the long beach at Marloes before you reach Westdale Bay with its Gothic-fantasy Dale Castle. The path runs round St Ann's Head from where you can look over Milford Haven.

The industrialization of Milford Haven, with its extensive oil refineries, dates from the late 1950s, but the town has managed to retain something of its history. A planned town dating from 1800, it developed quickly simply because it had such a superb harbour – Lord Nelson described the harbour here as the best in Britain.

Above: *Playful grey seals are commonly spotted off Skomer Island, which lies just off the southern tip of St Bride's Bay.*

Back on the path, and keeping Milford Haven in view all the time, we pass Mill Bay, Dale Point and then Monk Dale, where medieval pilgrims set off for, or arrived from, Ireland and Spain, or took boats to the shrine at St David's. Then comes Great Castle Head, where there are the remains of an Iron Age hillfort, and Sandy Haven before you reach the town of Milford Haven itself.

Beyond Milford the path continues to Neyland before running on across the Cleddau road bridge to Pembroke Dock. Based at the former Royal Naval dockyard, Pembroke Dock has a major deep-water, dry-cargo dock and the port handles general cargo and oil-rig support vessels. There are also twice-daily ferries to Ireland.

The south Pembrokeshire coast

Beyond Pembroke Dock the path makes its way to the River Pembroke and the town of Pembroke with its magnificent 13th-century castle. As you approach the castle, its rocky position and sheer walls are a reminder of how these Norman strongholds must have cowed the local populace. From Pembroke, a one-street town with a market, the path heads towards Moncton with its 11th-century priory, and then on across fields to Popton Point and Angle Bay. Angle village comes next and it's worth looking out for the long narrow pattern of medieval fields that is still visible. You must then climb higher until you are opposite Thorn Island and continue to the sandy beach at Freshwater West, behind which is a vast area of sand dunes, Broomhill Burrows.

From Freshwater West to Bosherton there are army ranges, so you must take to the road. When there is no firing (look out for the flags) you can return to the coast at Elegug Stacks, part way through the ranges, before continuing to Bosherston. The cliffs here are open to walkers at weekends, with the exception of the live-firing ranges, which are permanently closed.

Nere Elegug Stacks, giant limestone pillars standing a little way out to sea, is the spectacular Green Bridge of Wales, a natural limestone arch; some people dare to walk over this, but it is dangerous and not recommended. All along here are sea caves and potholes excavated by thousands of years of driving seas and heavy storms. One of the most spectacular features along this coast is the Huntsman's Leap, a narrow gorge more

Below: *In medieval times Tenby was a flourishing port and its long decline from prosperity was only halted by 20th-century tourists attracted to the town's three equally great beaches.*

than 100 feet (30m) deep but in places just 6 feet (2m) across. Don't try to jump it!

Best of all on this stretch is St Govan's Chapel, a miniscule, stone-built cell dating from the 13th century that still clings to the cliff-face. It is difficult to imagine a more austere, unworldly spot. From St Govan's, head for the broad sands of Barafundle Bay and then up a limestone cliff path to Stackpole Quay and on to Greenala Point and Freshwater East.

Now the cliffs and bays crowd one upon another – Westmoor Cliff comes first, then Swanlake Bay, then Eastmoor Cliff and Manorbier Bay. The historian Gerald of Wales was born in Manorbier Castle, probably in 1145. From Manorbier Bay you reach Lydstep and then a good stretch of beautiful, National Trust-managed land.

Caldey Island sits solidly out in Lydstep Haven. The path leads along the clifftops to Giltar and then Carmarthen Bay. Next comes Tenby, a popular holiday resort and long declined since its heyday as a medieval port, but still home to a glorious National Trust-owned late 15th-century merchant's house, with original frescoes and fireplace.

From Tenby the path goes to Monkstone Point and then Saundersfoot, from which anthracite was once exported by the shipload; the industry was at its height during the 19th century. From here it's just a few miles to the end of the walk at Amroth, originally a small mining settlement, but now a holiday spot with a wonderful beach.

Above: *A few miles beyond St Govan's Chapel you will reach the limestone cliffs at Stackpole Head. In spring the cliffs are a riot of colour as wild flowers thrive in the limestone habitat.*

THE RIDGEWAY

Above: *Following the re-introduction of red kites to the region, the endangered species can regularly be seen soaring above the M40 motorway near the Chiltern Gap.*

The brainchild of the Countryside Commission, the Ridgeway long-distance footpath was opened in 1973 after years of consultation with landowners. It has an immensely rich history, as it takes advantage of what has been described as the oldest road in Europe, a route that was used for millennia to trade goods and move animals, and one that has fascinated artists and writers in more recent times.

The Ridgeway once formed part of a prehistoric trading route that ran from Axmouth in Devon to The Wash in north-east England, a broad highway that effectively gave access to the heart of England via a diagonal route from south-west to north-east. The path came to life in modern times with Richard Jefferies' book *Wild Life in a Southern County* (1870). Jefferies, a writer and naturalist, loved the Ridgeway and probably began that romantic attachment to it that led more than a century later to its designation as an official long-distance path. But other writers and artists have found themselves moved by the ancient route: Edward Thomas, who was killed in the Great War, was uniquely alive to the pleasures of the Ridgeway, while Kenneth Grahame, author of *The Wind in the Willows*, wrote of the path: 'Out on that almost trackless expanse of billowy down such a track is in some sort humanely companionable: it really seems to lead you by the hand'. While Tom Hughes, author of *Tom Brown's Schooldays*, said of The Ridgeway: 'Was there ever such turf in the whole world... it is delicious!'

A city escape

The Ridgeway today appeals to walkers and those eager simply to get away from crowded cities and towns. The route joins together two Areas of Outstanding Natural Beauty – the North Wessex Downs and the Chilterns.

From Overton in Wiltshire the Ridgeway follows the top of the Wiltshire Downs for more than 40 miles (64km) except in just two places – the valley of the little River Og

GETTING AROUND THE RIDGEWAY

Start: Overton, Wiltshire.

Finish: Ivinghoe Beacon, Buckinghamshire.

Distance: 85 miles (137km).

Transport Links: *Overton Hill*: By car: located on the A4361, off the A4; by bus: buses run from Swindon and also Devizes and Marlborough, by train: Swindon, approximately 10 miles (16km) away. *Ivinghoe Beacon*: By car: can be accessed from the B488 and B489; by bus: a bus runs between Aylesbury and Luton and Dunstable via Ivinghoe Green and surrounding villages; by train: Tring is the nearest station, 3 miles (5km) away.

Ordnance Survey Maps: Explorers 157 Marlborough & Savernake Forest, 170 Abingdon, Wantage & Vale of White Horse, 171 Chiltern Hills West, Henley-on-Thames & Wallingford, 181 Chiltern Hills North, Aylesbury, Berkhamsted (1:25,000).

Guidebooks: *The Ridgeway* (National Trail Guides), Neil Curtis (Aurum, 2001); *Exploring the Ridgeway*, Alan Charles (Countryside Books, 2000); *The Ridgeway National Trail Companion*, Jos Joslin (National Trails Office, 2002).

Website: www.nationaltrails.gov.uk/ridgewayframeset.htm

Above: *The Neolithic long barrow known as Wayland's Smithy is shrouded in legend, and gets its name from the ancient myth that if you leave your horse and a coin here in the evening, when you return the next morning you will find your horse shod and your coin gone.*

and the point at which it crosses the great scar caused by the M4 motorway. So, roughly speaking, the walk is made up of two distinct kinds of landscape: open downland and wide skies to the west, wooded and gently undulating countryside to the east. Much of the downland has been ploughed for crops in the past century, but for centuries much of the land was given over entirely to sheep.

At Streatley, that pretty town that faces Goring across the Thames, the path ceases to be the Ridgeway and, strictly speaking, becomes the Icknield Way. This was essential in the planning stages, as much of the original Ridgeway route would take modern walkers along roads. At Princes Risborough, some 20 miles (32km) from the end of the walk at Ivinghoe Beacon, the Ridgeway takes you through Chiltern beechwoods before the final open chalky downland that leads to the beacon.

Throughout its length the Ridgeway passes ancient monuments, earthworks and tombs, tiny hamlets and farms, churches and splendid 17th- and 18th-century mansions. It is also richly endowed with the evidence of thousands of years of human activity. Recent research suggests that what we now call the Downs were almost certainly heavily wooded at the time they were settled by prehistoric humans, some 4,000–5,000 years ago, and they were gradually cleared by fire and axe.

Prehistoric origins

The inhabitants of the Avebury area between 2000 and 3000 BC are often referred to as the Windmill Hill people. These pre-literate tribes, who may have migrated here from the Mediterranean, built long barrows for their dead as well as the 130-foot-high (39.5-m) Silbury Hill, the exact significance of which is still disputed. One thing about Silbury Hill is certain: it is the largest man-made mound in Europe and was almost certainly constructed using antler picks and other primitive tools – an extraordinary achievement.

Next came the bronze-working Beaker People, who took their name from the characteristic vessels they produced, and who were followed in about 700 BC by the Iron Age settlers. All left their mark on the landscape, and in some areas land management practices that may have been thousands of years old were still in use at the turn of the 19th century: dew ponds, for example, were dug on the Downs in ancient times to collect water, and were still being utilized in places until World War I.

By the time the Romans arrived, the Ridgeway was probably little used, and the Saxons seem to have left little evidence of their passing. Sheep tracks dating from medieval times crossed the Downs, but sheep were driven on early unmetalled roads until 18th-century turnpikes pushed them back to the hills. When the railways came in the early and middle decades of the 19th century the Ridgeway sank back into quiet obscurity until the 20th-century enthusiasm for walking inspired the Countryside Commission to make it an officially designated walk.

The natural history along the route is another attraction: chalk downland plants include dropwort, bird's-foot trefoil, greater knapweed, restharrow and orchid. Butterflies include chalk-hill blue and small heath; deer thrive along the route, but particularly among the beechwoods, and the secretive, introduced muntjac deer is now among the most common species seen.

Surveying the stones

It's worth starting at Avebury, situated a little before the official start. There is a wealth of prehistoric evidence in the area, including the East Kennet long barrow and West Kennet long barrow and stone row, as well as the Wansdyke, an extraordinary 50-foot-deep (15-m) earthwork. West Kennet long barrow has been dated to a little before 3000 BC.

Immediately ahead of the barrows and the dyke is Avebury proper. The River Kennet that runs through the area is one of the cleanest and most beautiful chalk streams in

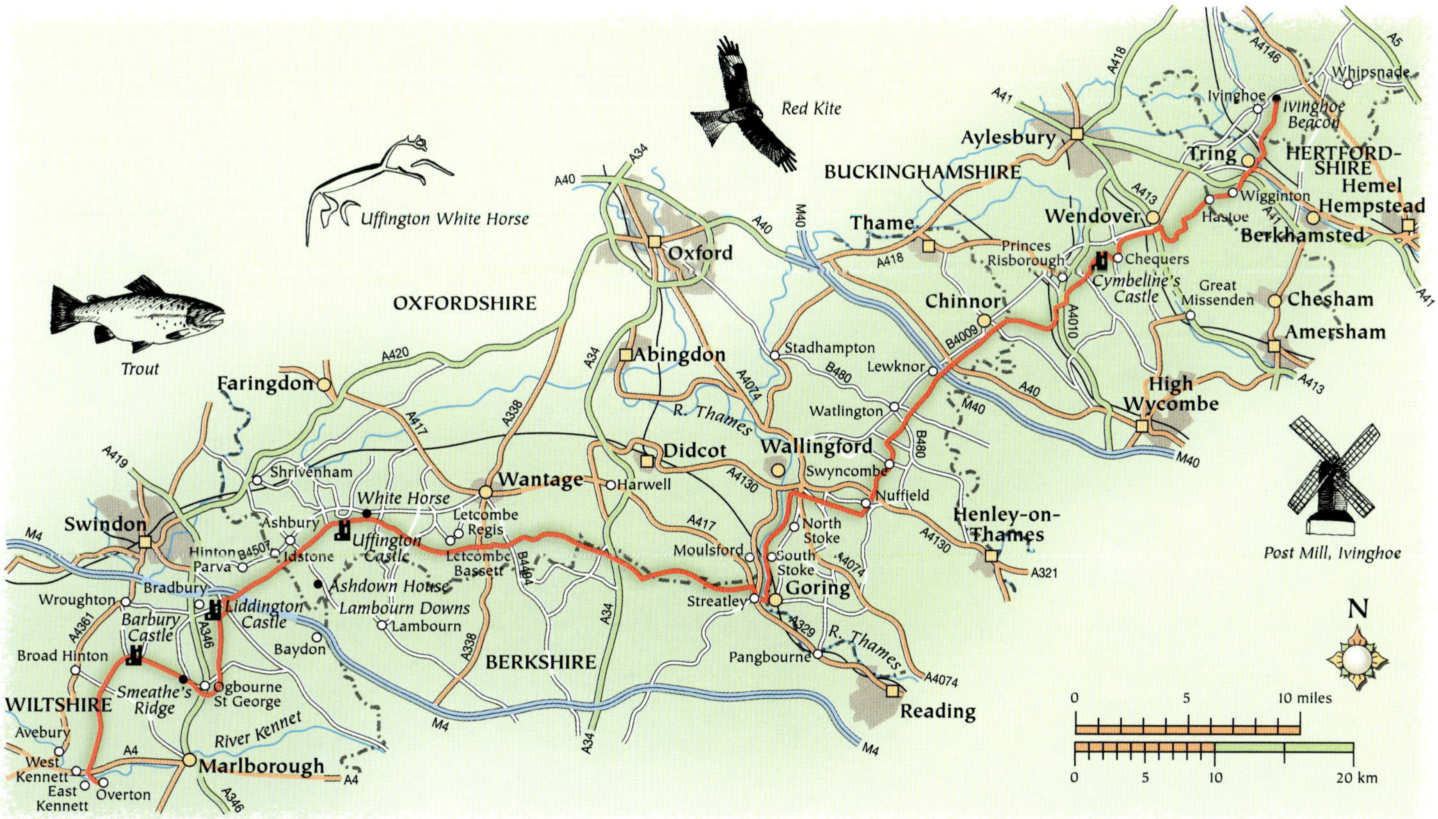

England. Here wild trout, fat chub and huge barbel glide through the green water and out across the golden gravel. Avebury was established long after the Windmill Hill people had vanished. It retains its manor house, its church and a row of tiny cottages, still largely undisturbed by modern development but very popular with tourists.

Avebury is the world's only village built within an ancient stone circle; in fact it is surrounded by several circles. For centuries local people left the stones pretty much to themselves, but by the early 19th century the stones were being plundered for building material. But enough remains for the design of the whole to be guessed at. A huge ring of stones enclosed two smaller rings, within which were larger stones. Outside the larger 1,500-foot (457.5-m) ring there was a ditch and bank 40 or 50 feet (12 or 15m) deep in places. Leading into the great circles from the north, south, east and west were stone-flanked causeways; little of the original work here survives.

Above: *The village of Avebury has the distinction of being built within an ancient stone circle thought to have been constructed* c. 2500–2000 BC, *possibly by the Beaker people.*

Over chalk downlands

Having feasted on Avebury it's time to begin the walk proper. It starts at Overton, along a trackway trod by countless earlier generations. In these early stages waymarkers are almost superfluous since the route is so clear. Whether you only have time for a morning's walk, or a full day's march of 15 miles (24km) or more, you are still using the route in time-honoured tradition.

The first broad curving sweep of the walk takes you roughly north-east to Hackpen Hill and – a little farther on – to the edge of the Vale of the White Horse, but still some way short of the monument itself. From Overton to Barbury Castle you will see clumps

Above: *Small clumps of beech trees here and there along the Ridgeway are testimony to the efforts of 18th- and 19th-century landowners to beautify the landscape.*

of beech trees dotted about. These were planted by 18th- and 19th-century landowners captivated by the idea of beautifying the landscape.

The trail passes Barbury Castle hillfort before going to the right to Smeathe's Ridge, from which there are wonderful views. Continue down into Ogbourne St George. All along the way it's worth pausing for a while in the villages at the foot of the Downs as most are unspoiled and some are uniquely beautiful. This part of the walk has a wonderfully open feel, with wide views across the countryside. Ogbourne is named after the little chalk stream that runs through it and is simply a single street. Having crossed the stream it is a short distance to yet another ancient hillfort at Liddington Hill. Also near Ogborne is the fascinating abandoned village of Snap, not a deserted medieval village, but a community that died out towards the end of the 19th century as cheap grain imports destroyed its economic viability. Piles of rubble mark the sites of long-vanished cottages.

Unfulfilled passions

After Liddington the path crosses the mighty M4 and you come to Fox Hill where the Ridgeway meets the Roman Ermine Way that runs from Silchester to Gloucester. From here you soon cross into Oxfordshire, passing the Earl of Craven's beautiful 17th-century Ashdown House. Now owned by the National Trust, this Dutch-style house has wonderful views across the countryside. The house is famous for its associations with the so-called winter queen – Charles I's sister, Elizabeth. The Earl of Craven consecrated the house – to use the National Trust guide's words – to Elizabeth, for whom he harboured a lifelong passion. This was a love story without a happy ending: he never told Elizabeth of his feelings and died, still a bachelor, in his nineties.

A little under 5 miles (8km) further on you reach Wayland's Smithy. Remote and windswept, this long barrow was excavated in the 1950s and found to contain ancient skeletons. It is said that if you leave your horse and a coin at the smithy in the evening and return next morning you will find your horse shod and your coin gone. Where and when the legend began is something of a mystery.

A clear, chalk track leads on to the famous White Horse, which is deeply etched into the hillside, and from where there are wonderful views north to the hills that surround Oxford. Some doubt has been thrown on the ancient origins of the horse, which would have had to be scoured regularly by generations of local people – even during times of religious intolerance – for it to have survived in its original state. It is difficult to understand why the medieval church would have permitted this attention for a pagan site. Strangely the horse seems to exhibit a heavily stylized, almost modern, design. The artist

Paul Nash (1889–1946) said of it, 'It is a piece of design… more a dragon than a horse'. The site, which includes Uffington Castle hillfort, is now looked after by the National Trust. Tradition says the the White Horse was carved to commemorate the defeat of the Danes by King Arthur in AD 870, but whatever the truth of the matter the horse had become the site of an annual fair by the 18th century. Booths and stalls were set up each summer on Uffington Castle and a cheese-rolling competition was held, with huge bets taken on the likely winners. The annual fair came to an end in the 1850s.

Towards the Thames

The Ridgeway heads towards the Thames Valley and the distant Cotswolds. Soon Didcot power station hoves into view; monumental and unsettling, it is unlikely ever to look at home in its rural setting, though some modern critics have grown fond of it. The power station stays in view for miles, but moving ever northward and eastward the Ridgeway reaches the Wantage-to-Lambourn road and then skirts the edge of Crowhole Bottom. Having taken this long curving route you reach Letcombe Bassett, once – like so many south-country, chalk-stream villages – a mass of watercress beds. Interestingly, many of the houses in the village are built from solid blocks of chalk cut from the Downs.

Next comes Wantage, a market town to which the green lanes and hollow ways of the Downs all once descended, for goods and animals came here for generations to be bought and sold. The path continues south of Wantage, with the famous Lambourn gallops visible across the Downs. If you want to see the horses exercising you will have to be an extremely early riser, however. Soon the path leads along Grim's Ditch, another ancient earthwork. Grim was Odin, the Norse equivalent to the Greek god Zeus.

In the distance the Thames makes its way eastward, and a few miles on you slip quietly into Berkshire. Soon you come to Lowbury Hill and the gentle descent to a steep-sided gap through the hills around the Thames Valley, flanked on either side by the twin villages of Streatley and Goring. Both are popular with wealthy London commuters. Streatley was formerly famous as a company village, the company in question being Morrell's brewery. The whole village was once entirely inhabited by its workers.

Below: *The mysterious Uffington White Horse, a stylised image of a horse carved into the steep chalk downs that the Ridgeway traverses. It was described by the artist Paul Nash (1889–1946) thus: 'It is a piece of design … more a dragon than a horse.'*

The Thames at Streatley and Goring marks the divide between the Berkshire Downs and the Chilterns. When the Countryside Commission designed the Ridgeway as we know it today they routed the last part – from Goring to Ivinghoe – along the Icknield Way, cleverly avoiding as many roads as possible.

The Chiltern ridge

The Ridgeway leaves Goring and heads north, parallel to more modern lines of communication – the railway and the river – and on to South Stoke. Here, as at Goring, the

very rich now have their rural retreats. Following the river the path takes you under one of Isambard Kingdom Brunel's railway bridges and on to the pretty village of North Stoke. The Thames part of the walk here takes us along in tandem with another long-distance walk – the Thames Path (see pages 142–51). At Watlington, with its old pubs and houses, the Ridgeway recrosses the river and heads back the way it came, following the line of Grim's Ditch eastwards to Nuffield. William Morris (1877–1963), otherwise known as Viscount Nuffield, of car fame is buried in the church here.

All along this part of the walk the Chilterns' distinctive wooded hills rise about us, covered with beeches. From Nuffield the path continues directly north to Swyncombe, a broad sweep of down that shelters a farm and the ancient chapel of St Botolph. This glorious little church has recently been restored and is well worth a visit. The path descends from Swyncombe and follows the Icknield Way below the hills until it reaches the M40 and the underpass. Much of the beechwood around here was important for the production of furniture (especially chairs), an industry centred on High Wycombe. Bodgers, working alone in the woods with their pole lathes, would have turned out countless chairs and other bits and pieces until mechanization took the industry into factories in the towns. The last bodgers only disappeared in the 1920s.

On either side of the M40 you can now regularly see red kites soaring high above the motorway. These large birds of prey were recently reintroduced after being exterminated more than a century ago and appear to be thriving. Their size and distinctive forked tails make them easy to distinguish from other common birds of prey.

Below: *The Grand Union Canal, which was formed between 1929 and 1932 by the amalgamation of several existing canals, leaves the River Thames at Brentford and climbs over 50 locks up into the Chiltern Hills, where the Ridgeway crosses it near Tring.*

A few miles on and you reach Princes Risborough and Buckinghamshire. Princes Risborough suffered badly from the attentions of car-obsessed town planners of the 1960s, but there is a fascinating National Trust property – early 17th-century red-brick Princes Risborough Manor House. After your visit rejoin the path to the south of the town. This will take you on a meandering route to the north and to Lower Cadsen where you climb once again, with a sense of relief, to open downland. Soon you are crossing the park at Chequers, the Prime Minister's country house. It was given to the nation in perpetuity by Lord Lee in 1921.

Rare wonders

With the park soon behind you the path heads north to Combe Hill and Wendover. Combe Hill is a glorious National Trust-owned Site of Special Scientific Interest. Here numerous rare butterflies and plants are protected from modern intensive farming and pesticides. Combe Hill is the highest peak in all the Chilterns at a little over 850 feet (259m). At the top is a monument to the dead of that now largely forgotten conflict, the Boer War.

Soon you will reach Wendover, a remarkably unspoiled little town with a pub that, until recently, had genuine Jacobean furniture in everyday use in most of the rooms. For a mile or so after leaving Wendover, the Ridgeway wanders lazily but ever upwards to reach the higher slopes and a clear route to Hastoe and then Wigginton village beyond. Here the path reaches the A41, built directly over the Roman Akeman Street that ran from St Albans to Cirencester. Cross the A41 on a high, specially built bridge and you will soon leave the noise of the busy road far behind. Next, the path crosses the Grand Union Canal and the railway. Tring station sits here, more than a mile (1.6km) from the town; it is a delightful monument to the townspeople's nervousness about the new-fangled railway. When they were told the train could come to a station right in the middle of their town the local worthies decided it was too dangerous, and rather than get the train to come to them they decided they would go to it.

From here the Ridgeway continues north and uphill. Soon the wide downs open up again, the chalk returns and it is a clear run to Ivinghoe Beacon where it is worth pausing to admire the early 17th-century windmill – more properly post mill – saved and restored by the National Trust.

Above: *The 17th-century windmill near Ivinghoe Beacon is strictly speaking a post mill, the earliest form of windmill construction. That is, it is not fitted with a fantail or elaborate shuttered sails, but is luffed or turned to face the wind by means of the tail pole. The 'common' sails are covered with separate sail cloths, which can be reefed and furled by hand according to the strength of the wind.*

SAINTS' WAY

Above: *An ancient milestone near Lostwithiel has directed travellers to the village of St Columb for centuries.*

The Saints' Way is believed to recreate roughly the route taken for centuries by those drovers and traders from Wales and Ireland who were reluctant to tackle the treacherous sea journey round Land's End. The way cuts across that narrow part of Cornwall between Padstow in the north and Fowey in the south. Most of the Cornish saints of the area were actually Welsh, and they left their mark right across the county. The Saints' Way takes in many of their churches, chapels and shrines.

The route begins at Padstow. Here fishing was the mainstay for centuries. St Petroc came here in the early 6th century; although nothing from that time survives, the town still has its lovely medieval abbey house and numerous fishermen's cottages. Before Petroc, Padstow was known by the Celts as Lanwethinoc, meaning 'the church site of St Gwethinoc'; it was Gwethinoc who founded the place. When the Vikings sacked Padstow in AD 981 it was known as Sancte Petroces Stow – in Old English or Anglo-Saxon 'stow' meant 'Holy Place'.

A historic route across Cornwall

From the harbour the path takes you uphill to the church but take time to visit – via a slight detour – Sir Nicholas Prideaux's 16th-century manor house, Prideaux Place. Most Cornish landowners were small squires who built such houses. Some are on the edge of towns, but many are hidden in remote wooded valleys and their discovery is one of the great pleasures of wandering in Cornwall. Prideaux is still a private house – though open to the public – and is one of those rare examples of a house still occupied by descendants of the family for whom it was originally built. Sir Nicholas is buried in Padstow church. But if Padstow is ancient, so are its traditions: the Padsow 'obby 'oss still parades through the town each May Day, for example. Green boughs are laid against houses around the town, and revellers follow the 'horse' as it dances and wheels its way through the narrow streets, accompanied by a drumbeat. The ceremony is undoubtedly pagan in origin.

GETTING AROUND THE SAINTS' WAY

Start: Padstow, Cornwall.

Finish: Fowey, Cornwall.

Distance: 26 miles (42km).

Transport Links: *Padstow*: by car: located on the A389 (which can be accessed from the A39); by bus: local buses run from the Eden Project, Wadebridge, Bodmin, Newquay and Truro; by train: Bodmin Parkway, 17 miles (27km) away. *Fowey*: by car: located on the AA3082 (which can be accessed from the A390); by bus: the number 24 bus runs from St Austell via various local towns including St Blazy and Par; by train: Par, approximately 3 miles (5km away).

Ordnance Survey Maps: Explorers 106 Newquay & Padstow, 109 Bodmin Moor, 107 St Austell & Liskeard (1:25 000).

Guidebooks: None available.

Padstow sits on the Camel Estuary, where the cry of the gulls is continual. The haunting call of the curlew can also be heard here – a sound long associated with bad luck, especially if heard at night.

The churchyard gate at St Petroc's is where the walk officially begins. Like most Cornish churches, which are either of flint or granite, St Petroc's dates back to Tudor times, but set against the church door is a Celtic cross, a reminder that Christianity came early to Cornwall. The church that bears St Petroc's name is of beautifully cut slate, silvery now with age.

From the church you must walk along Hill Street into Dennis Road and then Dennis Lane, keeping the estuary on your left. Climb then to the top of Dennis Hill with its wide views across the sea. From here descend to Trerethern Creek and along the Petherick Creek to Seamills, which until the 1890s used the ebb and flow of the tide to power its wheels and cogs. Next you reach Credis Creek with its abandoned copper mine. Much of the old prosperity of Cornwall was based on mining, most famously of tin, but there is evidence that the Bronze Age people of the area mined copper.

March on to climb a track formerly used to carry fine yellow sand up to the high fields to improve the soil, and the Way soon reaches Little Petherick, a village that has known many incarnations: some still call it St Petroc Minor, but in earlier times it was Nansventon, meaning the spring in the valley. Here there is another church dedicated to St Petroc, but alas this was almost completely rebuilt in the 19th century.

Above: *A small hill near the village of Lanivet is the site of Helman Tor, also known as the Logan Stone or 'rocking stone', believed to be part of the wall of an enclosed Neolithic settlement.*

Right: *Padstow, on the western side of the Camel Estuary, has a picturesque harbour. Fishing boats are often moored alongside yachts seeking shelter in the Inner Harbour, while along the quay catches of edible crab and lobster can be seen.*

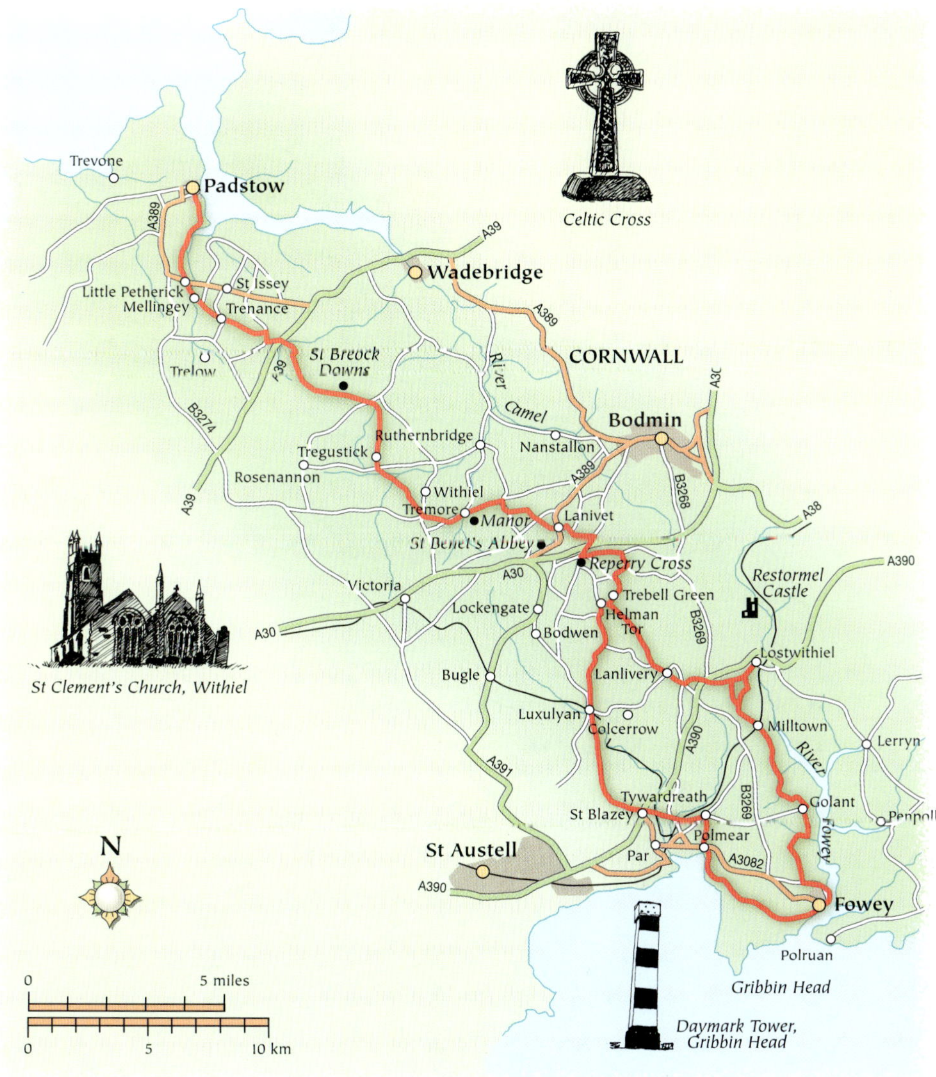

Local resources

From the church, cross the bridge and continue for a short distance along the A389, before turning right through fields towards Mellingey. Many of the stiles around here are made of slate which is, like granite, locally available. The Cornishmen who carved and worked both materials were masters of the art. Slate carvings from earlier centuries can be seen in churchyards throughout Cornwall, and many of the churches are made from granite – in some cases individual blocks of this hardest and most difficult of all materials are, as the poet Sir John Betjeman pointed out, 'as big as a chest of drawers'. Incidentally, the former poet laureate was buried at St Enodoc's Church, across the Camel from Padstow, in 1984.

At the village of Mellingey (the name means 'mill house') there are a few cottages and the impressive five-storey mill, now used as a willow workshop and

Above: *Old and new stand side by side on St Breock Downs, where ancient standing stones remain undisturbed by the advent of modern technology and the harnessing of natural energy on the St Breock windfarm.*

restaurant. Here, baskets are made from willow grown round about. Go on to the little village of Trenance. You can take a little detour north from here to St Issey, which was known long ago as Egoskruk or 'the church by the barrow'. St Issey's church has unusual painted decoration dating from Victorian times – the piers and arches are stencilled with bright colours.

All around this area are Stone, Bronze and Iron Age burial sites. Back at Trenance the path makes its way to and across the A39 and then climbs steeply past a lonely farm at Pawton Springs and onto St Breock Downs. As far as the eye can see on this, the highest non-granite upland in Cornwall, are the burial mounds of ancient peoples. The 16-foot-high (5-m) St Breock Longstone dates to the Bronze Age, weighs 16½ tons and is the heaviest example of a monument in Cornwall. Like all the monuments of these pre-literate peoples its exact significance is unknown. It is a reminder, however, that Christianity has not always been worshipped in Cornwall, and that the Cornish once believed in very different gods. During the Dark Ages and right through the medieval period local people met at the St Breock Longstone. Its name in Cornish – a language closely related to Welsh and Breton – is Men Gurta, or 'the stone of waiting'. Although a number of people understand the Cornish language today, the last native speaker died in about 1780.

If you look back towards the sea from the Longstone you will see the shining Camel Estuary. The Camel River still has a decent run of salmon and trout. Far away to the east are the bleak heights of Bodmin Moor; to the south the massive china-clay spoil tips, pink in the evening sun; to the west one of Cornwall's most impressive ancient monuments, the Iron Age hillfort of Castle an Dinas.

Above: *The houses in pretty Withiel village are, as throughout Cornwall, built mostly of granite, and though the village is small it has a church big enough for a town.*

A martyred saint

From the Longstone head for Hustyn Wood, past wind turbines and more ancient burial sites. The path leads to Higher Tregustick and then along an old track down into the Tregawne Valley and to the Ruthern (red) River where there is a choice of two footbridges. From here you continue through Blackhay farmyard to Withiel, one of the nicest little villages in the area. Here, out of all proportion to the small cottages of the village, is St Clement's. This big, airy church with its grand Georgian windows is dedicated to a saint who was martyred in AD 98 by being thrown into the Black Sea with an anchor tied round his neck. Opposite the church is the splendid, battlemented, early 16th-century Old Rectory.

From the village the well-marked path crosses fields to Lanzota, from where the path enters Withielgoose Lane and passes Withielgoose Manor before reaching Tremorebridge with its ancient houses, some with their tiny medieval windows. Leave the village, passing Tremore Manor gatehouse – the house itself is 18th-century – to reach the crossroads where there is a beautiful Celtic cross. Continue to Higher Woodley and then on to Lanivet where you cross the A389. In the churchyard at Lanivet are a number of Celtic crosses. The path then heads, via an underpass under the A30, to Reperry Cross. Celtic crosses and standing stones seem almost to clutter this part of the way – several were rescued from use as gateposts as recently as 1990. The route goes through Fenton Pits, passing another ancient cross, and then on to the little village of Trebell Green, then to Helman Tor Gate. Soon after this the path splits in two and you can choose which way to go.

Cornwall's ancient capital

The first route takes you through Lanlivery, where you can make a slight detour to the ancient town of Lostwithiel on the River Fowey. Climb to the top of Helman Tor – almost 690 feet (210m) above sea level – just for the spectacular views: on a good day you can see the Atlantic on the north side of Cornwall, and the English Channel to the south. On the top of the tor there is still evidence of a Neolithic stone enclosure. The path continues through ancient granite-hedged ways towards Lanlivery. No one knows how old this stone-lined path is, but it was certainly in use during the Dark Ages. The trackway comes to an end at Menawink Cross, which was placed here after being discovered in a field.

At Lanlivery the big 15th-century church is made from solid granite. Anyone who has

Above: *The open Cornish landscape is enchanting, and the well-maintained route makes the Saints' Way a joy to walk.*

ever tried to work granite in any way will marvel at the skill of the stonemasons who built with this incredibly unyielding material. The nearby Crown Inn is said to date in parts from before the Norman Conquest. Certainly it was for centuries a stopping place for thirsty drovers bringing animals from the Atlantic to the Channel-coast port of Fowey.

The path leaves the village and follows the road towards Lostwithiel. When you reach Pelyntor Cottage turn into the field and go up as far as the B3269 before turning right to the village of No Man's Land. From here follow the A390 into Lostwithiel. Lostwithiel, the ancient capital of Cornwall, is actually a detour from the path, but it is well worth it. The quays on the River Fowey (pronounced 'Foy') date back to medieval times; the bridge was built in the 1200s and this was the first of the Cornish stannary towns, where tin ingots were weighed, measured and given a stamp of approval. The great shire hall built by Edmund, Earl of Cornwall, still exists and was the place from which the county was once governed.

Daphne du Maurier

Leave Lostwithiel and go back up Castle Hill and turn left in front of the cemetery. From here follow the path down to the river where you can pick up the path to Milltown. From Milltown the path passes under the London–Penzance railway line past the medieval Lantyan farmhouse and on to Lantyan and Woodgate woods. It continues past the church of St Winnow, past Penquite – a 19th-century century mansion that is utterly Italian in design – and on to Golant church. This 15th-century building has wonderful carved oak beams as part of its barrel roof.

From Golant the path descends steeply, crosses a road and then climbs out of the

village on to the downs. There are glorious views across the Fowey Estuary from this high point. Descend to Sawmill Creek, cross the stepping stones, turn left at the road and continue until you hit the main road. From here it is a short walk into Fowey itself. Ferryside – an ivy-covered house visible on the other side of the river – was once the home of novelist Dame Daphne Du Maurier (1907–89).

The path threads its way through Fowey to the church of St Fimbarrus which, unlike the majority of Cornish churches, is not Tudor. It was built in the early 14th century and here our walk ends.

An alternative route

The alternative route runs from Helman Tor Gate towards St Blazey. Leave Helman Tor Gate and head towards Gunwen Chapel at Lowertown. Head south to Breney Common Nature Reserve (owned by the Cornwall Wildlife Trust) and continue past Tredinnick Farm before leaving the road for Luxulyan. Cross fields and a stream and on the way note the granite stiles whose discovery in 1984 by two local men led to the whole idea of the Saints' Way. Cliff Townes and Alf Fookes were fascinated by the number of Celtic sites and remains in this part of Cornwall, and – both keen walkers – they sought funding for a clearance project that would take the route from coast to coast.

From the valley bottom the path climbs steeply to meet the road, and skirts the centuries-old Luxulyan granite quarry. In Luxulyan itself the older houses and church are built entirely from granite. Just past the post office is an ancient well, the Well of St Cyor.

The path continues out of the village (via the back of the post office), crosses a railway line and descends to a valley bottom before rising again into an area famous for its free-standing granite boulders; the biggest is at nearby Colcerrow. The path carries on through Trevanny Farm and then on towards Prideaux Farm via the medieval manor house of Methrose, where the Methodist John Wesley (1703–91) stayed on one of his mammoth preaching tours of England.

Above: *Spring is the best time of year to embark on the Saints' Way as wild flowers will line much of the route just as they do here outside Fowey.*

On to Fowey

Go through Prideaux farmyard and turn left into Nanscowen Fields, then down to the road and to St Blazey along the A390. The village was once on the sea – it is now 2 miles (3.2km) away due to years of silting up – and was once known as Llandreath, meaning 'the church on the sands'. St Blaise was a 4th-century bishop martyred by the Romans. Candle wax that has dripped onto his altar is said to cure colds, sore throats and toothache.

Above: *The seaside town of Fowey, as seen from Boddinnick, was for some years the home of author Dame Daphne Du Maurier (1907–89). Du Maurier wrote many novels based in and around Cornwall, and lived at Ferryside just outside the town.*

Go back out to the A390 past some cottages and then uphill to Kilhallon. Take the sign for Lanescott before you reach Kilhallon. The path takes you to Treesmill Creek, and then under the London–Penzance railway up Marsh Lane to Tywardreath (Cornish for 'house on the strand'). Before the River Par silted up this was indeed a village on the strand (beach).

The path takes you past Wesley's Chapel and then climbs to Polmear, goes under a road and reaches a lovely row of almshouses built in the early 17th century. From here carry on uphill, then bear left across fields until you reach the Fowey road. A short distance along the road turn right towards Polkerris. The path continues to Polkerris itself with its stone pier, one pub and a few cottages. Walk up the lane, and right at the top, then left at the chapel at Tregaminion. If you kept straight ahead here you would reach the entrance to 18th-century Menabilly, Daphne Du Maurier's home for the last years of her life.

Continue through Tregaminion farmyard, cross a field and a stream and reach Tenant. To the right now you should be able to make out a red-and-white striped tower, the Daymark, built on Gribbin Head in the early 19th century to guide fishermen into Fowey Harbour. Before it was built the church tower was painted white as a landmark instead. The path goes on through Lankelly Woods, under a bridge over a stream, and into another farmyard before reaching the road. Follow the signs until you turn down an old packhorse road called Love Lane. The path then goes on the road into Fowey and ends at the church.

SOUTH DOWNS WAY

One of six long-distance walks recommended by the government in 1947, the route opened in 1972 from Eastbourne to Buriton in Hampshire. Twenty years later the Countryside Commission persuaded the Government to extend it a further 20 miles (32km) to Winchester. The South Downs Way now runs for mile after mile over what was once the bottom of the sea.

Above: *Among the glories of the South Downs are several species of blue butterfly: this is the Chalkhill Blue.*

The Downs are the remains of uncountable billions of ancient sea creatures compacted together on what was once the seabed and then pushed up over the millennia by tectonic plate movements. The Downs were created roughly 70–100 million years ago during the heyday of the dinosaurs, which is why the chalk cliffs, particularly farther west (see Jurassic Way, pp.82–9) are such a delight for fossil hunters.

The path along the South Downs starts at the west end of Eastbourne, that sleepy south-coast town beloved of the retired. The resistant chalk hills here – rising to Beachy Head's 530 feet (162m) – have weathered less than the surrounding areas of clay (the inland Weald, for example) because chalk is porous. Rainwater tends to go straight through the strata rather than wearing it away.

There is no doubt that man has used paths across the South Downs for at least 200,000 years, but the earliest peoples were Neolithic hunter-gatherers and not settled farmers. The area has only been settled during the past 4,000–5,000 years, so the Downs have not always looked as they do today. They were once tree-covered, although probably less densely than the valleys, and were therefore easier to clear. The soil on the Downs was always thin, and there is evidence that early man ploughed them. The fascinating remains of linchets (boundary ridges or unploughed strips) can be seen in places where ancient field systems have caused a distinctive landslip and created a bank of soil at the bottom of slopes. Right along the South Downs long barrows, Bronze Age tumuli, hill carvings and Iron Age hillforts testify to man's presence. There is also a Neolithic flint-mine at Cissbury.

GETTING AROUND THE SOUTH DOWNS WAY

Start: Eastbourne, Sussex.

Finish: Winchester, Hampshire.

Distance: 100 miles (167km).

Transport Links: *Eastbourne*: by car: located on the A259; by bus: local buses from Brighton, Hastings, Seaford and Bexhill; by train: Eastbourne, served by South Central. *Winchester*: by car: A3090/ A272 (both accessible from Jct. 9 of the M3); by bus: there is a frequent service from Southampton and Portsmouth, plus many other local services; by train: Winchester.

Ordnance Survey Maps: Explorers 123 South Downs Way – Newhaven to Eastbourne, 122 South Downs Way – Steyning to Newhaven, 121 Arundel & Pulborough, 120 Chichester, South Harting & Selsey, 132 Winchester, Alresford & East Meon (1:25 000).

Guidebooks: *South Downs Way* (National Trail Guides), Paul Millmore (Aurum, 2001); *The South Downs Way*, Kev Reynolds (Cicerone, 2001).

Website: www.nationaltrails.gov.uk/southdownsframeset.htm

Above: *Evening at Beachy Head: the 500-foot (162-metre) high chalk cliff is, like all these chalk downs, made from the bodies of countless billions of ancient sea creatures.*

Tens of thousands of the famous South Downs' sheep once grazed these hills, until European Union subsidies, encouraging farmers to grow ever more cereals using chemicals on land that would otherwise be suitable only for grazing, led to much of the higher ground being ploughed. The huge wealth of medieval England – wealth that built thousands of churches – was based on the wool trade.

The chalk grassland of these Downs provides one of Britain's richest wildlife habitats, with as many as 40 plant species recorded in just one square metre, so it is well worth taking a plant field guide along with you.

Villages tended to be sited at the foot of the Downs at the 'spring line', where the springs, formed as water percolated through the chalk, emerged. On the high tops, other than where dew ponds had been created, water was always scarce. Many small village houses were built from squared-off blocks of chalk, while flint that has been knapped (chipped and flaked) using a special hammer has been used in church construction in the area since medieval times. Knapping is a skill dating from Neolithic times, and survives today, though only a few specialists remain.

Above: *Pyramidal orchids and other wild flowers: as many as 40 different plants have been recorded in just one square metre of these burgeoning chalk downlands.*

A tough start along the coast

The sleepy Victorian town of Eastbourne comes to a sudden end and the beginning of the path could not be clearer. It's a steep climb, as are the Seven Sisters cliffs to come. Beachy Head (from the French *beau* for 'beautiful'), the tallest of all these cliffs, is notorious for suicides, with a sheer drop of just under 530 feet (162m). Tough short grass once cropped by sheep and now nibbled largely by rabbits typifies this early part of the walk. But these cliffs will not, in geological terms, be here for long: the sea, hundreds of feet below, continually undermines them. The cliff above then collapses, the debris disperses under the relentless pounding of the waves, and the process begins again. In 1999 Belle Tout lighthouse, built in 1830, was mounted on wheels in an extraordinary feat of engineering and inched back from the cliff edge in order to prevent it disappearing into the sea.

Having crossed the Seven Sisters the path descends to the valley of the River Cuckmere, meandering towards the coast with an almost primeval air. It seems strange, in such a busy county, for a river not to have a port, and this is the only river on this part of the south coast that does not have a settlement at its mouth.

Artistic connections

Just inland from here and worth a detour is a remarkable survivor: the medieval Charleston Manor Barn at Westdean is nearly 180 feet (55m) long and quite spectacular. Also a short distance inland is Alfriston, where the church is known as 'the cathedral

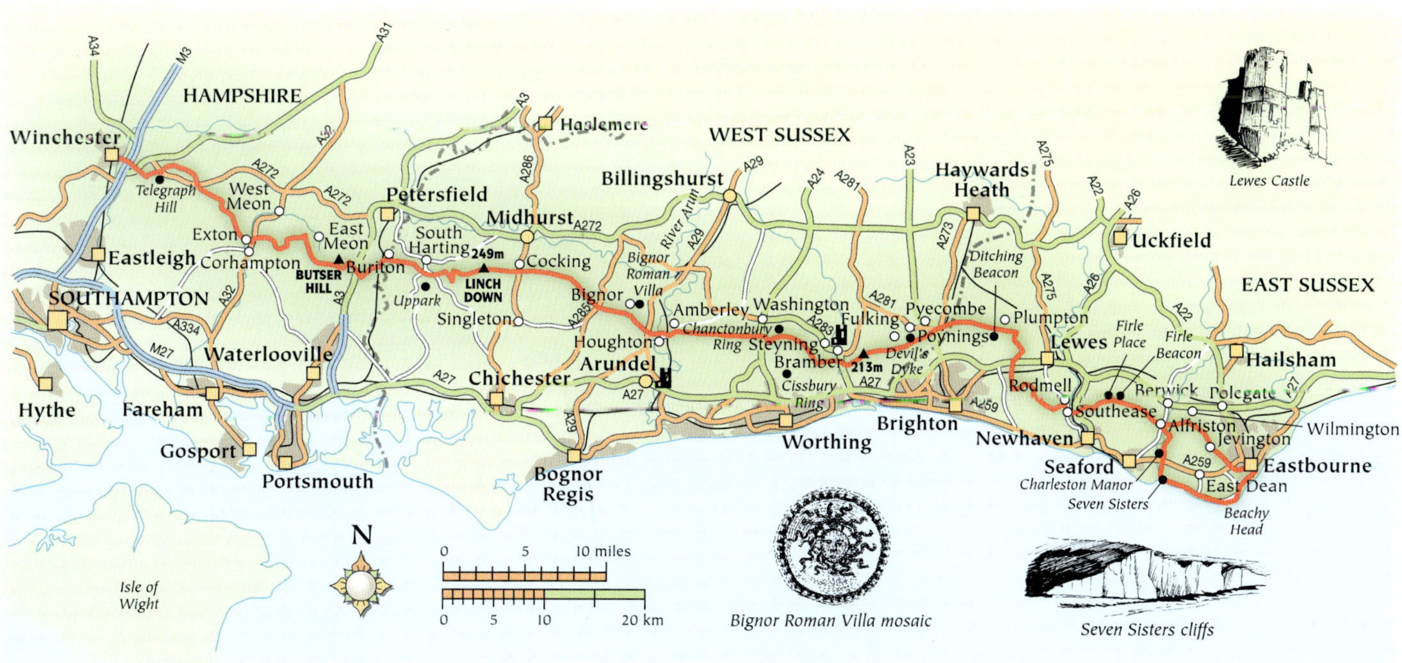

of the Downs'. An 8-mile (13-km) route would have taken you from Eastbourne to Alfriston via Jervington, but to take this would be to miss the spectacular cliffs. Alfriston is also famous as the birthplace of the National Trust, which acquired its first property – the beautiful late-medieval Clergy House – here in 1896. This timber-framed 14th-century building was in a dilapidated state when the Trust bought and restored it, complete with its rammed chalk floor. Alfriston has old pubs and a Saxon church, and from here you can take a further detour to Berwick church. This ancient church was decorated during World War II by England's best-known post-impressionist painters, Duncan Grant and Vanessa Bell.

Grant and Bell lived at nearby Charleston Farmhouse for more than 50 years, and are buried side-by-side in Firle churchyard. Their home can be visited, and it is a wonderful monument to the Bloomsbury Group of which they were central figures. They never owned the house, but were tenants of the Gage family who lived at nearby Firle Place, a lovely 18th-century house now open to the public. An earlier Gage bred a new and very sweet plum – the greengage.

Above: *The Long Man of Wilmington, mysterious guardian of the South Downs, has baffled archaeologists and historians for hundreds of years. It could be anything from a fertility symbol, an ancient warrior or an early 18th-century folly, but the not knowing is half the fun.*

Near Alfriston is the Long Man of Wilmington, a 200-foot-high (60-m) chalk carving on the north-facing slope of the Downs. No one knows exactly how old the figure is, but it was certainly there in the 18th century and there is some evidence that it is at least pre-Roman. Many of the houses in Wilmington, your next stop, date from the 15th and 16th centuries, and the image of the village in a time warp is enhanced by the fact that very little was built in the 20th century. Crossing the river the path reaches Southease with its round-towered church, climbs Iford Hill and then reaches Rodmell, where the novelist Virginia Woolf (1882–1941) lived. Woolf's home, Monks House, is owned by the National Trust, and her ashes were scattered in the garden after her death by suicide.

From Rodmell it's straight up to the Downs and wonderful views of Lewes some miles inland. Lewes is a still-lovely Georgian town with a ruined Norman castle and a house where Anne of Cleves, the fourth wife of Henry VIII, once lived.

Along the chalk ridge

Back on the path you must head for a little hidden valley known as Cold Combes. From here the path crosses the main London–Brighton road and then continues up to Plumpton

Above: *The South Downs Way crosses Grander Down near Titchbourne. All along the way there is a wonderful sense of wide skies, space and distant horizons.*

Plain back on the high chalk ridge. The way continues to Ditchling Beacon, the great hill that sees many cyclists on the London-to-Brighton cycle ride pushing their bikes forlornly uphill. Ditchling is more than 800 feet (244m) above sea level, the second highest point on the South Downs. The highest point is at Toplease in West Sussex at 836 feet (255m).

From Ditchling the path makes its way to Pyecombe via two windmills, known as Jack and Jill, rare survivors of dozens that once dotted these hills. From Pyecombe the path again crosses the main London road, and then climbs West Hill to Saddlescombe before reaching the Devil's Dyke, a hillfort inhabited on and off from Neolithic times until the end of the Bronze Age.

Six miles (9.7km) on, the path reaches the River Adur just after crossing the Shoreham road. Close to the path here is 11th-century Bramber Castle, one of several Norman strongholds built to guard the gaps through the chalk hills leading to London and beyond. It's worth taking a little detour to Steyning church, which is remarkably unaltered for a Norman building. The stone from which it was built was shipped here from Caen in France, testimony to the wealth generated in this area by wool. The path continues to the tiny village of Botolphs and across Annington Hill and Steyning Round Hill to the River Arun.

Cissbury Ring – a slight detour from the path – covers more than 60 acres (24 ha.). It was built around 200–300 BC and must have required a huge number of labourers as hundreds of tons of chalk and timber were involved in its construction. The whole area is now looked after by the National Trust.

From Cissbury it is a short distance north to the Iron Age hillfort of Chanctonbury Ring. The trees on the ring were damaged in 1987 by the great storms. The Irish composer John Field (1782–1837), inventor of the nocturne, a form perfected by Chopin, lived nearby. The path now descends to cross the Worthing–London road before climbing again to hills more wooded than we have yet encountered.

And on to Winchester

The Way continues to Washington and Amberley – Amberley Chalk Pits Museum is a 36-acre (14.5ha) open-air museum of industrial railway equipment – then rises to the top of Sullington Hill and leads on to Rackham Hill. From Rackham you may just be able to spot the Isle of Wight in the English Channel. From the hill you soon reach the River Arun itself and here it's worth making another detour, this time to Arundel Castle. Built in the 11th century, Arundel has been the family home of the dukes of Norfolk for 850 years.

The path crosses the Arun at Houghton, where the future Charles II is said to have stayed at the George and Dragon pub in 1651 en route to exile in France. From Houghton the path climbs to Bignor through wooded country. At Bignor there is a wonderful Roman villa with superb intact mosaics, now carefully preserved under specially built buildings. The path crosses the route of the Roman Stane Street at Gumber Corner, and then the A286. Just to the north is the Weald and Downland Museum, which has a fascinating collection of buildings, including medieval timber hall houses and tiny cruck-framed cottages, dating from the 13th to the 19th centuries.

March on to Barlavington, Woodavington Downs and then Cocking, a few miles from which are the Devil's Jumps, a long line of Bronze Age burial sites. Continue past isolated farms, very much a feature of this part of the world, to Beacon Hill's Iron Age hillfort and then Uppark, a beautiful late 17th-century house painstakingly restored by the National Trust after a disastrous fire in 1989. The novelist H.G. Wells (1866–1946), whose mother worked in the house, lived here as a boy. From Uppark we soon reach Hampshire and the walk descends slowly to Buriton.

The path now crosses the Queen Elizabeth Country Park and climbs to the Iron Age hillfort on Butser Hill, the highest point on the walk (886 feet/270m). Exton village follows, then Beacon Hill and Cheese Foot Head, before reaching Telegraph Hill. Descend to the lovely valley of the Itchen – world famous for its trout fishing – and finally into Winchester, whose magnificent cathedral is one of the wonders of Europe.

Below: *This ancient gateway into the precincts of the 11th-century cathedral is just part of the historic fabric of Winchester, a town that was known to the Romans as Venta Belgarum and was later capital of England under Alfred the Great (827).*

THAMES PATH

The great thing about the Thames Path is that it's very difficult to get lost – just head for the river! There's also something enormously appealing about a walk that largely follows a towpath that was used commercially for centuries. The survival of this towpath, which runs from Lechlade in Gloucestershire to Putney in west London, was the inspiration for the National Trail.

Opposite: *At the beautiful 18th-century bridge in Henley the Thames Path changes banks. The annual regatta has made the town world famous.*

At the turn of the 20th century the Thames was both the most important trade route into London and a highway for simple journeys for more than 2,000 years. Great palaces and gentlemen's houses were sited along the banks of the river for ease of transport and royal processions were by water; the last of the great royal barges is kept in the National Maritime Museum at Greenwich. By the 1920s rail and road transport had made the old Thames barges virtually obsolete, and the river was losing its commercial value, but the Thames Conservators realized that it was always going to be a focal point for a host of leisure interests. Apart from boating and fishing, writers like Jerome K. Jerome in his best-selling *Three Men in a Boat* had shown how a journey down the river could capture the public imagination. Pressure from the Ramblers Association and long hard negotiations with landowners followed, and in 1989, nearly 60 years after the idea was first mooted, the Thames Path was officially designated a National Trail.

The source of the Thames

A stone by a spring in a field near the village of Kemble, Gloucestershire marks the source of the Thames and the start of the Thames Path, but changes in the water table mean that the spring is often dry. In winter you can follow the little stream over the fields towards Kemble before crossing the Fosse Way Roman road. Near here is the route of the disused Thames & Severn Canal, which enabled goods to be taken by water to Gloucester.

The tiny River Thames reaches Parker's Bridge, just outside Kemble, and the way follows a path through Ewen (from the Anglo-Saxon word for 'source of the river'). The

GETTING AROUND THE THAMES PATH

Start: Ewen, Gloucestershire.
Finish: Thames Barrier, London.
Distance: 184 miles (294km).
Transport Links: *Thames Head*: By car: Kemble is located on the A429; by bus: infrequent local services from Cirencester to Kemble, just south of Ewen; by train: Kemble. *Thames Barrier*: By car: located on the A1020 on the north side and the A205 on the south side; by bus: many London bus services run to Woolwich and Charlton; by train: Charlton, a short walk away.
Ordnance Survey Maps: Explorers 168 Stroud, Tetbury & Malmesbury, 169 Cirencester & Swindon, 170 Abingdon, Wantage & Vale of White Horse, 180 Oxford, Witney & Woodstock, 159 Reading, Wokingham & Pangbourne, 171 Chiltern Hills West, Henley-on-Thames & Wallingford, 172 Chiltern Hills East, High Wycombe, Maidenhead, 160 Windsor, Weybridge & Bracknell, 161 London South, Westminster, Greenwich (1:25 000).
Guidebooks: *The Thames Path*, David Sharp (Aurum, 2001); *The Thames Path* (A Cicerone Guide), Leigh Hatts (Cicerone, 1998); *Walks along the Thames Path*, Ron Emmons (New Holland, 2001); *The Thames Path National Trail Companion* (National Trails Office, 2001).
Website: www.thames-path.co.uk

The Angel

Above: *This statue of Old Father Thames at St John's Lock, near Lechlade, once stood at the spring where the Thames begins.*

trail crosses the river before following it along meadow paths. Upper Mill Farm and a footbridge across an old mill-race are reminders that the river was once an important power source.

Soon you reach Somerford Keynes, its church a classic silhouette on the skyline. Neigh Bridge Country Park follows with its wide lakes, and then a mass of now-flooded gravel pits leads to Ashton Keynes where the river follows several routes. Head through the village where, Venice-like, at least one stream rushes between houses.

Set off through fields before crossing another wide expanse of gravel pits. The route is mostly clear past Waterhay and on to Hailstone Hill. A short detour away from the river follows before a long stretch of river walking through North Meadow to Cricklade.

The Roman Ermine Street runs near Cricklade, where the church of St Sampson is tucked behind the houses. Soon the path returns to the river bank; the Thames, augmented by the waters of the Clun, is widening. The path goes under the A419 and continues along the river with a small detour towards Castle Eaton, passing through the middle of the village – with its attractive old stone cottages – before returning to the water's edge. Trout, perch and chub thrive here in the well-oxygenated, clean water.

The path makes a long detour across fields to Upper Inglesham where medieval ridge-and-furrow patterns can be seen in the fields. Sadly, from Upper Inglesham to Inglesham the path is forced onto the road, but the journey is worth it for the Church of St John the Baptist, which still has its Georgian box pews. Just beyond the village return to the river where the River Coln and the long-disused Thames & Severn Canal meet the Thames. The old towpath to London began here, but the trail takes to the fields again with Lechlade's tall church spire visible over the fields.

Lechlade was once an important market town, but with the end of commercial river traffic it entered a long decline. The beautiful church was built on the profits of the wool trade, and Percy Bysshe Shelley (1792–1822) once wrote a poem in the churchyard. Morley House, which faces the church across the square, has had a number of highly eccentric owners over the centuries.

The upper Thames – towards Oxford

Back at the river the path goes under Ha'penny Bridge, so-called because that was once the toll. More fields – frequently flooded in winter – follow to St John's Lock, where there is a statue of Old Father Thames; this once stood at the spring where the walk began. A priory existed here until the Dissolution of the Monasteries (1536–40), and legend has it that the pleasant Trout Inn was built with stones from the priory.

A lovely walk through fields leads past concrete World War II pill-boxes. At Buscot Lock barbel weighing as much as 20lb (9kg) are said to inhabit the deep water beneath the weir, and a tiny lock-keeper's cottage, situated on a little island, is available for rent from the National Trust. Buscot village is less than half a mile (0.8km) from the weir and nearby is beautiful Buscot Park, home of Lord Faringdon, and the Old Parsonage (both National Trust).

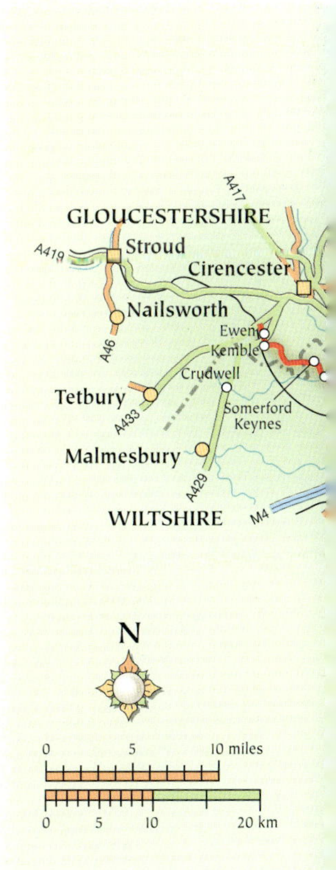

The southern route

On the southern side, the path runs from Teddington Lock through a surprisingly rural landscape to reach Ham House (National Trust), a Jacobean gem, hardly altered since it was built in the early 1600s. A little farther along look across at Marble Hill House, a beautiful white Georgian mansion built for a mistress of George II. Next comes Richmond, with its spectacularly famous view along the river from the hill, and then Kew with views across to old Isleworth and Syon House, London home of the dukes of Northumberland for more than 500 years. Kew Bridge follows, with lovely riverside cottages below the bridge, then Chiswick; the path here has a very rural feel. The path passes Mortlake, Hammersmith and the splendid Wetlands Centre, formerly Barn Elms Reservoirs.

At Putney Bridge the path leaves the river for a short distance (this was the downstream limit of the towpath), skirts Wandsworth Park and goes into Battersea. Much of the route towards Battersea Bridge is along the Embankment, as is the stretch past Battersea Park. Battersea's former power station lies abandoned. At Chelsea Bridge there's a detour to Nine Elms (site of the new Covent Garden) and Vauxhall, an unholy mass of railway lines and roads. The Embankment is reached again a little before Lambeth Bridge; note the Tudor gatehouse of magnificent Lambeth Palace and the Tradescant Gardening Museum.

Above: *For centuries the rich built their mansions along the river – as with this splendid Gothic house overlooking the Thames at Oxford – in part, at least, because travel by boat was so much easier than by road in earlier times.*

The Embankment continues to Waterloo Bridge, Royal Festival Hall, National Theatre, London Eye and Blackfriars Bridge. Pass the magnificent re-creation of Shakespeare's Globe Theatre, near the sites of many great Elizabethan playhouses. Just before the Globe is a narrow stuccoed house opposite St Paul's Cathedral. Henry VIII's first wife Catherine of Aragon is reputed to have stayed here when she came to London; a later tenant was the architect of St Paul's, Sir Christopher Wren (1632–1723). The house is still privately owned. The Old Bankside power station houses the Tate's collection of modern art, and the Millennium Bridge crosses the river to St Paul's.

The path reaches an area that recaptures what the riverside must have been like before World War II. Beyond the Anchor Inn, largely 18th-century and once part of the infamous Clink Prison, a narrow lane – Clink Street – twists through tall warehouses to a reproduction of Sir Francis Drake's 16th-century *Golden Hind* and Southwark Cathedral, once part of the great monastic foundation of St Mary Overie. Nothing remains of this foundation apart from the west wall of Westminster Palace.

The impressive Victorian Tower Bridge still opens regularly to admit ships and epitomizes London for many tourists. Below Tower Bridge a riverside walkway leads past restored warehouses and the Design Museum, through St Saviour's Dock and Jacob's Island (once a notorious slum), and the foundations of a 14th-century moated manor house to Rotherhithe, a wonderful piece of old village London. Rotherhithe's church still sits within a group of early houses and a Georgian school looks out over the churchyard. The captain of the *Mayflower*, which took the Pilgrim Fathers to the United States in 1620, is buried in the church. Next comes Brunel's foot tunnel under the river and its pumping house: the Underground now uses the tunnel.

Endless wharfs, restored into upmarket accommodation, follow and the river broadens considerably. Surrey Docks, Canada Wharf and Barnard's Wharf exist now only as names, but recall the time when this was the hub of the commercial world. At last, via a detour through Deptford – where the great Elizabethan playwright Christopher Marlowe was murdered in 1593 – we reach Greenwich. Here the last of the great tea clippers, the *Cutty Sark*, is preserved. The walk passes along the front of the Royal Naval College, built in the late 17th century and designed not to obscure the view of the river from the Queen's House (designed by Inigo Jones) further up Greenwich Hill.

At the top of Greenwich Hill is the world-famous 17th-century Observatory, housing John Harrison's five clocks. Harrison was the first to invent a clock that would be accurate on a ship, thus solving the problem of determining a ship's longitudinal position.

The path continues back alongside the river past the Trafalgar Tavern, a lovely Victorian pub where the Thames at high tide laps almost to the windowsills. A little group of Georgian almshouses follows, then a long industrial stretch past the now-disused Millennium Dome. Eventually we arrive at the Thames Barrier, an extraordinary futuristic construction that will prevent London flooding again.

Above: *The Tower of London is a major feature on the northern bank of the Thames in London. In Tudor times, the water entrance to the tower came to be called Traitor's Gate as many political prisoners entered the tower from the river. Few who entered the Tower by this route were ever seen again.*

The northern route

From Teddington Lock the northern alternative follows a road to Twickenham, then past Eel Pie Island and the 17th-century Swan pub before continuing to Marble Hill House and Richmond. Beyond Richmond weave through old Isleworth and past the splendid pub The London Apprentice. Continue on through Syon Park, once a monastic foundation.

Follow the River Brent through a marina before doubling back to Brentford High Street. Kew is next, then a lovely interlude along Strand on the Green (once home to Johann Zoffany, the 18th-century portrait painter) and then by road to Chiswick Bridge, Dukes' Meadows and Chiswick. Chiswick Mall, with its 18th-century houses is delightful.

The path is lovely from here to Hammersmith, passing The Dove, a little pub where the Thames watermen once drank. Walk on to reach Putney Bridge; it's worth taking a short detour to the largely Tudor Fulham Palace. From Putney the way skirts round 18th-century Hurlingham House (famous for croquet and exclusivity) and then reaches Wandsworth Bridge, Battersea Bridge and 18th-century Cheyne Walk, where the National Trust owns the former home of 19th-century Scottish writer Thomas Carlyle. The Embankment starts here, and the route follows it past the Chelsea Physic Garden (established in 1670 and the oldest herb garden in the world) to Chelsea Hospital, Christopher Wren's masterpiece.

The Embankment walk passes the Tate Gallery, then Lambeth Bridge and the Houses of Parliament (rebuilt after a disastrous fire in the 1820s). The path continues past 18th-

century Somerset House, former home of the Public Records Office; parts of the building and its riverside terrace are open to the public.

The Embankment was built by Joseph Bazalgette between 1855 and 1859 to carry London's sewage out to sea; it also provided a perfect route for a major section of the Underground. Sadly, it destroyed the pleasant riverside aspect of many communities, and led to the disastrous decision to route a major highway through the most historic part of the City of London. Between Waterloo Bridge and Blackfriars Bridge the Inns of Court can be found between the river and Fleet Street. Lawyers have been here for hundreds of years, and many early buildings remain in the maze of courtyards and alleyways.

From Blackfriars continue past St Paul's Cathedral, London Bridge and the Monument, built to commemorate the Great Fire of London. Many medieval churches and Wren masterpieces were destroyed by bombs in this area, but traces can still be found, hemmed in by giant office blocks and the huge riverside road. The College of Arms is an almost complete 17th-century building. The walk passes in front of the famous Tower of London, and on to Tower Bridge and the 18th-century St Katherine's Dock, today popular with the owners of expensive pleasure cruisers.

Soon you reach Wapping High Street – one of the most dangerous districts in Victorian London – Wapping Pierhead (a lovely group of Georgian houses built for dock company officials) and Shadwell. En route the way passes The Prospect of Whitby, a historic riverside pub, and skirts Shadwell Basin. Ratcliffe comes next (formerly notorious for muggings and murders) and then Limehouse Reach and Millwall, where the path leaves the river and takes to the road to the Isle of Dogs. This part of the walk is about as far from idyllic as you can get, but nevertheless it has a certain charm. At Greenwich this alternative route ends, and you take a subway to rejoin the way on the south bank.

Above: *Canaletto made famous this view of Greenwich when he painted it from the Isle of Dogs in the 1750s. In the centre is the Palladian Queen's House, now a museum, designed by Inigo Jones (1573–1652). The rest of the buildings are now the Royal Naval College and part of the National Maritime Museum.*

WOLDS WAY

Yorkshire's Wolds Way, which runs from the Humber Estuary to the rocky windswept coast at Filey, took 15 years from inception to creation. It is a chalk ridge walk offering wonderful views across the Vale of York and wandering through numerous ancient historic villages.

Above: *Huggate village: a typical Wolds settlement, it still has its largely unspoiled 14th century church.*

The Yorkshire Wolds have been inhabited by man for at least as long as the southern chalk uplands, but are probably less densely populated now than at any time in the past thousand years. There is evidence of Neolithic, Bronze and Iron Age occupation, as well as Roman, Saxon and Danish remains. As in the south of England, sheep once dominated the landscape. Now, most of the land is under intensive arable farming. Some sheep remain and there is cattle farming. Although once-common farmland birds – such as yellowhammer and lapwing – have declined as a result of modern agricultural techniques, you will still hear the song of the skylark along the way. Kestrels and other birds of prey have made something of a comeback since the 1960s and '70s when they almost vanished completely. The Humber Estuary is also home to countless waders and wildfowl.

From the Humber to the Wolds

The walk starts at the Ferryboat Inn at Hessle. Head for the estuary and then turn towards the gigantic Humber Bridge, which soars to a staggering 525 feet (160m). Continue along the beach under the giant bridge supports; you may be lucky enough to see the last local cargo sailing barge, or 'keel', on the estuary; she still plies her trade up and down the river, under the protection of the Humber Keel and Sloop Preservation Society.

At North Ferriby the way turns sharply inland, crosses a railway and the A63, passes a quarry and reaches Welton, a typical and very pretty Wolds village. Beyond Welton the path goes through woodland, passing an early 19th-century monument to the Raikes family (local landowners) and then over fields to Wauldby. Here there is a church and an artificial lake (Wauldby Dam), but the village once served by the church is long vanished.

The path follows a gently undulating track, and soon there are far-reaching views to the west over the flat industrial heartland of Yorkshire. The way passes Brantingham

GETTING AROUND THE WOLDS WAY

Start: Hessle, East Yorkshire.
Finish: Filey, North Yorkshire.
Distance: 79 miles (127km).
Transport Links: *Filey*: By car: Located on the A1039, which can be accessed from the A165); by bus: local services run from many local towns; by train: Filey. Northern. *Hull*: By car: take the A63, A165 or A1079; by bus: hourly buses from York and Leeds; by train: Hull.
Ordnance Survey Maps: Explorers 293 Kingston upon Hull & Beverley, 294 Market Weighton & Yorkshire Wolds, 300 Howardian Hills & Malton, 301 Scarborough, Bridlington & Flamborough Head (1:25 000).
Guidebook: *Wolds Way* (National Trail Guides), Roger Ratcliffe (Aurum, 1992).
Website: www.woldsway.gov.uk

village, which is well worth a detour, and on through Brantingham Dale to the ancient village of South Cave, with its Georgian market hall and Regency Gothic manor house.

Above: *High in the Wolds near Market Weighton: this land is probably less densely populated now than at any time in the last thousand years.*

Romans and Christians

Back on the Wolds Way itself the path goes through a plantation and on into Comber Dale and Weedley Dale. It then follows the route of the old, long-gone Barnsley–Hull railway and on to Swin Dale, from where a detour to North Newbald is a must. One of Yorkshire's best, least modernized villages, North Newbald's greatest treasure is its Norman church of St Nicholas. Back on the path continue past a number of ancient burial mounds and the site of a Roman ampitheatre – sadly no trace remains – to cross the A1079 and join the bridlepath that was once the route of the Beverley–Market Weighton railway. Head on to Goodmanham and its lovely little church, where much Norman work remains. Goodmanham is said to be the place where Edwin, King of Northumbria, was converted to Christianity. From the church the path goes under an old railway bridge and then uphill until it reaches a trackway that was once part of a Roman road. From here enjoy wonderful views across the Vale of York. If you have time you can detour into nearby Market Weighton, which has been a market town for 750 years.

Continue on through Lord Burlington's Londesborough Estate, across a stream and uphill before joining another trackway. Keep on the ascent from here, unless you are an inveterate church visitor in which case leave the path and visit Londesborough's All Saint's

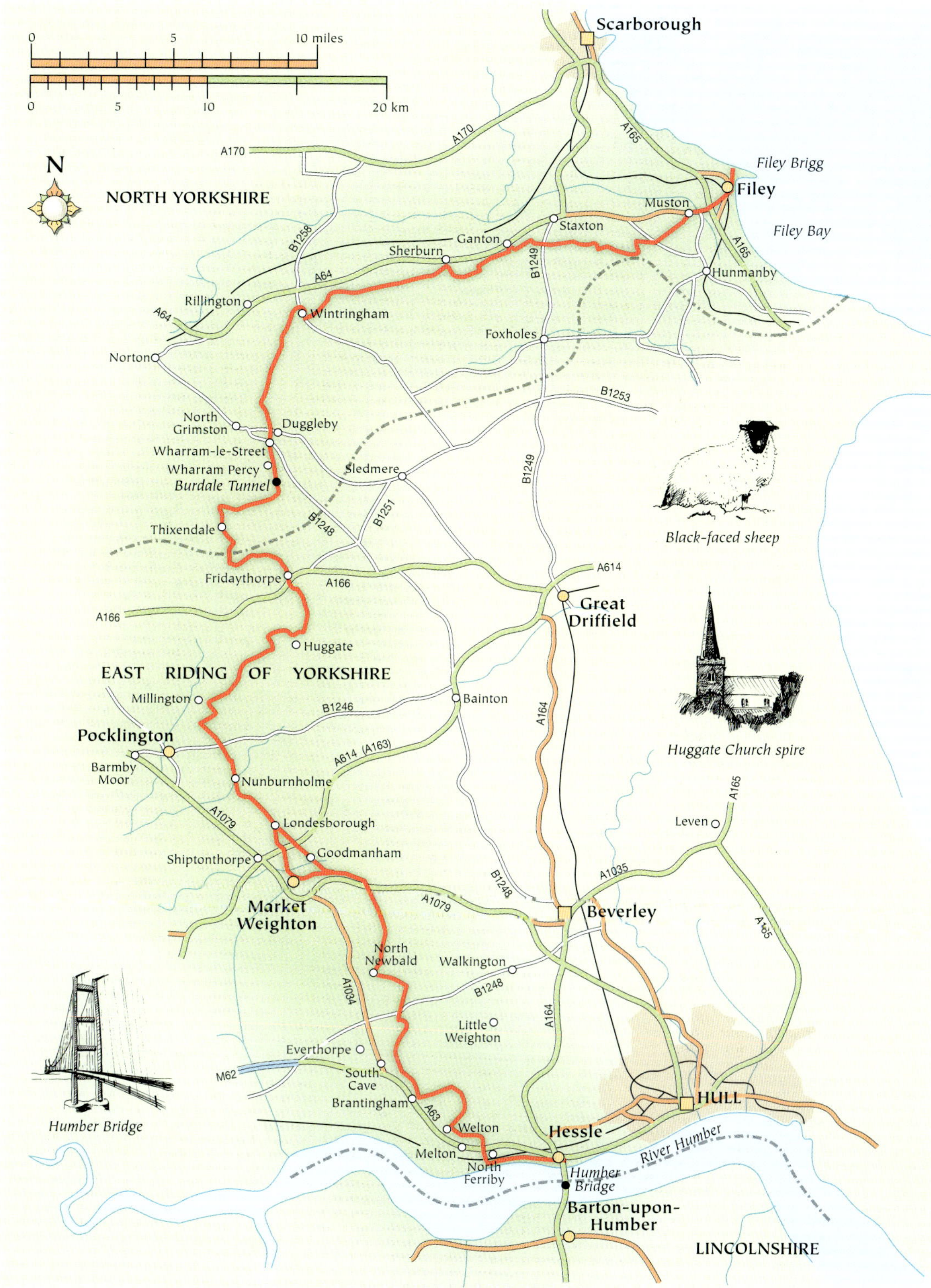

Black-faced sheep

Huggate Church spire

Humber Bridge

Church. Back on the way you will reach a small road, which must be followed for a mile or so before cutting into a farmyard. From here the path circles a wood and crosses a stream before continuing to Nunburnholme. From the village head uphill to a wood, cross several fields and a road and you will then reach another wood before passing close to Millington village.

Viking origins

Soon you reach a spectacular high ridge that continues for several miles. All along here there are wonderful views and in the distance can be seen the almost surreal outline of the giant Drax power station.

From the ridge, descend into Sylvan Dale and then climb again past an Iron Age earthwork before reaching Nettle Dale. The path continues on up to Huggate Sheep-walk and then reaches its highest point, a splendid ridge 650 feet (200m) above sea level, with views back to the Humber Estuary. York Minster can also be glimpsed to the west.

From the sheepwalk descend to pass close to Huggate village with its lovely 14th-century church. Beyond Huggate the path crosses fields and reaches Horse Dale before passing a deserted medieval village and climbing Holme Dale. The way then emerges in the village of Fridaythorpe – the 'thorpe' revealing its Viking origins – with its 12th-century church. This is roughly the half-way point.

A deserted village

Cross farmland to West Dale and then on to Thixen Dale, a steep valley famous for its uncultivated and plant-rich slopes, before entering the village of the same name. Thixendale village is tucked away in its little valley, only accessible by tracks, footpaths and minor roads. The path leaves the village and heads north and uphill, then crosses fields until it reaches Vessey Pasture Dale where it descends before rising again, following an ancient earthwork and then a green lane. At the end of the green lane take a detour of about half a mile to the deserted medieval village of Wharram Percy, one of the best preserved examples in the country. The site was inhabited from prehistoric times; the Romans were here

Right: *The Black Death, sheep farming and isolation reduced the population of Wharram Percy until the last house was abandoned in 1500, making it just one of 100 deserted villages in the Wolds.*

Below: *The evening sun warms a mown field near Heslerton. Though much land is now intensively cultivated, odd pockets of wilder ground provide havens for numerous wildlife species.*

Above: *The Wolds Way is clearly way-marked, leaving walkers little difficulty finding their way to the next village where refreshment can be found.*

too, as well as the Danes and Saxons. In the late 14th century the Black Death, which is estimated to have killed a third of Europe's population, sealed Wharram Percy's fate. The mounds that reveal the sites of houses and barns are still clear and the church, though ruined, still stands.

Fine churches

The path crosses above Burdale Tunnel, which runs for nearly a mile (1.6km). Dug in the 1850s, the tunnel closed almost exactly a century later along with the railway line from Malton to Driffield. Continue north to Wharram-le-Street where St Mary's Church has a splendid and rare Anglo-Saxon nave. Another detour here – of about a mile (1.6km) – will take you to Duggleby with its 130-foot (40-m) diameter Neolithic barrow.

The path continues through Wharram-le-Street, then along a bridlepath. It crosses a minor road and stream before entering steep-sided woodland, best seen in spring when it is alive with colour. The path twists and turns along here until, without warning, you reach a breathtaking view across the Vale of Pickering to the North York Moors.

Head across fields and over another stream – or beck – to Wintringham, with its lovely limestone church. The inside of this church is particularly special. Most early churches were modernized by the Victorians, and this often involved ripping out

early pews and other woodwork. Not so in Wintringham: the church boasts a glorious collection of still-used early 17th-century pews and other furniture.

Beyond the village the way climbs through a wood then continues along another ancient earthwork and past more woodland. Soon you reach West Heslerton Brow from which it is possible – just! – to glimpse the distant North Sea. From here the path heads steadily east, passing the village of Sherburn (where the church has some interesting Saxon remains), crossing fields and woods to the pretty village of Ganton.

The way now climbs through fields before following a farm road and then crossing more fields to Raven Dale where, once again, the path follows an ancient earthwork before reaching Camp Dale, whose high top the path follows on a circular route into Stocking Dale. Beyond Stocking Dale the path leads to a wood, crosses a road and a field and then goes down into the village of Muston. From here the path crosses the A165 and soon reaches Filey.

The path finally makes for the coast, passes the lifeboat station and heads out to the high rocky cliff of the Brigg itself. All along the cliffs here, surrounded by spectacular views, you may see fish being hauled up hundreds of feet by men wielding long beach-casting rods. The path continues some way past Filey Brigg and up the coast, ending abruptly at a fence a little beyond North Cliff.

Above: *The town of Filey earned its living from fishing for centuries, and in Victorian times it became a popular seaside resort. The expansive beach still attracts holiday-makers today.*

INDEX

Page numbers in *italic* refer to illustrations

PICTURE ACKNOWLEDGEMENTS

All the photographs in this book were taken by Paul Felix with the exception of the following:

David Tipling: 12 (top); 30 (top), 36 (bottom); 47 (top & bottom); 111 (bottom); 117 (top); 120 (top); 136 (top); 138

John Mason: 112 (top); 139

David Paterson: 151

GEOGRAPHICAL CASE STUDIES

THE DEVELOPING WORLD

Worldaware

Editors: Vincent Bunce,
Alexandra Studd

Authors: Hazel Barrett, Vincent Bunce,
Garrett Nagle, Steve Scoble,
Kris Spencer and Alexandra Studd

Hodder & Stoughton
A MEMBER OF THE HODDER HEADLINE GROUP

Acknowledgements

The editors would like to thank: Dr David Simon, Department of Geography, Royal Holloway and Bedford New College, University of London; WWF-UK; Data Support for Education Service and Carol Inskipp.

The publishers would also like to thank the following for giving permission to reproduce copyright photographs in this book:

Ace, Figure 11.4; Vincent Bunce, Figures 4.15, 5.2, 5.4, 5.18, 6.2, 6.4, 6.6, 7.3, 7.11, 8.5, 8.18, 10.1, 10.5, 10.6, 10.7 and 10.9; Sylvia Cordaiy, Figure 9.5; Sue Cunningham, Figures 3.11, 9.9 and 9.13; Halcrow, Figure 9.17; Robert Harding, Figures 6.26, 6.28, 6.33 and Life File, Figure 3.4 and 8.13; Link, Figure 6.11, Garrett Nagle, Figures 1.2 and 1.10; Panos, Figures 5.13, 7.19, 8.16, 12.3 and 12.18; Popperfoto, Figures 3.17, 7.21, 7.22 and 9.15; Steve Scoble, Figures 3.12, 3.14, 3.15, 4.10, 7.8, 7.12, 7.16, 8.6, 8.10 and 10.14; SIPA-Press, Figure 4.7; Still, Figures 3.9, 9.3, and 11.6; Topham Picturepoint, Figures 6.17 and 12.6; Trip, Figures 3.2, 3.8, 4.2, 4.5, 5.8, 6.15, 11.8, 11.11, 11.15, 12.4 and 12.14.

Inside artwork by Tom Cross, Jilly Luff at Bitmap Graphics and Gary Rees at Linda Rogers Associates.

British Library Cataloguing in Publication Data

The developing world. – (Geographical case studies)
1. Developing countries – Geography – Juvenile literature
I. Bunce, Vincent II. Studd, Alexandra
910'.02'1724

ISBN 0 340 670037

First published 1997
Impression number 10 9 8 7 6 5 4 3 2 1
Year 2000 1999 1998 1997

Typeset by Wearset, Boldon, Tyne and Wear
Printed in Hong Kong for Hodder & Stoughton Educational, a division of Hodder Headline Plc, 338 Euston Road, London NW1 3BH by Colorcraft Ltd.

Contents

What is development?

The term 'development' is difficult to define. In geography, development refers to a number of characteristics such as population change, economic progress, increased use of resources, higher levels of technology and political freedom.

Statistics can be used to measure many aspects of development including such as population growth, life expectancy, health, education, urbanisation, income distribution and energy consumption (Figure 1.1). Gross National Product (GNP) which is an indicator of a country's wealth is one of the most common ways of measuring development (see Figure 1.3).

One view of development divides the world into three groups of countries:

- the First World: Western Europe, North America, Australia, New Zealand and Japan
- the Second World: state-controlled Communist countries such as the former USSR
- the Third World: all the other less developed countries.

In the 1960s and 1970s the terms Less Developed Countries (LDCs) and Developed Countries (DCs) were used. Then in the early 1980s the terms **North** (developed) and **South** (less developed) started to be used. However, many so-called LDCs were in fact quite advanced socially and politically, such as the Mayas in central Mexico and the Shona in Zimbabwe. Moreover, the oil rich countries in the Middle East and Newly Industrialising Countries like South Korea did not really fit into any category very well.

Figure 1.2 People living below the poverty line

Figure 1.1 Indices of development

	UK	BRAZIL	INDIA	NAMIBIA
GNP per capita (US $)	18 110	2810	310	1670
Adult literacy (%)	99	82	50	40
Life expectancy (years)	75.6	66.3	60.4	58.8
Daily calorie supply (% of needs)	125	114	105	90
Without access to water (millions)	–	21.4	–	0.7
Malnourished children ('000)	–	1250	69 345	75
Malnourished children (%)	–	7	63	33–50
Infant mortality rate (per '000)	8	57	93	71
Cars per 100 people	41	8.5	0.7	–
% employed in agriculture	2	26	62	43
% employed in industry	28	26	11	22
% employed in services	70	48	27	35
% of total income going to poorest 40%	17.3	7	21.3	–
Human Development Index	0.916	0.804	0.439	0.611

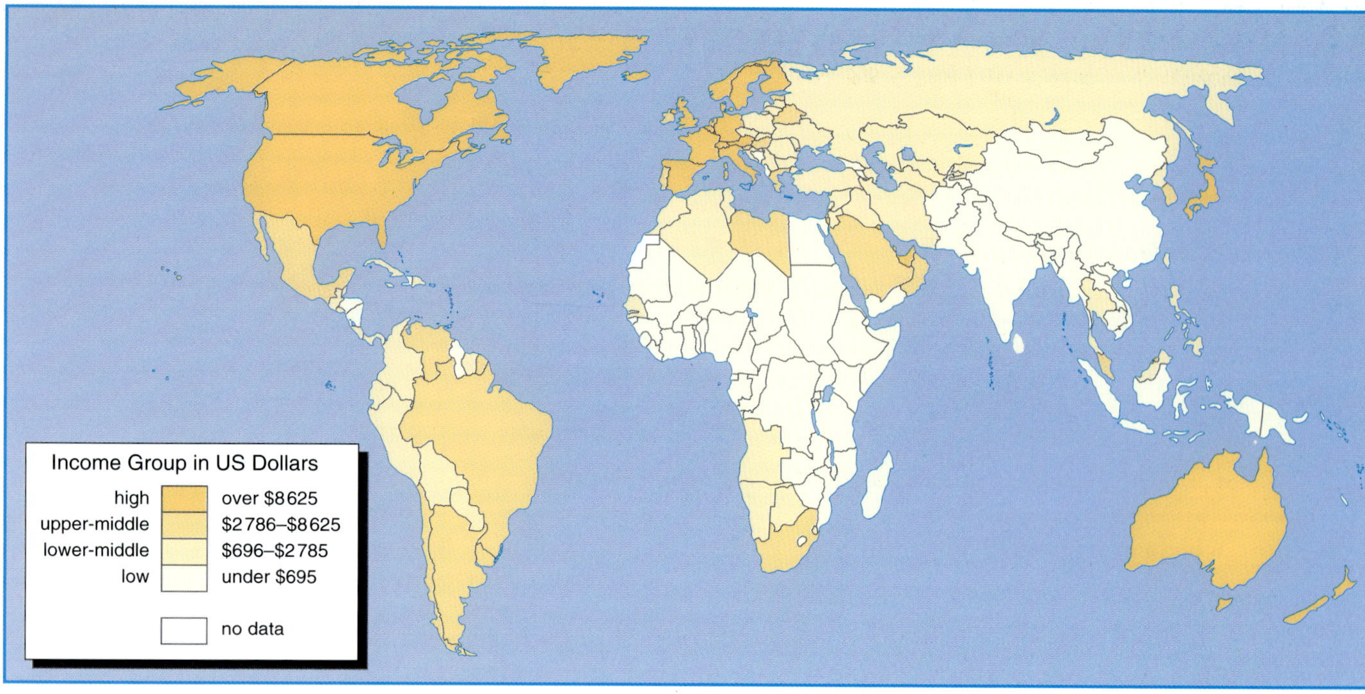

Figure 1.3 Gross National Product (GNP) per capita, 1993

Countries are now classified as follows:

More Economically Developed Countries (MEDCs): e.g. the UK and the US. These are the most 'developed' countries and have a high standard of living.
Less Economically Developed Countries (LEDCs): e.g. Namibia and India. These countries are at a lower stage of development and have a lower quality of life.
Centrally Planned Economies (CPEs): e.g. North Korea. These are socialist countries whose economies are strictly controlled by the government. Living standards are higher than LEDCs although freedom of speech is limited.
Oil rich countries: e.g. Saudi Arabia and Libya. These countries are very rich although their wealth may not be distributed evenly. Without oil, many of these countries would be LEDCs.
Newly Industrialising Countries (NICs): e.g. South Korea and Taiwan. These countries have experienced rapid industrial, social and economic growth since 1960.

Development is difficult to define. It means different things to different people. Even within a single country there are often huge differences in levels of development.

1 What do you understand by the term 'development'? How would you go about deciding whether a country is developed or not? Explain your answer.

2 Using Figure 1.3 and an atlas, name:
- **a** three high-income countries (GNP per capita over US $8625)
- **b** three low-income countries (GNP per capita less than US $695)

3 Study the following categories of countries:
- First, Second and Third Worlds
- Developed and Less Developed
- MEDC, LEDC, NIC and oil rich
- North and South

- **a** Are any of these terms offensive? Give reasons for your answer.
- **b** Are any of the classifications too simplistic? or too detailed? Again, suggest reasons.
- **c** Which do you think is the best classification? Support your answer with details from Figure 1.1.

4 Are there any features of an MEDC such as the UK that you dislike? Are there any features of an LEDC that you find attractive? What do these suggest to you about the terms More and Less Developed?

Measuring development

Figure 1.4 Who benefits from development

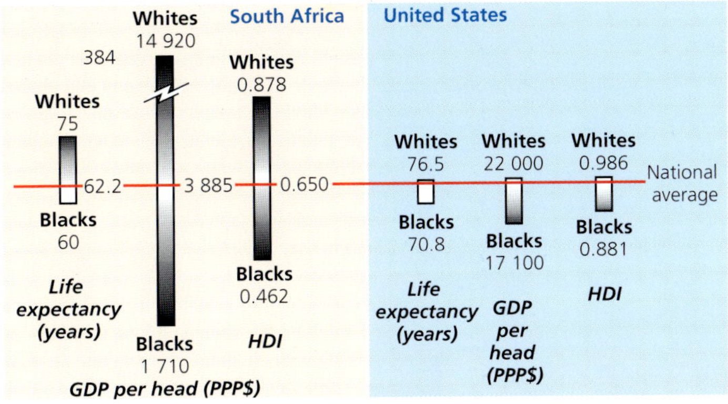

Figure 1.6 Differences in development between whites and blacks in South Africa and the US

The most common way of measuring development is by using GNP per capita. The world map of GNP per capita (Figure 1.3) clearly shows that the MEDCs of Western Europe, Japan, North America and Australia have much higher levels of GNP per capita, over US $8626, than the LEDCs such as India, Bangladesh, Nigeria and Zimbabwe, which have less than US $695. Only 15 per cent of the world's population live in areas with a high GNP per capita whereas 56 per cent of the world's population live in areas with a low GNP per capita. Some countries including Rwanda, Burundi, Ethiopia, Tanzania and Mozambique even have a GNP per capita of less than US $200.

However, average GNP per capita as a way of measuring development has its shortcomings. It:

- hides differences between one part of a country and another
- does not take into account local costs of living
- does not take account of the informal economy
- ignores the environmental and social costs of economic growth.

Figure 1.5 Human Development Index, 1994

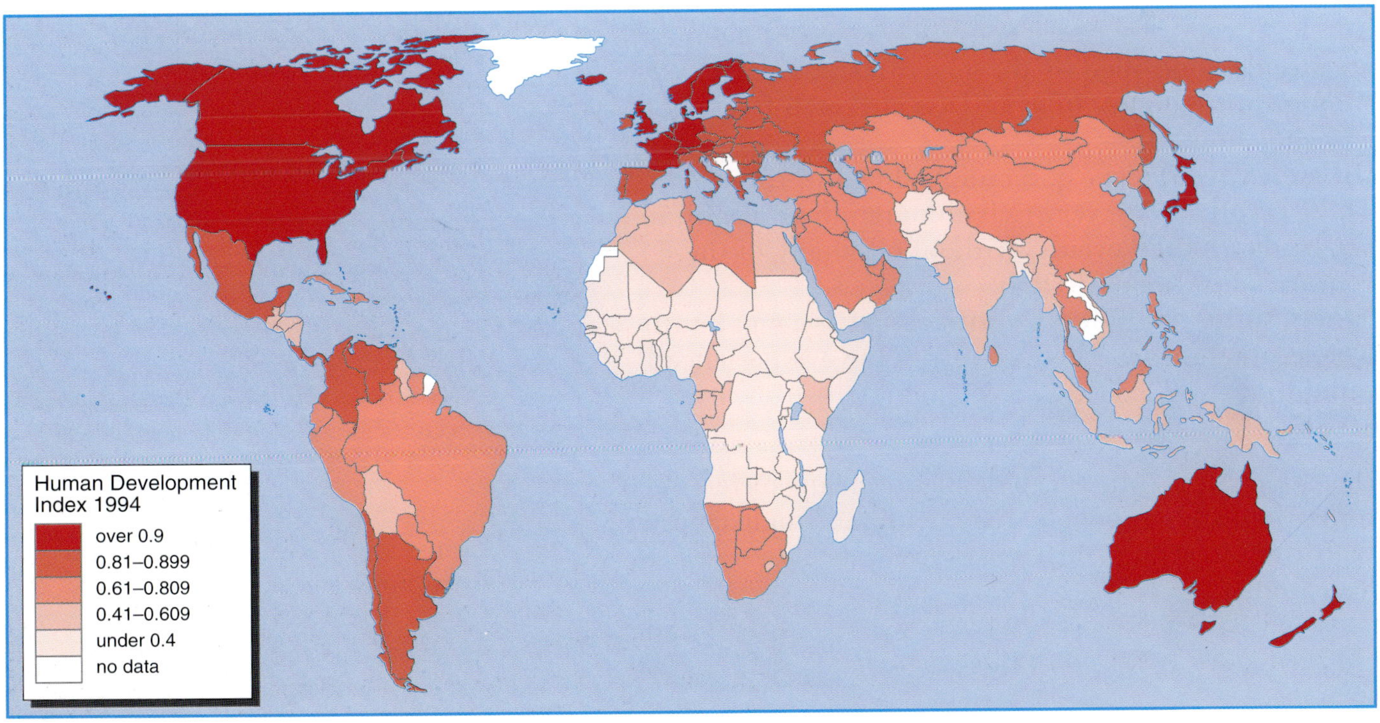

	Human Development Index (1992)	Life expectancy (years)	Purchasing Power Parity (US $)	GNP per capita (US $)	Adult literacy (%)
Bangladesh	0.364	55.6	1290	220	36.4
Brazil	0.804	66.3	5470	3020	81.9
Germany	0.921	76.0	20 990	23 560	99.0
India	0.439	60.4	1250	290	49.9
Iraq	0.617	66.0	3500	3785	54.6
Namibia	0.611	58.8	3930	1660	40.0
Nigeria	0.406	50.4	1480	310	52.5
South Africa	0.705	62.9	3885	2900	80.6
UK	0.916	76.2	17 750	17 970	99.0
US	0.937	76.0	24 750	24 750	99.0

Figure 1.7 Some measures of development in selected countries

Several other measures of development have been used. These include the **Physical Quality of Life Index (PQLI)** and the **Measure of Economic Welfare (MEW)**. Since 1990, however, the United Nations has used the **Human Development Index (HDI)** (Figure 1.5). This index is based on three aspects of development:

- life expectancy
- a measure of literacy and schooling
- income (based on PPP – see below).

According to the 1994 figures Canada has the highest HDI, with a value of 0.932 (1.0 is the maximum value). MEDCs dominate the higher levels of the HDI while LEDCs such as Afghanistan (0.208), Burkina Faso (0.203) and Guinea (0.191), are at the bottom (Figure 1.7). As with GNP per capita, national HDIs can conceal widespread inequalities. However, regional and racial HDIs can be developed and these show interesting patterns within a country (Figure 1.6).

The World Bank prefers to use an **Index of Purchasing Power Parity (PPP)**. This is a measure of GNP which has been adjusted to reflect local costs of living.

1 What point do you think the cartoon (Figure 1.4) is making about development?

2 Study Figure 1.5.
- **a** In which continent are the lowest HDI figures to be found?
- **b** Name two countries in South America with very low HDI figures.
- **c** What evidence is there to suggest a North–South divide between countries with high and low HDI figures?

3 Compare the differences between measures of development for blacks and whites in the US and South Africa (Figure 1.6).
- **a** Which racial group does best in both countries?
- **b** In which country is the difference between black and white the most significant?
- **c** Can you suggest reasons for your answers to **a** and **b**?
- **d** What do these graphs tell us about levels of development between the US and South Africa?

4 Some measures of development are shown in the table (Figure 1.7).
- **a** Which two countries listed in Figure 1.7 do you think are the 'most developed'?
- **b** Which two countries listed in Figure 1.7 do you think are the 'least developed'?

For your answers to **a** and **b** explain your choice of countries. What development indicators did you think were the most important?

Spreading the effects of development

Development is often concentrated in particular places. These places grow by attracting jobs, people and investment. Governments may try to spread development, for two reasons:

- so that all the people in a country can benefit from its advantages
- to prevent a few 'very developed' areas suffering from too much development e.g. congestion, pollution, high land prices etc.

Attempts to spread development vary with the type of development. For example, economic development often results from industrial growth, whereas human development is more closely linked to the provision of services such as water or schools.

TYPES OF DEVELOPMENT

Development is often associated with a change in a country's employment structure from largely rural and agricultural to urban and industrial (Figure 1.8). However this is just one type of development. Not all countries will follow the same 'route to development'.

There are three main ways in which development may occur:

Natural under free market conditions countries exploit their resources to generate growth. Most MEDCs have taken this route.

Forced in socialist countries, such as North Korea, the government controls the resources and what sort of growth takes place and where.

Planned Newly Industrialising Countries such as South Korea have progressed by changing their import-substitution industries into export-orientated industries.

THE MULTIPLIER EFFECT

When development occurs it is often concentrated in particular places. Why do some regions prosper while others fail? It is mainly because some places have a comparative advantage over others, e.g. a good supply of natural resources, power or labour. This advantage stimulates industrial growth. **Multiplier effects** then occur as **acquired advantages** e.g. improvements in infrastructure and a trained workforce reinforce the area's reputation and attract further investment (Figure 1.9).

As a region grows and develops, skilled workers and new investment are attracted to it. The growing region becomes the **core**. Other areas called the **periphery**, are flooded by manufactured goods from the core (the **backwash effect**), thus preventing the development of the periphery. The **spread effect** occurs when the core stimulates the surrounding areas to develop.

Figure 1.8 Rural agricultural area changing to urban area

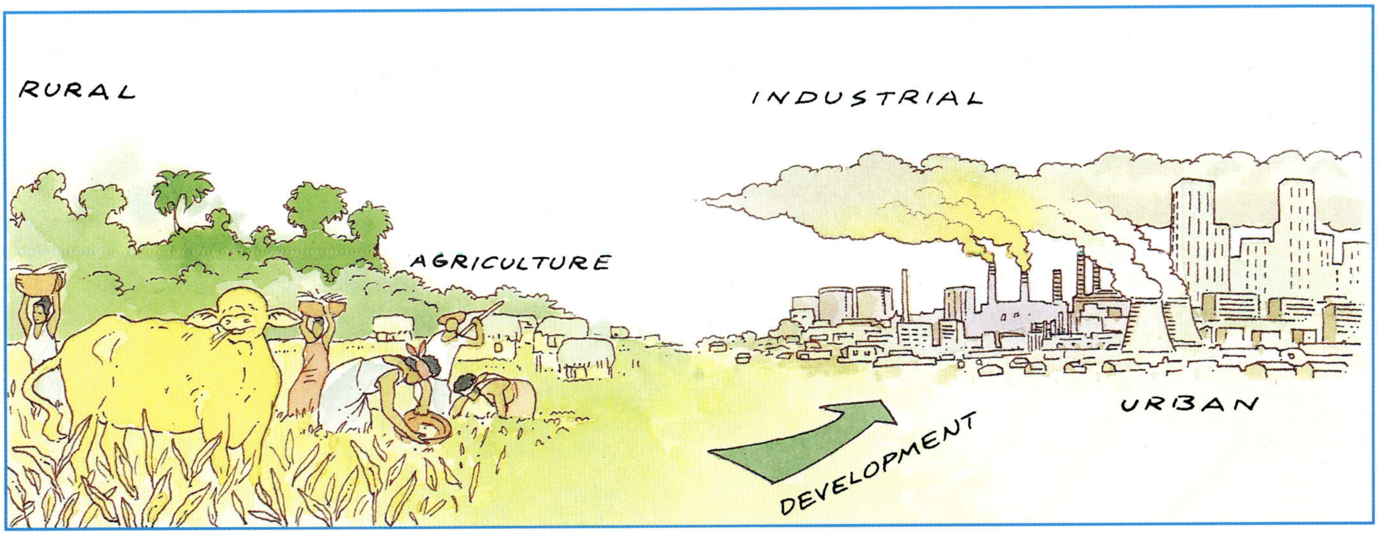

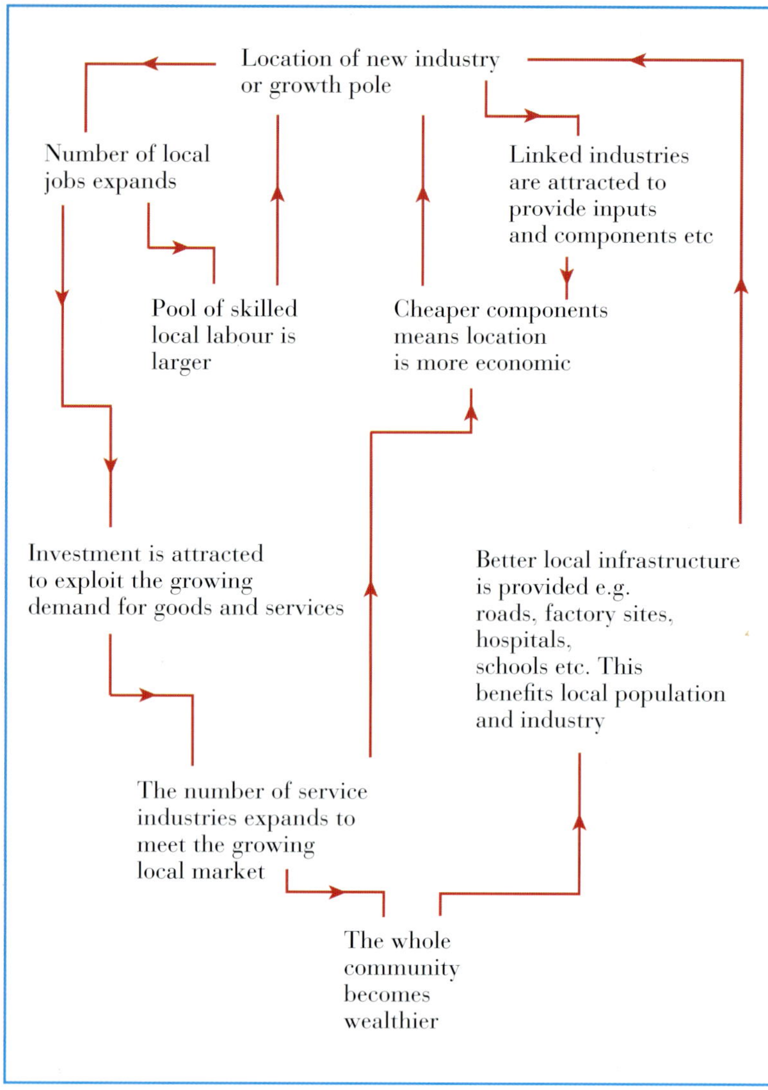

Figure 1.9 Multiplier effects and the formation of growth poles

1 Figure 1.8 shows how development can mean a change from a rural to an industrial economy.
   a Is it appropriate for every country to follow this route?
   b List three disadvantages for a country of developing a series of major urban and industrial complexes.

2 In what ways has development differed between MEDCs and socialist countries? Give examples.

3 What are the advantages and disadvantages of a 'growth-pole' strategy?

4 Study the two photographs in Figure 1.10 which show two types of development in a rural area in South Africa. Discuss the likely advantages and disadvantages of each scheme to:
   a the national economy
   b local residents
   c the environment.

Places or districts which are favoured because of a good location, labour supply, resources or market access are economically more attractive and are often used by planners to form natural **growth poles**.

By developing growth poles, however, regional inequalities may be worsened, because resources have been concentrated in favoured locations. Rural areas may not benefit. If development projects are large in scale, such as the irrigation scheme at Keiskammahoek (Figure 1.10a), then the resources may only benefit the small surrounding area, with few spread effects. Increasingly, attention is turning to **appropriate development**, which uses local resources, needs and ideas, at a price which is affordable to the local community. Examples include check dams, earthen terraces, vegetable gardens etc (Figure 1.10b).

Figure 1.10 Large and small projects, South Africa

2 country spotlights

Spotlight on Brazil

Official name	Federal Republic of Brazil
Area	8 511 965 km^2
Position	6° North to 33° South and 35° to 73° West
Capital	Brasilia
Currency	Real (R)
Language	Portuguese
Religion	Mainly Catholic

Key Exports

Coffee	Footwear
Iron ore	Preserved fruit

Economic and Social Indicators

GNP per capita (US $)	2810
% population with access to safe water	87
TVs per 100 people	21
Adult literacy rate (%)	81.9
Life expectancy at birth (years)	66.3
Population per doctor	847
Maternal mortality rate (per 100 000 live births)	200
Total fertility rate	2.9

Brazil's three largest cities

São Paulo	9.7 million people
Rio de Janeiro	5.5 million people
Belo Horizonte	2.1 million people

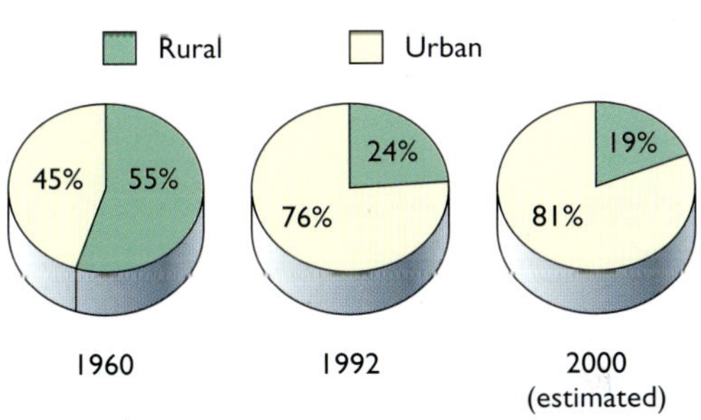

Rural – urban population balance (%)

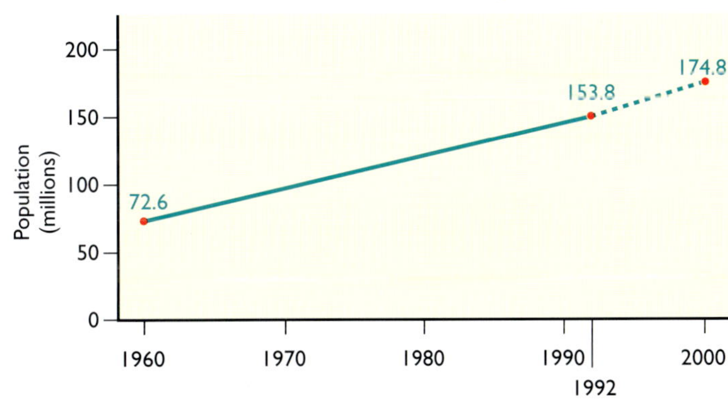

Brazil's population growth

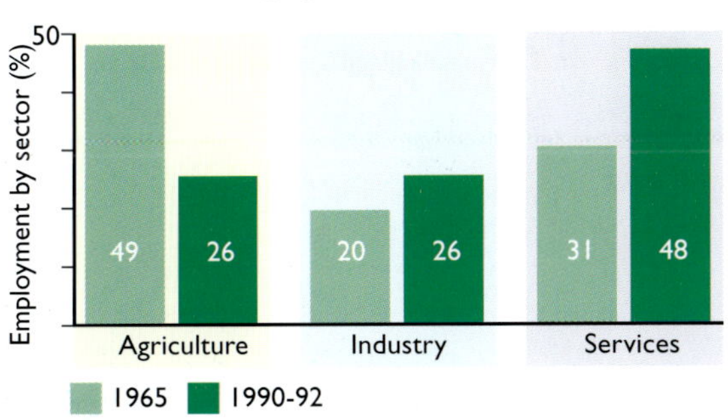

Employment by sector (%)

Population Indicators (1992)

(rates per 1000 population)

Birth rate	24.6
Death rate	7.5
Infant mortality	58
Population doubling date (year)	2032
Population density (people per km^2)	17

Map of Brazil

Spotlight on India

Official name	Republic of India
Area	3 287 590 km^2
Position	33° to 8° North and 68° to 97° East
Capital	Delhi
Currency	Rupee (Rs)
Language	Hindi (official); English (associate)
Religion	83% Hindu; 11% Muslim

Key Exports

Gems and jewellery
Ready made garments
Engineering products
Leather and leather goods
Chemicals and allied products
Cotton products

Economic and Social Indicators

GNP per capita (US $)	310
% population with access to safe water	79
TVs per 100 people	4
Adult literacy rate (%)	49.9
Life expectancy at birth (years)	60.4
Population per doctor	2439
Maternal mortality rate (per 100 000 live births)	460
Total fertility rate	3.8

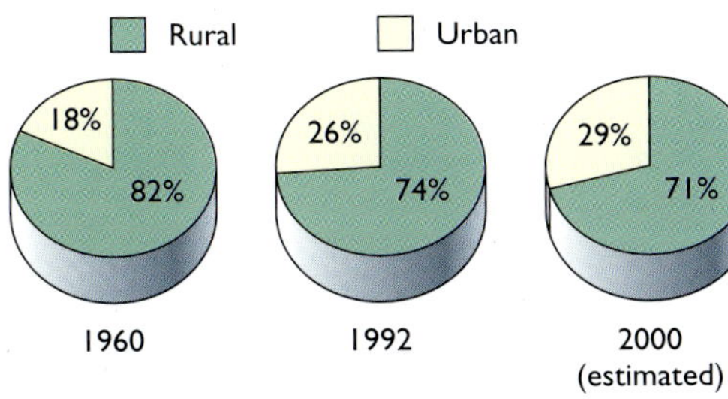

Rural – urban population balance (%)

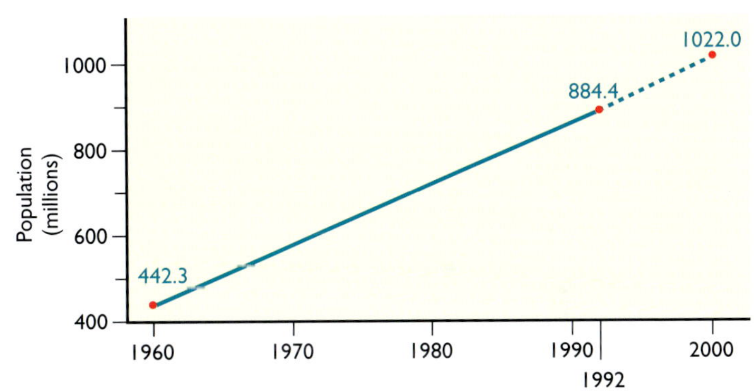

India's population growth

India is the world's:

- largest tea producer
- second largest sugar cane producer
- second largest rice producer
- third largest pool of scientific labour
- third largest milk producer
- fourth largest producer of cement, cotton and potatoes

India's three largest cities

Calcutta	11 million people
Bombay	9.5 million people
Delhi	5 million people

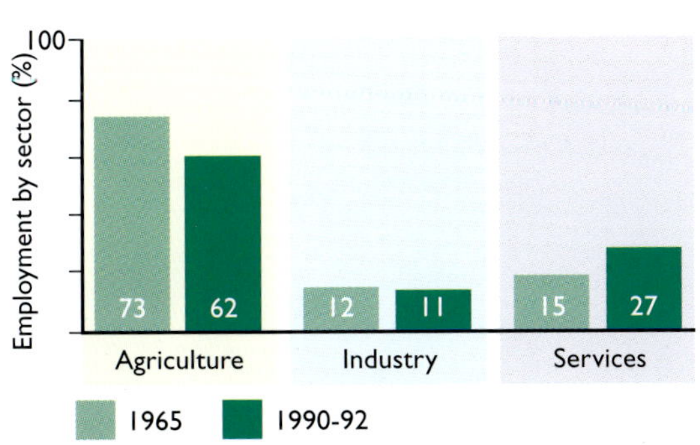

Employment by sector (%)

Population Indicators (1992)

(rates per 1000 population)

Birth rate	29.1
Death rate	10
Infant mortality	82
Population doubling date (year)	2028
Population density (people per km^2)	247

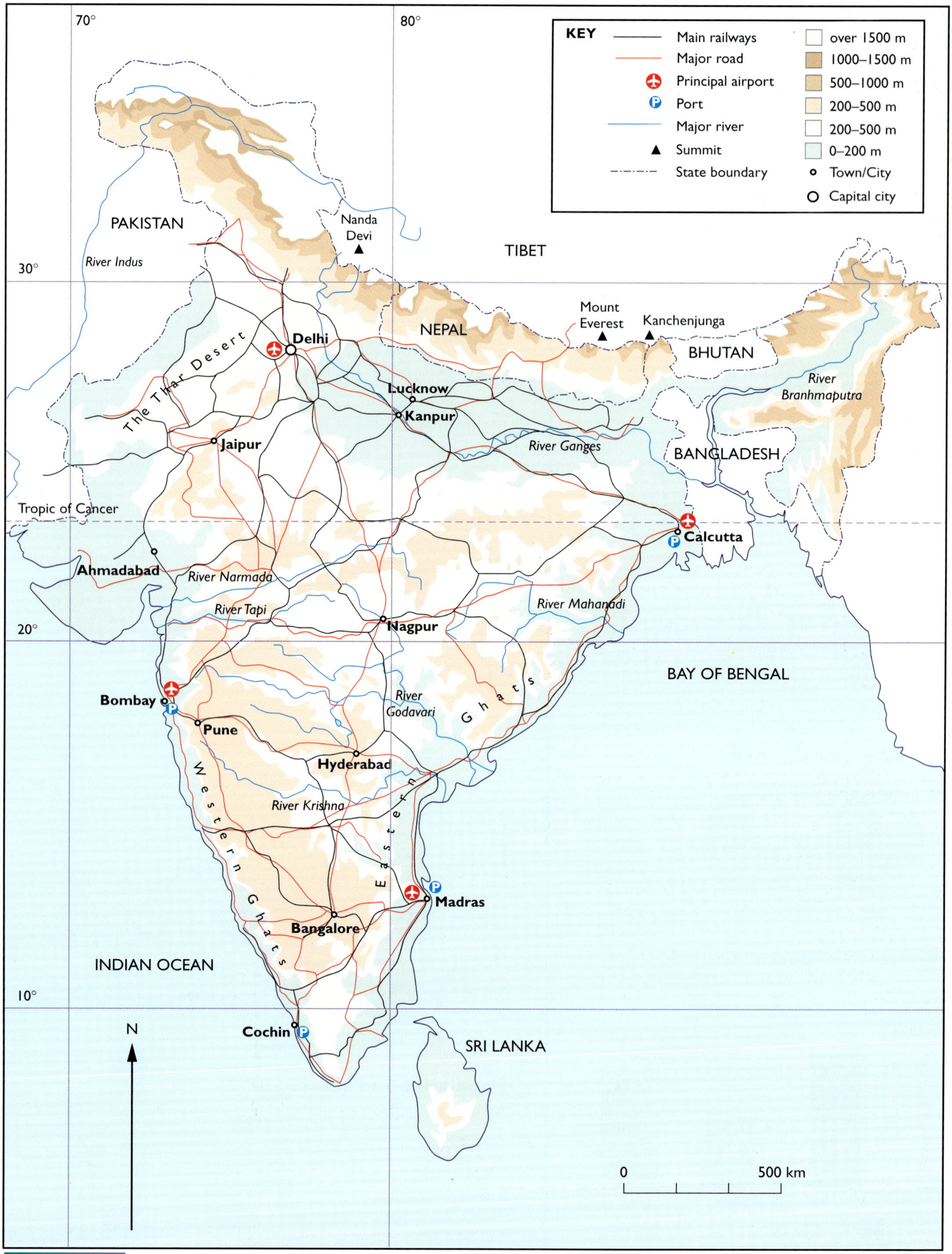
KEY
Main railways
Major road
Principal airport
Port
Major river
Summit
State boundary
over 1500 m
1000–1500 m
500–1000 m
200–500 m
200–500 m
0–200 m
Town/City
Capital city
70°
80°
30°
20°
10°
Tropic of Cancer
PAKISTAN
River Indus
Nanda Devi
TIBET
NEPAL
Mount Everest
Kanchenjunga
BHUTAN
River Branhmaputra
BANGLADESH
The Thar Desert
Delhi
Lucknow
Kanpur
Jaipur
River Ganges
Calcutta
Ahmadabad
River Narmada
River Tapi
River Mahanadi
Nagpur
BAY OF BENGAL
Bombay
Pune
River Godavari
Eastern Ghats
Hyderabad
Western Ghats
River Krishna
Madras
Bangalore
INDIAN OCEAN
Cochin
SRI LANKA
N
0
500 km

Map of India

Spotlight on Namibia

Official name	Republic of Namibia
Area	824 269 km^2
Position	17° to 29° South and 12° to 25° East
Capital	Windhoek
Currency	Namibian Dollar (N$)
Languages	English, Oshikwanyama, Afrikaans, Otjiherero
Religion	Mainly Christian

Key Exports

Minerals (diamonds, uranium, copper)
Manufactured products (meat, fish)
Agricultural products (live cattle, sheep, goats)
Electricity

Economic and Social Indicators

GNP per capita (US $)	1670
% population with access to safe water	52
TVs per 100 people	2
Adult literacy rate (%)	40
Life expectancy at birth (years)	58.8
Population per doctor	4545
Maternal mortality rate (per 100 000 live births)	370
Total fertility rate	5.3

Namibia's three largest cities

Windhoek	115 000 people
Swakopmund	15 500 people
Rehoboth	15 000 people

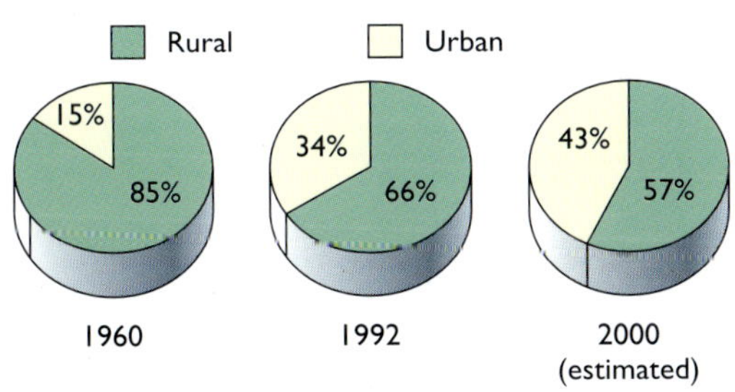

Rural – urban population balance (%), 1992

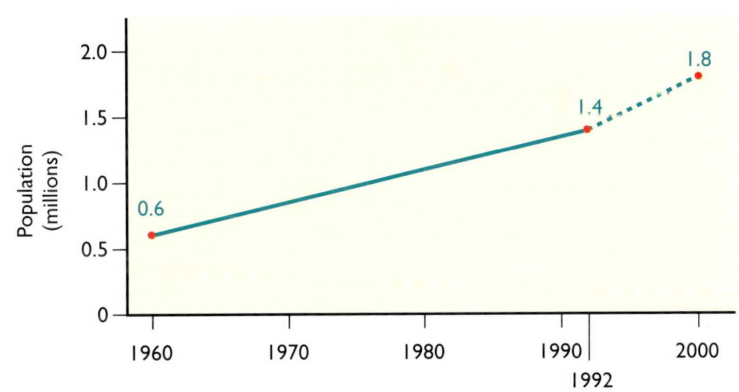

Namibia's population growth

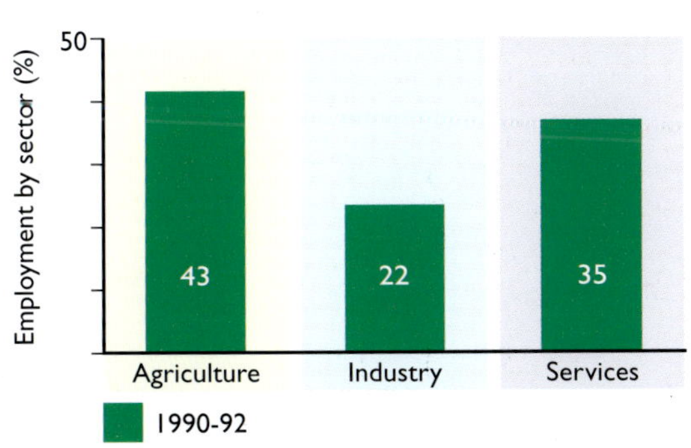

Employment by sector (%)

Population Indicators (1992)
(rates per 1000 population)

Birth rate	37
Death rate	10.5
Infant mortality	60
Population doubling date (year)	2018
Population density (people per km^2)	1.7

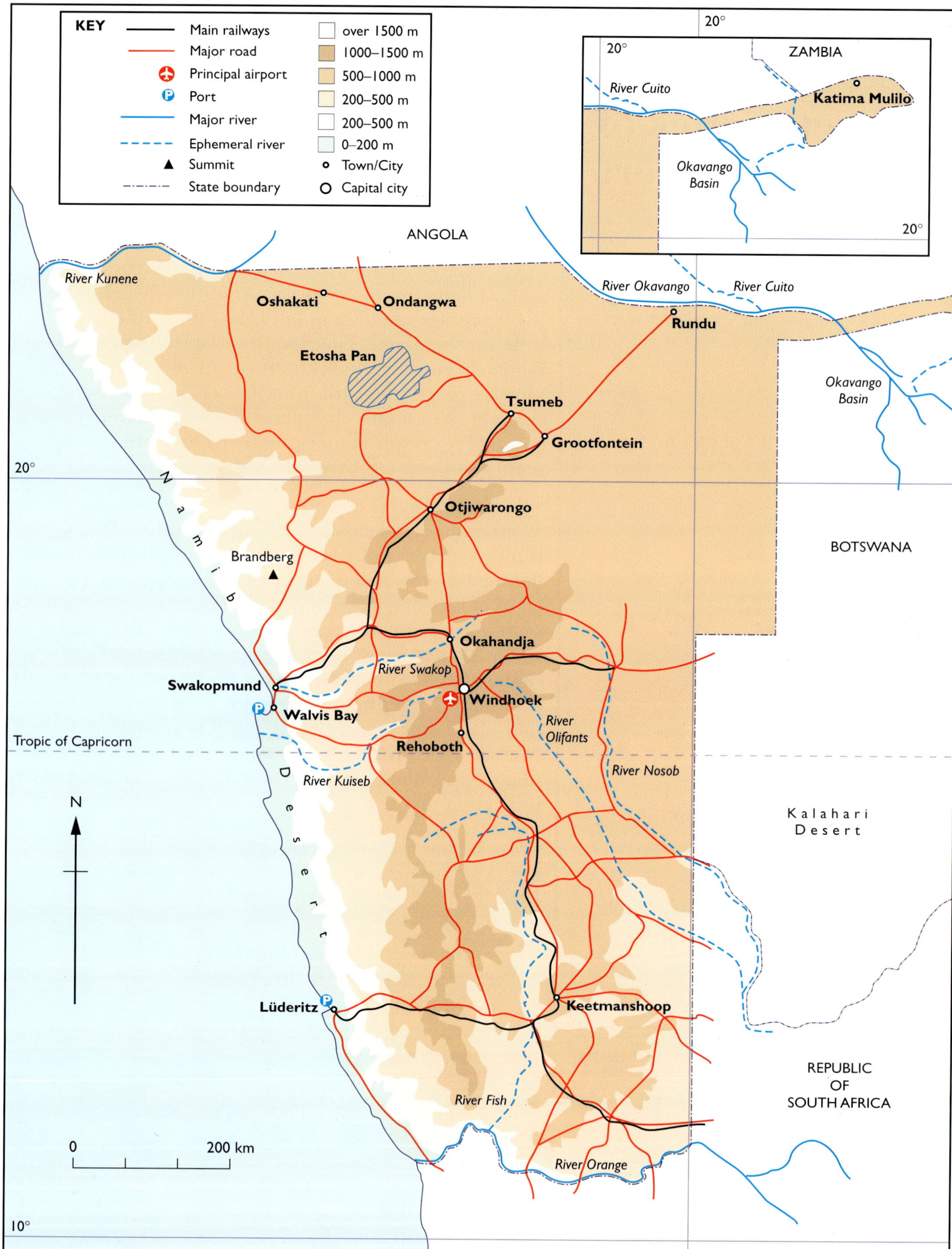

Map of Namibia

Characteristics of a desert environment: the Namib Desert

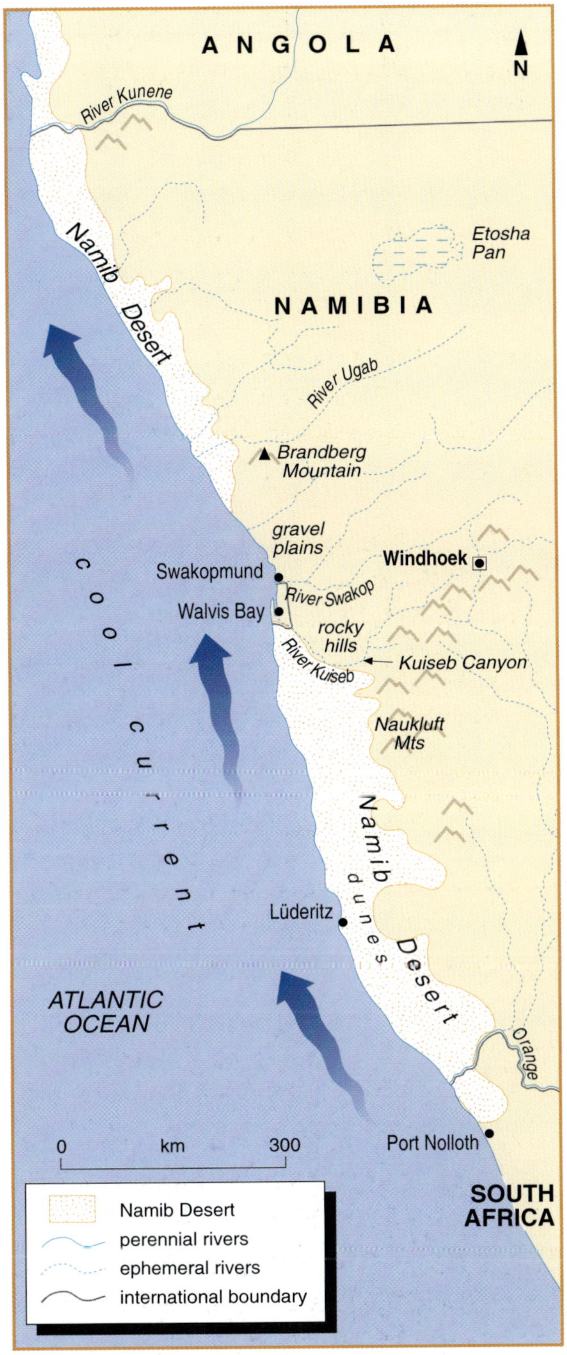

Figure 3.1 The Namib desert

The Namib is one of the world's oldest deserts. It extends in a narrow strip, along the entire 1600 kilometres of Namibia's Atlantic coast (Figure 3.1). Average annual rainfall is less than 100 mm, and it decreases inland. The Namib is the result of the cool Benguela current which captures any moisture which is blown towards the land from the ocean. Deserts are thought of as totally dry places. In the Namib however, coastal fogs result in moisture being available for the plants and animals living there.

The Namib Desert is dominated by three processes: weathering, wind erosion and water erosion. Weathering is a slow process which includes the disintegration and flaking of rocks and the growth of salt crystals. The wind erodes fine materials by **deflation** and uses these materials to **abrade** more resistant rocks. Erosion by water is short-lived but forms spectacular landforms such as wadis and alluvial fans. Almost all the rivers of the Namib are **ephemeral**, and run for only short periods of time before drying up. Where they cross the Namib desert, **linear oases** are formed. Trees and plants grow along these dry watercourses, giving a clear indication that water is sometimes present (Figure 3.2).

FEATURES OF THE NAMIB

Like many deserts the Namib contains a range of features (Figure 3.3):

- granite mountains and inselbergs
- grass, gypsum and quartz plains
- sand dunes.

Figure 3.2 Trees growing along dry valley of river in Namib desert

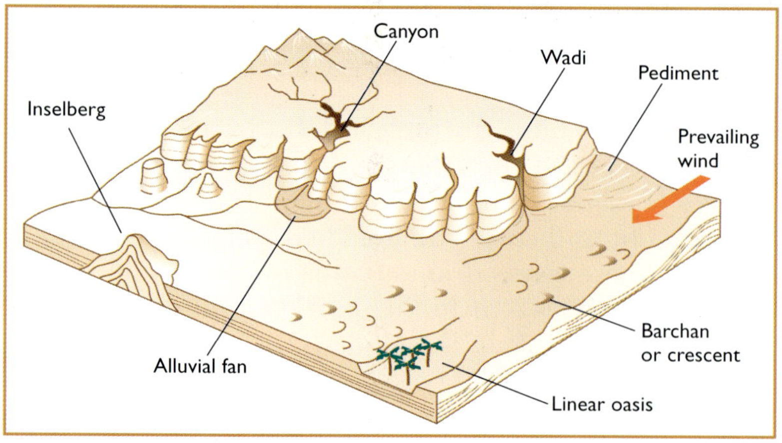

Figure 3.3 Desert landforms

Canyons e.g. the Fish River Canyon are very deep gorges, which are usually dry. If there is a river it rises outside the desert and is known as an **exotic** river.

Sand dunes are common in the Central Namib. Where dunes occur they exist in a number of shapes and sizes depending upon wind speed and direction, the amount of sand available, and the nature of the ground.

Figure 3.4 The Orange dunes at Sossusulei, Namib desert are over 300 m high

Wadis are dry gullies that have been eroded by flash floods. Heavy rainstorms (100–250 mm) create rushing torrents on steep slopes. Run off on the slopes is via **rills**, small water channels, which join to form **gullies**.

Inselbergs or **kopjes** are isolated domes of resistant rock. The Brandberg, south of the Ugab River is one such example, and is Namibia's highest mountain.

Alluvial fans are cones of sediment which spread outwards and away from the mouth of a wadi or canyon. Once a river leaves the confines of a wadi deposition is rapid, owing to a broadening of the river's channel.

A **pediment** is the typical desert slope profile. The pediment is a low angle slope (1–7°) at the foot of a steep debris slope and cliff.

1 a Name the cold current which runs along the Namibian coastline.
b In what way is the current responsible for the area becoming a desert?

2 a Using an atlas mark the locations of the world's hot deserts onto a blank world map outline.
b What do you notice about the general location of the hot deserts? Think about their latitude, and the position within continents where deserts are found.

3 Figure 3.2 shows a dry river valley. What evidence is there to suggest that the river is a potent agent of erosion and transport?

4 a What is the difference between weathering and erosion?
b Evaluate the importance of wind and water in the creation of desert landscapes.

5 Imagine you are taking a holiday with Namib Desert Tours (Figure 3.5).
a Using evidence drawn from this page, describe the clothing you would pack.
b What other precautions might you take to prepare for the conditions you will face:
i) before you arrive in Namibia?
ii) each day?

Figure 3.5 The desert is a growing tourist attraction

A river delta: the Ganges

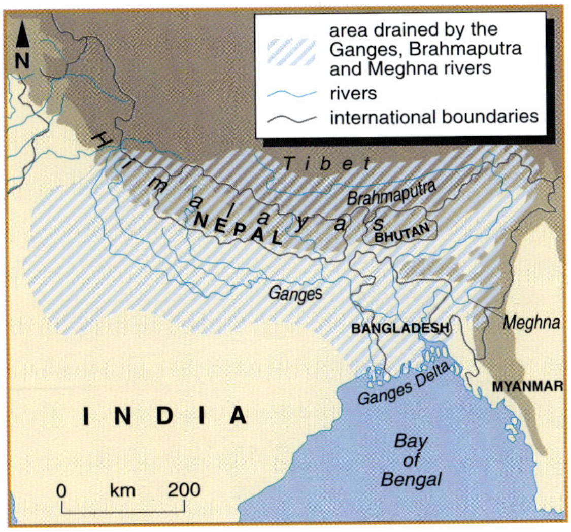

Figure 3.6 Location of Ganges delta

The Ganges Delta is the largest **delta** in the world. It has formed at the **confluence** of three huge rivers: the Ganges (Padma), Jamuna (Brahmaputra) and Meghna (Figure 3.6) and covers an area of 130 000 km^2. Together these rivers drain an area of over 2 million square kilometres – including parts of India and Nepal as well as the whole of Bangladesh.

The delta exerts a massive influence on the geography of Bangladesh. Much of the country is very low-lying – few areas exceed 10 metres above sea-level. As a result, flooding is a frequent problem. However as the rivers **overflow** their banks they wash fertile **silt** onto the land, helping to make it better for agriculture. The land is therefore attractive for settlement, even though flooding occurs regularly.

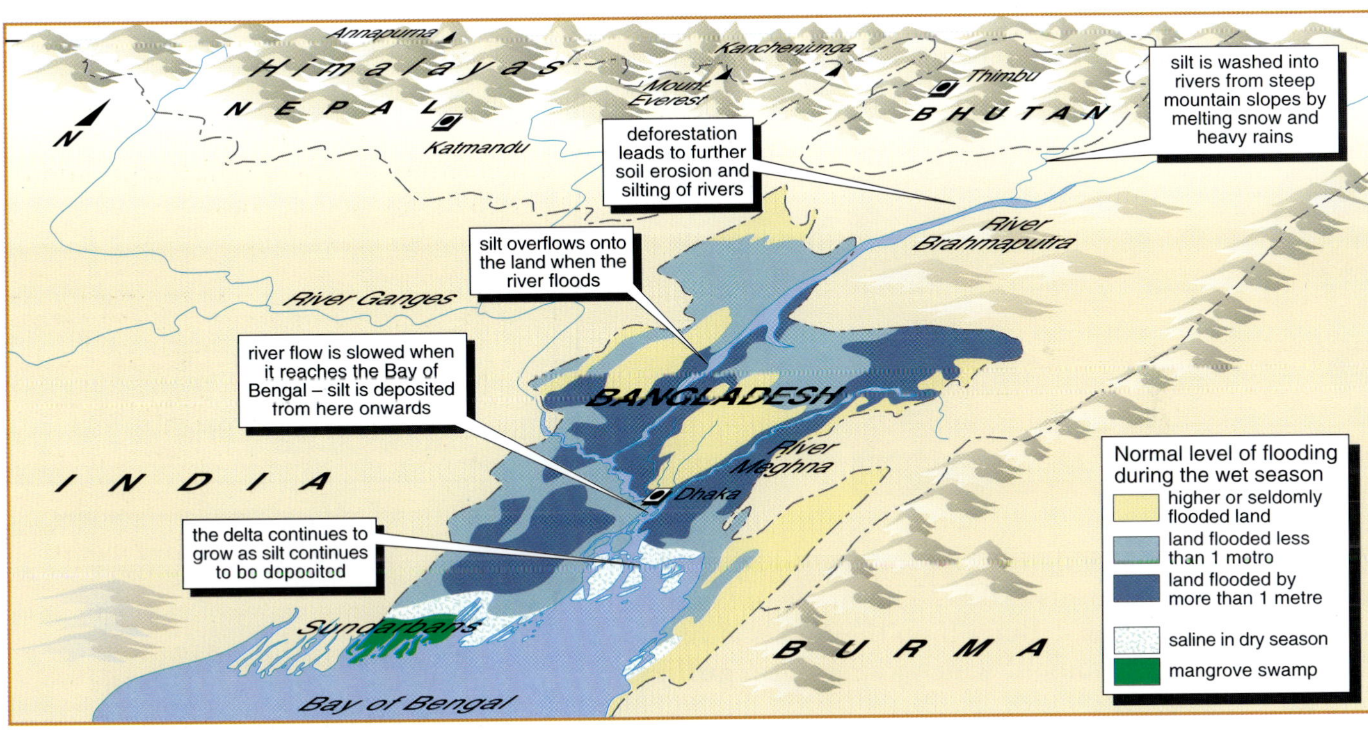

Figure 3.7 How the delta is formed

A delta is created when a river flows into the sea and deposits the sediment (silt) it has been carrying (Figure 3.7). Several factors have led to the growth of the Ganges delta:

- the river (the lower Meghna) is heavily laden with silt (2.4 million tonnes per year)
- its velocity, and thus its ability to carry silt, is reduced when it reaches the Bay of Bengal
- salt water, in the Bay of Bengal causes particles of clay in the silt to stick together.

The processes which caused the delta to form continue to operate, and so the delta is a dynamic landform continually changing in size and form. Each year the river pattern is altered as new islands and sand bars appear (Figure 3.8).

Bangladesh's population of over 116 million people live at one of the highest population densities in the world (over 800 people per km^2). This means that land must be farmed intensively. Over two-thirds of Bangladesh is used for arable cultivation. Many people live in the extremely fertile Ganges delta, where they are at risk from both river and coastal flooding (Figure 3.9).

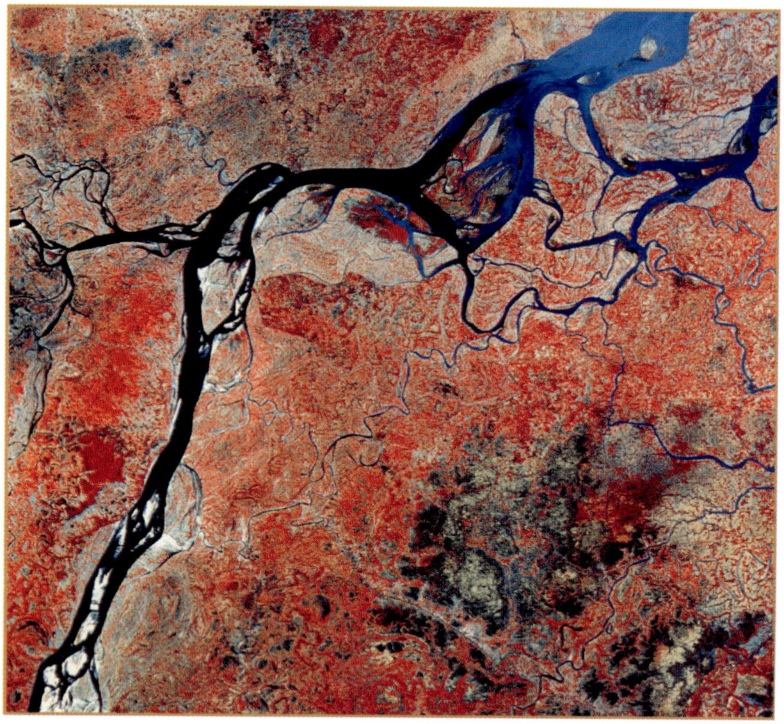

Figure 3.8 Satellite image of the Ganges delta

Figure 3.9 Ganges delta – in flood

In Bangladesh, rivers usually flood during the **monsoon** season between June and September. When this happens, up to 25 per cent of the country is covered in water and a thin layer of fertile silt. River floods rarely cause deaths. Tropical cyclones in the Bay of Bengal are largely responsible for more damaging floods. The cyclone in April 1991 was the worst for nearly thirty years – more than 140 000 people died and over 10 million were made homeless. Waves almost five metres high swept away whole communities. Some were lucky – in the island of Sanadia, 650 people climbed up on a 6 m high cyclone shelter – and survived. However it would cost at least US $66 million to provide shelters for all of Bangladesh's 'at risk' population. Only ten per cent of these 'raised shelters' have so far been built.

1 Which of the following sentences are **True** and which are **False**?
   - **a** The river Ganges speeds up as it reaches the Bay of Bengal.
   - **b** Silt is very fertile and helps farmers.
   - **c** The Ganges delta is getting smaller.
   - **d** Salt water helps in the formation of deltas.

2 Using an atlas and Figures 3.6 and 3.7, explain:
   - **a** why the Ganges Delta is so large;
   - **b** why the River Ganges carries so much silt.

3 **a** Explain why deltas are attractive places to live as well as hazardous environments.
   - **b** What do you think the people shown in Figure 3.9 feel about living near the river?

4 Why are Bangladesh's flood control measures unable to cope at present. How is this likely to change?

Conflicts along a coastline: Rio de Janeiro

The coastline marks the boundary between land and sea. There are often conflicts at this point between different activities. This is especially true along Rio de Janeiro's scenic coastline. The area has changed greatly over time (Figures 3.10 and 3.11).

Figure 3.10 View along Leme beach in Rio de Janeiro, 1890

PHYSICAL CHARACTERISTICS

Rio de Janeiro's coastline has many different natural features:

- dramatic **cliffs** and **headlands** are the result of continuous erosion by the strong waves
- between the rocky headlands there are wide **bays**. The city of Rio de Janeiro is built around Guanabara Bay.
- over thousands of years the coastline has been eroded to produce sand which has been transported by longshore drift and deposited elsewhere
- in some places **sand spits** have formed with **lagoons** behind them. Sometimes the coastline suddenly changes direction like at the Restinga de Marambaia and this allows the sand to pile along the coast as a long bank of sand. There are many coastal **dunes**.

Figure 3.11 The same view of Leme beach in 1990

Figure 3.12 Coast near Restinga de Marambaia

1 Study Figures 3.10 and 3.11. Describe all the changes you can see between the two views along Leme beach.

2 **a** In Figure 3.12, name coastal feature 'X'.

b Look at its location on the map (Figure 3.13) and describe the direction of the sea currents which would have brought the sand to here.

c Why are features like sand spits likely to form along these parts of the coast?

Some parts of Rio's coastline are more useful to people than others (Figure 3.13). This creates conflicts over how the land is used.

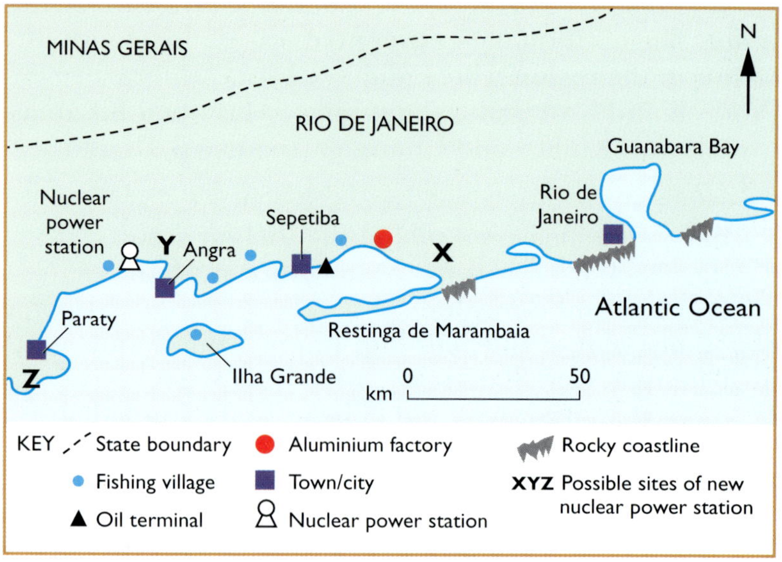

Figure 3.13 Coastline south of Rio de Janeiro

COASTAL CONFLICTS

The coastline around Rio de Janeiro has attracted many types of land use:

- when Brazil became a Portuguese colony in 1500 the coast was a good location for early settlements and a base for exploring the interior
- in the 18th century, gold from nearby Minas Gerais was sent by ship to Europe
- fishing, industry and tourism have developed more recently (see Figure 3.13).

Figure 3.14 Paraty is now a World Heritage site

Efforts have been made to preserve areas such as Paraty (Figure 3.14), an old historic town which has been made a World Heritage Site. However, as Rio de Janeiro grows, more and more conflicts over land use have developed along the coast. One of these concerns is the nuclear power station at Angra, which could result in radioactive pollution in the bay. The government has been urged by Greenpeace and other environmental groups to close the power station, but in 1995 it was announced that a second nuclear power station, Angra 2, would be built.

Figure 3.15 Ilha Grande is a popular place to visit from Rio de Janeiro

3 Consider the different ways in which Rio's coastline is used and protected. Which of the activities would the following people be **in favour of** and **against**? Explain the reasons for your choices.

a A marine biologist working for the Foundation for the Preservation of Ilha Grande.

b An industrialist who owns an aluminium factory needing imported ore and a large supply of energy.

c A tourist visiting Rio de Janeiro.

d An unemployed school-leaver in Angra.

4 Study sites X, Y and Z on the map (Figure 3.13). In small groups decide which site is best for the building of the new Angra 2 nuclear power station.

Khilari Earthquake, India (1993)

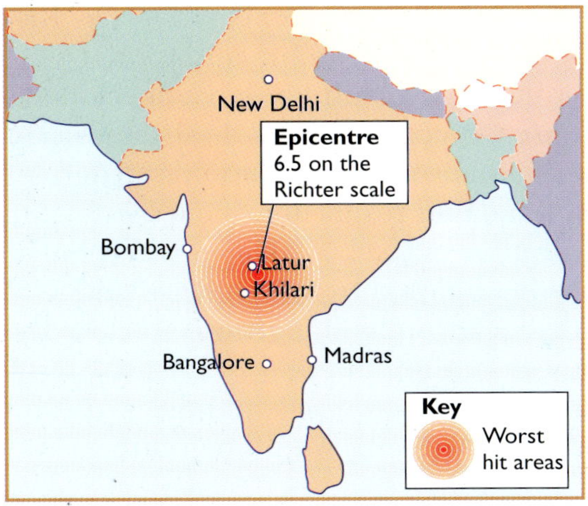

Figure 3.16 Khilari earthquake – the worst hit areas

Most of the major Indian earthquakes have struck along the edge of the Himalaya mountain range in the north of the country as Figure 3.18 shows. Plate boundaries like this are usually the focus for tectonic activity. Southern India, like Britain, is a low risk earthquake zone and Maharashtra state was thought to be geologically stable. The earthquake was probably caused by tensions in the **fault lines** within the Indo-Australian plate (Figure 3.19).

Several factors about the Khilari earthquake combined to result in a massive loss of life. People around Latur had no reason to expect an earthquake, so they were totally unprepared. The area was heavily populated and building standards were poor. At the time of the earthquake almost all the victims were indoors and asleep when their houses collapsed on top of them. If the houses had been better built, the damage would have been less. Many of the houses in this rapidly expanding region were constructed hastily from concrete and breeze-block, and were not properly reinforced.

In the early hours of the morning, on 30 September 1993, a massive earthquake hit Maharashtra state in India. The earthquake's **epicentre** was 32 km south of Latur, in the region where Maharashtra, Andhra Pradesh and Karnataka states meet. The worst hit areas were Latur, Khilari and Umargao (Figures 3.16 and 3.17):

- the quake measured 6.5 on the Richter scale
- the shock itself was felt as far away as Madras, Bombay and Bangalore
- 80 per cent of the houses in Latur, Khilari and Umargao were flattened
- more than 40 towns and villages in the immediate area were destroyed
- over 10 000 people lost their lives and many more were injured
- damage was apparent over an area of 1500 km^2.

Figure 3.17 Damage caused by Khilari earthquake, 1993

Date	Place	Richter scale	Deaths
15 January 1934	Bihar – Nepal	8.4	10 700
31 May 1935	Quetta (Pakistan)	7.5	30 000
15 August 1950	Assam	8.7	1530
20 August 1988	India/Nepal border	6.5	1000
20 October 1991	Himalayan foothills	6.2	1600

Figure 3.18 Major earthquakes in the Indian subcontinent

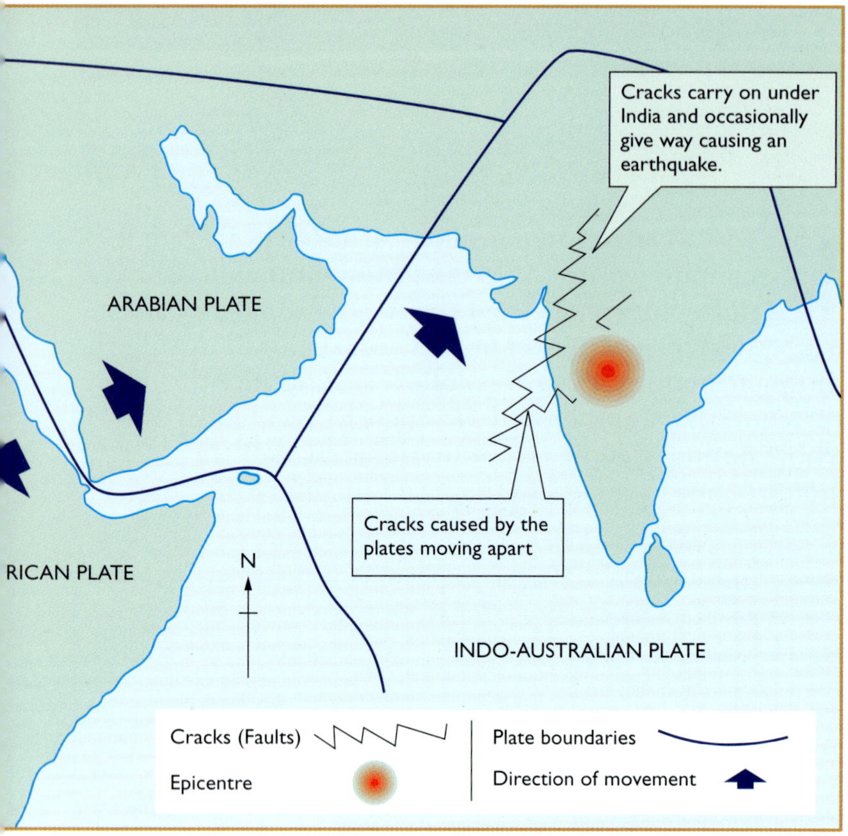

Figure 3.19 The cause of the Khilari earthquake

India is an old, stable continent riding on an ocean-floor plate which moves a few centimetres a year. India detached herself from a larger landmass, opening up the Indian Ocean, moved slowly northwards and crashed into Asia, throwing up the Himalaya Mountains.

The Himalaya Mountains are still rising. Most major earthquakes on the Indian subcontinent occur at this plate boundary. The Khilari earthquake, some distance south of the main danger area, seems to have occurred because of movement in an ancient fault line associated with the widening of the Indian Ocean which runs deep below the continental crust and under the Indian landmass.

The area around Khilari is not easily accessible, which made it difficult for rescue workers to reach the disaster area. They were hampered by a lack of local hospitals, poor telecommunications and incessant thunderstorms.

1. What factors contributed to the high death toll in the Khilari earthquake?
2. Why was an earthquake not expected in this area of India?
3. Draw a map of India marking in the three areas which suffered most damage in the earthquake of 30 September 1993. On the same map mark in any other earthquakes that have occurred in India in the last twenty years.
4. What do you think are the most important tasks in the immediate aftermath of this sort of disaster? Why?
5. Find out as much as you can about how buildings in earthquake zones should be constructed in order to minimise loss of life.

To minimise damage from earthquakes, houses need to be constructed carefully as Figure 3.20 shows. They should, whether made of rubble, stone or adobe, be cubic in shape. Doors and windows should be well away from corners. The walls should be anchored on deeply dug foundations, with well laid stone at the base. Buildings should avoid vertical joints.

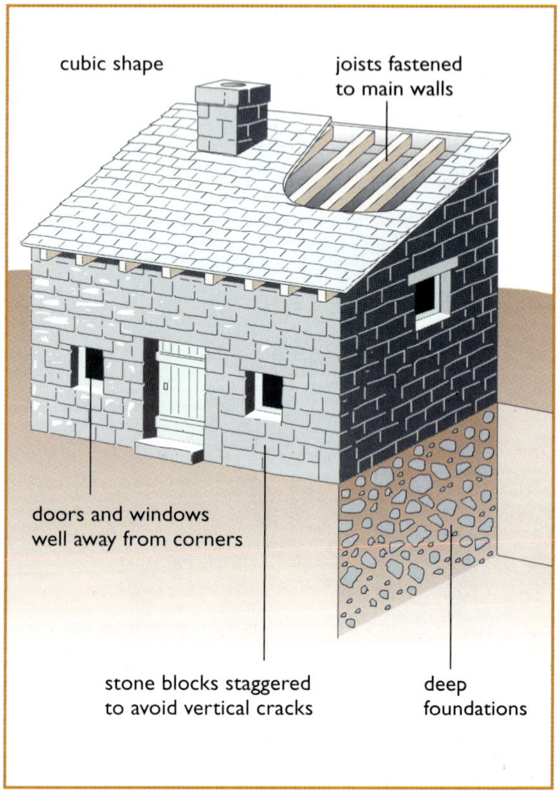

Figure 3.20 Building design in an earthquake zone

The Indian Monsoon

Every year in India millions of farmers rely on a climate feature called the **monsoon**. The word monsoon comes from the Arabic word *mausim* which describes a period of very high rainfall during the summer months. The rains follow several months of very hot, dry weather and are eagerly awaited by the whole nation. People celebrate the arrival of the monsoon and even go to the beach to enjoy the rain!

Figure 4.1 Summer and winter climates in India

Figure 4.2 Rice farmers depend on monsoon rain

The monsoon is mainly caused by the heating up of the Indian sub-continent during the hot months, which draws in air from the sea (Figure 4.1). These winds, which blow from the south-west, are moisture-laden having travelled across the Arabian Sea. At the beginning of June the monsoon 'breaks', starting from the southern tip of India and advancing northwards (Figure 4.3). By early July the monsoon rains have covered the whole country. This is how one writer has described its movement:

> 'One morning it is at Kovalam beach, by midnight it has moved many miles northwards over the green coastal plains of Kerala. The next day it is in Cochin blowing through the fishing nets, first the wind bending the palm trees to its will, then the rains. . . . It gathers the clouds along the way and then, one early morning they burst over Bombay.'

from *Chasing the Monsoon* by Alexander Frater.

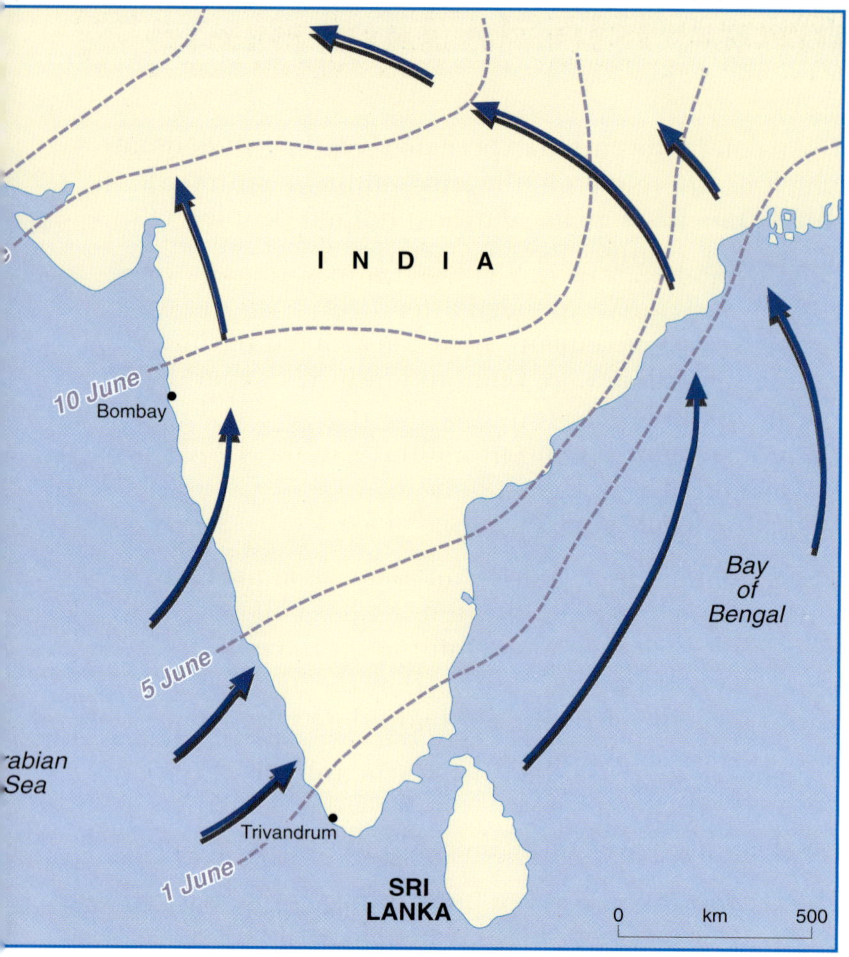

Figure 4.3 Dates and directions of India's monsoon

1 What does the word 'monsoon' mean?

2 Study the map and diagram of the monsoon in India (Figures 4.1 and 4.3).
   a In which direction do the two main branches of the monsoon winds travel?
   b How many days does it take for the monsoon to reach Bombay from Trivandrum?
   c Use an atlas to find out where rice is grown in India. Describe how closely it is linked to rainfall from the monsoon.

3 Study the climate graph for Bombay (Figure 4.4).
   a Draw your own copy of the climate graph.
   b Mark on your graph the period of the Monsoon and the hot, dry season.
   c What proportion of the annual rainfall occurs in the four months of the monsoon?
   d What type of weather will Bombay have during the monsoon season? What problems might this cause?

4 Write a poem describing how an Indian might feel about the arrival of the monsoon.

Most rain falls along India's western coast, but part of the monsoon spreads through the Bay of Bengal bringing rains to the fertile Ganges valley. In these areas rice, the country's main subsistence crop, is planted. Although the monsoon can cause many problems, the rains are vital to India's farmers, representing almost 75 per cent of the annual rainfall in most years. By October, the monsoon retreats back to the south and dry winds begin to blow from the north-east, bringing a cooler, drier period until the arrival of the next year's monsoon.

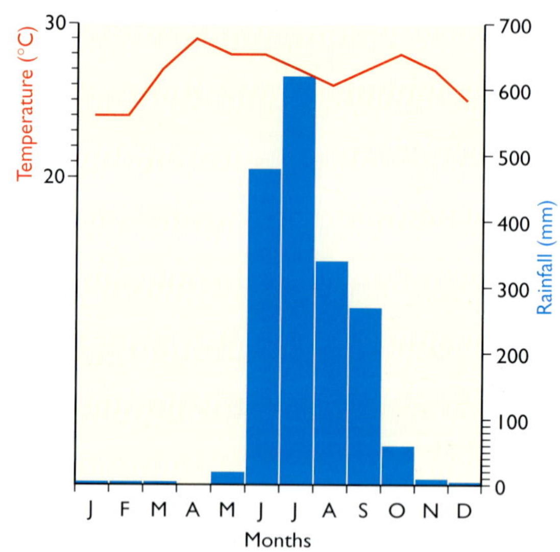

Figure 4.4 Climate graph for Bombay

Figure 4.5 The monsoon rains arrive after many dry months

Changing urban climates: Rio de Janeiro

Figure 4.6 Temperature clock found in Rio de Janeiro

Figure 4.7 Mudslides in Rio de Janeiro

Towns and cities often experience weather and climate which is different from the surrounding countryside. Rio de Janeiro is a city of over 5 million people. As it has grown, changes have occurred:

- the city's area expanded after 1900
- roads and pavements were constructed in the 1920s
- high-rise flats were built and industry expanded in the 1930s
- industry moved into the suburbs in the 1950s and 1960s
- traffic levels have increased since 1970.

These changes have caused an increase in average temperature and rainfall (Figure 4.8). This has occurred because heat has built up in the city's atmosphere. Figure 4.9 shows that the air becomes hotter near the city centre. In addition:

- rainfall increases because warm air can hold more water than cold air
- there are fewer rainy days but more heavy storms.

Higher rainfall in Rio is a hazard for people living close to rivers or on steep slopes, where landslides and mudflows occur. Many *favelas*, like Dona Marta (Figure 4.10) are built on the steep mountains close to the city centre and in February 1988 heavy rains killed 277 people and made 22 000 homeless. If Rio's climate continues to change then solutions must be found to protect lives and property.

	Temperature °C	Rainfall (mm)	Days with Rain
1900–1910	22.7	1211	141
1910–1920	22.7	1024	132
1920–1930	22.8	1014	134
1930–1940	22.8	823	131
1940–1950	23.1	1176	131
1950–1960	23.7	1168	122
1960–1970	23.7	1216	121
1970–1980	23.8	1114	122
1980–1990	23.9	1258	116

Figure 4.8 Rio's changing climate

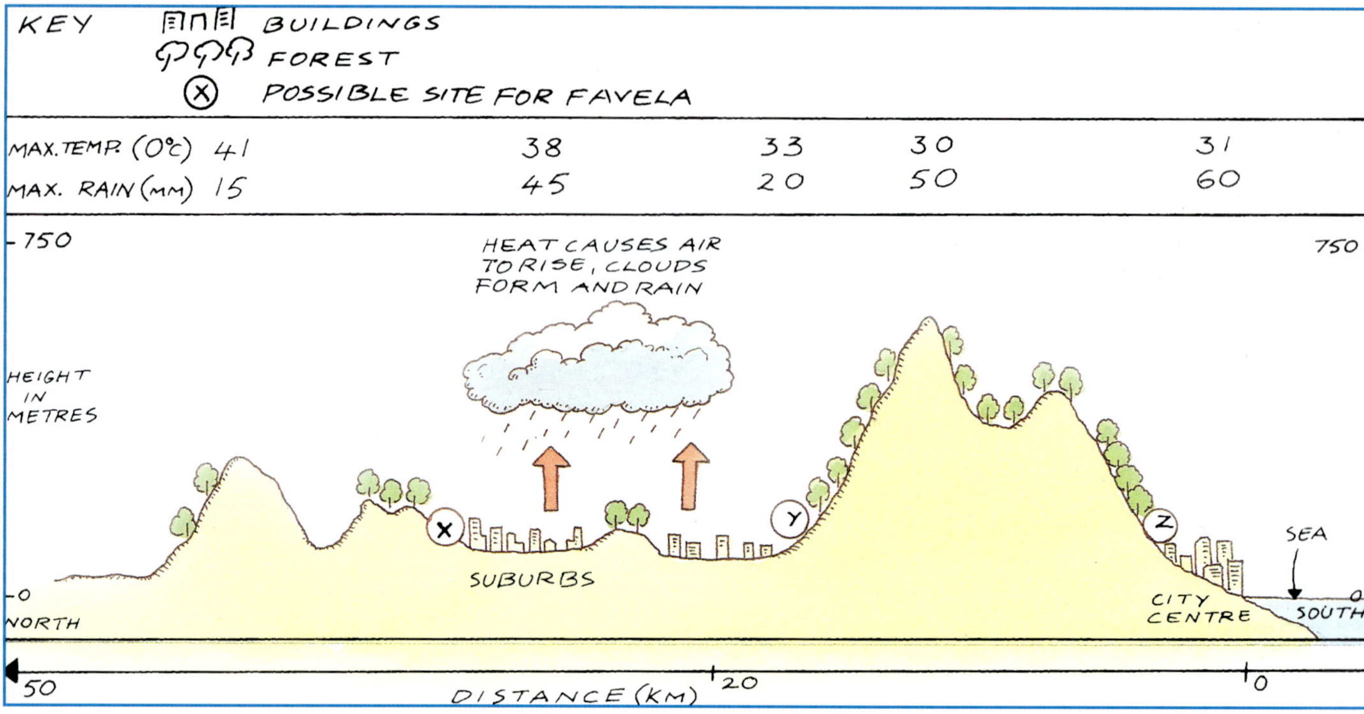

Figure 4.9 Cross section of Rio de Janeiro showing climate in January 1989

Figure 4.10 Rain clouds over Dona Marta favela

1 a Draw line-graphs (using Figure 4.8) to show the changes in Rio's climate.

b Write a sentence describing the changes in each graph.

2 a Explain how each of the following can increase air temperature in a city:

- more buildings
- industries
- cars and lorries

b On the temperature graph you have drawn write in these changes at the date when they occurred in Rio.

3 Make a copy of the cross-section (Figure 4.9). Why does more rain fall in the suburban area about 25 km from the city centre?

4 Imagine that you are a member of Rio's city council. Due to increasing rain storms, some of the sites where *favelas* are being built are unsafe. Only one of the sites marked X, Y and Z on Figure 4.9 is safe. Which one would you allow building on? Why?

Drought and desertification: Namibia

Namibia is an arid nation. Rainfall is very low over most of the country (Figure 4.11) part of which is a desert (see page 15). This low rainfall is made worse by other factors:

- high temperatures lead to high evaporation rates. As a result, the amount of surface water is minimal. Only a handful of rivers are **perennial** (contain water all year round);
- rainfall is very variable, especially in the desert areas. Swakopmund on the west coast has an annual rainfall of just 15 mm, and may go without rainfall for many years. Even Windhoek in the centre of the country has a variable rainfall as Figure 4.12 shows.

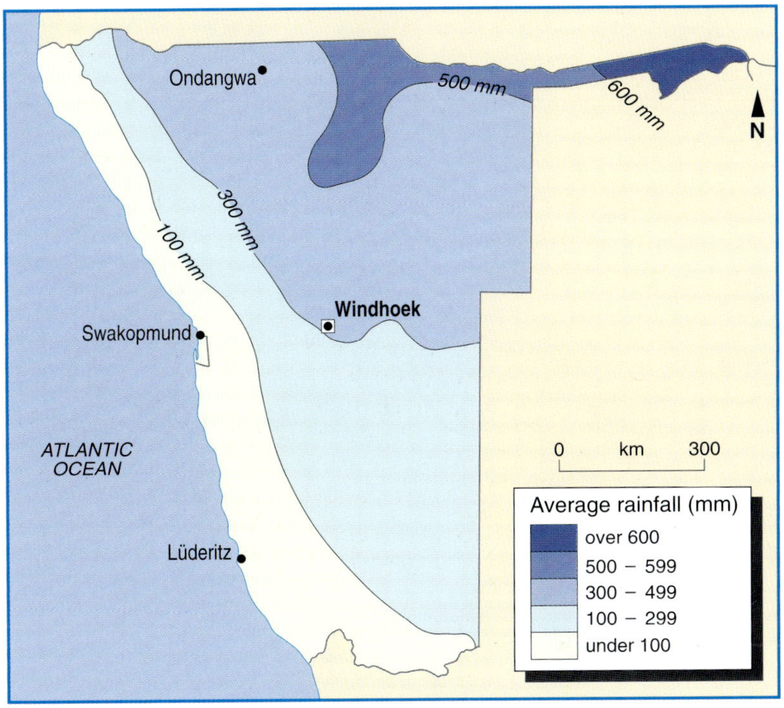

Figure 4.11 Average rainfall in Namibia

DROUGHT

Drought is a deficit of water due to high evaporation rates and low rainfall. Countries with low rainfall are likely to suffer from occasional droughts. The rains in Namibia are **seasonal** with June to mid-October usually dry. The vegetation is adjusted to this seasonal pattern as Figure 4.13 shows. However, in 1991–2, the situation worsened. The rains stopped four months earlier than normal – in January, the middle of the growing season. By April, Namibia was suffering from a severe drought:

- most reservoirs were almost empty and many crops were failing
- a state of emergency was declared by the President of Namibia
- water had to be brought to many communities by tanker (Figure 4.13).

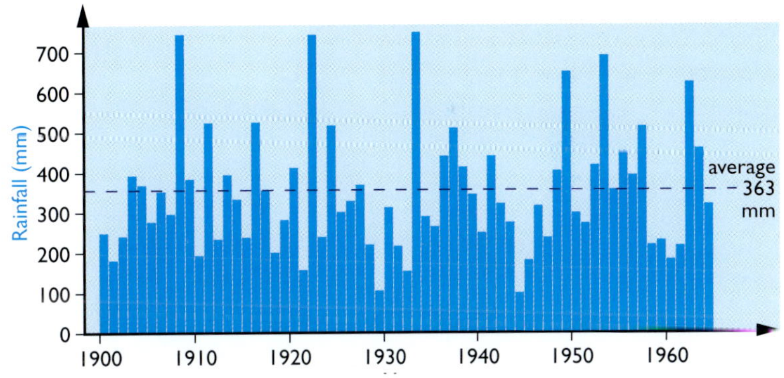

Figure 4.12 Rainfall in Windhoek, 1900–1965

Figure 4.13 How seasonal rainfall affects vegetation

Drought relief: Ten tankers deployed

As part of its drought relief programme the Government will deploy ten huge water tankers, each carrying about 10 000 litres.

The tankers were commissioned by the Department of Water Affairs from a special fund set up for the drought in an attempt to bring relief to the areas which have been hardest hit.

So far four tankers have been deployed in the Kaokoland, Gobabis, Swakopmund/Okahandja and Rundu regions. Four more will be deployed in the Ovambo region shortly, and two will be kept as reserves at Okahandja.

An engineer in the department, Mr Adrian Cashman, said the water situation in the country could be described as "severe but not critical". The situation in parts of Hereroland and Damaraland were severe and soon rural folk would be moving to other areas which offered greater security, he said.

Figure 4.14 Drought relief in action

In a country of less than 1.5 million, more than half a million people were affected by the drought. A *National Drought Relief Programme* was instituted, and this helped to alleviate the worst effects. Since then, several measures have been taken which place Namibia in a better position if a similar event occurs again.

DESERTIFICATION

Desertification – the process of arid land becoming less productive over the years – is also a problem in Namibia.

Natural causes of desertification include reduced rainfall and increased seasonality. This results in vegetation dying. With less vegetation, the soil is increasingly exposed to erosion by wind and water. This is usually a long-term process.

Desertification can also be caused by human activities and by poor land management. In Namibia, overgrazing and deforestation which has been caused by using wood for cooking, shelter, heating and fencing, are the factors responsible. Huge areas of the country are suffering from desertification and **bush encroachment** (Figure 4.15).

1. Copy and complete the following passage using the text and Figure 4.11 to help you.

   Rainfall in Namibia is very _____. Rainfall decreases as you move _____. Swakopmund on the coast has _____ mm of rainfall each year, while the capital, Windhoek, enjoys _____ mm. As a result of very high temperatures, much of the rain that falls in Namibia is lost through _____. This can lead to _____.

2. Study Figures 4.12 and 4.13.
   - **a** What normally happens to vegetation in the dry season?
   - **b** Describe how rainfall in Windhoek varies from year to year. What problems do you think this variation might lead to?

3. The area shown in Figure 4.15 was once grassland. How has it changed? Suggest some causes of this change.

4. Outline two things that the Namibian government can do in order to reduce the effects of a future drought.

Figure 4.15 A grassland area transformed by bush encroachment

Mineral extraction: Rössing Mine, Namibia

Figure 5.1 The location of Rössing mine

Rössing mine (Figure 5.2), about 70 km inland from Swakopmund on Namibia's west coast is the world's largest open-pit uranium mine. It was established in 1976, to take advantage of a large low-grade uranium deposit in the area. The RTZ–CRA Group is the largest shareholder in the mine.

About 18 per cent of the world's electricity comes from nuclear power stations, where uranium is used to generate heat to turn water into steam. This steam drives turbines, which in turn produce electricity. The uranium found in the rocks at Rössing is very low-grade and must be refined into uranium oxide (U_3O_8) before it can be used. One drum of uranium oxide contains the energy equivalent of 25 000 barrels of oil!

Figure 5.2 Rössing mine is a huge open-cast pit

Figure 5.3 Plan of Rössing mine showing operations

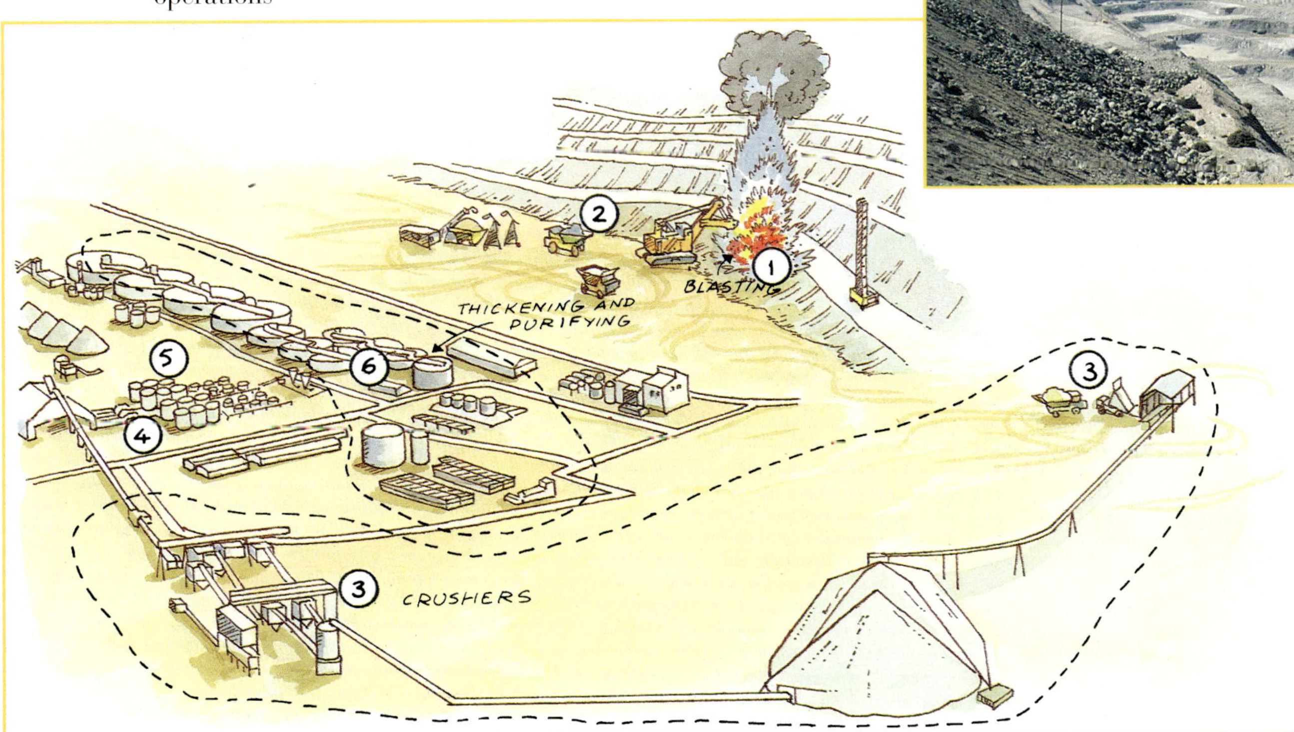

MINING OPERATIONS

Figure 5.3 shows how uranium oxide is produced from the rocks which come from the open pit. Try to follow the different stages in the operation.

1 The ore containing uranium is found in the rock close to the surface. It needs to be loosened by blasting. Some 100 tonnes of explosive are used each week.
2 After each blast the rock is loaded into 150-tonne trucks (Figure 5.4) and taken to the crushers.
3 Crushers reduce the large boulders to pieces of about 14 cm in size in just two minutes. Three more crushing stages produce particles the size of coarse sand.
4 Wet grinding further reduces the particle size to a mud-like slurry.
5 Sulphuric acid is added to dissolve the uranium out of the rock. The waste from this part of the process is pumped to the tailings dam for disposal.
6 The solution containing the uranium goes through a series of processes designed to concentrate and purify it.
7 Finally the liquid is removed from the solution and the resulting yellow cake is dried and roasted at a high temperature to produce uranium oxide. This is packed into steel drums ready for dispatch.

RÖSSING AND THE ECONOMY

The Rössing Mine was, in the 1980s, the largest single contributor to Namibia's Gross Domestic Product (GDP), export earnings and tax revenues. World prices then fell due to lower demand for uranium from the electricity generators, and cheap supplies of uranium becoming available from the former Soviet Union.

Rössing is still important to the economy as Figure 5.5 shows. The Rössing mine produces 14 per cent of Namibia's mineral exports (by value) and employs 1250 people, most of them Namibians. However, in the 1990s the mine has been working at about half capacity – 1994 output of uranium oxide was 2254 tonnes. The company has established the Rössing Foundation to assist Namibia's development. This is done through support for a variety of agricultural and educational projects.

Figure 5.4 A 150 tonne truck at Rössing mine

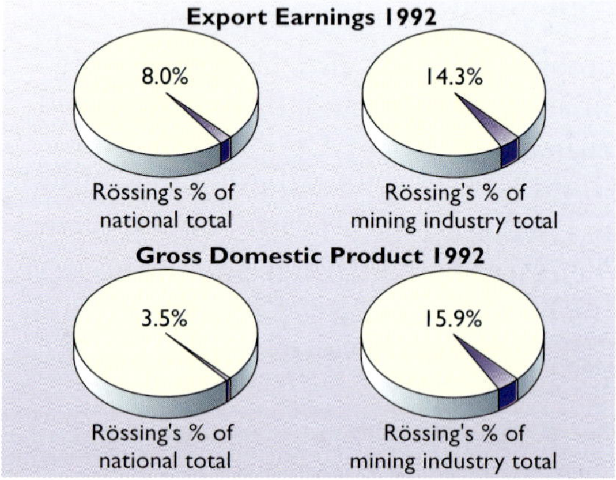

Figure 5.5 Rössing mine's contribution to Namibia's economy

1 a What type of energy is uranium used to produce?
  b How is this achieved?
  c Why are people concerned about the production of this type of energy?

2 Draw a flow chart to show the different processes which take place at the Rössing mine. Use Figure 5.3 to help you.

3 Which aspects of the mining operation at Rössing must be controlled to ensure that as little damage as possible is done to the environment?

4 a Use Figure 5.5 to help you explain how important Rössing mine is to Namibia's economy.
  b Refer to the map of Namibia on page 15 and your atlas to help you explain how important Rössing mine is to the local economy.

Hydro-electric power: the Itaipu dam in Brazil

Hydro-electric power (HEP) is a source of electricity produced by the force of water passing through large **turbines** which are built into dams, across rivers or reservoirs. Hydro-electricity supplies 37 per cent of Brazil's total energy needs. This is likely to increase in the future as between 1997 and 2005 almost 50 new hydro-electric projects are planned.

Many large rivers flow across Brazil. The areas which they drain are called **drainage basins**. A good HEP site should have land available for building the HEP station, and must have fast flowing water. In Brazil one of the best sites for developing HEP is the Parana drainage basin (Figure 5.6).

1 **a** Name the rivers on the map in Figure 5.6, using an atlas to help you.
b Copy the table (Figure 5.7) and complete the final column stating the correct letter for each drainage basin.
c What is surprising about the amount of HEP which may come from the River Amazon? Suggest reasons for this.

Drainage Basin	% of HEP	Letter
São Francisco	28	
Paraguai	0	
Amazon	7	
South East Brazil	3	
Tocantins	1	
Parana	58	
North East Brazil	1	
Uruguai	2	

Figure 5.7 Potential contribution of each major drainage basin in Brazil

Figure 5.6 Map of Brazil's drainage basins

Figure 5.8 Itaipu dam

ITAIPU: THE WORLD'S LARGEST HEP SCHEME

The Itaipu dam (Figure 5.8) was built on the Parana river on the border with Paraguay as a joint project between the two countries. The 18 massive turbines which make up the Itaipu HEP scheme started to operate in 1983. They produce six times as much electricity as Egypt's Aswan Dam:

- the dam is two kilometres wide and 120 metres high
- total cost was US $18.5 billion
- a large lake of 1400 km^2, the Lago de Itaipu, has formed behind the dam to store the water needed
- the dam produces 25 per cent of Brazil's hydro-electric power
- electricity from Itaipu is transmitted 650 km to Curitiba and 1000 km to São Paulo.

As the lake filled up with water behind the Itaipu dam a number of wildlife habitats were lost, some 20 000 people had to be resettled in a town nearby, and famous waterfalls were submerged. Local people and environmental groups criticised the project, but its supporters argue that water power has many advantages over the burning of fossil fuels like oil and coal for energy.

Figure 5.9 Sketch diagram of Itaipu dam

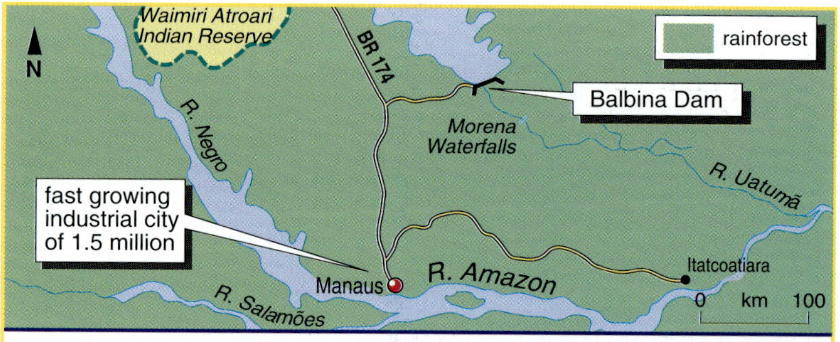

Cost per unit of power (kw) in US $

Balbina – 3000
Tucurui – 675
Itaipu – 1206

Ecological impact

* 31 times more forest was submerged than the Tucurui Dam
* Drowned forest has increased the water acidity. Fish found dead downstream

Figure 5.10 Amazonia's Balbina project

2 Study the sketch diagram of the Itaipu project (Figure 5.9). Make a copy of the sketch, including these labels in the correct positions:

Lago de Itaipu
Brazil
New housing for local people
Turbines
Spillway for controlling excess water
Electricity generator
Electricity pylons
Dam wall
Paraguay

3 Examine the information in Figure 5.10 about the Balbina HEP scheme in the Amazon region. With a partner:

a Describe the location of the project
b Why do you think the project was started?
c List the good and bad points of the scheme.
d Discuss with the rest of your class whether you think the HEP station should have been built.

Energy in India

India's population is expected to reach one billion by the year 2000. At the moment average annual power consumption is low at around 300 kilowatt hours a head, but demand is soaring by nine per cent a year. The country's ability to develop is closely linked to the expansion of the energy sector. Here we look at two approaches to energy supply.

TOP-DOWN DEVELOPMENT: THE NARMADA PROJECT

The Narmada Valley Scheme is set to become the world's largest hydro-electric power (HEP) and irrigation complex. It involves 30 major dams, 135 medium sized dams and 3000 small dams. It is designed to irrigate 20 000 km^2 of land in the drought-prone states of Gujurat and Madhya Pradesh, provide drinking water for the whole region and generate 500 megawatts of electricity. The scheme which will cost US $40 billion, mostly borrowed from the World Bank, has been criticised by environmentalists, farmers and some politicians (see Figure 5.12).

Top-down development
- decision-making comes from centralised government or organisations outside the country
- little responsibility is given to local communities
- projects are large involving huge amounts of money and western technology.

Bottom-up development
- decision-making is passed to the people
- responsibility is given to local communities
- projects are small-scale and appropriate to the needs and technology of the area.

Sustainable development
- designed to meet the needs of the present without affecting the ability of future generations to meet their own needs.

Figure 5.11 Approaches to development

Figure 5.12 Opposition to the Narmada river scheme

Figure 5.13 Sustainable energy sources

BOTTOM-UP DEVELOPMENT: HARYANA STATE

An alternative to big schemes like the one at Narmada is the sustainable energy project in Haryana State, to the north-west of New Delhi. The project is centred on one village, Dhanawas, which has about 300 inhabitants. Participation by the villagers is an important part of this initiative. Energy comes from three **sustainable** sources:

- bio-gas digesters (Figure 5.13) which are fuelled by a mixture of cow dung and water. They produce enough energy for five hours cooking or ten hours lighting. The aim is to make the village self-sufficient in renewable fuels, thereby reducing the consumption of fuelwood
- a gasifer (Figure 5.13, top) which is fuelled by a mixture of shredded mustard stalks, cow dung and water in the form of small pellets. This mixture is converted into gas. The equipment can generate enough energy to light the whole village
- solar powered water heaters.

1 Explain the difference between bottom-up and top-down development. Figure 5.11 may help.

2 Study Figure 5.14.
  a Which sector is India's largest energy user?
  b Which fossil fuel provides most electricity?
  c State two reasons why demand for electricity in India is likely to increase over the next ten years.

3 Copy and complete the table below outlining the advantages of the Narmada Valley Scheme.

	Advantages	**Disadvantages**
power supply		will benefit urban areas not rural areas
water supply		water will be taken away from rural areas for use in cities
irrigation		irrigation can waste water due to evaporation and can lead to salinisation
environment		1500 km^2 of forest will be lost

4 The Haryana energy scheme was developed after talking to the villagers of Dhanawas. Give three advantages of this bottom-up approach.

5 What would be the problems of using sustainable energy projects to supply all of India's energy needs?

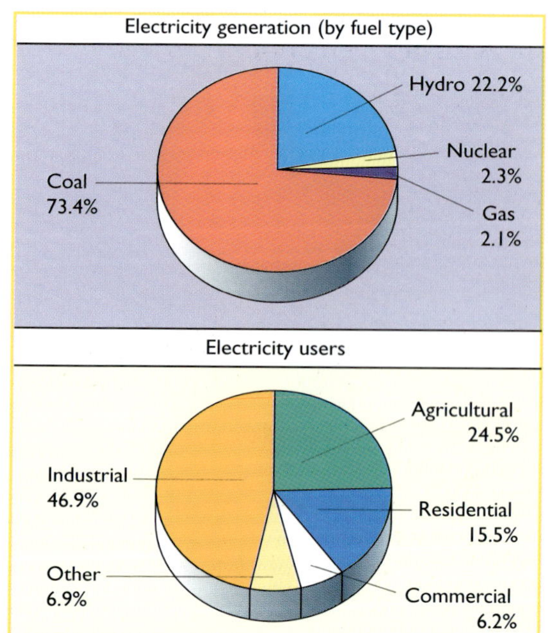

Figure 5.14 Energy in India: electricity generation and consumption

Resource scarcity: water in Namibia

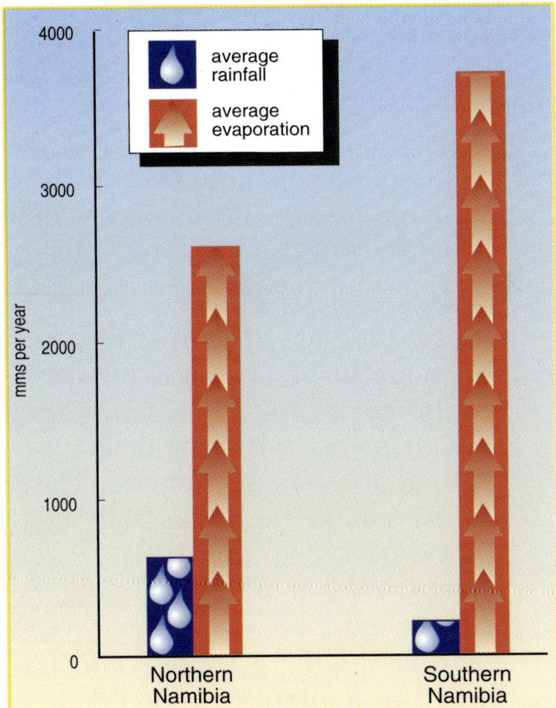

Figure 5.15 Rainfall and evaporation rates in Namibia

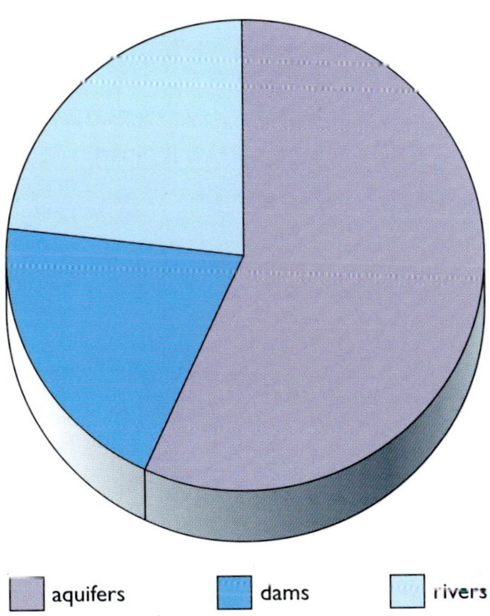

Figure 5.16 Where Namibia's water supply comes from

Namibia is the driest country in Africa south of the Sahara Desert. Water is a precious resource, and its scarcity affects the geography of the country, and the way of life of most people, in many ways:

- the vegetation shows adaptations to the harsh conditions
- agricultural output is limited
- population distribution is influenced.

Not only is rainfall low (Figure 5.15), but it varies greatly from year to year, and high temperatures lead to huge water losses by evaporation. In fact, rates of evaporation far exceed the supply of rainfall, so there are very few rivers which flow all year round. Most of Namibia's rivers are **ephemeral** (Figure 5.17). That is they may be dry for month after month. The only **perennial** rivers are found near Namibia's northern and southern borders.

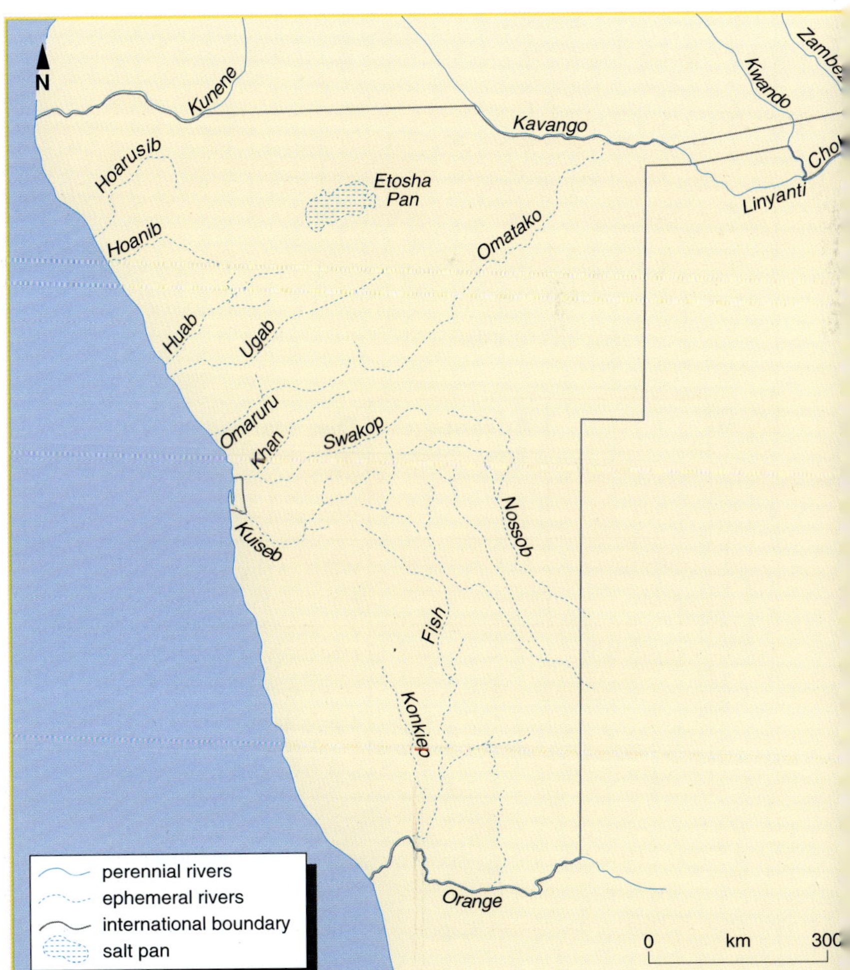

Figure 5.17 Rivers in Namibia

Figure 5.18 The Von Bach dam

1. Look at Figure 5.15.
   - **a** Describe how rainfall and evaporation rates differ between northern and southern Namibia.
   - **b** Suggest reasons for these differences.
2. Suggest how each of the following may have been affected by Namibia's low and unreliable rainfall:
   - vegetation
   - river flow
   - agricultural output
   - population distribution.
3. **a** Look at the pie-chart (Figure 5.16) and estimate the proportion of Namibia's water supply which is drawn from each of the three sources shown.
   - **b** Explain the limitation of using dams and reservoirs to supply water in Namibia.
   - **c** Apart from storing water, what other benefits might result from building dams in Namibia?
4. **a** Devise a poster which will encourage people in Namibia to conserve water.
   - **b** What problems might the government encounter in mounting a campaign to reduce water use?

WATER SUPPLY

The problems mentioned above make it difficult to store and supply water. Protecting scarce resources and improving the supply of water to people for domestic, industrial and agricultural uses is essential for a growing nation like Namibia. The heaviest demand for water comes from the arid central region, which has no perennial rivers. The largest city, Windhoek, is located here. Much of its water comes from the Von Bach Dam, north of the city.

Most of the country's water comes from **aquifers**, or water-bearing rocks, under the ground. The remainder is supplied by dams and rivers. A number of large schemes have been developed to transfer water from the wetter, northern parts of Namibia to drier regions. One such scheme is the Eastern National Water Carrier (ENWC). This transfers water from the Kavango river in the north, to the central region. The Von Bach Dam (Figure 5.18) which supplies water to Windhoek, is part of this system.

Subsistence agriculture: northern Namibia

Agriculture is Namibia's second most important economic activity after mining – it involves 70 per cent of the population and contributes 10 per cent to GDP. There is a great contrast between the large privately owned ranches found in the **commercial farming** areas of southern Namibia, and the **communal areas** in the north where subsistence farming dominates (Figure 6.1).

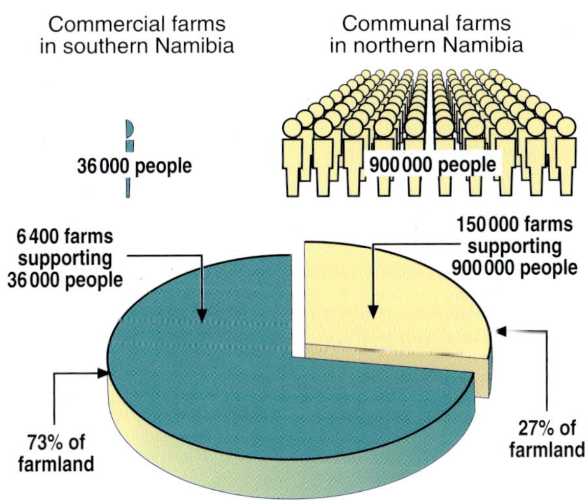

Figure 6.1 Division of farmland

1 Why is farming in Northern Namibia marginal?

2 a How does the way in which land is organised differ between northern and southern Namibia?

b State three other differences in farming between northern and southern Namibia.

3 Using Figure 6.3 to help you, suggest reasons why millet is:

- planted in December and January
- harvested in April and May.

Figure 6.2 Scrub vegetation and bushes in Namibia

The majority of Namibia's population live in the north of the country, on just 5 per cent of the agricultural land. In this area there are 120 000 smallholder families whose farms support almost 1 million people. This is the only part of Namibia where conventional rainfed arable farming can take place – although even here, low rainfall and poor soils make it a **marginal** activity.

Land in northern Namibia is communally owned – so grazing land can be used by anyone in the community who owns sheep, cattle or goats. Village elders or chiefs decide how land is allocated to households. Agriculture here is mostly for subsistence, with the produce being used to feed the families that live on the land. Most farming is mixed, with millet (locally called *mahangu*) and maize the most common crops, although livestock are also found, especially cattle.

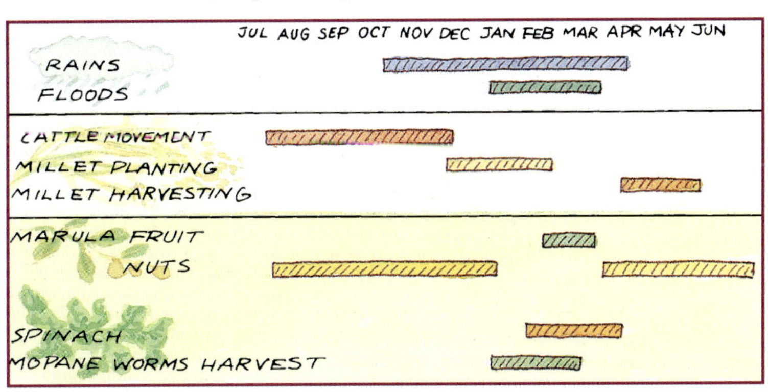

Figure 6.3 Agricultural calendar in northern Namibia

Cash-crop farming: bananas in St Lucia

Figure 6.4 Bananas growing in the Roseau valley

Bananas are grown on 85 per cent of St Lucia's farming land. Half the island's population depend on this crop to make a living and St Lucia's economy is **dependent** on bananas for half of its total export income. Since the mid-1980s banana exports have exceeded 100 000 tonnes a year. However changes in world trade have made it harder for St Lucia to sell bananas in Europe.

The island's climate makes it well-suited to cultivating bananas:

- annual rainfall is over 2000 mm
- average year-round temperatures are 27°C.

Bananas grow best on flat, fertile land (Figure 6.4) but are found almost everywhere in St Lucia. The banana plant grows a sappy stem with long, broad leaves at the top of the plant (Figure 6.6). Once cut, the bananas are taken to the nearest packing shed and dipped into insecticide. The fruit is then packed into boxes and transported to the docks in Castries or Vieux Fort. Here, the bananas are inspected, weighed and graded before being loaded onto the ship which will carry them across the Atlantic (Figure 6.5).

Figure 6.5 The banana chain

Figure 6.6 Banana cutter at work

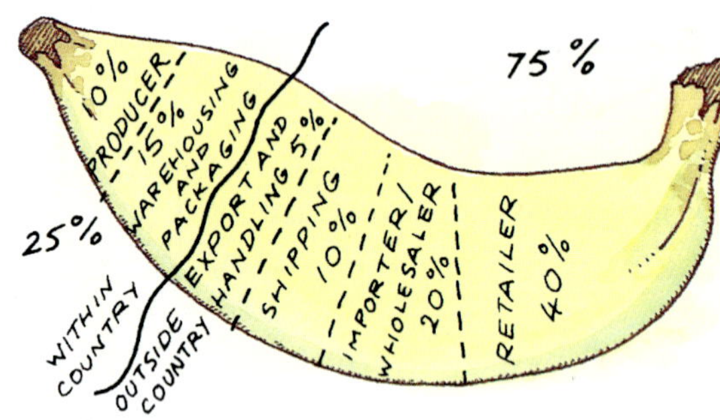

Figure 6.7 The banana trade – who does best?

1 **a** How is St Lucia dependent on bananas?

b List two dangers for a country relying heavily on one crop.

2 Suggest six different types of work involved in getting bananas from St Lucia to the UK. Figure 6.5 may help you.

3 **a** Banana growers get about twenty pence per kg for their fruit. How much do you pay for bananas (per kg) in your local supermarket?

b How much of the money spent on bananas in UK supermarkets do you think goes to the grower?

c Use Figure 6.7 to find out the truth. Is this situation fair?

Fishing in Namibia

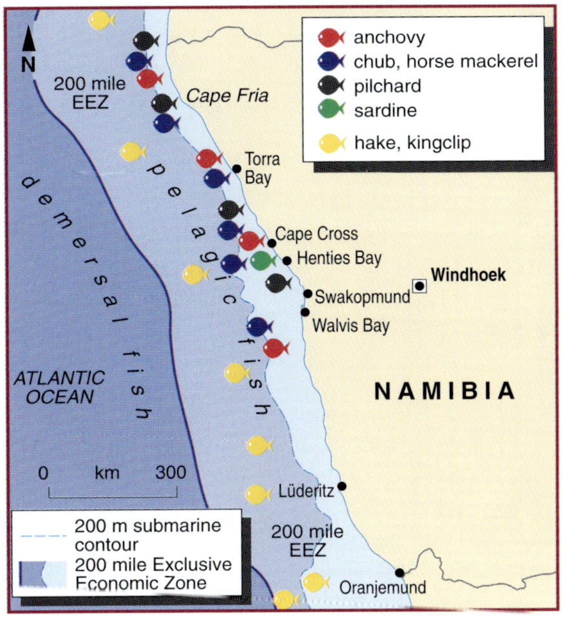

Figure 6.8 Namibia's fishing grounds

During the 1990s, Namibia's fishing industry has been one of the main sources of economic growth, employing about 6000 people in the Walvis Bay area, 800 in the White Fish factory at Lüderitz and up to 950 people in the rock lobster industry.

The nutrient rich waters of Namibia's 1850 km Atlantic coastline are one of the world's richest fishing grounds (Figure 6.8). The cold upwelling Benguela current provides huge supplies of plankton which are a rich food supply and attract fish. These waters have relatively few species but large stocks of each, unlike most tropical areas which have many species but small stocks. This favours large-scale fishing and attracts factory ships.

The industry is divided into two main groups, **pelagic** and **demersal** fishing. Pelagic species such as pilchards, anchovies and mackerel, are found in the shallow waters from Walvis Bay to Cape Frio in the north; demersal or white fish species, such as kingklip and hake, are found in the deep continental shelf along the entire coastline. Rock lobsters are important around Lüderitz, and the coastline also provides other resources including seaweed and guano (bird droppings) which is used as fertiliser.

Figure 6.9 Part of Namibia's fishing fleet

Figure 6.10 Changing fish catches before Independence

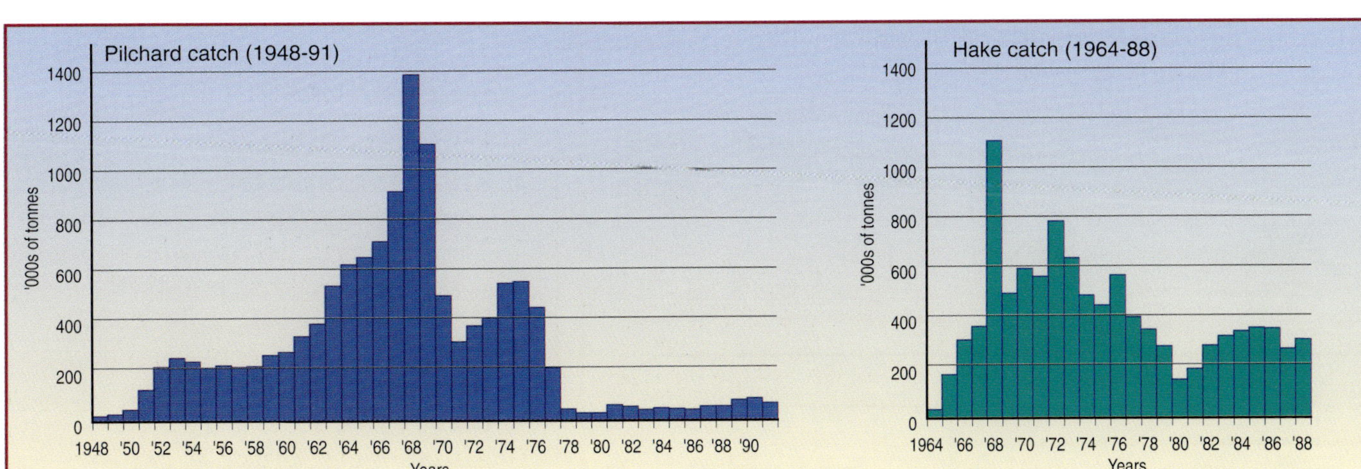

Figure 6.11 Fish being unloaded at Walvis Bay

Prior to Independence, Namibia's waters were overfished, resulting in a severe depletion of fish stocks, in particular hake and pilchards, as Figure 6.10 shows. To rectify this situation and allow the fish stocks to recover, the government has taken several steps since 1990:

- there is a 370 km exclusive economic zone (EEZ) in which trawlers from other countries are prohibited from fishing. Fines of up to £200 000 can be made if the EEZ is violated and vessels can be confiscated;
- shore based processing of fish caught in Namibian waters is to be maximised;
- most fishing companies should be Namibian owned or controlled.

Namibia's fishing policy has a number of objectives. They want to ensure that the country's rich fish resources are the basis of an economically viable industry.

	1989	1990	1991	1992	1993	1994
Anchovy	79	51	17	39	63	25
Hake	14	55	56	87	108	108
Kingklip	–	408	395	295	747	732
Mackerel	32	144	436	427	475	362
Monk	–	1499	4622	8123	9233	9351
Pilchard	76	92	69	81	115	116

All figures for catches in '000 tonnes

Figure 6.12 Fish catches 1989–1994

It is also intended to develop links with other local industries by increasing the amount of local processing and increase foreign exchange earnings.

Strict catch limits and the ban on unlicensed trawlers in the EEZ has allowed fish stocks to recover (Figure 6.12). Stocks of about 500 000 tonnes of hake and pilchards exist, and up to 120 000 tonnes may be caught yearly. Prior to Independence stocks were higher but foreign trawlers were removing up to 750 000 tonnes annually. It may take until at least 2005 for fish stocks to return to their original level.

1 a Why are the waters off the Namibian coastline attractive to fish?
  b Why is the fishing industry important to the Namibian economy?

2 Why is Namibia's fishing industry unlike that of the rest of tropical Africa?

3 Which is better for a fishing industry: large numbers of a few species of fish or a greater variety of fish but fewer numbers? Explain your answer.

4 a What problems did the fishing industry face before Independence? Use Figure 6.10 to illustrate your answer with examples.
  b What steps did the government take to resolve the problems?

5 a Use the data in Figure 6.12 to draw line graphs to show catches of fish since 1989.
  b Is there any evidence to suggest that government measures to replenish fish stocks are working?

6 What is meant by harvesting the fish in a sustainable way?

7 Why are Namibian waters so clean?

Electronics industry: Bangalore – India's 'silicon plateau'

Figure 6.13 Major centres of India's electronics industry

A cluster of high technology companies from India and the West have been drawn to Bangalore (Figure 6.14) as a base for supplying software and computer systems to customers in India and abroad. They have located in Bangalore for a number of reasons:

- there is already a skilled workforce as Bangalore is home to several national research laboratories and higher education establishments with a ready supply of well educated engineers
- low labour costs attract foreign multinationals – a first class graduate can be recruited for 12 000 Rupees a month (about £2800 a year)
- with an altitude of just over 900 m and relatively light rainfall, Bangalore has been described as having 'an air-conditioned climate'
- India has a growing market for computer products. It is an important Asian base for several large European and American high-tech firms.

Bangalore is the capital of Ķarnataka, a largely agricultural state, which is becoming one of the most important industrial regions in India. Bangalore's computer software industry has grown rapidly in recent years, – the area is known as India's 'Silicon Plateau'.

Indian Company	U.S. Partner	Product
Citicorp Overseas Software	Citicorp	Software services
HCL-HP	Hewlett Packard	Workstations, PCs, software
ITC	Lotus Development	Software services
Mastak	Ingres	Software services
Onward Computer Technologies	Novell	Software services, maintenance
Pertech Computers	Dell Computers	Motherboards, PCs.
Rotta India	Intergraph	Computer-aided design workstations, services
Tata Information Systems	IBM	Software services
Tata Unisys	Unisys	Workstations, software services
Wipro infotech	Sun Microsystems	Workstations, software services

Figure 6.14 Some of the US–Indian partnerships in electronics production

Figure 6.15 Woman worker in Bangalore electronics factory

CASE STUDY 1:
INFOSYS – AN INDIAN HIGH TECH FIRM

Infosys is one of India's best regarded software companies. It is located in 'Electronic City', a government sponsored industrial site some 18 km outside Bangalore. The grinding journey out from Bangalore illustrates one of the region's problems – poor roads clogged with slow moving trucks. The company's customers include Reebok and the Holiday Inn Hotel group.

CASE STUDY 2:
MOTOROLA – INVESTMENT FROM THE US

Motorola, the US electronics communications and equipment company has also located in Bangalore. In 1993, it established a plant with western style equipment but also with a generator so that operations could continue despite the daily power cuts which plague businesses in Bangalore. Motorola chose Bangalore for four reasons:

- it is the high-tech centre of India
- other multinationals like Hewlett-Packard and 3M have located there
- labour is inexpensive and high quality
- to supply India's growing domestic market.

Mr. Xerxes Desai. Managing Director of Titan Industries

This is by far the nicest city in which to live and work in India. There is no comparison.

Mr. Dinash Raghavan. Managing Director of Motorola

I came here with a lot of negative perceptions but I have been pleasantly surprised.

Figure 6.16 Views on foreign investment in Bangalore

HIGH TECHNOLOGY INDUSTRIES

Conventional high technology industries manufacture computers, silicon chips, lasers, robotics, aerospace and medical equipment. Sometimes biotechnology and telecommunications are included.

Figure 6.17 The city is a pleasant place to live

1 The following is a list of things which high-tech companies look for when locating their industries. Finish each sentence to explain why the factor is important.
   a Labour costs should be low because . . .
   b Efficient transport links are important because . . .
   c Closeness to universities and an educated workforce are important for high-tech firms because . . .

2 The rapid growth of Bangalore in terms of population and business ventures has caused a number of problems. Describe three problems faced by rapidly growing cities in the developing world.

3 In Figure 6.16, Dinesh Raghaven mentions 'negative perceptions'.
   a What do you think his 'negative perceptions' might have been?
   b Why do you think he has been 'pleasantly surprised'?

4 Read the two case studies. State two problems faced by industries in Bangalore's Electronic City.

An industrial region: Brazil's south-east

South east Brazil is made up of the states of São Paulo, Rio de Janeiro, Minas Gerais and Espirito Santo. Although the region only covers 11 per cent of Brazil's area, it is responsible for most of the country's industrial production and energy consumption (Figure 6.18) and houses some 62 million people. Here is the industrial heartland or 'golden triangle' of Brazil.

Until 1900, south east Brazil was mainly a coffee growing region where the rich soils, a good railway network and the port of Santos all contributed to a booming export farming economy. The **profits from farming** were used to build industries and the growing population of immigrants from Japan and Italy increased the **workforce**. This led to many factories being built in São Paulo. Industry expanded between São Paulo and Rio de Janeiro along the Paraiba valley when the government built the Volta Redonda steelworks in 1941.

In the 1950s the government set up car factories, steel mills and chemical works along the **railway and highway** leading to Rio de Janeiro. Since then more industries have been attracted to the region whose growing population provides an important **market** for machinery and consumer goods. In addition, the **government** has attracted **multinational companies** like Fiat and Coca Cola. Belo Horizonte, a city of 1.5 million people, with **reserves of iron ore** nearby has developed a steel industry, a large car factory and chemical works. Today, the Rio–São Paulo–Belo Horizonte Triangle is the largest industrial area in South America.

	Percentage of national				
	area	population	GDP	industrial production	energy used
North	42	5	4	2	2
North East	18	29	14	16	13
Central West	22	6	5	5	2
South East	**11**	**44**	**59**	**55**	**71**
South	7	16	18	22	12

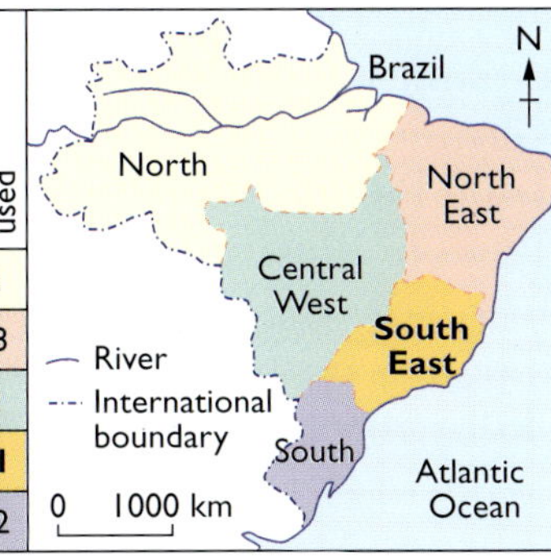

Figure 6.18 Regional differences in Brazil

1 a Make a copy of the cross-section across part of south east Brazil (from X to Y on Figure 6.20).

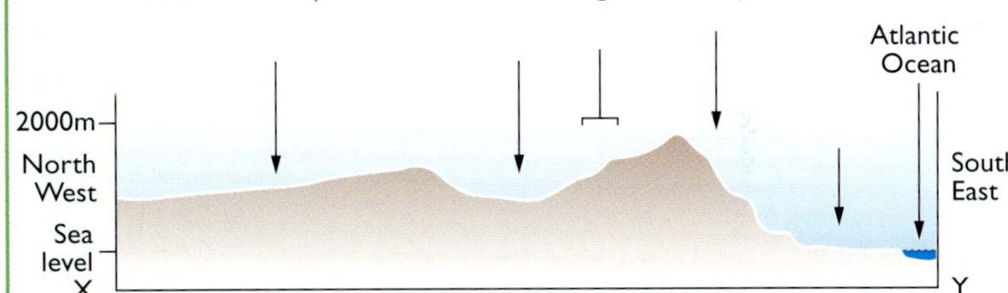

b Add the following labels to the diagram in the correct places using the information on this page and the map to help you.
- Flat coastal strip
- Fertile soil for coffee growing
- Escarpment
- Paraiba valley
- Main industrial area

2 Write a sentence about each of the reasons for the growth of south east Brazil. These are highlighted in **bold** in the text.

3 Using Figure 6.20, list the main industries found in:
- the São Paulo–Santos area
- Belo Horizonte

Figure 6.19 The steelworks at Volta Redonda

GROWTH IN THE CAR INDUSTRY

In July 1995, Volkswagen decided to build a new factory to make trucks and buses in Resende, about 50 km from Rio de Janeiro. A number of different locations in Brazil were considered before Volkswagen chose Resende. Figure 6.21 explains why. Once built, the factory will employ 1500 workers directly and 30 000 in related industries and services. The government of Rio de Janeiro offered incentives to persuade Volkswagen to locate in Resende including not having to pay taxes and water bills for 15 years.

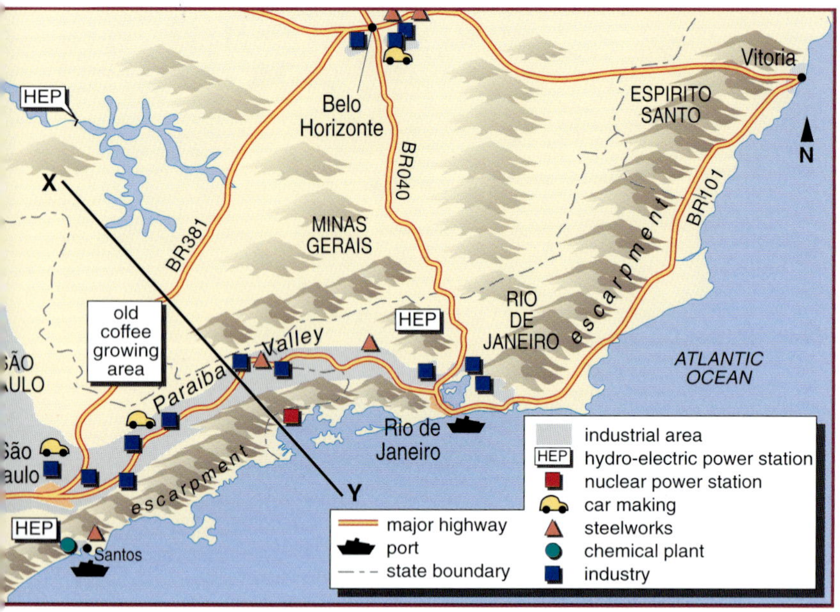

Figure 6.20 The industrial areas of south east Brazil

Volkswagen in Resende: the perfect profile

With a growing industrial area, large consumer market, easy access and a high quality of life, Resende has all the requirements for a new Volkswagen bus and truck factory. Resende is 150 km from Rio, 260 km from São Paulo and 490 km from Belo Horizonte. Eighteen other large companies have come here in recent years and its position gives good access to the ports of Rio, Santos and Sepetiba. São Paulo is linked by the Presidente Dutra highway (BR 116) and Minas Gerais by a railway line. Raw materials from the nearby steel factory at Volta Redonda and gas by pipeline from the Campos basin make Resende a perfect choice.

Figure 6.21 A new factory for Resende

Figure 6.22 Resende's location

Figure 6.23 Aluminium do Brasil in Minas Gerais

4 Study the map of the Resende area (Figure 6.21).

a List three reasons why you think that Volkswagen chose Resende to build a car factory.

b What other reasons, not on the map, might have helped Volkswagen decide?

5 In three years time the French car maker Renault will build a car factory in Brazil but hasn't decided on the location. The government would like the factory built in São Paulo. Design an advert to attract Renault by showing the possible benefits of this location, and the help the government might give.

A Newly Industrialising Country (NIC): South Korea

Figure 6.24 The world's NICs

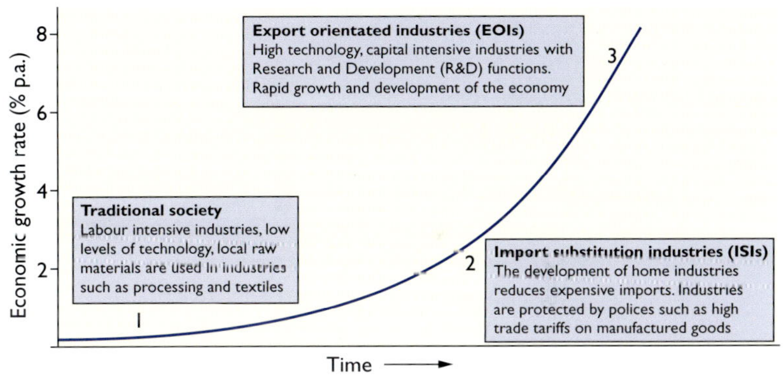

Figure 6.25 Stages in the development of a newly industrialised country

NEWLY INDUSTRIALISING COUNTRIES

Newly industrialising country (or NIC) is a term given to a country whose economy has been growing quickly for several successive years and where industry is growing rapidly.

An NIC is characterised by:

- an increasing proportion of the workforce in manufacturing industries
- significant growth in manufacturing production
- an increasing share of the world's manufacturing output.

Figure 6.24 shows where the original and more recent NICs are located. Although they have many different characteristics, NICs tend to develop in a similar way as Figure 6.25 indicates.

Figure 6.26 Ship-building in South Korea

Figure 6.27 Changes in South Korea, 1963–1992

	1963	1992
GNP per capita (US $ per head)	82	7220
Infant mortality rate (per 1000)	85	11
Urban population (%)	29	77
Population with access to safe water	63	93
Employment in primary industry (%)	63	19
Employment in secondary industry (%)	9	28
Employment in services (%)	28	53

Figure 6.28 Microelectronics in South Korea

SOUTH KOREA

Over the last 30 years, South Korea has undergone something of an economic miracle which has transformed it from a largely agricultural nation to a thriving industrial one (Figure 6.27). The economy has sustained an average growth rate of 7 per cent a year over the last 25 years.

Korea was the scene of a bitter war during the 1950s which resulted in the creation of two countries, communist North Korea and capitalist South Korea. The growth of the new South Korea has been helped by:

- aid from the US and Japan
- loans and grants from development banks
- government incentives to promote economic growth
- investment by multinational companies.

The first industries developed in South Korea were **import substitution industries (ISIs)**. These produced iron and steel, ships, textiles and chemicals in order to reduce dependence on costly foreign imports. Industrial development was assisted by South Korea's skilled and cheap labour force and its excellent location. Access to raw cotton from neighbouring countries helped the textile industry, while artificial fibres were generated by the rapidly expanding chemicals industry.

South Korea has now turned its attention to **export orientated industries (EOIs)** in an attempt to secure foreign currency and export earnings. Computers, televisions and microwave equipment are at the forefront of the country's electronics industry. South Korea's workforce has a well-earned reputation as hard-working, aggressive, imaginative and innovative. Future growth industries are likely to be in research and development, and high-value industries, including computers, biotechnology and aerospace.

1 **a** Draw two pie charts to show how South Korea's employment structure changed between 1963 and 1992. Use the data in Figure 6.27.
b Describe the main changes shown in your pie-charts.
c Look at the information in Figure 6.27. What do you think was the most important change in South Korea apart from employment structure?

2 **a** South Korea's growth has been assisted by some external help. What form has this taken?
b Using a map, show why South Korea's geographical location is 'excellent'.
c Explain in your own words how its position may have helped it grow.

3 **a** Why is South Korea hoping to develop its electronics, biotechnology and aerospace industries. Where do you think the markets for these will be?
b Explain why South Korea's workforce is so important for its economic development.

Maquiladora development: US companies in Mexico

Presto Lock, an American Company, opened a padlock factory in Mexico in 1983. They moved out of California because of strict environmental laws. The factory is now located in Ciudad Juarez, a town very close to Mexico's border with Texas.

Ten years later, the area is an environmental disaster. The following passages describe the pollution:

> 'In July, a girl playing in the street suffered burns to her feet. The city water department tested the drain outside the factory and found concentrations of heavy metals up to ten times the permitted level.'
>
> 'One hundred yards north runs a ditch of foul-smelling black water, covered with a film of white mould. The millions of gallons of raw sewage that Juarez produces every day eventually collects in this ditch. Mixed with industrial waste, some of it toxic, the sewage is used to irrigate cotton fields. Some of it ends up in the river.'

Figure 6.29 Slum areas in Ciudad Juarez

For many years the Mexican government has encouraged American industries to locate in Mexico, especially near its border with the US. The border zone has been established as a 'zona libra', or free-trade zone. Wages here are higher than elsewhere in Mexico, but much lower than across the border in the US.

Figure 6.30 The US–Mexican border area

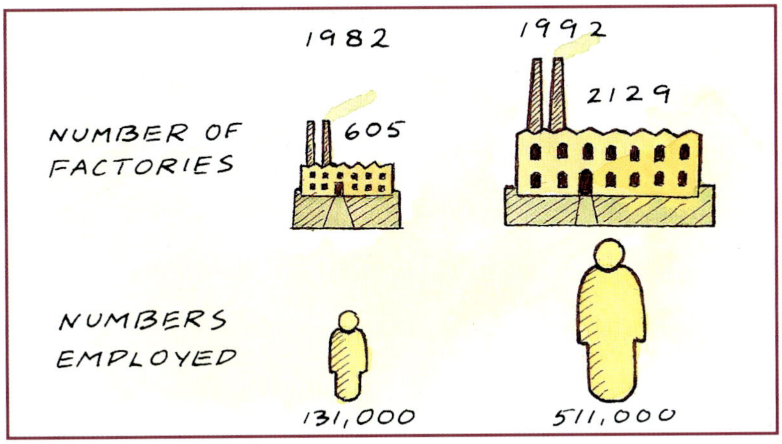

Figure 6.31 Maquiladora growth, 1982–1992

MAQUILADORA DEVELOPMENT

Mexico has attracted US-owned corporations to build assembly plants and other low wage factories in border cities such as Ciudad Juarez (Figure 6.29). These factories are known as *maquiladora* operations, and are foreign-owned, although the labour force is local.

Since 1989, more than 2000 manufacturing plants have set up in Mexico's border cities. The US firms are attracted by:

- low labour costs
- lenient environmental laws
- close proximity to US markets.

The firms are obliged by law to ship hazardous solid waste back to the United States, but illegal dumping on the Mexican side is common. For several months of the year a brown smog hangs over Ciudad Juarez and El Paso, its Texan neighbour across the Rio Grande.

ADVANTAGES AND DISADVANTAGES OF MAQUILADORA DEVELOPMENT

In spite of the environmental problems they cause, many Mexicans approve of maquiladoras. They argue that this type of development brings wealth to the north of Mexico. Over half a million people are now employed in maquiladora factories. As a result many labourers remain in Mexico when they might otherwise emigrate illegally to the US.

Critics of maquiladora development point out that it makes Mexico increasingly dependent on the US. They also recognise that the manufacture of textiles, electronic components and other products is likely to affect conditions in Mexico. If these firms sell their products in Mexico, it could result in factory closures elsewhere. The workforce is not likely to become more skilled as many of the factories are only involved in simple assembly operations.

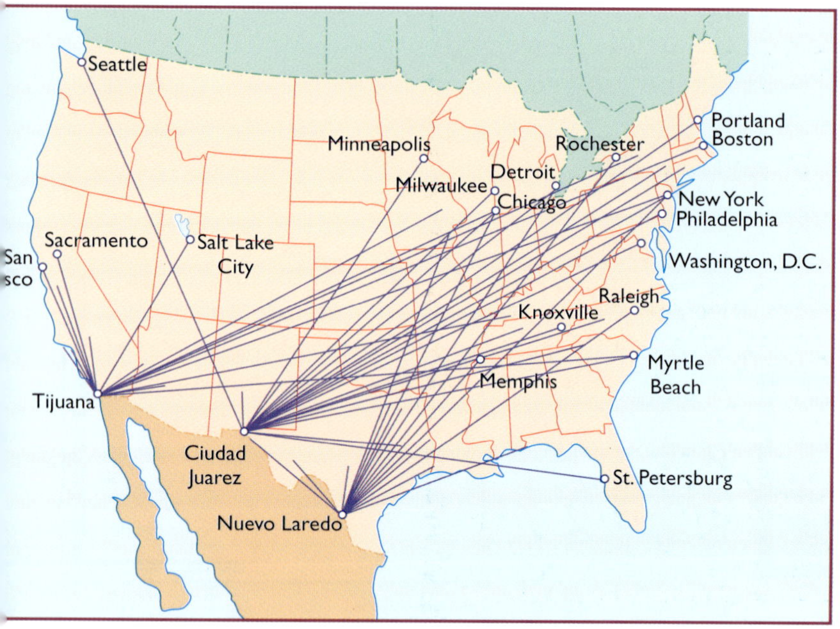

Figure 6.32 Trade from maquiladora plants in northern Mexico

Figure 6.33 Many maquiladora industries pollute the environment

1 Pedro Antonio Mendoza is a shopkeeper who has lived near the Presto Lock factory for 40 years. This is what he says about the factory:

'It was small at first, but as it grew so did the problems of pollution. These people throw their waste into the street. Each evening there is a smell like paint thinner, only worse. People complain of headaches, vomiting and skin allergies.'

Use his comments and the passage describing pollution at the start of this unit to draft a letter to the Mayor of Ciudad Juarez asking for the factory to be closed down.

2 **a** What is a maquiladora operation?
b Explain what the *zona libra* is.
c Give three advantages to US firms of locating in Mexico's border cities.
d What benefits do maquiladora operations bring to northern Mexico?

3 What does the map in Figure 6.32 show about where different factories in the maquiladora zone send their goods to in the US?

4 Imagine you are a Mexican worker living in Ciudad Juarez with a young family. You have a chance to migrate to California in the US. Give three reasons to stay in Mexico and three to leave the country.

5 Environmental problems are one disadvantage of maquiladora operations. Why else might foreign firms cause problems for Mexico?

Uneven Population Distribution: Namibia

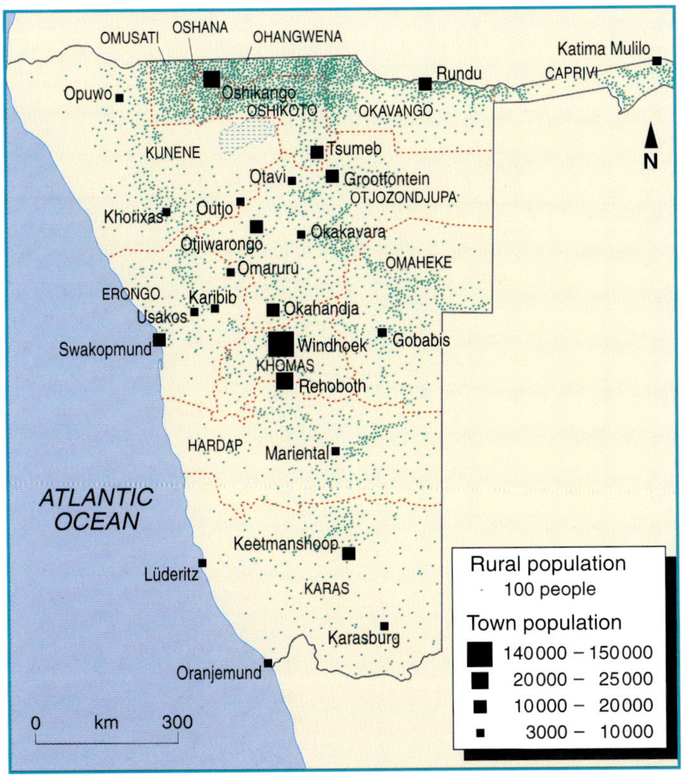

Figure 7.1 Population distribution in Namibia

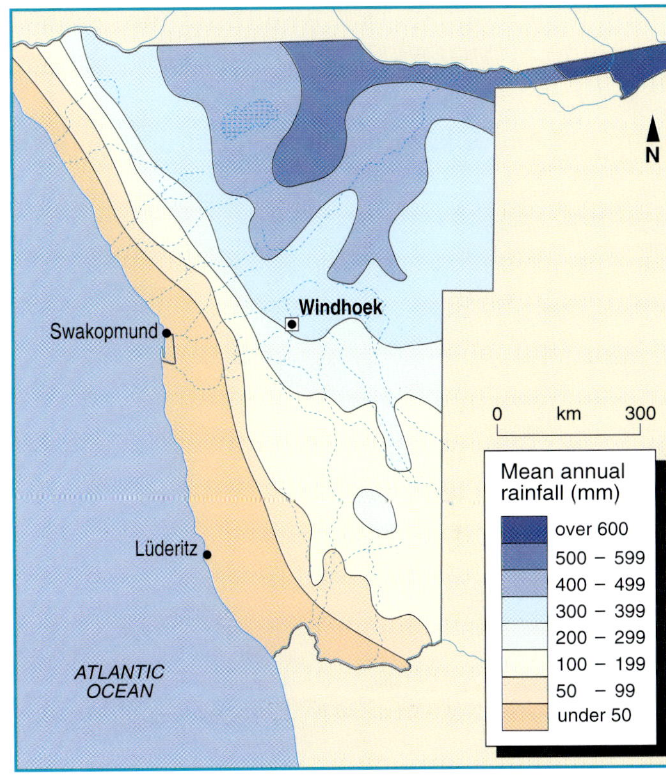

Figure 7.2 Rainfall in Namibia

Figure 7.3 Work in progress to reduce water shortages

In 1992, Namibia's population was estimated at 1.4 million. It is one of Africa's most sparsely populated countries. The population is very unevenly distributed as Figure 7.1 shows. With the exception of a few major settlements, ports and mining centres, large parts of the country are virtually uninhabited. The average **population density** of 1.7 people per km^2, compares with the African average of 18 people per km^2. Regional density varies from over 10 people per km^2 in the north, to less than 0.25 people per km^2 in southern parts.

Namibia is the driest country south of the Sahara. Water is scarce, rainfall is low and variable and evaporation rates are high (see Unit 4, page 28):

- there are no permanently flowing rivers between the southern and northern borders
- Namibia's coastal strip is an arid desert. Rainfall here averages less than 100 mm per year
- only 8 per cent of the country (the extreme north-east), receives over 500 mm of rain per year

Region	Population	Area km^2	Density people/km^2
Caprivi	92 000	19 532	
Erongo	98 500	63 719	
Hardap	80 000	109 888	
Karas	93 000	161 240	
Khomas	161 000	36 804	
Kunene	58 500	44 254	
Ohangwena	178 000	10 582	
Okavango	136 000	43 417	
Omaheke	55 600	84 731	
Omusati	158 000	13 637	
Oshana	159 000	5290	
Oshikoto	176 000	26 607	
Otjozondjupa	85 000	105 327	
Total	1 511 600	822 269	

Figure 7.4 Population by region

- the Caprivi region enjoys the highest rainfall – over 600 mm per year (Figure 7.2)
- rainfall patterns are erratic. The driest areas suffer most variation, even in drought free years.

The availability of groundwater and the seasonal distribution of rainfall have an important influence on settlement patterns (Figures 7.1 and 7.4). Over half the population are concentrated in the far north and eastern parts of the country, where more than a quarter of the total population live in just over 1 per cent of the land area. Population density in Caprivi is as high as 100 people per km^2. Densities across the four northern regions Ohangwena, Omusati, Oshana and Oshikoto average between 5 and 15 people per km^2 compared to less than 0.5 people per km^2 over much of the rest of the country.

Windhoek, the capital, is the single most densely populated area of Namibia, with some 159 000 inhabitants – 11 per cent of the total population. Windhoek has eight times as many people as the next largest town, Swakopmund.

The average population growth rate is estimated at 3.05 per cent a year which will result in a doubling of the population in 23 years. The 1991 census data reveals considerable variations in regional growth rates, some are stable, others are declining. There is a significant trend of **urban migration**. Growth rates in urban areas are estimated at 5–6 per cent a year, almost three times higher than rural areas. Urban migration is particularly significant in areas where mining or commercial farming predominate. In Windhoek the population growth rate is around 10 per cent per annum.

1 Using all the resources (text and figures) in this unit, explain in your own words why large areas of Namibia are uninhabited? Draw an annotated map if this helps your answer. You could refer back to the map of Namibia in Unit 2, page 15.

2 Explain what is being built in Figure 7.3. What has this got to do with population distribution?

3 **a** Use the data in Figure 7.4 to calculate the population density for each region. Remember:

$$\text{Population Density} = \frac{\text{Population}}{\text{Area}}$$

b Copy and complete the table in Figure 7.4, by including your answers from **a**.

c Why does population density in Namibia vary so much?

4 **a** If you were to move to Namibia which part of the country would you like to live in? Explain your answer.

b List **three** reasons why people are migrating from Namibia's countryside to the cities?

Population growth: Brazil

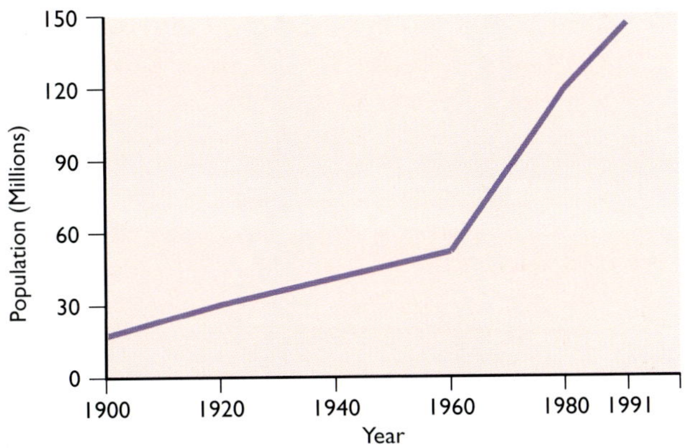

Figure 7.5 Population increase in Brazil since 1900

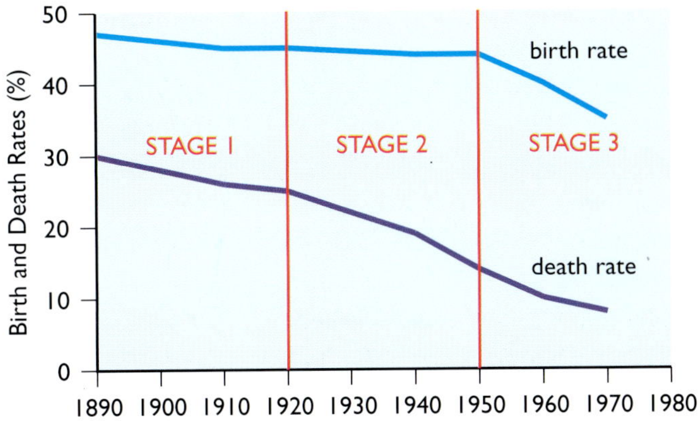

Figure 7.6 Changes in birth and death rates 1940–1980

- the average number of children per family is now three instead of six
- immunisation programmes for chil dren have been introduced
- most people live in the countryside and need large families to work in farming
- raising children is more expensive due to higher education and health costs
- two-thirds of women use contraceptives to prevent pregnancies.

Figure 7.7 Reasons for change in birth and death rates

Figure 7.8 Poster in Rio de Janeiro 'Your child deserves to be born healthy'

Brazil's population has steadily increased since 1900 (Figure 7.5). In 1960 it was thought that the population would reach 213 million people by the end of this century. Recent estimates put the figure at 179 million. There are several reasons why Brazil's population has not grown as quickly as predicted. The rate of population growth has been influenced by the relationship between birth and death rates.

If the birth rate is higher than the death rate, the population will grow. When the difference between them is large, the population increase is high. Many things have affected birth and death rates in Brazil (Figure 7.7). It is often thought that as a country becomes richer the speed of population growth slows down. In Brazil most of the population have a low income but the population growth rate has still slowed. One reason for this is that since 1960 most people have lived in cities. How might this have defused Brazil's 'population time-bomb'?

1. **a** Was the population estimate for the year 2000 made in 1960 too high or too low?
   b What is the difference between that estimate and more recent estimates?
2. Make a large copy of Figure 7.6.
   a Describe what is happening to birth and death rates in each of the three stages shown.
   b Study the list of reasons for changing birth and death rates (Figure 7.7). On your copy of the graph write in the correct reasons for each stage which explain why birth or death rates have changed.

Rural–urban migration: Brazil

'After a journey of several days from Barreiras in Bahia, Claudinior Pereira arrived in Salvador with his wife, two daughters and their three children. In the beginning Claudinior made his living painting walls, selling fruit and car cleaning. The family lived in several different places, at first on the pavement. Later they moved to the edge of the city. When they were short of cash the Pereira's received money from their neighbours. The women cooked on the open pavement with a small stove, and a four month old baby, grandson of Claudinior – already a grandfather at 37 – slept in a cradle nearby. Whenever it rained the person nearest covered the cradle with a plastic sheet.'

Figure 7.9 The story of Claudinior Pereira

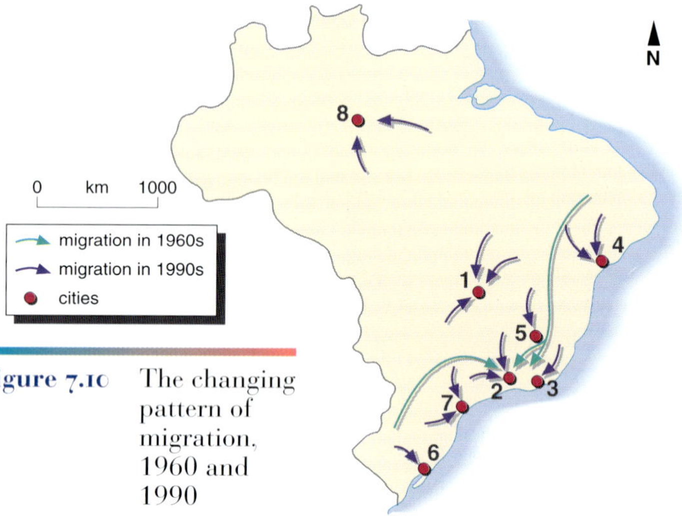

Figure 7.10 The changing pattern of migration, 1960 and 1990

1 **a** The journey which Claudinior and his family undertook lasted several days. How do you think he and his family travelled to Salvador?
b What hardships might a journey like this involve for a family with young children?

2 **a** List the reasons why people move to cities. For each reason explain:
i) why it will make people move to towns and cities
ii) if the reason is **forcing** or **encouraging** people to move.
b What attractions does a city like Rio de Janeiro (Figure 7.11) offer to people moving there from the countryside?

3 Study Figure 7.10.
a Name the cities which people migrated to in i) the 1960s and ii) the 1990s.
b Describe the main differences between movements in these two years.

Read Claudinior's story (Figure 7.9). It is a common one for thousands of families who have migrated to the large Brazilian cities since the 1950s. They either chose, or were forced, to uproot their lives in the countryside and travel, sometimes long distances, to the urban areas. Making this change was an improvement for some, but for others like Claudinior it led to great hardships.

Figure 7.11 Brazil's cities attract people living in rural areas

Why are people deciding to live in towns and cities in Brazil?

- modern farming methods, using tractors, fertilisers and machinery require fewer labourers
- prospects are poor for those living in rural areas
- the growth of trade and tourism is creating more jobs in ports and other cities
- the growth of town and city-based industries such as car making, steel making and oil refining has led to a demand for workers.

The reasons which force people to leave their homes are called **push factors**. Those that attract them to cities are called **pull factors**. In 1960, only 45 per cent of the population lived in Brazil's towns and cities – today this figure has increased to over 75 per cent.

Population policies: India

India's population reached 844 million in 1991. It continues to grow at around 2 per cent each year. Many people fear that a rapid increase in population will cause problems for India. More people will put a strain on the country's resources – and these are already stretched. India is a relatively poor country and many problems make it difficult for it to develop (Figure 7.14). These problems will probably get worse, so why do some families in India have so many children?

India's birth rate is 30 per 1000 of the population compared to 20 per 1000 in China and 13 per 1000 in Britain. This is the main reason why the population is growing so quickly. There are several reasons why the rate is high (Figure 7.15).

Figure 7.12 The Hindu religion encourages large families

1. Draw a line graph to show India's population growth since 1911.
2. Copy the table (Figure 7.14) and with a partner think of one effect of population growth on each of India's development problems.
3. Discuss as a group how India's birth rate might be reduced.

Year	**1911**	**1931**	**1951**	**1971**	**1991**
Population (millions)	252	279	361	548	844

Figure 7.13 Population growth in India 1911–1991

Development problems	**Effect of population growth**
1 Land shortage for growing food	
2 Lack of education	
3 Women not given enough importance	
4 High number of babies die	
5 Poor medical services	
6 Large number of poor people	
7 Some cities grow very quickly	

Figure 7.14 Development problems and their effects

Religion	Hinduism and Islam both encourage large families. Some religious tasks can only be performed by boys so more children are born.
Tradition	Large families are considered important.
Poverty	Children are needed to help with farm work and to look after parents in their old age.
Child health	Many children die young and so a family often has to be large to ensure that some survive.
Family planning	The main form of contraception is sterilisation for women. This is usually done after the second birth. Less than 30 per cent of the population use birth control.

Figure 7.15 Reasons for India's high birth rate

HOW POPULATION IS BEING REDUCED

In several parts of India attitudes are changing towards the number of children women should have. In the southern state of Tamil Nadu one family planning worker explained this: 'I have three children. My mother had nine. I want my daughter to have just one child.' So what exactly is making people want to have fewer children? Many different **population policies** have been tried. Which ones do you think are the best?

Figure 7.16 Family planning clinics such as this one in Tamil Nadu, are of growing importance

> **4** Which policies for reducing population growth do you think are likely to be the most successful?
>
> **5** Design a poster to persuade people in some Indian states that a smaller population is better.

- In some rural areas men and women, even childless couples, were forced to have **sterilisations** to meet the population growth limit. Radios and money rewards were given to women who agreed to be sterilised.
- In villages and towns **health centres** have been set up to help with contraception, pregnancy advice and sterilisation. Nurses visit mothers and babies to check their health and promote contraception. In Tamil Nadu, because of this system, only 40 new births out of 1000 die – half the national average. If the number of infant deaths falls then women will realise that having many children is not necessary.
- Educating women helps to delay the age of marriage and reduces the number of children each woman is likely to have. Providing more girls with **primary education** and free meals, as happens in Kerala and Goa, can help to achieve this.

The success of these policies has varied across India (Figure 7.16). However, many problems remain especially the low use of contraception apart from sterilisation. More serious, is the practice of killing girl babies. This happens because boys are favoured, and receive land and property when the father dies. When girls get married their family must give money and gifts (a dowry) to her husband's family. Although this is now illegal, it is still widely practised.

In the 1950s India was one of the first developing countries to start family planning but since then the population has nearly doubled. Only now are there signs that the rate of population increase might be slowing down.

Refugees: the Rwandan crisis

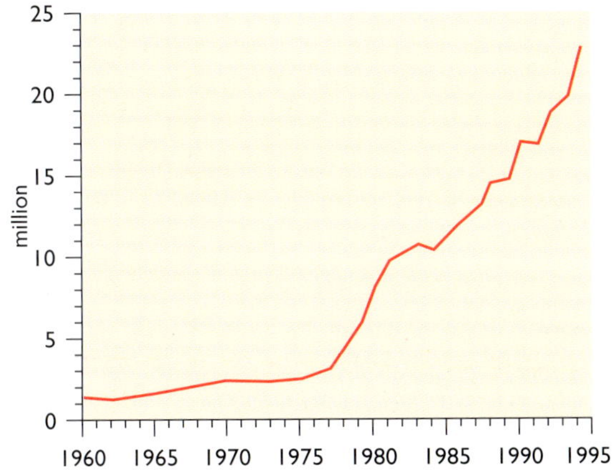

Figure 7.17 The number of refugees worldwide

Figure 7.18 Where the Rwandan refugees went

Figure 7.19 Conditions inside refugee camps are harsh

Refugees are people who are 'outside their own country, owing to a well-founded fear of persecution, for reasons of race, religion, nationality, membership of a particular social group or political opinion'. In 1994 there were over 23 million refugees worldwide.

The number of refugees is increasing due to war, economic collapse and the loss of basic human rights. This increase is so large that international relief agencies are often unable to cope with the numbers. One country that has faced a refugee crisis recently is Rwanda. Since 1993, millions of people have been forced out of their homes and into refugee status.

WHAT HAPPENED IN RWANDA?

The Rwandan crisis is rooted deeply in history. Members of the Hutu tribe dominated the Rwandan government from independence in 1962 and fiercely resisted any power sharing with the minority Tutsi tribe. In 1993 following the murder of 300 Tutsis, other Tutsis responded by killing the Rwandan president and seizing political control. Up to 500 000 Tutsis were slaughtered by Hutus and a further 2 million were forced out of Rwanda into neighbouring countries. Renewed conflict between the minority Tutsi government and the Hutus resulted in more Hutu deaths and over 2 million refugees were forced out of Rwanda into neighbouring countries.

The Rwandan crisis has not only caused death and relocation, but has had an adverse effect upon Rwandan agriculture and the rainforest. In Rwanda crops rotted in fields as fleeing farmers were unwilling to return, for fear of being killed. In the huge refugee camps which sprang up around several of Rwanda's borders diseases spread quickly.

1 **a** Study Figure 7.17. What has been happening to the number of refugees worldwide?
b What do you understand by the term 'human rights'?

2 **a** What was the main cause of Rwanda's refugee crisis?
b Where were the main refugee camps set up?

3 Describe the conditions associated with refugee camps.

Economic migration: Mexico to the US

Throughout history people have migrated across international boundaries. Some, like Africans captured into slavery and shipped to the Americas, were forced migrants. Others have moved because of political and religious persecution. People also migrate in response to poverty, seeking out better economic opportunities.

ECONOMIC MIGRATION OF MEXICANS

In 1993, the US Immigration Service caught 1.2 million people trying to enter the US over its Mexican border. Many migrants try several times before succeeding. The main destinations are California and Texas. There are border patrol agents (almost 5000 in total) as well as fences to keep the migrants out, but the border is 3112 km long (Figure 7.20) and cannot be patrolled along its entire length. Some 1700 trucks cross the bridge between Juarez in Mexico and El Paso in Texas every day. It would be impossible to search every one. There are many other road crossings along the border as well as the Rio Grande River.

Some 300 000 people cross the border illegally each year. This huge exodus takes place because of Mexico's low standard of living. Migrants go to the US in search of work which is:

- low-paid by US standards, but still better-paid than it would be in Mexico
- seasonal (often as agricultural labourers)
- unskilled.

The industrialisation of the border zone (see Unit 6, pages 48–9) has increased migration.

Figure 7.20 Migration along the US–Mexican borders

Most migrants are male. They leave their families behind but regularly send wages home. These earnings are one of Mexico's largest sources of foreign exchange. Many migrants actually return to their homes in Mexico after 6–12 months in the US. From an American point of view immigration is a mixed blessing. While employers welcome the migrants as cheap labour, some American workers resent them, blaming them for helping to depress wage levels.

1 Define these terms:
forced migration; political migration; economic migration.

2 **a** Which river runs along much of the US–Mexican border.
b What benefits do the migrant workers produce for Mexico?

3 **a** Give four reasons why Mexicans are migrating to the US. Identify each reason as either a 'push' factor or a 'pull' factor.
b Why is it difficult to keep Mexican migrants out of the US?
c Why do you think the Californian authorities want to keep illegal immigrants out of the state?

Figure 7.21 US border patrol agents

Figure 7.22 Illegal entry into the US

A village case-study: Patanusar, Bangladesh

Some eight million people live in the cities of Dhaka and Chittagong, but the majority of the population in Bangladesh (83 per cent) live in rural areas. There are nearly 60 000 villages. These villages or *mouzas* are at the bottom of the **administrative hierarchy** in Bangladesh (Figure 8.1).

Bangladesh division	Number of units	Average Population per unit
Division	5	22.3 million
Zila	64	1.74 million
Thana	490	227 000
Union	4451	2500
Mouza	59 990	1900

Figure 8.1 Administrative hierarchy

Patanusar is a village in the Sylhet region of north east Bangladesh. It is located quite close to the border with India, and close to Srimongal, in an area which is best-known for growing tea. The village is situated on rich fertile low-lands, near the River Lagata (Figure 8.2). These two factors enable a food surplus to be produced in most years. However, the river and the nearby land is regularly covered in floodwater.

Patanusar was established in the 15th century. The village population of just over 2500 people are all Bangladeshis, although a number of people from other villages have come to Patanusar to live and work. In part this is because the village is quite rich. Money is sent to some villagers by members of their families who have gone to the Middle East to work. This money has been used to develop local craft industries.

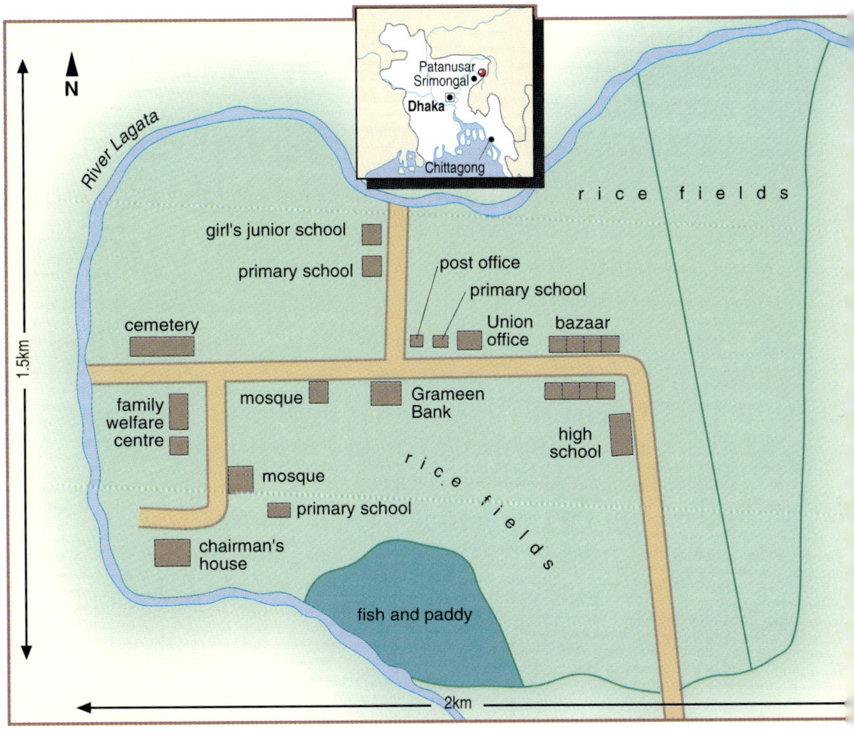

Figure 8.2 The site and layout of Patanusar village

Figure 8.3 Patanusar

The village has quite a young population, although the three oldest residents are 84, 96 and 100 years of age respectively. Four village women have loans from the Grameen Bank.

Patanusar Fact-File

Population	2508
Number of houses	246
Households with TV	97
Village centre buildings	Family Welfare Centre, Grameen Bank branch, Post Office, Mosque
Economic activities	rice cultivation and milling, welding, woodworking, furniture-making
Water supply	50 tube wells
Schools	3 primary, 1 girls junior school, 1 high school

Figure 8.4 Patanusar fact-file

We are trying to improve the village for all the people who live here. Next year we must decide between building more culverts to help take floodwater away more quickly, or providing leisure facilities for the children to use.

Figure 8.5 Mr Chowdhury the village chairman

HOW IS THE VILLAGE CHANGING?

- electrification under a USAID scheme 3 years ago, means that most homes now have electricity, and many run fridges and a TV. Power is also available for the village's rice mill.
- a road has been provided to the village, which means that:
  - any crop surplus is more easily transported to nearby markets
  - traders visit the village selling clothes and household goods
  - cars can come to the village (before 1976 only rickshaws could reach it)
- the population is slowly increasing
- more *pucca* houses are being built – these are more solid than existing houses
- the village layout is changing as it becomes more planned: houses are being built together in the village centre.

In the future, it is planned to provide an all-weather surface for the road which leads to the village and to improve the leisure facilities by building a playground and football pitch. The villagers also plan to construct more **culverts** to carry floodwater away.

Patanusar is part of Union Parishib, a group of villages which is presided over by Mr Zaharuddin Chowdhury. Villagers hold elections every 5 years for this position. Altogether there are 12 elected councillors. They are responsible for allocating government money to various improvement projects e.g. extending electrification; flood relief schemes; and administering local justice (through a village court system).

1 Using the text and Figure 8.2, outline the advantages of the site which was chosen for the village of Patanusar.

2 Copy and complete these sentences, using the text and all the sources:
- New road links to the village mean that . . .
- The village layout is changing . . .
- The village water supply comes mainly from . . .

3 Study Figure 8.1. Try to suggest British equivalents for the different administrative 'divisions' in Bangladesh.

4 **a** Write a profile of Patanusar under the following headings:
- Population
- Economic activity
- Change

b Compare Patanusar with a village in the UK which you have studied.

c Are all the changes which are happening in Patanusar good ones?

5 Read what the Union Chairman is saying in Figure 8.5. What would your advice be to his committee about how to spend their money next year?

Favelas in Rio de Janeiro

Figure 8.6 Dona Marta favela

1 Study Figures 8.6 and 8.7 carefully.
   a Describe what the *favelas* shown are like.
   b What difference can you see in the construction of *favela* buildings in the two photographs?

2 Using Figure 8.8, draw line graphs to show the growth in the size of Rio's population and the number of *favelas*. What is the link between the two lines?

The richest 20 per cent of Rio de Janeiro's population live in very comfortable high-rise apartments in expensive areas of the city like Copacabana and Ipanema. But more than 25 per cent of the city's population live in poor quality housing known as *favelas* or slums (Figures 8.6 and 8.7).

Figure 8.7 Favela housing

Favelas are scattered throughout the city but are often found on steep hillsides or on flat land far from the city centre. They are often close to major industrial areas. In *favelas*, the houses are small, and made of brick and tin or any other available scrap materials. The rapid growth of Rio de Janeiro due to the influx of poor migrants from the countryside and the low paid jobs that people work in means that this is the only type of housing the poorest people can afford. The facilities are usually sparse with no mains water, proper sewage or gas.

Until recently the city council tried to solve the problem of *favelas* by simply knocking them down or even burning the homes. Many areas have been improved now by building proper roads, installing electricity and water supplies. For the majority of people who live in *favelas* life is still difficult with low income and threats from diseases, crime and landslides.

Year	1920	1940	1960	1980	1991
Population (million)	1.2	1.8	3.3	4.1	5.3
Favelas	20	34	56	269	575

Figure 8.8 The number of favelas in Rio 1920–1991

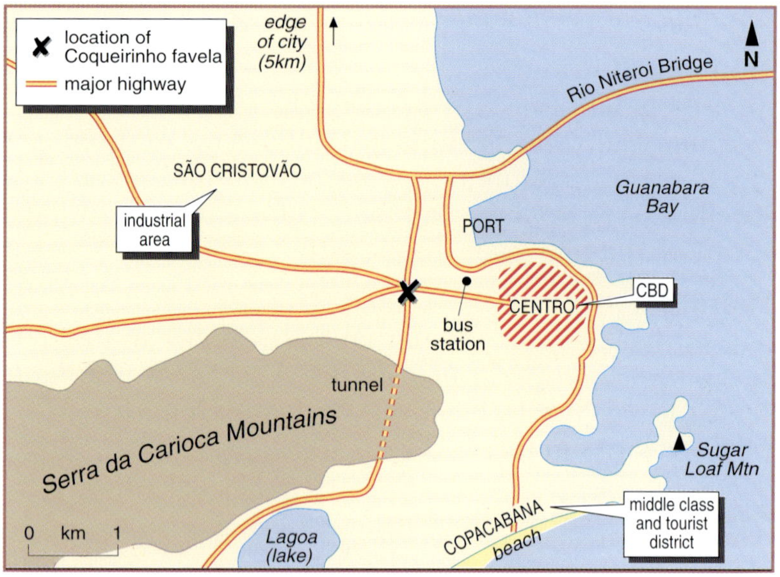

Figure 8.9 Location of the Coqueirinho favela

Figure 8.10 Views about the favela

COUNCIL TO REMOVE FAMILIES FROM NEW FAVELA

One thousand five hundred people living in dozens of wooden shacks under a motorway bridge in the *favela* of Coqueirinho will be removed during this year, announced the housing leader of Rio's city council. This is part of the 'Live Without Risk' scheme for resettling families living under bridges, close to rivers or on steep slopes and moving them to the edge of the city. Meanwhile, new houses continue to be built. Without water, electricity and gas the residents survive how they can.

Not everyone is in favour of this decision to move them away from their homes, and many would like proper houses built on the present site.

Figure 8.11 Coqueirinho favela

3 a Using Figure 8.9, describe the location of the Coqueirinho favela.
  b Why does the city council want to move many of the families on the site?

4 Imagine that you have just been appointed Rio de Janeiro's new housing leader. What decision would you make about the favela's future? Explain what answers you would give to Sergio Fonseca and Ivone Berezza.

A planned industrial city: NOIDA, New Delhi

Figure 8.12 The location of New Delhi

Figure 8.13 Pollution in New Delhi

New Delhi is the capital of India. Its tree-lined avenues and pleasant gardens have been replaced by an overcrowded and polluted city. The city's population is nearly nine million and it has a population density five times that of New York. New Delhi's growth has created a number of problems:

Housing Shortages

More than half the city's residents live in sub-standard housing. Many live in slums without access to running water or proper sanitation. Tens of thousands of city dwellers have been on waiting lists for government flats for more than 15 years.

Pollution

The air has become so foul that traffic police at the busiest junctions wear face masks. A recent World Bank report listed New Delhi as one of the seven most polluted cities in the world.

Congestion

The city's streets are clogged with slow moving traffic. Two million motor vehicles compete for space with tens of thousands of cycle rickshaws, carts and pedestrians. Seven hundred new vehicles go on the road each day.

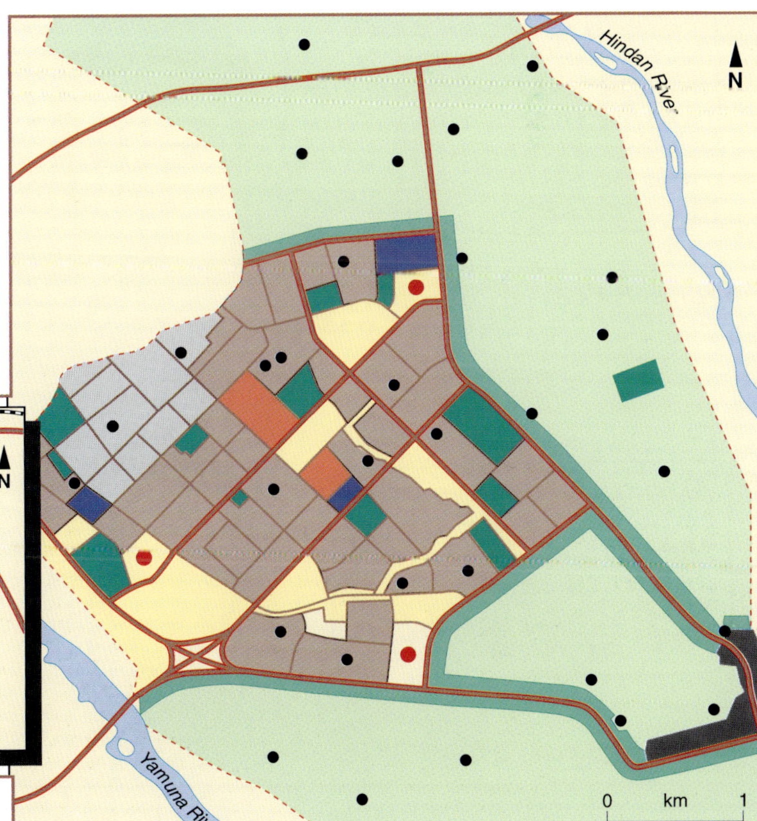
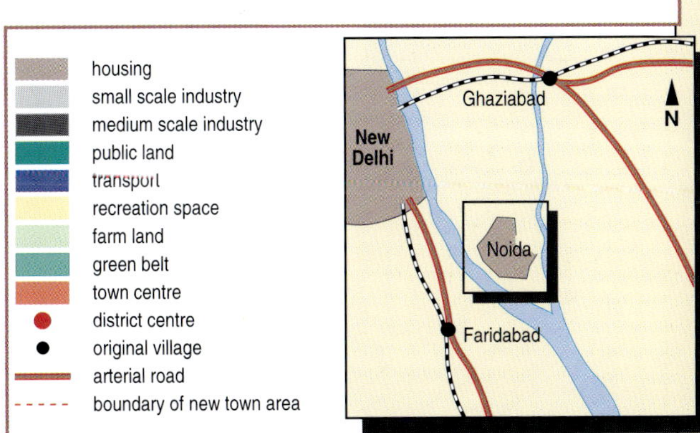

Figure 8.14 Land use in NOIDA

Figure 8.15 Industries are moving out of New Delhi

NOIDA: A PLANNED INDUSTRIAL CITY

NOIDA – the New Okhla Industrial Development Area – is a planned industrial city. NOIDA is located east of the Yamuna River some 12 km south east of New Delhi (Figure 8.14). It was built because New Delhi had become very overcrowded.

NOIDA aims to provide:

- housing at reasonable prices with good access to New Delhi
- an alternative location for a large number of small and medium-sized industries away from the congestion found in New Delhi (Figure 8.15).

NOIDA is a development similar to a British new town. Land-use has been carefully planned with industry and housing largely kept apart. Houses and flats have been built for people on low incomes. These dwellings are heavily subsidised by NOIDA and can be bought in easy instalments over a period of up to 13 years. The urban area encloses 21 villages and is surrounded by a green belt area which will supply agricultural produce. In 1990 the population was 200 000. In order to limit the population to half a million by the year 2001 the number of residential plots has been restricted.

1 New Delhi's population doubled in size between 1984 and 1995. Give two reasons why the population of cities in the developing world grows so rapidly.

2 New Delhi suffers from housing shortages, pollution and congestion. Draw a table like the one below and complete it to contrast the types of problems faced by New Delhi with those faced by a British city such as London.

	New Delhi	**London**
Congestion		
Housing shortages		

3 **a** How did the scheme set out the needs of people on low incomes?
b Is NOIDA a good solution to the problems of housing shortages, pollution and congestion suffered by New Delhi? Explain your answer.

4 **a** Why might the factory owner in Figure 8.15 choose NOIDA to relocate to?
b Describe and explain the location of these small and medium-scale industries in NOIDA.

There are more than 3000 businesses now located in NOIDA, mainly involved in electronics, engineering and the manufacture of garments. They are attracted by low-cost factory units. The emphasis has been on attracting pollution-free industries.

Figure 8.16 NOIDA

A growing city in an LEDC: Windhoek, Namibia

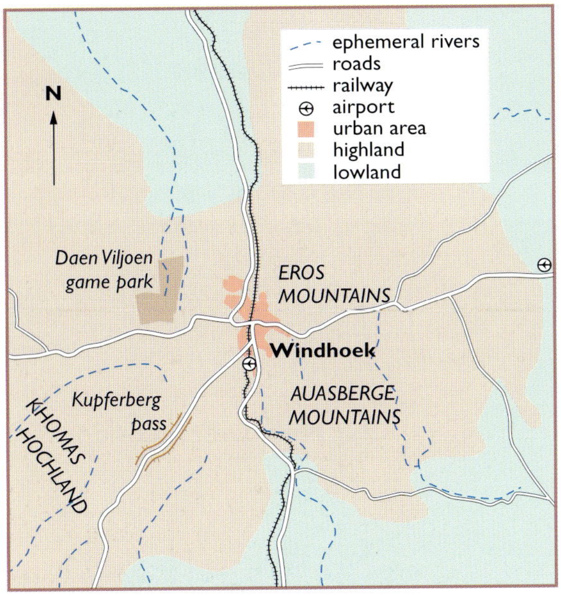

Figure 8.17 Windhoek's location

Figure 8.18 Modern Windhoek does not really look like an 'African' city

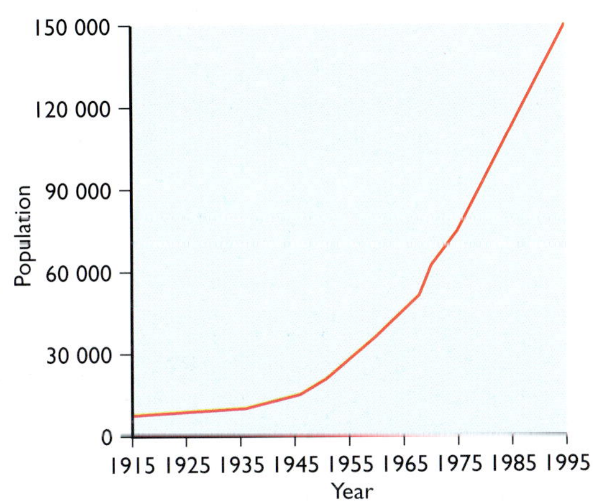

Figure 8.19 The growth of Windhoek

WINDHOEK POPULATION, 1991	
Windhoek	41 517
Katutura	86 640
Khomasdal	18 900

Figure 8.20 The areas of Katutura and Khomasdal are heavily populated

Windhoek has a population of nearly 200 000. The city looks very modern and has a thriving centre (Figure 8.18). As well as serving as Namibia's capital, Windhoek is an important commercial and industrial centre with a concentration of health and educational facilities. In many ways central Windhoek, with its enclosed shopping malls, modern office blocks, fast-food restaurants and German architecture, does not resemble a typical African city.

The city occupies a fairly central location in Namibia (Figure 8.17). It lies in a sheltered valley, with the Eros mountains to the north, the Auas mountains to the south and the rolling highlands of the Khomas Hochland to the west. Windhoek's site was probably chosen by early settlers as a result of the **perennial springs** found in what was otherwise a semi-arid area.

HISTORY AND RACIAL SEGREGATION

Once it became the main German garrison and capital city in 1890, Windhoek grew steadily. This growth quickened after a rail link was opened with Swakopmund in 1902. A number of trading companies and hotels were attracted to the town.

At first Windhoek was ruled under German colonial administration. After 1915, control passed to South Africa. A policy of racial segregation (apartheid) had been implemented under German rule and was continued by the new administration. Africans were prevented from owning property and were also excluded from many local services such as education and health. As far as housing was concerned, Africans were confined to two or three 'native locations', outside the city boundaries.

In 1959 two new townships were established some 5 km north west of the city – Katutura (for Africans) and Khomasdal (for coloureds). Black Africans and coloured people were forced to move to these new areas, which were separated from each other and from white Windhoek by buffer strips.

RECENT DEVELOPMENTS

Since the 1930s, the city has developed fast (Figure 8.19). In the decade up to 1991, the city's population has grown at over 5 per cent per annum. Although racial segregation is no longer practised, its legacy still remains. Data from the 1991 census shows that the overwhelming majority of Windhoek's population is concentrated in the two former townships and their newer equivalents to the west and north west (Figure 8.20). Many people in Katutura live on or below the poverty line. Average annual incomes here of N$1500 (£250) are much lower than those elsewhere in Windhoek, though they are higher than incomes in communal farming areas of northern Namibia.

1 Write a sentence to explain each of the following terms:
- racial segregation
- land-use zoning
- colonial

2 a Study Figure 8.18. List five words which would best describe Windhoek to someone who could not see this photograph.

b i) In what ways does Windhoek resemble an African city?

ii) How does Windhoek differ from your idea of an African city?

3 Draw a sketch of the site of a city you have studied. Using Figure 8.17 to help you, compare its site with that of Windhoek.

4 a How do the prospects for people living in Katutura differ from those of other residents of Windhoek?

b Explain how these differences came about.

The city is expanding as its population grows. Planning means that industry and housing are zoned in separate areas (Figure 8.21).

However, Windhoek's growth has brought some problems:

- water is a scarce resource and the government are having to plan carefully to keep up with demand especially in a growing area like Windhoek
- unemployment levels are high.

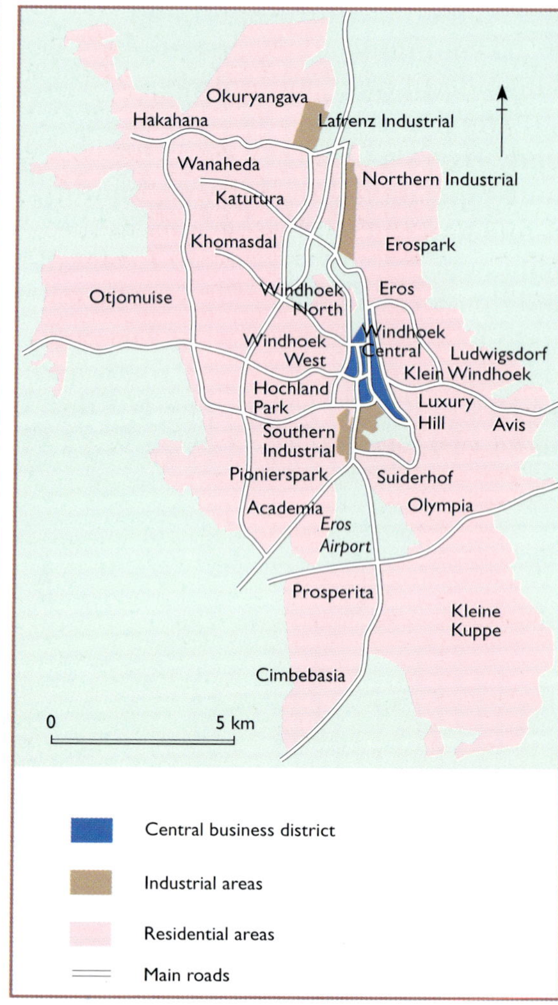

Figure 8.21 Landuse in Windhoek

9 *transport and communications*

Transport development: the Jamuna Bridge Project, Bangladesh

Economic development relies on an efficient transport and communications system. In Bangladesh, road and railway construction is made difficult by the many rivers which criss-cross the landscape and by the low-lying nature of much of the land, especially in the delta area (Figure 9.1). Heavy rainfall and flooding can affect large areas for up to four months each year. The cost of building and maintaining roads and bridges in Bangladesh is amongst the highest in the world.

Figure 9.1 Bangladesh's river system

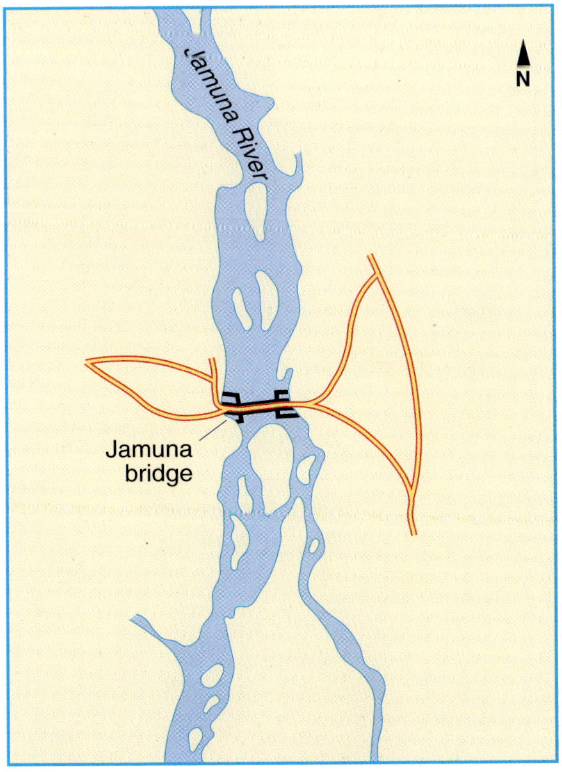

Figure 9.2 The Jamuna bridge

A COUNTRY DIVIDED BY RIVERS

The Jamuna river physically divides Bangladesh into two parts. Two virtually independent railway networks operate, one in the east and another in the west. The river, which can only be crossed by ferry is a major obstacle to overland traffic moving from east to west. Traffic crossing the Jamuna river faces a delay of one to two days before a two to five hour crossing, depending on the season. The Padma river further divides western Bangladesh into north and south.

THE JAMUNA BRIDGE

To help overcome these problems, a bridge is being constructed 100 km north west of Dhaka (Figures 9.2 and 9.3). This is the largest infrastructure project in Bangladesh. When it opens in 1998, the Jamuna Multipurpose Bridge will be the first fixed-transport link between east and west Bangladesh. The bridge will carry road and railway traffic, an electrical power line, a high pressure gas pipeline and telecommunication cables. It will connect people in the north west of Bangladesh with electricity, gas and telecommunication facilities.

The Jamuna is one of the world's largest rivers and has a maximum discharge of about 90 000 m^3 per second. It has two to four channels, which vary their courses from year to year. The total width of the river varies from about 3 km to 15 km between the dry and wet seasons.

Figure 9.3 The site where the bridge is being constructed

This behaviour of the river presented a major challenge to the engineers who designed the bridge. In order to overcome the natural movement of the channels, two very large banks are being built, between which the river will be contained. The bridge, which will be approximately 4.8 km long, will connect the two artificial banks. New approach roads are being constructed across the surrounding **flood plain** on embankments with an average height of 4.5 metres. Raised areas are being built at each end of the bridge, also above maximum water level, to accommodate the toll booths and other bridge end facilities.

The Jamuna Multipurpose Bridge is likely to bring huge benefits in terms of greater mobility of people and resources (Figure 9.4) and should lead to new industrial growth in western Bangladesh.

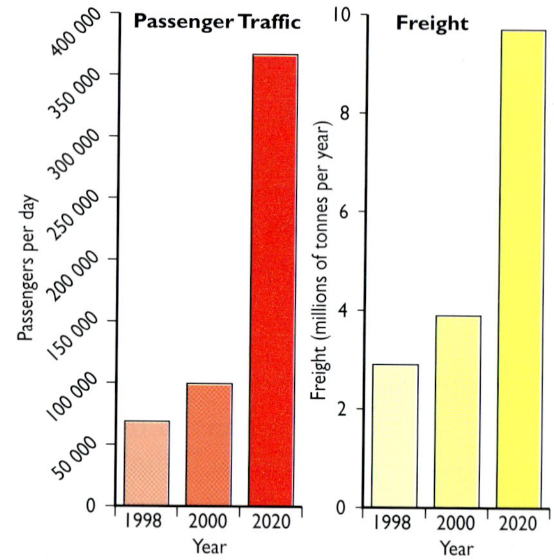

Figure 9.4 Estimated passenger and freight traffic

1 Explain some of the difficulties which engineers face in building roads and railways in Bangladesh.

2 **a** State three ways in which transport and communication links are important to a country's development.

b How important do you think the Jamuna Multipurpose Bridge is to the future of Bangladesh?

3 How have engineers overcome the problem presented by the variation in width of the Jamuna river, according to season?

4 Draw an outline map of Bangladesh.

a Mark onto your outline the Jamuna river, the Padma river and the Meghna river. Add the approximate position of the Jamuna Multipurpose Bridge.

b Using different types of line, include Bangladesh's major roads and railways on your map.

A railway system: Indian Railways

Today, Indian Rail is one of the largest **railway systems** in the world. This is partly because the area of the country is so large. More than 7000 railway stations are spread over a route length of over 60 000 kilometres, and there are some 11 000 locomotives in the fleet (Figure 9.5). The Indian Railway is one of the world's largest single employers, with 1.6 million employees. This is more than the combined population of Birmingham and Manchester!

Figure 9.5 Indian train

COLONIAL ORIGINS

The railway has its origins in the mid-nineteenth century, when India was a British **colony**. The first railway line, covering 34 km from Bombay to Thana, was opened in 1853.

The railways were built by the British, and unlike many other countries at this time, whose railways were built mainly to carry export produce and minerals to the nearest port, they were initially used:

- to help internal and external trade
- for military and strategic reasons in order to be able to rush troops to the borders
- to transport food from surplus to deficit areas in times of famine.

India's railways have greatly contributed to the internal development of the country – accelerating economic, industrial and social development.

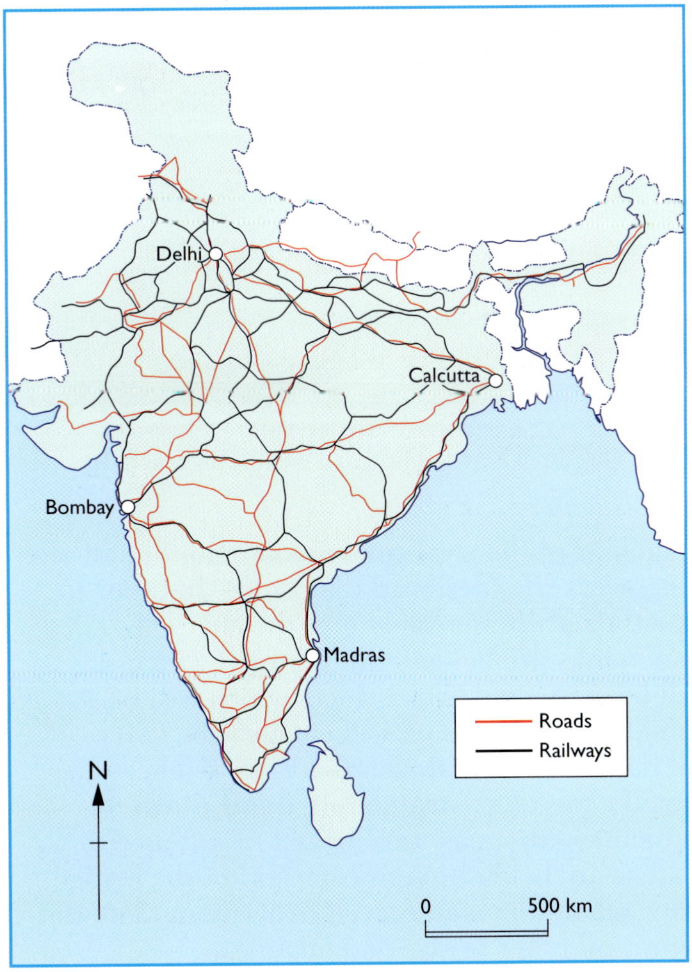

Figure 9.6 Major road and railway networks in India

	1988–89	1989–90	1993–94
Passengers (billion)	3.50	3.65	4.06
Freight (million tonnes)	329	334	362

Figure 9.7 Growth in passenger and freight traffic

THE NETWORK

India's **rail network** has several important characteristics:

- there is no single **route focus** (Figure 9.6)
- most major towns and cities are well served by rail, and across central India railway lines criss-cross each other, providing passengers with choice of route
- there are some areas e.g. the Thar Desert in the west and the Eastern and Western Ghats where the network is less well developed
- there are some **international links**. Routes cross India's borders with Bangladesh and Pakistan.

PASSENGERS AND FREIGHT

The railways in India are an important **mode of transport** for freight and passengers (Figure 9.7). In part this is due to the fact that the network is so extensive and because the railways provide a cheap and efficient means of transport, in both rural and urban areas. Some 11 million people travel by train every day. A variety of freight is handled, including mineral ores, food grain, cement and fertilisers. Rail is ideal for transporting bulky goods like these.

1 Why did the British build railways in India?

2 a Using Figure 9.6, compare the network pattern for major roads with railways in India? Which network is the more complete?

b Now find maps showing the motorway and intercity railway network of the UK. Which is the most complete?

c Suggest reasons for the difference in the relative importance of road and rail between India and the UK?

3 a Using an atlas suggest three reasons why India's rail network is not very well developed in some areas.

b What advantage does rail travel have over road travel in India for freight transport?

4 Draw two line graphs to show the trend in passenger and freight traffic using the figures in Figure 9.7.

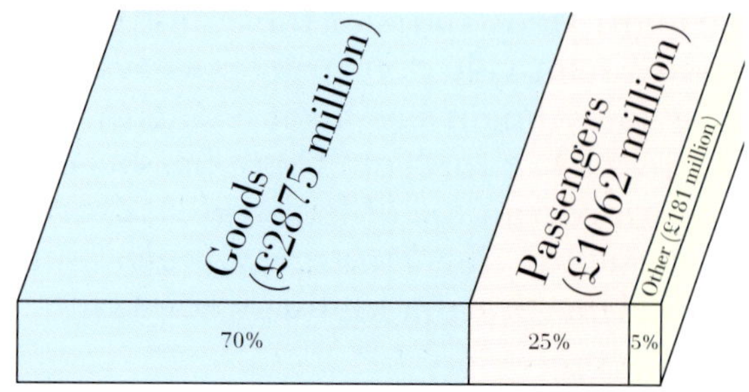

Figure 9.8 Indian railways' earnings 1990

SELF-RELIANT RAILWAY SYSTEM

The rail industry is almost entirely **self-reliant**, importing less than 10 per cent of equipment and parts from abroad. Diesel and electric locomotives, coaches, components and signalling equipment are all manufactured by Indian railways. Britain however maintains strong links with Indian rail – in 1994 British Steel supplied 40 000 tonnes of rail to the Ministry of Railways. The high standard of Indian railway expertise is proven by the fact that India is now helping other developing countries to run or modernise their own railways.

Improving transport: developments in Brazil

Brazil is the fifth largest country in the world. Its huge size means that the cost of transporting people and goods can be high. Many parts of the country have a relatively poor transport system. The government has been trying to address this problem. There has been a major programme of highway construction, the *Transamazonica* and the Belém–Brasilia highway are two examples.

Figure 9.9 New glass bus stop in Curitiba

Figure 9.10 Paraguai–Parana–Plate waterways

Other developments are helping to improve transport in Brazil. Here we will look at three of them:

- Curitiba's integrated public transport system
- an attempt to improve river transport in southern Brazil – the Hidrovia Project
- plans for a South American 'super-highway'.

PUBLIC TRANSPORT IN CURITIBA

Curitiba, a city in southern Brazil, has developed an integrated public transport system:

- passengers can travel from home to work with one ticket, however many buses they need
- minibuses connect the residential areas with the city's twenty bus stations. Passengers transfer to express buses to take them to work or to the shops
- buses travel in special bus lanes
- there are bus stops at 400-metre intervals (Figure 9.9). They provide telephones, newspaper kiosks and post office facilities.

THE HIDROVIA PROJECT

This scheme will allow ocean-going ships to travel 3400 km inland along the rivers Paraguay and Parana (Figure 9.10). Already many farming companies are starting to benefit. The Itamarati company in land-locked Mato Grosso is exporting sugar through the river ports of Caceres and Corumba. Ships, loaded with sugar, travel down the Parana–Paraguai–Plate waterways to Argentina and return with flour.

Figure 9.11 The river Paraguai

Environmental groups are worried that the Hidrovia project will destroy the Pantanal – the world's largest wetland area (Figure 9.13). This huge swamp is a refuge for thousands of species of animals and birds such as the cayman crocodile, jaguar and Jaibiru stork. It has been argued that the Hidrovia scheme will lower the water levels in the Pantanal, so damaging animal and plant habitats.

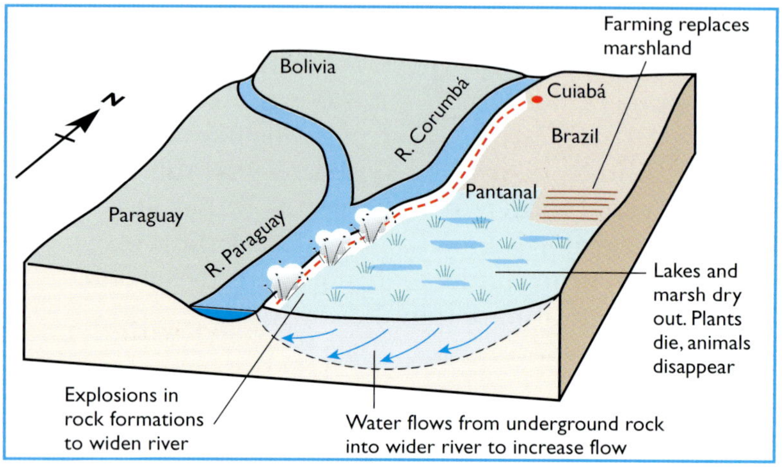

Figure 9.12 Possible impacts of the Hidrovia project on the Pantanal

Figure 9.13 The Pantanal – a rich wildlife reserve

THE PLANNED SOUTH AMERICAN SUPER HIGHWAY

A 2500 km expressway is planned to link the cities of São Paulo and Buenos Aires (Figure 9.14). If it goes ahead, the road which will cost at least US $2.5 billion, will link three countries: Brazil, Uruguay and Argentina.

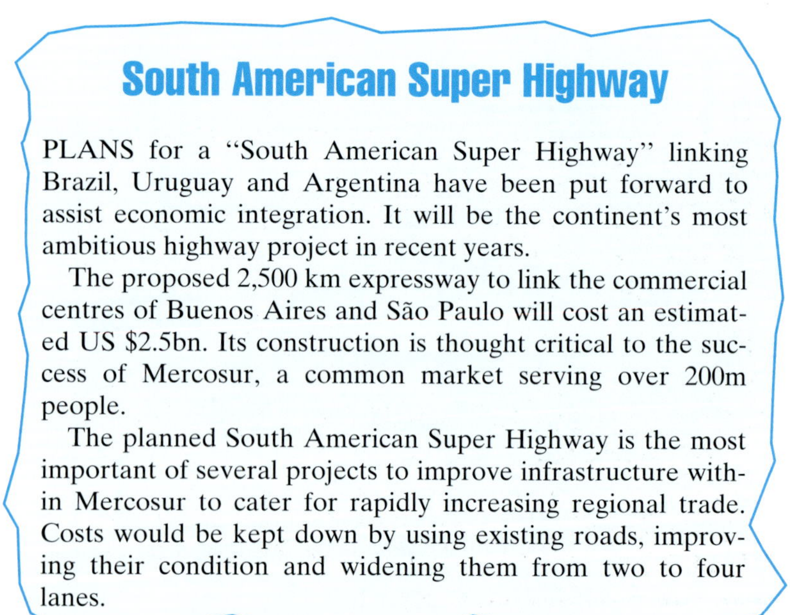

South American Super Highway

PLANS for a "South American Super Highway" linking Brazil, Uruguay and Argentina have been put forward to assist economic integration. It will be the continent's most ambitious highway project in recent years.

The proposed 2,500 km expressway to link the commercial centres of Buenos Aires and São Paulo will cost an estimated US $2.5bn. Its construction is thought critical to the success of Mercosur, a common market serving over 200m people.

The planned South American Super Highway is the most important of several projects to improve infrastructure within Mercosur to cater for rapidly increasing regional trade. Costs would be kept down by using existing roads, improving their condition and widening them from two to four lanes.

Figure 9.14 Reports on the super highway plans

1 Using an atlas, write brief notes about Brazil's rail and road networks. How complete are they? Which regions are covered? Why are the networks not more complete?

2 How has Brazil's size affected the development of transport?

3 Trace a copy of Figure 9.10.
   - **a** Colour in blue the Rivers Paraguai and Parana up to 3400 km away from the coast.
   - **b** Explain why the new waterway system is helping the farmers of Mato Grosso.

4 Write a letter to the Brazilian environment minister explaining how you think the Hidrovia scheme may affect the environment. Should the scheme proceed?

5 **a** Outline three benefits the new South American highway (Figure 9.14) might bring.
   - **b** What economic and political difficulties must be overcome before this project goes ahead?

Hong Kong's new airport

Figure 9.15 A plane landing at Hong Kong's Kai Tak airport

Hong Kong is an important port linking Europe with Asia. Hong Kong is also an **entrepôt**. An entrepôt is a trading centre where goods are imported and re-exported without incurring duty. Trade is at the centre of Hong Kong's success.

The existing Kai Tak Airport, is located in the shadows of skyscrapers close to the city's downtown district (Figure 9.15). Many people feel its location, close to the central business district, presents considerable dangers to the city and risks to its inhabitants. It has also limited the airport's growth – Kai Tak is the world's fourth busiest international airport and the second busiest cargo destination in the world.

BUILDING THE NEW AIRPORT

In 1992 work began on a new airport for Hong Kong. It is being built on the artificially created Chek Lap Kok island just north of Lantau Island (Figure 9.16). This is west of the current site on the densely populated Hong Kong Island. It took over two and a half years, working 24 hours a day, to create the 1214 hectare site. It also required the world's largest fleet of dredgers. The combined excavation and reclamation project was completed by the end of 1995. The task of building and fitting out the airport then began.

Figure 9.16 Hong Kong's new airport and linked developments

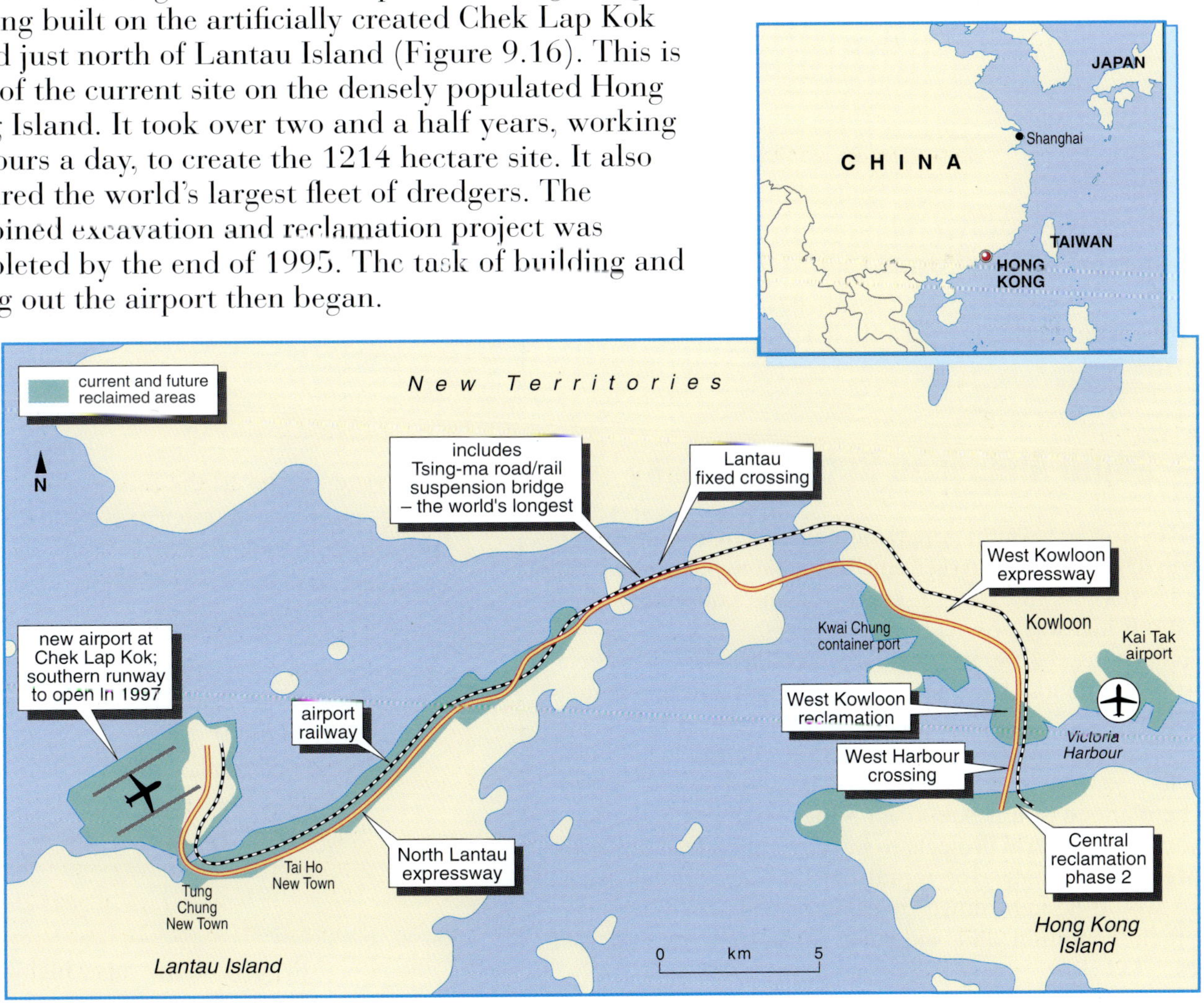

When it opens in April 1998, the new airport will:

- have cost £4.1 billion
- have an annual capacity of 35 million passengers and three million tons of cargo
- operate round the clock (unlike Kai Tak Airport)
- handle up to 40 aircraft movements every hour.

RELATED DEVELOPMENTS

As well as building the airport itself, a number of linked developments are planned as Figure 9.16 shows. Further land reclamation will result in extensions to both Lantau and Hong Kong Islands. There is a £1 billion plan to extend the Lantau container port. Both the airport and the container port are linked to Hong Kong Island and the mainland by a network of bridges, expressways, tunnels, a high speed rail link, a new harbour crossing and a new town.

Victoria harbour, the entrance to Hong Kong, is shrinking rapidly as land reclamation projects gobble up its waters. The whole island is being reshaped as mountains are levelled off to make way for bridges, tunnels, roads and rail links, more offices and housing. Figure 9.18 shows some of the less positive responses to this loss of land.

Figure 9.17 Lantau fixed crossing being built for Chek Lap Kok airport

Figure 9.18 Views on reclaiming land in Victoria Harbour

1 Hong Kong has a successful economy. It is a small island, with very few natural resources of its own. Why has it become so successful? An atlas may help you with this answer.

2 **a** Why are airports so important to modern commercial centres like Hong Kong?
b List four essential locational requirements for a busy modern passenger airport.

3 **a** Explain what the following words mean:
i) reclamation; ii) entrepôt
b Give three reasons why Hong Kong's airport is moving its current location to Chek Lap Kok island?

4 Study the views expressed in Figure 9.18 about reclamation in Victoria Harbour.
a Why do you think that land is being reclaimed?
b Give three arguments against the reclamation scheme.
c Decide whether you think that reclamation is a good idea, then draft a letter to a local newspaper setting out your views on the reclamation of Victoria Harbour.

A game park: Etosha National Park, Namibia

With an area of over 22 000 km^2 (the size of Wales) the Etosha National Park in northern Namibia is one of Africa's finest game parks. The word etosha means 'huge white area'. This refers to the Etosha Pan – a vast salt pan – inside the park (Figures 10.1 and 10.2).

Etosha was created by Friedrich Von Lindequist, the Governor of German South West Africa in 1907. The park is a six hour drive north from the capital city, Windhoek, and is home to a huge range of wildlife (Figure 10.3).

Etosha is very flat. Much of the park is covered by mopane savanna and woodland, with dwarf shrub savanna close to the fringes of the salt pan. Little more than this can grow in the area's extremely dry climate (Figure 10.4). The dry season, between May and October, is the best time to visit Etosha, as the animals congregate at the waterholes around the edge of the pan. It is here that the park's three rest camps are sited – at Halali, Okaukuejo and Namutoni.

Figure 10.1 A waterhole on the fringe of Etosha Salt Pan

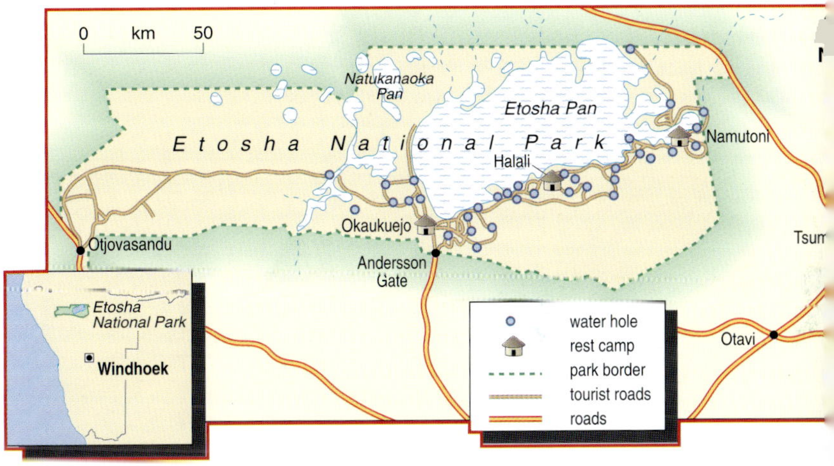

Figure 10.2 Etosha National Park

340 species of bird
114 species of mammal
50 species of snake

Black-faced impala	700	Giraffe	2000
Black rhino	300	Kudu	2000
Burchells zebra	6000	Lion	300
Eland	250	Ostrich	1500
Elephant	1500	Red hartebeest	600
Gemsbok	4000	Wildebeest	2600

Figure 10.3 Etosha's rich stock of animals and birds

WILDLIFE IN ETOSHA

Many tourists visit Etosha to see the 'big five' (elephant, giraffe, lion, leopard and rhinoceros). There are many other species of animal including springbok and gemsbok as well as wildebeest. The number of animals in the park has fluctuated in response to climatic and other factors. A ban on poaching and the drilling of 50 boreholes has increased elephant numbers from just 50 at one point, to around 1500. The number of lions has also increased from 200 to around 300.

ETOSHA PAN	J	F	M	A	M	J	J	A	S	O	N	D
Average temperature (°C)	27	25	24	23	19	16	16	18	23	26	26	26
Rainfall (mm)	76	108	75	26	18	2	0	0	2	8	31	68
Hours of sun per day	8	7	8	9	10	10	10	10	9	9	9	10
Days of rainfall per month	15	13	10	5	1	0	0	0	1	5	9	13

Figure 10.4 Etosha Pan – climate figures

PROBLEMS IN ETOSHA

Three actions of people have had negative effects.

- Fifty waterholes have been constructed to attract wild animals and so improve viewing prospects for visitors. The animals now concentrate around the new waterholes resulting in excessive grazing in their vicinity.
- A fence has been erected along the park's 850 km boundary to control the spread of disease and keep out domestic stock. This has obstructed migration patterns by stopping animals like wildebeest from leaving the park during droughts. This can lead to overgrazing and a consequent reduction in animal numbers: the wildebeest population has declined from 25 000 to 2500 in just 30 years.
- A gravel road network has been developed to improve access.

Figure 10.5 Some of the wildlife found in Etosha

1 Copy and complete the following paragraph:

Etosha is a large _____ park in northern _____. The park is covered by _____ savanna and is named after a large flat _____ pan. Visitors to Etosha can stay in one of the park's _____ rest camps. Most of the game concentrates around the _____ which are south of the Pan. The best time to visit Etosha is between _____ and _____

2 **a** Draw a climate graph using the figures for rainfall and temperature in Figure 10.4.
b Which months are the winter months? Why?

3 Design a poster to attract tourists from Europe and North America to Etosha. Think about the Park's unique selling points, and try to refer to them. Make your poster as attractive as possible, and include some pictures or symbols that you think are relevant.

4 **a** Study Figure 10.2. If you were to build another rest camp for visitors, where would you locate it? Give three reasons for your answer.
b Do you think that a fourth rest camp should be established?
c If you were working for a firm of consultants advising the Government of Namibia, what additional information would you need in order to give them a better answer to part **b** above?

Tourism and the environment: beautiful St Lucia

Over the last few years, the tiny Caribbean island of St Lucia has attracted increasing numbers of tourists. Cruise liners often call into St Lucia on trips around the Caribbean and new hotels mean that more and more visitors are staying on the island. Over a quarter of a million people visited St Lucia in 1995 – the island's population is just 140 000! The increase in the number of tourists is placing a growing burden on the fragile environment of this tiny island.

One area which has been the subject of controversy has been in the south west of St Lucia around the famous Piton mountains (Figure 10.6). In 1987 it was decided that the area around the Pitons should become a National Park so that the special landscape (much of it tropical rainforest), could be protected for the future. But the following year, a decision was made to develop the Jalousie Estate, an old sugar plantation in the middle of this area. A large 5-star luxury hotel complex was planned – complete with tennis courts, swimming pool and cottages for visitors to stay in. This hotel, which is now open, has been the subject of controversy for more than 10 years (Figures 10.8 and 10.9).

Building a large hotel in a rainforest area like this (Figure 10.7) is difficult without changing the environment in many ways:

- some of the rainforest had to be cut down to make way for the new buildings and access roads
- there was a loss of wildlife habitats
- roads needed to be widened
- large quantities of building materials were brought onto the site.

Figure 10.6 The Pitons, a symbol of St Lucia

Figure 10.7 The Jalousie Plantation Hotel under construction

Outrage over plan to defile St Lucia's famous landmark

A plan by overseas investors to use an area surrounding two of St Lucia's most famous landmarks for tourism development, has erupted into a major controversy here. The landmarks in question are the majestic twin Pitons – two cone-shaped mountains in the south western town of Soufrière.

The Pitons have for decades thrilled locals and visitors alike with their breathtaking beauty. There is hardly a visitor in St Lucia who has left the island without seeing them.

But now, a proposal by foreign investors to develop the area is threatening to create deep divisions among St Lucians who are being forced to choose between the jobs that the project promises to bring, and the need to preserve intact, what they consider to be part of their natural heritage. St Lucia's acclaimed playwright Derek Walcott has publicly threatened to do whatever it takes, to stop any developer from tampering with the Pitons.

The main proposal is to set up a 120 room hotel complex with sporting facilities, a health spa and docking facilities for yachts. The project has attracted criticism from those who argue that it will have a negative impact on the environment, lying as it does smack between the two Pitons.

Several protesters claim that bulldozers crushed archaeological artifacts while they were preparing the site. The development also drew opposition because of the government's failure to heed a recommendation by the Organisation of American States (OAS), that the area should be converted into a National Park.

Figure 10.8 Protest against development around the Pitons

There are concerns too that the many extra people who visit this area each year to stay in the hotel, will also damage the environment.

Deciding how to manage the growth in the number of visitors to St Lucia is a difficult problem. The government wants tourists to visit the island because of the money they bring, but they also need to protect the fragile environment, which is the reason why many tourists visit the island in the first place.

1 What benefits does tourism have for a small island like St Lucia?

2 What views do you think the following groups would hold about the hotel development at Jalousie?
- Government of St Lucia
- St Lucia National Trust
- St Lucia Tourist Board
- Soufrière Development Council

For each group, give a reason to explain your answer.

3 Look at the Pitons landscape shown in Figure 10.6 and read the Prime Minister's comments in Figure 10.9 about the way St Lucians value the Pitons. Do you think that this area should be used for tourism?

4 **a** Why have some people and groups objected to the development? The newspaper article in Figure 10.8 may provide some clues.

b What advice would you give to the government of St Lucia about how they should manage the growth of tourism in the future? Should the number of visitors be controlled in any way, or encouraged to grow?

'The Government is committed to preserving the Pitons Valley as an area of outstanding national landscape beauty. We are all aware that the Pitons are our national symbol. We will not permit any degradation of the quality of these landmarks. The approach taken to develop this area is one which recognises that it is possible for development and for conservation to co-exist and to be pursued in a harmonious manner.'

Figure 10.9 Prime Minister John Compton's views on developing the Pitons

Developing tourism: opportunities and constraints in Brazil

In recent years Brazil has become more popular as a holiday destination. It has many attractions for visitors (Figure 10.10) and travel companies often describe the country as a tropical paradise.

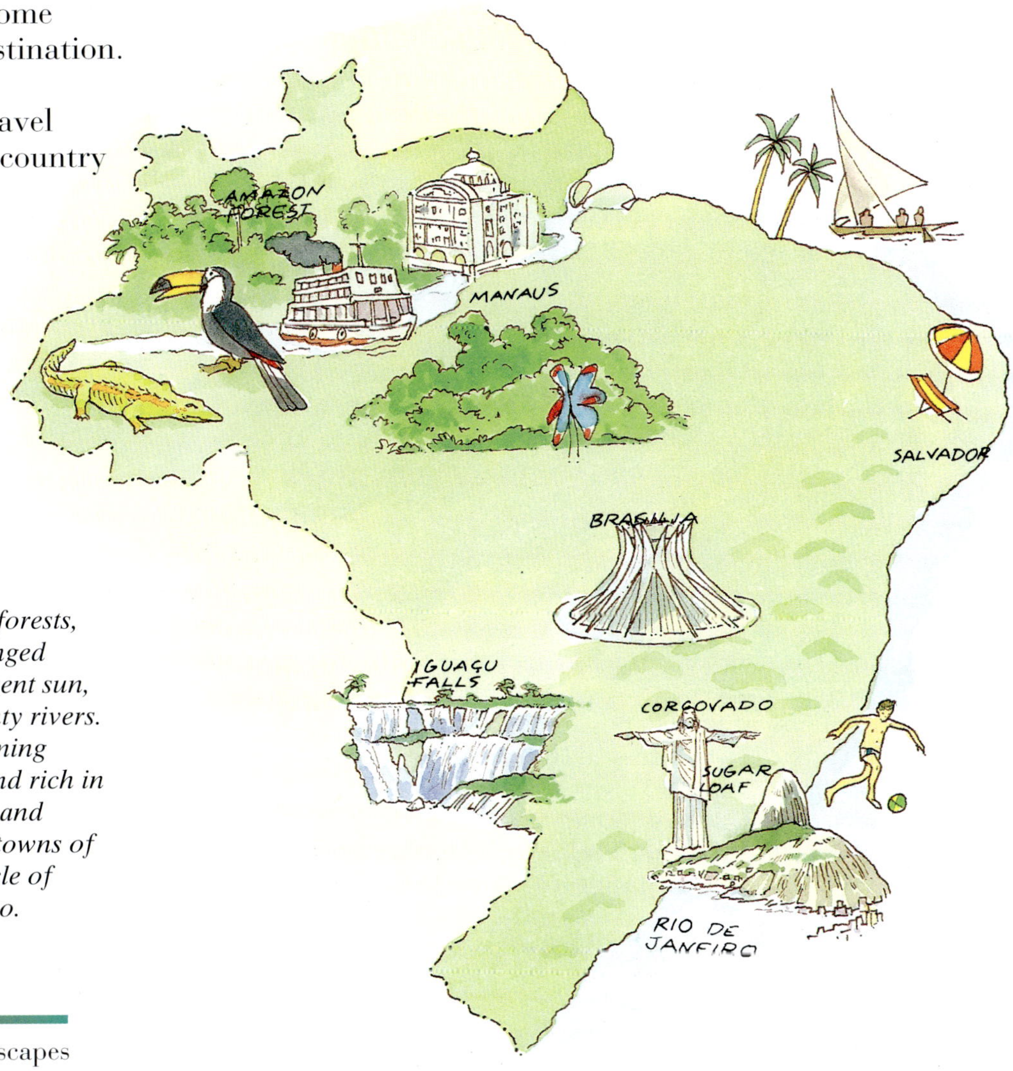

Brazil

A paradise with lush tropical forests, bleached white beaches fringed by coconut palms, an ever present sun, magnificent waterfalls and mighty rivers. Forests and grasslands teeming with wildlife, combine with a land rich in popular traditions of song and dance, from the quiet colonial towns of Minas Gerais to the spectacle of carnival in Rio de Janeiro.

Figure 10.10 Brazil's tourist landscapes

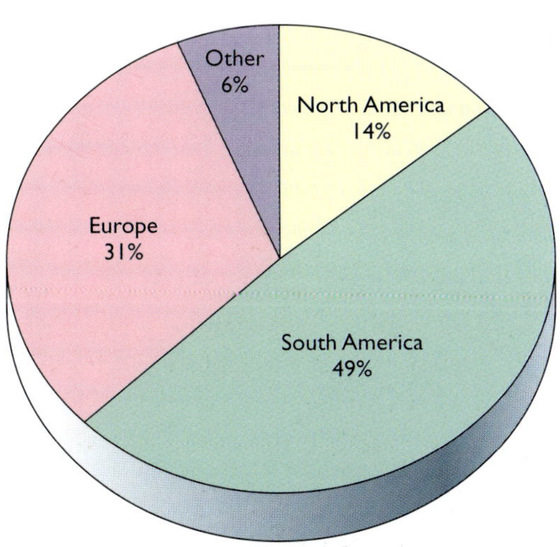

Figure 10.11 Origins of Brazil's tourists, 1995

Despite the many real or possible attractions, there are problems with developing the tourist industry in a country like Brazil. The natural landscapes of mountains, beaches, forests and waterfalls are spread throughout the size of an area greater than Europe and are often difficult to reach. People can spend two or three weeks travelling around Brazil, and still see only a few of the tourist attractions and places of interest.

1 Study Figure 10.11. Explain the relatively high numbers of tourists coming from:
i) South America
ii) Europe
Use an atlas to help if necessary.

2 A government organisation called EMBRATUR encourages tourists to visit Brazil. Imagine you are the director of a travel company and have received the map, graphs and photographs from EMBRATUR (Figures 10.12 to 10.14). These are to help you plan a two week holiday to Brazil. You are aiming to attract tourists who want to:

- see attractive scenery
- spend time on the beach
- visit Carnival in Rio

a With a partner, use the map of Brazil to plan a two week itinerary for the tour. Study all the information and pay particular attention to the weather for the south east region, popular holiday periods and the location of the main sights. All travel within Brazil will be by air.

Produce a report which will include:

i) a labelled map of the tour route starting from Rio de Janeiro. Draw a line to show your air routes between the sights and places you will visit.

ii) a schedule for the 14 days. State the exact time of year you have chosen with dates. The example below shows how to do this.

Day	Destination	Activity
1 (15 Feb)	Heathrow – Rio de Janeiro	Book into hotel
2 (16 Feb)	Rio de Janeiro	Visit to beach and Sugar Loaf Mountain

b If your holiday was planned for people concerned about the environment, which places would you visit?

c Find a travel brochure from a company which organises Brazilian holidays and see if your holiday plan is similar.

3 Write a letter to EMBRATUR explaining what you think are the good and bad points of tourists visiting Brazil. Use information from other pages in this book to help you.

Figure 10.12 Brazil's tourist areas

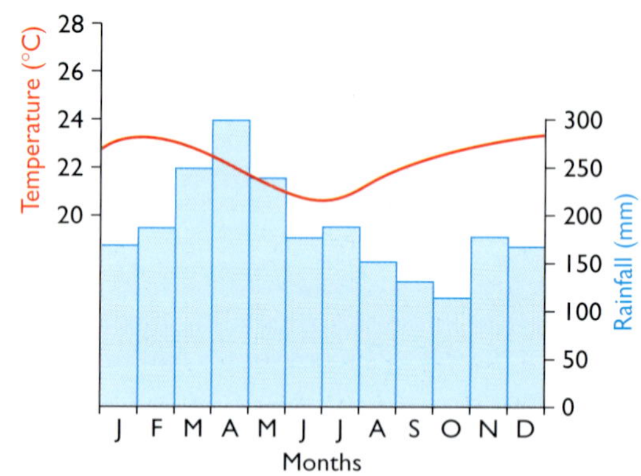

Figure 10.13 Climate graph for south east Brazil

Figure 10.14 Tourism in Brazil

Aid from Britain: the Overseas Development Administration

Bilateral aid is given by the government of a donor country (usually industrialised) directly to the government of an aid recipient country (usually an LEDC).

Multilateral aid is given by the government of a donor country to international institutions which work to support development in the LEDCs e.g. The World Bank, The Asian Development Bank, The United Nations. Contributions are pooled together and paid out to LEDCs to finance specific projects or activities.

Figure 11.1 Types of aid

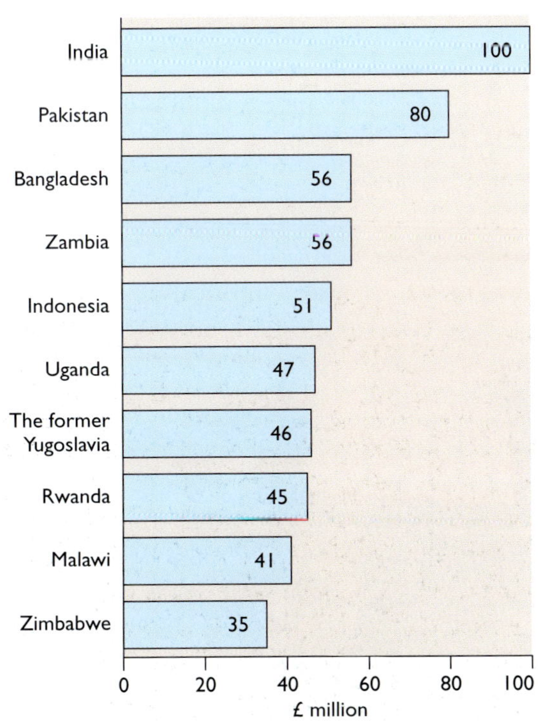

Figure 11.2 Countries receiving the most aid from Britain

The world's more economically developed countries (MEDCs) assist less economically developed countries (LEDCs) by many different means, one of which is **aid**. Official foreign aid is given to LEDCs by Governments worldwide and by multinational donor agencies. Aid is normally **bilateral** or **multilateral** (Figure 11.1).

Britain's official aid programme is administered by the Overseas Development Administration (ODA), the aid wing of the Foreign and Commonwealth Office. Aid is given to over 150 countries. The programme is the fifth largest in the world. Britain divides its aid fairly evenly between bilateral and multilateral aid. The major recipients are shown in Figure 11.2.

The aim of the ODA's overseas aid programme is to 'improve the quality of life of people in poorer countries by contributing to sustainable development and reducing poverty and suffering'.

Aid from Britain takes many different forms:

- projects to improve water and power supplies, build roads and bridges, or improve health and education
- money to buy essential materials like fertiliser and seeds, or equipment such as tools and vehicles
- technical assistance to help people develop skills, or to help countries develop their institutions
- emergency aid for refugees and the victims of disasters such as wars, floods or earthquakes.

1 **a** What are the two main types of government aid to developing countries?
   b Name three organisations through which multilateral aid is provided.

2 On an outline map of the world mark the ten countries which receive most British aid. Use the data in Figure 11.2. In which continents are most of these countries located?

3 Why do you think that no country in Central or South America is on the list?

4 Four different forms of aid are listed. In small groups discuss the advantages and disadvantages of each type. Try to rank them according to how important they are.

A Non-Governmental Organisation: Save the Children

Save the Children is a British **non-Governmental Organisation** (NGO) operating in many countries (Figure 11.3). It was founded in 1919 and has grown massively since then. In 1994–95 it spent more than £91 million.

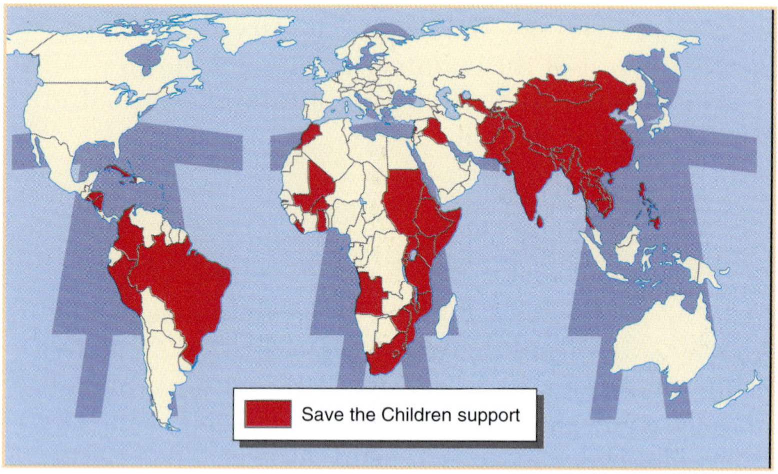

Figure 11.3 Countries where Save the Children is supporting projects

SAVE THE CHILDREN IN INDIA

Save the Children's work in India started in 1935 following the Baluchistan earthquake, and later provided emergency aid to victims of the Bengal Famine in 1943. Today, the India programme concentrates on:

- supporting work in remote areas and urban slums
- assisting people from ethnic minorities
- working with low caste groups, landless migrants and refugees.

Much of the money spent by Save the Children India is channelled through a network of Indian NGOs. One of these is Bhuvaneshwari Mahila Ashram (BMA). The BMA rural development programme works to improve the living conditions of communities in the remote hilly areas of Uttar Pradesh. Communities are helped to identify their own problems and then find appropriate solutions. The special needs of women are particularly emphasised. BMA carries out training in health education and farming techniques. It also trains pre-school teachers and supports the government's adult literacy programme. BMA-trained workers support local health services including mother and child health care, immunisation and health education.

NON GOVERNMENTAL ORGANISATIONS
Unofficial aid is provided by Non Governmental Organisations or NGOs. These organisations, most of which are charities, operate at 'grassroots level' often focusing on primary health care, basic literacy and education, clean water and family planning.

1 What advantages do organisations like Save the Children have, when providing aid, compared with governments?
2 Explain the following terms:
   - grassroots level
   - immunisation programme.
3 Save the Children spends 1 penny out of every pound on information and education. Why do you think these things are important to such organisations?
4 What is the main focus of Save the Children's work in India?
5 Why do you think that NGOs often focus attention on primary health care, sanitation and education?

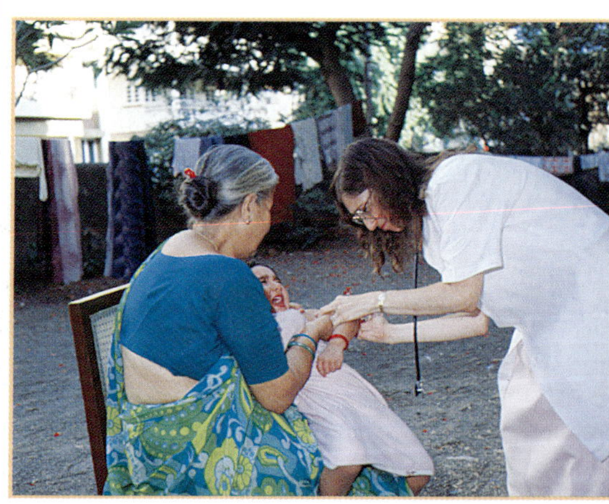

Figure 11.4 Save the Children project in India

A water development project: Sri Lanka's Victoria Dam

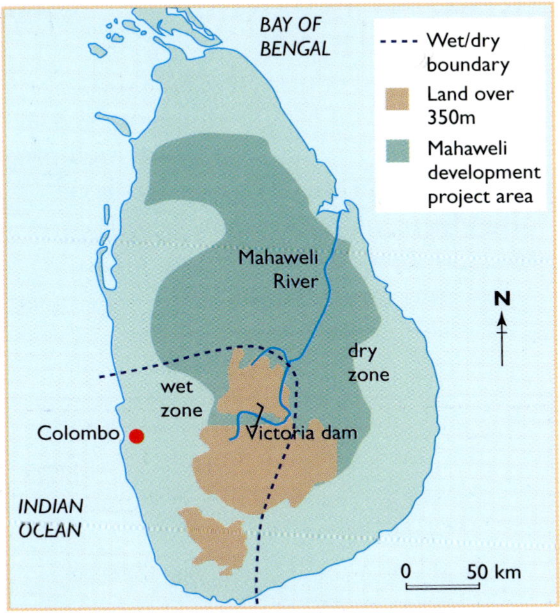

Figure 11.5 Sri-Lanka's wet and dry zones

Figure 11.6 The Victoria dam

Sri Lanka can be divided into two main geographical regions (Figure 11.5). The Wet Zone in the south west, receives over 2000 mm of rainfall per year and includes the hilly region famous for its tea plantations. All Sri Lanka's major rivers originate in this region, including its longest river, the Mahaweli. The Dry Zone which covers the rest of the country, has a much shorter rainy season with less than 1000 mm of rainfall. Agriculture here relies on irrigation.

THE ACCELERATED MAHAWELI DEVELOPMENT PROJECT (AMDP)

In 1970, Sri Lanka embarked on an ambitious project to transfer water from the Wet Zone to the Dry Zone. By using water from the River Mahaweli, the government planned to irrigate 175 360 hectares of land in the Dry Zone, and hence increase rice production. The project would also produce hydro-electricity. The AMDP required channels, dams, reservoirs and hydro-electricity stations to be built (Figure 11.7).

One of the three dams built along the Mahaweli River was the Victoria Dam (Figure 11.6). The British government put £100 million towards the project.

The Victoria Dam:

- is 122 m high and 520 m long
- cost £250 million to build
- was designed to provide water for irrigation and includes a hydro-electricity generating station with 210 MW capacity
- provides 20 per cent of Sri Lanka's electricity.

Despite local protests the dams were built, and the AMDP is now almost complete. The areas which receive irrigation water under the AMDP now provide 16 per cent of the country's rice. The three dams in the scheme produce 66 per cent of the country's electricity needs and have enabled the government to develop industries in Sri Lanka.

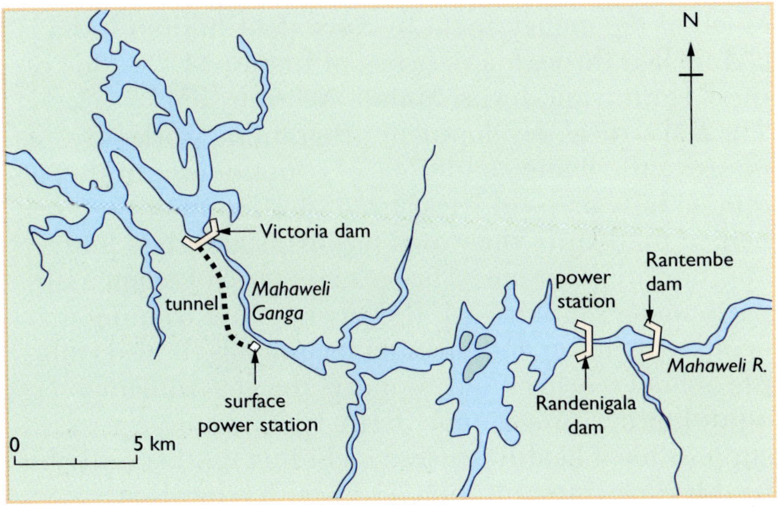

Figure 11.7 The Accelerated Mahaweli Development Project

Although the AMDP is regarded as a success by the government and by aid donors, the scheme was not without its costs:

- the reservoir behind the Victoria Dam flooded 3230 hectares of the Dumbara Valley and has inundated six towns, 123 villages, and 400 hectares of fertile land
- 6000 families had to be resettled
- Sri Lanka's national debt has increased
- wildlife habitats (including over 100 000 hectares of rainforest) have been destroyed
- 1.5 million people have been resettled.

In the last 15 years, there has been much concern about the impacts of large dam projects such as the AMDP in Sri Lanka and Narmada Scheme in India. Most countries and international organisations no longer give aid for such projects.

Figure 11.8 Rice cultivation in the newly irrigated lands

Positive	Negative
Electricity is generated	Destruction of wildlife habitats
Increased irrigation capacity	Displacement of people
Control of flooding	Increase in health hazards e.g. diseases such as hepatitis and malaria
Jobs are created	Poor economic returns and increased debt
National prestige and political credibility	Political instability and protest

Figure 11.9 Positive and negative impacts of large scale dam projects

	Pla[illegible] Total
Irrigable area (ha)	175 360
Farmer families settled	74 253
Schools	272
Health centres	112
Post offices	85
Banks	35
Wells	17 351
Roads (km)	3632

Figure 11.10 Main characteristics of the Mahaweli Development Project

1 **a** What was the main barrier to agriculture in Sri Lanka before the Mahaweli Development Project was started?
  b What other benefits has the project had?

2 List five ways in which increasing the production of hydro-electricity can benefit a poor country such as Sri Lanka.

3 What view of the AMDP do you think each of the following people would have?
- Minister of Agriculture
- Farmer who has lost fertile rice fields in the Dumbara Valley
- Teenager whose family has been resettled in the AMDP from a small town.

4 British consultants and companies have earned £150 million from the AMDP in orders and contracts. What do you think are the links between aid and trade? What benefits do developing countries get from aid? What are the advantages to the donors of giving aid?

5 Make a copy of the table in Figure 11.9. Use the table to evaluate the Accelerated Mahaweli Development Project. Tick each item on the list which applies to the AMDP. Give details, such as numbers, where you can.

Trade and investment: India and the UK

Figure 11.11 India exports clothes to the UK

India is the world's seventh largest industrial economy. With a population of nearly 900 million, and a growing middle class, India has a huge number of potential consumers.

Until 1991, India protected her domestic industry by imposing **tariffs** and **quotas** on all imported goods. In 1991 many of these restrictions were removed. Today, only 5 per cent of imports are restricted, and tariffs for many products are now much lower than in the past. Foreign investment is also welcomed.

IMPORTS AND EXPORTS

Britain is one of India's principal trading partners (Figure 11.11), accounting for about 6 per cent of total trade. The UK's main exports to India are machinery and equipment (often as part of an aid package for major development projects) and minerals. The UK's main imports from India include clothing, yarn and shoes (Figure 11.12). The value of trade between India and the UK now exceeds £3000 million each year.

UK exports to India

	1995
Electrical Machinery	72.0
General Industrial Machinery	111.4
Iron & Steel	57.1
Non-Metallic Minerals	556.0
Power Generating Equipment	123.4
Scientific Equipment	60.3
Specialised Industrial Machinery	104.4
Transport Equipment	117.9
TOTAL	**1682.7**

UK imports from India

	1995
Apparel & Clothing	317.1
Footwear	82.9
Leather Products	15.8
Metal Manufactures	71.2
Miscellaneous Articles	91.6
Non-Metallic Minerals	28.8
Power Generating Equipment	56.0
Tea, Cocoa, Spices etc.	41.6
Textile Yarn/Fabrics	286.5
TOTAL	**1435.5**

Figure 11.12 UK trade with India, 1995

UK INVESTMENT IN INDIA

With the opening up of the economy (Figure 11.13), India is being targeted by many overseas companies as a market and as a manufacturing base. Foreign companies are being encouraged to enter joint ventures with Indian companies, especially where 'technology transfer' is likely.

Many UK companies are now investing in India and are involved in economic activities ranging from construction to retailing, from chemicals to banking and financial services. The UK, with over £2 billion invested, is the largest foreign investor in India.

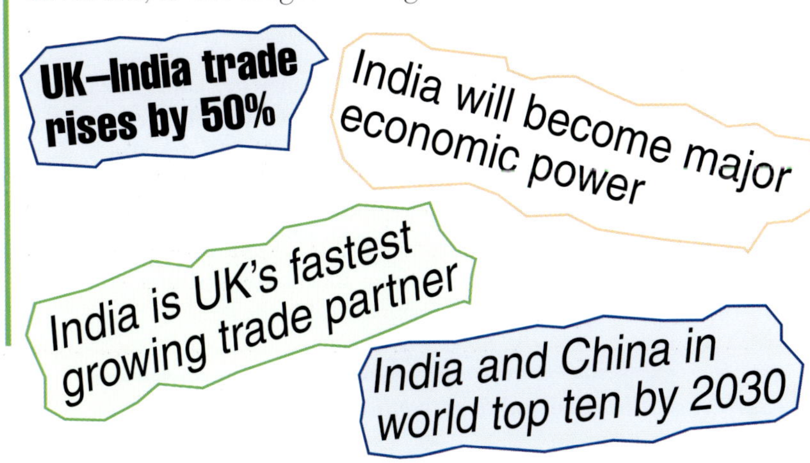

Figure 11.13 India's future prospects

CASE STUDY: LITTLEWOODS

In the next five years, the UK retailer Littlewoods plans to open 50 new stores across India. Most (95 per cent) of the products sold in the Littlewoods stores in India will be sourced locally.

Littlewoods opened its first Indian store in Bangalore in March 1996, followed by stores in New Delhi and Madras. They sell a range of clothing, toiletries and household textiles, a combination of Western style goods and items geared to the local market. The Bangalore store employs 50 people with senior staff coming to the UK for training. Bangalore was chosen as the first site because of its relatively large middle class population and because many people are credit card holders.

1 **a** Use Figure 11.12 to identify:
   i) the three most important UK exports to India
   ii) the three most important UK imports from India

   b Does India have trade surplus with the UK or a deficit?

2 Copy and complete the following sentences. Use all the information on these two pages to help you.
- India is attractive to overseas investors because . . .
- The Indian government are keen to attract industries where there is a likelihood of technology transfer because . . .
- Tariffs and quotas restrict trade between countries because they . . .

3 Why are many UK Companies investing in India? Include examples in your answer – referring to Littlewoods and to the Hilton Hotel Group.

4 Choose one of the newspaper headlines in Figure 11.13 and write a short article to accompany it, outlining why India has become more attractive to overseas investors.

5 RESEARCH ACTIVITY
Choose one of the companies named in Figure 11.14, and find out about its overseas operations. You could either write to the company and ask questions about its investment overseas, or find a copy of its annual report (perhaps in your local Reference Library). Do they give any details about the size of their investment in India? What do they plan to do there?

ANZ Grindlays	ICI
BAT	Lucas
BOC	Rolls Royce
Boots	Smithkline Beecham
Cadbury Schweppes	Standard Chartered
Coats Viyella	Unilever
GEC Alsthom	
Glaxo	

Figure 11.14 UK companies with a significant presence in India

Figure 11.15 India is now attracting large companies from many countries

CASE STUDY: HILTON INTERNATIONAL

Hilton International, the hotel group, is investing in India. In 1995 the company signed an agreement with Bharat Hotels of India to manage a hotel in New Delhi. Hilton plans to manage two more Indian hotels, in Bombay and Goa, by 1998. The Hilton Group is expanding into India because it is one of the world's fastest growing economies and because travel and tourism within India is forecast to grow at 15 per cent a year.

Trading blocs: NAFTA

The North American Free Trade Agreement (NAFTA) between the US, Canada and Mexico came into effect at the start of 1994, creating one of the largest **free trade zones** in the world (Figure 11.16). It is the first such agreement to join rich and poor countries (LEDCs and MEDCs).

NAFTA is an agreement to phase out restrictions on the movement of goods, services and capital between the three countries by the year 2010. It has created a market of some 380 million people (Figure 11.17). Its aims include:

- eliminating trade barriers
- promoting economic competition
- increasing investment
- improving trade between the US, Canada and Mexico.

Until 1982 Mexico followed a policy of government sponsored industrialisation based upon import substitution industries (ISIs). However, financial crises in the 1970s and 1980s forced the Mexican government to seek aid from the US, the World Bank and the International Monetary Fund (IMF). Aid was provided, but Mexico was instructed to rearrange its economy along free-market lines. The government agreed to do this, partly because they needed the aid, and partly in fear of being ignored by the US. Mexico hoped that joining NAFTA would increase economic growth and employment levels, and that it would take off as a Newly Industrialising Country.

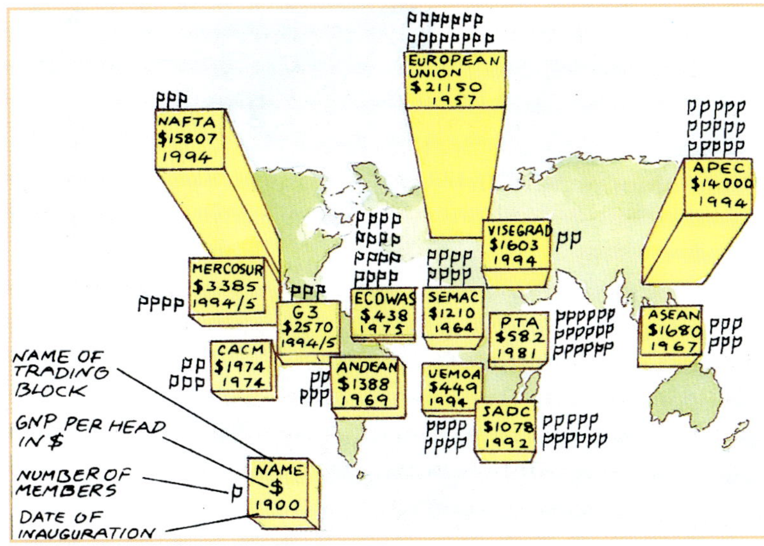

Figure 11.16 The world's major trading blocs

Figure 11.17 The North American Free Trade Association (NAFTA)

Country	Manufacturing	Textiles	Electronics
Mexico	1.40	1.27	1.04
US	10.80	9.74	14.31
Canada	12.30	11.23	13.99

Figure 11.18 Hourly industrial wage rates in NAFTA (US $)

However, there has been opposition to NAFTA. Critics argue that it will not necessarily bring economic growth. In Canada many small firms have closed due to competition with lower cost US firms – some companies have even moved to the US; in addition, mergers and takeovers have caused unemployment.

With respect to Mexico, the main concerns are that:

- US industries will move to Mexico to take advantage of its very cheap labour (Figure 11.18), so creating unemployment in the US
- up to 15 million farmers will be affected by the removal of subsidies, decline in communal ownership of the land and the removal of border restrictions on trade. US and Canadian grain producers will dump their surpluses in Mexico, forcing Mexican peasants out of agriculture.

According to NAFTA, Mexico's rural areas will become export orientated: industrial and service growth will replace agriculture. However, where there has already been growth its value has been questioned. Along the US–Mexican border there are about 2000 US-owned, labour-intensive, export-orientated assembly plants or *maquiladoras* (see Unit 6, page 48–49), employing about 500 000 Mexican labourers. Many of the workers are children, wages are low and working conditions unsafe. Critics argue that Mexico could be exploited even more for its huge ultra-cheap labour supply.

Environmentalists point to Mexico's poor record of enforcing environmental laws. The country's rivers and air (especially in urban areas) are already heavily polluted. They fear that Mexico may in addition become a dumping ground for hazardous materials.

1 Study Figure 11.16.
   a Which are the world's most important trading blocs?
   b In what ways does NAFTA differ from other trading blocs such as the European Union? Why is this important?
   c Find out a little more about one of the trading blocs shown on the map (other than NAFTA).

2 Using an atlas and Figure 11.17, compare and contrast the US, Canada and Mexico in terms of:
- population characteristics, such as birth rate and death rates
- size of markets
- standards of living
- employment structure.

3 Who are likely to be the main winners and losers as a result of NAFTA? Explain your answer.

4 How do wage rates vary in NAFTA's three member states (Figure 11.18)? What impact might these differences have for Mexico within NAFTA?

5 Briefly explain how NAFTA may effect Mexico's natural environment.

6 Chihuahua is a state on Mexico's US border. Study the advertisement in Figure 11.19.
   a What is the advertisement trying to achieve?
   b List four aspects of the state that Chihuahua is trying to sell to companies.
   c What does the advertisement claim in particular about the advantages for Chihuahua of NAFTA?

Figure 11.19 Come and locate in Chihuahua

Development strategies: what is best for India?

When India gained its Independence in 1947 it was a very poor country: infant mortality rates were high, life expectancy was less than 30 years, and only 30 per cent of the population were literate.

In 1996, India is still among the world's poorest countries. It has a low Human Development Index (see Unit 1, page 7) and a low per capita income. Despite India's huge economy, nearly three-quarters of the population live in rural areas and are largely unaffected by industrialisation and development.

THE NARMADA SCHEME

- Over 20 million people live in the valley
- Electricity and water will be provided by the scheme

BUT

- Over 1 million people will have to move to make way for the scheme
- Over 24 000 hectares of forests will be destroyed
- Construction will lead to widespread environmental destruction
- 144 000 hectares of land and over 570 villages will be flooded

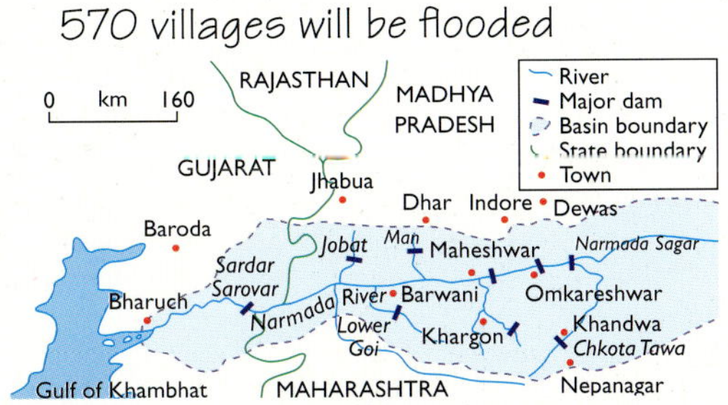

Figure 12.2 Large scale development: the Narmada Scheme

DEVELOPMENT IN INDIA

The main political leaders at the time of India's Independence were Gandhi and Nehru. Each leader favoured a contrasting approach to development (Figure 12.1). Gandhi favoured development that was centred in rural villages and would create self-sufficiency in food, clothing and housing.

small-scale development	village-centred	self-sufficiency in food, clothing and housing
large-scale development	nationally focused	growth in the economy and the volume of exports

Figure 12.1 Different types of development

By contrast, Nehru believed in national and industrial growth. As Prime Minister from 1947, Nehru was responsible for a series of Five Year Plans designed to enable India to pursue a policy of **large-scale industrial development**. India now has one of the world's largest economies and a skilled labour force that is second in size only to the US. This policy has been supported by several large development projects which are funded by international donors, like the Narmada Dam Project (Figures 12.2 and 12.3).

Nehru believed that the benefits of growth would **trickle down** to rural areas. Increased demand from the industrial workforce for agricultural products would stimulate rural areas. This did not occur. From the 1970s a series of Rural Development Programmes, Food for Work Programmes and a **National Minimum Needs Programme** tried to improve the standards of living among the poor, especially those in rural areas.

In some cases development projects have been planned and organised by the rural communities themselves. These projects are more **appropriate** as they take into account the needs, ideas and resources of the people.

Figure 12.3 The Narmada Dam Project

1 Look back to the statistics in Unit 2, page 12 and Unit 11, page 84. Make two lists: i) statistics which support the idea that India has developed; and ii) statistics which show that India is still a less economically developed country.

2 **a** Copy Figure 12.1. Extend the table by adding the name of the politician who favoured each type of development.
b Contrast the different views of Gandhi and Nehru about development in India.

3 What do you think are the advantages and disadvantages of large development projects like the Narmada Dam Project (Figures 12.2 and 12.3) for an LEDC like India?

4 **a** Briefly describe how Gandhi's view of development would have benefited the rural population.
b How was it thought that the benefits of development would 'trickle down' to rural areas?

5 What is meant by large-scale industrial development? Give an example from India, or another LEDC you have studied, to illustrate your answer.

The government is trying to modernise the economy by attracting foreign investment. Although it has been quite successful (see Unit 11, pages 84–5) there has been little development for the poor. The education system is still very undeveloped, especially in rural areas: on average most Indians spend just two and a half years at school! Secondly, child labour is widespread. As many as 55 million children work between 14 and 16 hours a day, in hazardous conditions for minimal wages.

Figure 12.4 Child labour is one of the less attractive aspects of India's development

Environmental improvement: cleaning up Guanabara Bay

A Portuguese visitor to Rio de Janeiro in 1553 wrote 'what can be said about her is that all is beauty.' Sadly, this can no longer be said about Guanabara Bay. This huge natural harbour where whales once used to give birth to their young has become heavily polluted since the 1960s with a cocktail of oil, chemicals and sewage. Guanabara Bay (Figure 12.6) covers 300 km^2 and is an estuary where the salt water of the sea mixes with the fresh water of the 35 rivers flowing into it. Just over 7 million people live around the bay in the densely populated urban area of Rio de Janeiro. They have played a major part in polluting the waters of the bay. Figure 12.8 shows the main source of pollution.

Figure 12.6 Guanabara Bay, Rio de Janeiro

Figure 12.5 A variety of domestic and industrial waste makes its way into the Bay

BRINGING LIFE BACK TO THE BAY

To reduce the high levels of pollution in Guanabara Bay, a plan has been launched by the government of Rio de Janeiro state. This plan, will affect most of the built-up area around the bay. The estimated cost of the scheme is US $793 million. Part of this money has been provided by the Japanese government and the Inter-American Development Bank.

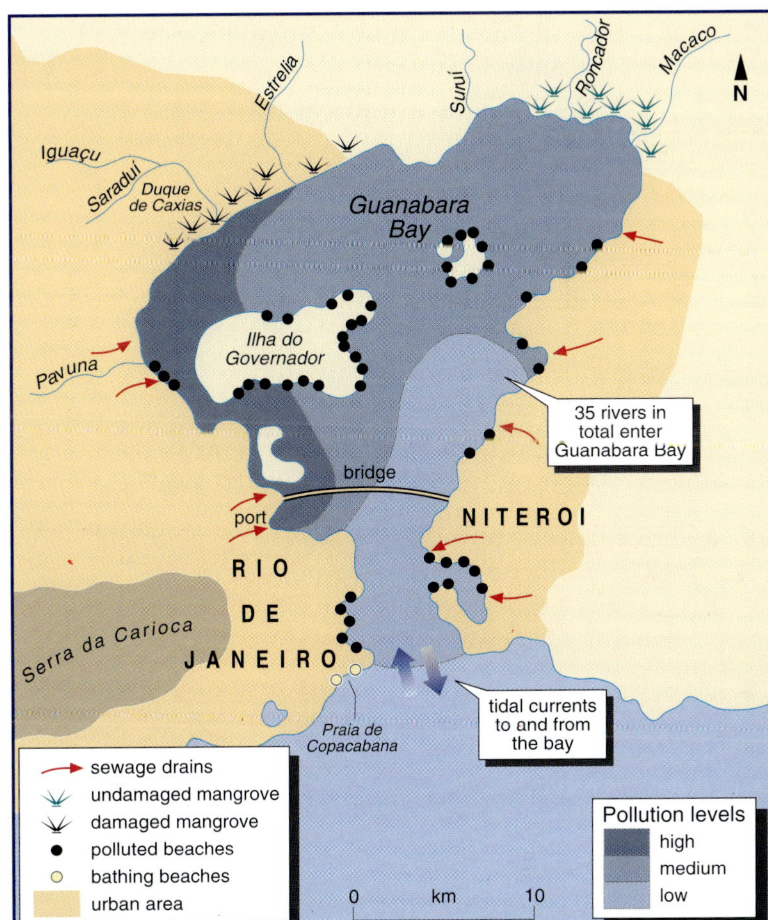

Figure 12.7 Pollution levels in Guanabara Bay

	Source of Pollution	Amount
1.	6000 factories	80% of pollution from 52 factories
2.	Duque De Caxias Oil refinery	1.5 tonnes of oil per day
3.	Port of Rio	2.3 tonnes of oil per day
4.	Sewers	17.5 million m^3 of sewage per day

Figure 12.8 Main sources of pollution in Guanabara Bay

Most of Rio's population do not have proper sewage disposal methods and it was decided that a programme of basic sanitation was essential for health reasons. This will help to reduce the amount of raw sewage which finds its way into the bay and will improve health. In Rio de Janeiro half the hospital beds are filled by people with diseases caused by contaminated water. Controls on industrial pollution are also being introduced. Some projects such as the re-planting of mangroves (Figure 12.9) will improve the appearance of the fringes of the bay as well as helping to improve water quality.

Figure 12.9 Replanting of mangroves

1 Use Figure 12.7 to describe where in Guanabara Bay you would find:
i) the highest levels and ii) the lowest levels of pollution

2 a Using Figure 12.8 to help you, make a list of the different kinds of pollutant which may be found in Guanabara Bay. For each one, state whether it is likely to have been produced by houses, industry or the Port of Rio de Janeiro.

b Try to explain why pollution levels vary in different parts of Guanabara Bay.

3 Study Figure 12.10.
Copy the diagram and complete the empty boxes to show the likely results of the depollution scheme on plants and animals living in Guanabara Bay.

Figure 12.10 How cleaning up the bay will affect plants and animals

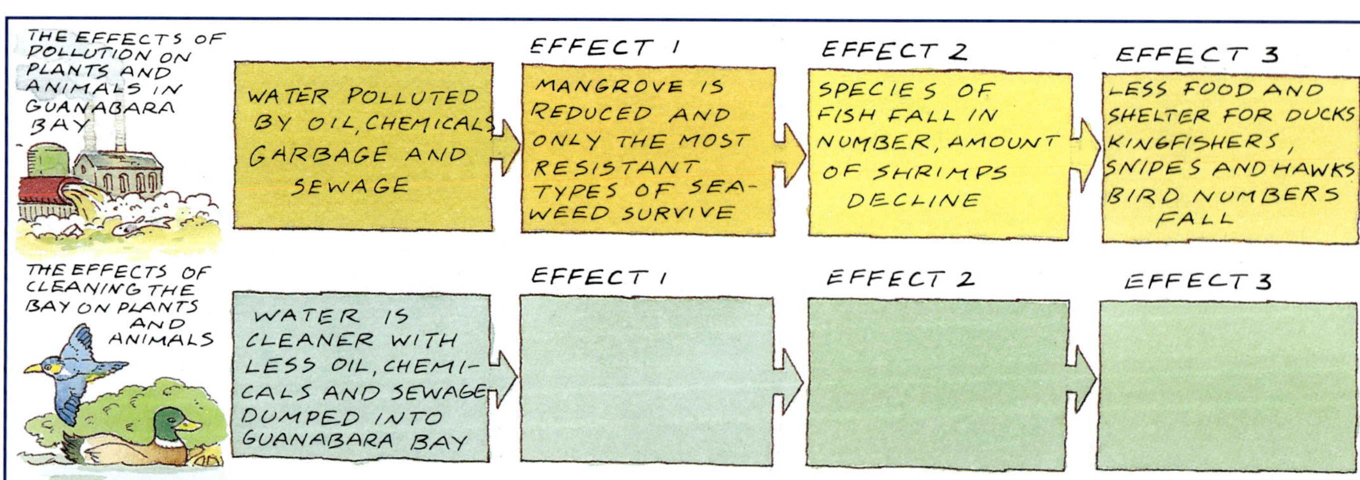

Women and development

The relatively low status of women in many LEDCs and continuing discrimination against them means that very few countries enable women to enjoy the same benefits as men. In fact 90 countries have not yet accepted the legal equality for women and men as set out by the United Nations in 1979. As a result, the roles played by women are often undervalued and ignored by policy makers. Women contribute to the development process but appear to benefit far less from it than men. They also represent 70 per cent of the world's poor.

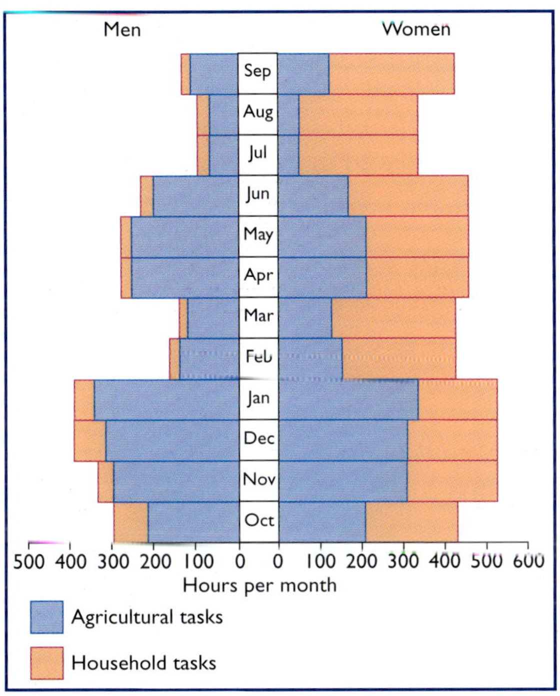

Figure 12.11 How women and men in Sri Lanka spend their working time

WHAT DO WOMEN DO?

Women in LEDCs make a valuable contribution to family and community life. Firstly, they are mothers and carers. They maintain the home, prepare food and collect fuelwood and water. In addition, women contribute economically to the family by working for wages or growing food. This heavy workload is reflected in the long hours that women work compared to men (Figure 12.11).

In many different sectors women suffer from disadvantages compared with men (Figure 12.13):

- women are less likely to be literate than men. In South Asia female literacy rates are only 55 per cent of males. Many regions and countries have even lower rates (Figure 12.12).
- although women tend to live longer than men, in many countries of South Asia and North Africa, neglect of women's health or nutrition means that they have a shorter life expectancy.
- in many LEDCs women have fewer opportunities of a paid job than men. China has the best opportunities where female employment rates are 80 per cent of males. The lowest rates are found in the Arab states where the proportion is only 21 per cent.
- women are often paid less than men. In Bangladesh for example, men are paid twice as much as women. In many instances women's work is unpaid. In sub-Saharan Africa, 80 per cent of food is produced by women, for which they receive no wages.
- women are under represented in the political world. Although women comprise over 50 per cent of the world's population, they make up just 10 per cent of the world's parliamentarians. This makes it difficult for women to fight for equality.

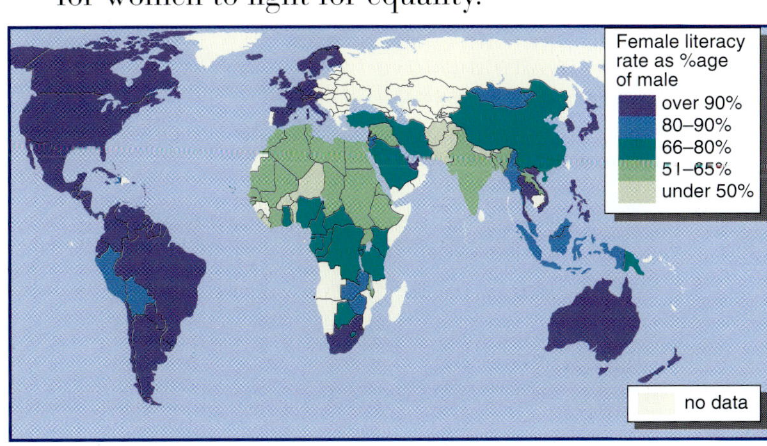

Figure 12.12 Female literacy rates as a percentage of males throughout the world

	Fertility Rate per Woman	Female Literacy as % of Male	Female Rates of Economic Activity as % of Male	% of Girls (10–14 Years) Economically Active	Share of Parliamentary Seats Held by Women
Arab States	4.8	61	21	5	4
East Asia	1.9	80	80	21	19
Latin America & Caribbean	3.1	97	37	2	10
South Asia	4.1	55	35	9	5
South East Asia	3.3	90	56	9	9
Sub-Saharan Africa	6.3	66	58	20	8
European Union (EU)	1.8	100	52	0	14

Figure 12.13 Some indicators of the status of women within society

Women are important agents of economic and social change. Development which discriminates against women or excludes them cannot be regarded as true development.

1 **a** Study Figure 12.11 and suggest reasons why women work longer hours than men.
b Suggest three ways that women's workloads could be reduced.

2 Women are energetic participants in the development process. How do they contribute to the economic and human development of their families, communities and nations?

3 **a** Describe the pattern of female literacy shown in Figure 12.12. In which parts of the world are levels of female literacy highest and lowest?
b Suggest two reasons to explain your answer to **a**?

4 Write a newspaper report describing the unfairness to women as shown in Figures 12.13 and 12.15. Include some statistics in your answer. You could also interview two or three people to get their reactions, and include these interviews in your report.

5 The status of women is often measured using three indicators: fertility rate per woman, female literacy and level of female economic activity. Discuss how each of these indicators can demonstrate the status of women within society. What other indicators could be used?

Figure 12.14 Woman working in West Bengal

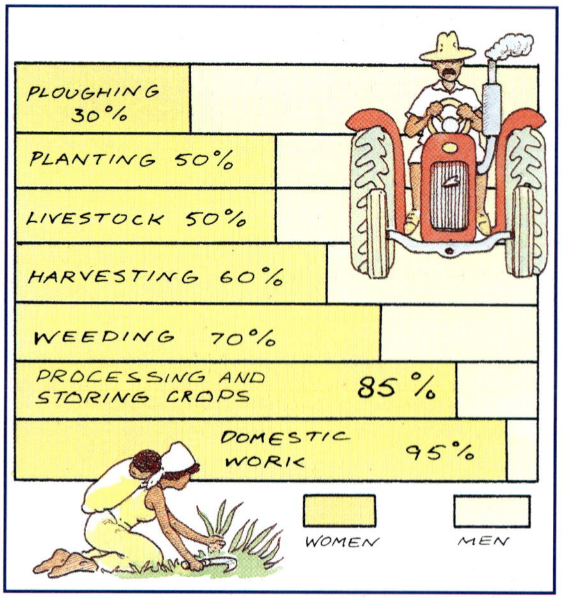

Figure 12.15 Division of labour between men and women in Africa

Deforestation: Northern Namibia

Much of Namibia is too dry for anything more substantial than scrub savanna to grow, and part of the land area is actually desert. The only forested area is confined to the wetter north and north west. However, because wood is in such great demand for a whole range of different uses (Figure 12.18), this forested area is under threat.

Figure 12.16 Carrying fuelwood home

Figure 12.17 Wood for fencing

1. Using Figure 12.18, list five different uses of wood in Namibia.
2. **a** Why do you think wood is used rather than other types of fuel?
   b What methods might the Namibian Government use to persuade people to use fuels other than wood?
3. Compare the reasons for deforestation in Namibia with those in any other area you have studied.

Figure 12.18 Some uses of wood in Namibia

It is estimated that around 1.7 million cubic metres of wood is consumed each year in Namibia. The uncontrolled felling of trees has been taking place over a long period. The problem is that areas of land are left bare and therefore open to rain and wind, the two main agents of soil erosion. Tree cover, even though it is confined to a small area of Namibia, has helped to conserve the environment, and sustain agricultural yields by protecting the land from **degradation**.

Rates of deforestation are highest in the Owambo, Kavango and Caprivi areas. As northern Namibia contains more than 60 per cent of the population, the land here is already under great pressure. Wood is mainly used as fuelwood, in the construction of houses, and for use in fencing (Figure 12.17).

The Namibian Government is now trying to conserve and regenerate the country's forests, with financial support from donor agencies and countries.

Glossary

abrasion the wearing away of rock by a rubbing action
aid assistance, often in the form of money, given by more economically developed countries (MEDCs) to less economically developed countries (LEDCs)
appropriate development development which uses local resources and ideas to meet local needs at a price which is affordable to the community concerned
backwash effect the movement of resources from the periphery to the core
bay curved inlet found along the coast
bilateral aid which is given by one country directly to another
colony country which was once occupied and run by another country usually for economic advantage
degradation deterioration of the environment, which may be due to soil erosion, bush encroachment, overcultivation or other factors
delta flat area made up of silt found at the mouth of a river e.g. Ganges, Nile
drought a long period without rain
entrepôt trading centre, usually a port, where goods are imported and re-exported without incurring duty
ephemeral river which runs for only a short period during the year
export-oriented industries economic activities which focus on producing items for export, in order to maximise a country's export revenue
family-planning schemes the use of birth control (contraception) to plan families
favela area of very poor housing (slums) where the houses are made out of scrap materials. Also known as a shanty settlement
gross national product (GNP) the wealth of a country. The total value of the goods and services produced
growth pole place or district which is a favoured place for economic growth, either through good location, labour supply or resource availability, and which as a result is a designated area for development
gulley small, steep-sided valley which has been cut by water
HDI Human Development Index; a method of measuring quality of life and level of development
headland promontory of hard rock which juts out into the sea
import substitution industries industries developed by a country in the early stages of economic development, to reduce its dependence on foreign imports e.g. iron and steel, shipbuilding and textiles
inselberg isolated dome or pillar of hard, resistant rock often found in desert or semi-arid areas
maquiladora foreign-owned factory, often an assembly plant paying low wages, located just inside Mexico's borders
MEW Measure of Economic Welfare. Statistical measurement of economic wellbeing, often used as a general development indicator
migration movement from one place to another to live and work
monsoon period of very high rainfall following a seasonal wind reversal
multi-purpose having various aims, e.g. a water-scheme including the generation of hydro-power, the improvement of navigation and the general control of water supply
multilateral aid which is given by governments to international agencies like the United Nations and The World Bank, who then distribute it to countries and organisations
multiplier effect economic growth which occurs as a result of some areas having a comparative advantage over others. Money invested in a locality has spin-off effects which lead to further growth
natural increase a measure of how quick a country's population is growing: the difference between birth and death rates
newly industrialising country (NIC) country whose economy has grown quickly, and for several successive years and where industry is expanding rapidly
oasis spring or waterhole in a desert area which makes human settlement nearby possible
perennial river or spring which is permanently flowing
population policy set of measures designed to regulate (positively or negatively) the rate of population change in a country
PQLI Physical Quality of Life Index: a measure of human wellbeing which incorporates several development indicators
pull factors perceived advantages, usually of cities, which attract people towards them to live and work
push factors perceived disadvantages, usually of rural areas, which encourage people to move away and live in cities
Sahel the semi-arid lands south of the Sahara Desert in Africa
sand spit linear deposit of sand or shingle transported and laid down by longshore drift, which often extends across an estuary
sustainable development development which improves people's lives without damaging the environment for future generations
transnational corporation (TNC) large business enterprise which has branches in many countries, and which is engaged in a range of different economic activities

Index